President and Nation

The Making of
Modern America

John Kentleton

First published 2002 by
PALGRAVE MACMILLAN
Houndmills, Basingstoke, Hampshire RG21 6XS and
175 Fifth Avenue, New York, N.Y. 10010
Companies and representatives throughout the world

PALGRAVE MACMILLAN is the global academic imprint of the Palgrave Macmillan division of St. Martin's Press, LLC and of Palgrave Macmillan Ltd. Macmillan® is a registered trademark in the United States, United Kingdom and other countries. Palgrave is a registered trademark in the European Union and other countries.

ISBN 0–333–43696–2 hardcover
ISBN 0–333–43697–0 paperback

This book is printed on paper suitable for recycling and made from fully managed and sustained forest sources.

A catalogue record for this book is available from the British Library.

Library of Congress Cataloging-in-Publication Data

Kentleton, John, 1941–
    President and nation : the making of modern America / John Kentleton.
        p. cm.
    Includes bibliographical references and index.
    ISBN 0–333–43696–2—ISBN 0–333–43697–0 (pbk.)
        1. Presidents—United States—History—20th century. 2. United States—Politics and government—20th century. I. Title.

E176.1 .K437 2002
973.9′092′2—dc21

                                                              2001060250

10 9 8 7 6 5 4 3 2 1
11 10 09 08 07 06 05 04 03 02
Printed in China

Contents

Acknowledgements

My thanks are due to Vanessa Couchman who commissioned this book, to Vanessa Graham who waited patiently for it, to Jonathan Reeve who helped me extend it, and to Terka Acton who brought it to completion. Two anonymous readers gave generous advice and encouragement. Peggy Rider typed a first draft and Adrian Kentleton provided unfailing IT expertise. David Dutton furnished a book I needed. Pandora Kerr Frost and Valery Rose edited the text, and Patricia Hymans compiled the index.

Joyce and Malcolm Lambert's kindness in frequent loans of their charming home allowed me to write parts of this book in the serenity of the Cotswolds. I owe a particular debt to my students over the years for their enthusiasm and interest in American history of which I was the beneficiary; the pleasure of teaching them taught me even more. My final thanks, impossible to quantify, must go to Pamela, my wife.

Meols, Wirral   J.K.

Introduction

The subject of this book is the role of the presidency in the political development of the United States since 1901. It concentrates exclusively on presidential politics, but this is not to deny the significance of other forces in a country as large as the United States under a federal system of government. Clearly, the implication that only what happens in Washington, DC, is important would be to misunderstand the nature of the democratic process in the United States, where so many of its citizens are active in politics and causes. It is simply that the American presidency is a unique institution and the president the only American politician who can claim a national constituency. Moreover, it was in this period that the American president began to acquire and utilize immense powers that were to have profound consequences in the making of modern America.

This has deeper implications, for the historical importance of the United States in the modern world is incontestable. No understanding of its evolution is complete without due recognition of the part America played in building up and strengthening a democratic and increasingly egalitarian society within a republican form of government, and of the impact she was thus to have on the wider world community. For many, the United States was to be both an example and an inspiration. Ex-President Theodore Roosevelt, as early as 1910, discerned this latent importance:

> Our country – this great Republic – means nothing unless it means the triumph of a real democracy,... of popular government, and,... of an economic system under which each man shall be guaranteed the opportunity to show the best that there is in him. That is why the history of America is now the central feature of the history of the world; for the world has set its face hopefully toward our democracy.

And that democracy increasingly invested its greatest hopes in its presidents, of whom Theodore Roosevelt was an important forerunner for later developments.[1]

This sense of the significance of American history lies deep in the national consciousness. It has really been there since the days of the early settlements. In a little-known speech in 1936 celebrating the fiftieth anniversary of the Statue of Liberty, President Franklin Roosevelt spoke of America as being 'mankind's second chance'. That was to be her destiny in over three centuries: 'Even in times as troubled and uncertain as these, I still hold to the faith that a better civilization than any we have known is in store for America and by our example, perhaps, for the world.'[2]

If those times were often to witness a considerable gap between hope and reality, the American willingness to try to bridge it remained. America is at heart an optimistic nation. It is one of her many attractive qualities and helps explain her consistent ability to rise to the occasion and to surpass her expectations. In this, too, the presidency was to play a crucial role.

'France,' wrote F. Scott Fitzgerald, 'was a land, England was a people, but America, having about it still the quality of the idea, was harder to utter.' Yet only by endeavouring to discern the power of the ideas that lie deeply embedded in the American experience, and explain her progress, can one hope to understand the inner meaning of American history.[3]

Indeed, for more than two centuries Americans have been endeavouring to work out the implications of a simple but devastating proposition: 'That all men are created equal, that they are endowed by their Creator with certain unalienable Rights, that among these are Life, Liberty and the pursuit of Happiness.'[4]

In so doing they have been conscious that they are not merely doing it for themselves: they are also doing it for others. The price of success or failure is quite simply the prospects for general human betterment. As another president, Lincoln, admonished his countrymen at the height of the Civil War: 'We shall nobly save, or meanly lose, the last best, hope of earth.'[5]

Again and again, Americans have returned to these simple verities. They have provided the integrity to American history, a coherence that the ablest American statesmen and thus her most successful presidents have intuitively recognized. History is inevitably about movement, and America was to change much in the years after 1901. Yet beneath the changes, momentous though they were, one can still see clearly the outlines of an agreed and ordered framework. 'This was the first nation in the history of the world to be founded with a purpose,' proclaimed President Lyndon Johnson in 1965. 'The great phrases of that purpose still sound in every American heart. North and South: "All men are created equal" – "government by consent of the governed" – "give me liberty or give me death". Well those are not just clever words or those are not just empty theories. In their name Americans have fought and died for two centuries.'[6]

Continuity and change hint at the creative tension of American history, and nowhere has this been more apparent than in the modern era; the challenges that America faced were stupendous and the stakes were of the highest. There would be a constant need to redefine the American purpose so as to balance objectives with resources. Again, the best of her presidents endeavoured to give a lead. Each generation had in Lincoln's words to 'think anew, and act anew'.[7]

Indeed, it is possible to see a certain pattern or movement every generation or thirty or so years as an overarching idea is first propounded, worked for, then established and finally superseded, its death and decay giving birth to a new impulse for change. Of course, the parameters are not that neat. If there are tides in history, there are also undercurrents; and one must also recognize that the concept of a generation cannot be too precisely defined. Yet such divisions serve a purpose; they remind us that it is possible to delineate certain salient characteristics of a period, and that the whole is greater than the sum of its parts.

Arguably, this forms the pattern of American history. One can see in the stirrings against British rule in the 1760s the creative impulse that was to lead to revolution, independence and a new national Constitution, before it ossified somewhat in the late 1790s, and was challenged and superseded by the Jeffersonian revolution of 1800. Nonetheless, this in turn represented republican rule by aristocrats, as the successive presidencies of Jefferson, Madison, Monroe and Adams in the first thirty years of the nineteenth century indicated. The egalitarian surge that a more established United States demanded centred round Andrew Jackson, a frontiersman entre-preneur first elected president in 1828 after an unsuccessful bid four years previously. And it was the failure of his party, the old Demo-cratic one, to speak for a nation rather than for a section over the issue of slavery, that required the emergence thirty years later of the new Republican Party, for whom Abraham Lincoln was the spokesman. And it was to take the carnage of the Civil War of 1861–5 for his words to be accepted. Yet Republican success, if it cemented the Union, did so at a price; and the victory of the North itself gave rise to problems. Battlefields don't just test armies but the resources of the societies that put them there. Thus the same Northern industrial might that crushed the Confederacy had, by the 1890s, put the United States into a position where, if the nation was to remain true to the principles of its founding, a fresh look at the role of American government was urgently required. The state needed to assert itself, to ensure that it, not a minority of its wealthy citizens, would ultimately prevail in the unending contest between individual freedom and collective betterment. It is at this juncture that modern America begins and the role of the president becomes increasingly significant.

This generational concept, however, fits into a broader category that argues that two generations, say some sixty years, is a more meaningful period. Such a view neatly sections American history since the mid-eighteenth century, establishing the movement towards Independence, the Jeffersonian revolution, the Civil War and the presidency of Franklin Roosevelt as the fundamental historical events that shaped their ensuing eras. As a refinement one might even suggest, for ideas come before events, that three presidents have shaped American history: Thomas Jefferson for its republican period, Abraham Lincoln for its national, and Franklin Roosevelt for its international. It is yet another illustration of the relationship between President and Nation.

Thus the United States by 1901 was at a halfway stage in one respect, though ready to receive a fresh infusion of creative energy within a shorter context. *The Development of Modern America* therefore spans the first three decades of the twentieth century. If they began in hope and resolution, they ended in despair and confusion. In this respect the Depression was a watershed and marked a decisive break with the past. Accordingly, these early years are crucial to an understanding of the evolution of the United States into its modern form, for they were fertile in innovation, witnessed great changes and offered new challenges. Nonetheless, they seem more a harbinger of what would come and less a rupture with what had gone before. Certainly, America moved a long way, as an examination of the problems with which the two dominating figures of the period, presidents Theodore Roosevelt and Woodrow Wilson, had to contend well indicates. Clearly the advent of the first Roosevelt to the presidency marked a decisive change in how that office was exercised; it was changed decisively by Wilson as well. And since the centre of focus is political development as practised in and seen from the perspective of the White House and Washington, DC, one must consider in general terms at least some of the major factors that marked their respective presidencies. In a broader context they can be seen as comprising the political creeds both men came to embrace, Progressivism and internationalism. And while not all supporters of either of these creeds embraced both, one can discern a balance between them so that they are mutually supporting. True, both these movements were to be in retreat by the end of this period but they were the seed-corn of the future. Clearly, ideas generated at the time were to be developed and extended later, whilst some of those who had their political baptism in this period were to play a major part in their later fulfilment.

Both these movements, however, required the exercise of presidential power operating within the confines of party politics. Thus the opening decades of the twentieth century witnessed this development of presidential power and influence that was to be one of the salient characteristics of modern American history. Accordingly, in looking at policies one is also required to look at how they were implemented. That necessitates an awareness of the role of party, and indeed this is another of the major features of the whole period. For what one first observes is the dominance of the Republican Party in national politics. In 1901 this seemed to be a basic fact of life, and how this dominance was eroded is one of the major themes of modern American political history. Clearly, when one is dealing with a continental nation, one must always be aware that selection can distort; here the concern has been with the impression given by the overall picture rather than with precise and particular detail. Nonetheless, if we are witnessing in retrospect *The Development of Modern America*, it must be conceded that future possibilities and latent potentialities are not preordained to reach maturity. If there is a greater continuity between these opening years and what followed, it is because the legacy of Roosevelt and Wilson was to find its most potent expression in the greatest of the modern presidents, Franklin Roosevelt.

This political giant was the most creative statesman of the modern world. A Protean figure, through him flowed and merged all the major currents of American politics. Building on the work of his predecessors but giving it a wholly new dimension, he stands at the confluence of modern American history. So vast was his achievement that it is impossible to confine it within the space of a single chapter, for his unique twelve-year tenure of the White House encompassed the most significant and dangerous years of world history. Here again there is a clear equation between domestic and foreign policy, though not all those who supported him in one or other of these directions would have accepted it. In the years immediately prior to the second Roosevelt taking office, both a shorter and a longer period of American development came to a halt. For if the Depression beginning in 1929 marks the end of that generational surge of creativity that started with the first Roosevelt, it also marks the end of that distinctive phase in national development that commenced after the Civil War's resolution and the South's surrender in 1865. Thus Franklin Roosevelt was uniquely poised, if he could rise to the occasion, to provide a leadership that might weld his own generation of Americans with the long-term future prospects of the United States. Perceptively, both Roosevelt in recognizing his opportunity and President Herbert Hoover in opposing him saw that what was at stake was more than immediate political concerns, however grievous. Roosevelt would say in 1936: 'There is a mysterious cycle in human events. To some generations much is given. Of other generations much is expected. This generation of Americans has a rendezvous with destiny.' Meanwhile, Hoover could warn his countrymen in 1932: 'This campaign is more than a contest between two men. It is more than a contest between two parties. It is a contest between two philosophies of government . . . It means deciding the direction our Nation will take over a century to come.' In both instances the words of these two men were to be proved prophetic.[8]

It is possible to discern four particular themes when considering Franklin Roosevelt's unique contribution to modern American history. The first, obviously, is *The Achievement of Liberalism*. This, Roosevelt only continued. The Depression forced Americans to think anew, to consider new ways of ordering their society. Here the example of Theodore Roosevelt and Woodrow Wilson was potent, but Franklin Roosevelt took their work much, much further. Given the constraints under which he laboured, the turbulence of the times and the pressure of events, his record was a stupendous one; in a very real sense he set the parameters of American politics for a generation. His successors performed in his shadow.[9] But in redefining the relationship between American government and society, in enlarging the possibilities open to political action, he had to recreate the political party through which he operated. He was to reorder the American political landscape, to effect a change of seismic proportions. *The Achievement of Liberalism* over the next thirty odd years was to see not only the implementation of liberal policies but also the creation of a liberal party. The Republican Party dominance that had lasted since 1860 was replaced by a Democratic one. Yet both these developments, fundamental though they were, also testified to the growth of presidential power without which they would have been impossible. Roosevelt's election as president in 1932 ushered in the most creative generation in the history of the United States since the time of the formative years of the Republic. The challenges that she faced and mastered transformed American history. The Roosevelt years were the fulcrum of modern American history.

Nor was it a matter for the United States alone. For the Roosevelt years also witnessed *The Attainment of World Power*. Here, once again, he built on the legacy of his predecessors Theodore Roosevelt and Woodrow Wilson. Yet their generation had refused the world leadership offered them. It had met the challenge of the First World War slowly, hesitantly and finally deliberately, but had then retreated into disillusioned isolationism. It must take some of the blame for the slide into anarchy of the interwar years. Here Franklin Roosevelt was as creative as in domestic politics. Patiently he educated the American people to world realities; the next time Americans went to war they would accept the obligations of their commitment. The coming of peace would not be an occasion for escapism. It was a slow process of self-enlightenment. But this time the lessons lasted. America did not merely respond to the Fascist and communist threat; she took on the role of world leadership. Almost sixty years were to elapse, two generations, between the advent of Roosevelt and Hitler to power, the American recognition of the Soviet Union, conceding that the old Bolshevik revolutionaries were there to stay, and the final overthrow of communist rule. Roosevelt had laid down the parameters of foreign policy for his successors. Again they operated in his shadow.

Moreover, these developments abroad, again and strikingly, augmented presidential power. Presidential initiatives in foreign policy enjoyed considerable latitude, but each incremental increase of presidential power made further increases more likely, whilst the scope of foreign policy decisions themselves required a strengthened executive. Roosevelt began that international phase in American history which has continued to the present. In so doing he committed the Democratic Party to internationalism, but the commitment was to prove its undoing. Just at that moment when liberalism could be said to have become the prevailing public philosophy and the Democratic Party its vehicle of expression, this political victory was undermined by an over-extension of ambition abroad that equally cost it dear at home. It was an example of that coincidence of circumstance in history that often spells impending change.

Thus whilst in foreign policy *the Attainment of World Power* brought about a Pax Americana which would ultimately prevail, in domestic affairs one witnessed a slow but inexorable sea change in attitudes. Distant stars are often at their brightest in the firmament when in fact their light has presaged their destruction.[10] And if, in domestic politics, the 1960s was to see a further burst of that creative spirit that had animated the New Deal, it did not long survive its makers. Perhaps the momentum of American history in the second third of the twentieth century was such that it was bound to produce a reaction. If the thrust of developments had been towards increased centralization and reform politics, there had always been a conservative counterpoint. Thus by the end of the 1960s one witnesses *The Resurgence of Conservatism*, a movement that gathered pace and became the predominant political creed in the waning of the century.

The first consequence of this, both as cause and effect, was the erosion of Democratic Party dominance. At first glance it might appear as if the Republican Party was bent on recapturing its once unchallenged ascendancy. But the process was slower and less clear-cut than earlier reversals of political fortune; only towards the end of the twentieth century was it beginning to look as if a prevailing conservative philosophy might find itself represented by a prevailing Republican conservative party. Here the pattern was still somewhat confused, even if clear pointers existed. If politicians adapt to public moods, they also help form them. One of the themes of this account is that one must not lose sight of the role of the individual and, indeed, accident in history. Had William McKinley not been assassinated in 1901, Theodore Roosevelt might never have become president or, alternatively, he might merely have succeeded McKinley three years later. Had Franklin Roosevelt not succumbed to polio in 1921 he might not have had to interrupt his political career and would possibly have seen it broken by defeat in the long years of Republican victories. Had a bystander not knocked the arm of Franklin Roosevelt's potential assassin in 1933 and deflected the bullets, would a President Garner in his place have effected the New Deal and the development of American internationalism? Had John Kennedy not been killed in Dallas in 1963, would liberalism ever have achieved the triumphant fulfilment that it did under Lyndon Johnson? But then again, though here the issue is much more speculative, would the war in Vietnam have happened quite as it did? The theme of this book is the importance of the presidency; but this in turn depends on who is president.

Inevitably, then, these chapters are but part of the making of modern America and its development could be followed from many different perspectives. Even the basic geographical configuration of the nation was altered, from 45 states at the start of the twentieth century to 50 thereafter. Meanwhile the very form of American government was modified. Explicitly in the number of amendments to the American Constitution that were ratified: there were no less than twelve during this period. And implicitly in the way that the constitutional balance has been altered between Executive and Legislature, and in how Americans came to see, and the Judiciary endorse, new notions of governmental powers and individual rights.

One of the strengths of America is that she is always changing. So, too, are Americans! In 1900 the nation already had a population of over 75 million; by 2000 this figure was over 280 million. And whereas there were just about 2 per cent more men than women in the former year, this proportion was reversed by the latter. Again, in 1900, 60 per cent of Americans lived in the country, 40 per cent in the towns; in 2000 scarcely one in four Americans was a rural inhabitant. Similarly, in 1900 just about one in eight Americans was non-white; by 2000 it was virtually one in four. Now almost one of any two Americans taken at random would be of a different ethnic origin to the other. As a young nation got older, so too did its citizens; at the beginning of the century the median age of the population was 23; by 2000 it was 35. In 1900 a white male could expect on average to live to 46, a white female to 48. By 2000 the respective figures were 75 and 80. Similarly, non-white life expectancies in 1900 were 32 and 33 respectively: in 2000, 68 and 75. In short, there were a lot more Americans as the century progressed, they had radically changed where they lived, their ethnic identity was more varied, and they were a lot older. And this is to say nothing about their extraordinary social and cultural diversity!

Accordingly, presidential history affords at best a partial insight into the lives of such a numerous people. Washington, DC, is not the United States, even if it is the focus of its politics. The Constitution of the United States begins with the phrase, 'We the People of the United States', from whom all political power ultimately derives.[11] Thus one may recognize that of all nations, for America politics is an expression of national will. Politics looms large in the ensuing chapters because Americans have the ability and capacity to take charge of their own destiny. If the emphasis is on presidential politics, that is simply because this is one important way they can do so. The United States has always been a society where individuals have felt that they had rights, a duty to defend them and an obligation to extend them. The words of Woody Guthrie still ring true: 'This land is your land, this land is my land, from California to the New York island; from the redwood forest to the Gulf stream waters, this land was made for you and me.'[12]

And because they believe it to be so, Americans further their private hopes by collective public action. As Lyndon Johnson noted to a Joint Session of Congress in 1965:

> Beyond this great chamber, out yonder in fifty states are the people we serve. Who can tell what deep and unspoken hopes are in their hearts tonight as they sit there and listen. We all can guess, from our own lives, how difficult they often find their own pursuit of happiness, how many problems each little family has. They look most of all to themselves for their futures. But I think that they also look to each of us.[13]

It was in this period that not only the American people, but also the world outside, looked to Washington. Of course, by the time the twentieth century opened, America as a concept had been in the European consciousness for at least 400 years, had been a society for almost 300, and an independent nation for 125. Certainly, it had served as an inspiration to many who aspired to enjoy the political freedom that the new United States practised. Millions of immigrants voted with their feet. But the practical impact of American policies on the rest of the world largely dates from this period.

There was the growth of the American empire or, at least, its interests overseas; its economic and industrial development; vitally, its entry into the First World War. For a brief moment an American president, Woodrow Wilson, held world leadership in his hands. The opportunity was missed. Then the American Stock Market Crash in October 1929 reverberated round the world. It was the overture to the Great Depression. This was the first great international challenge since the First World War. Franklin Roosevelt met it by concentrating on his own country's needs. He thus ensured that, when this grave economic threat to the nation's survival was followed by an explicit military one, the United States would have the strength to overcome it. The leadership that America gave the world in those years she has never lost, though subsequent presidents did not always command such unquestioned moral authority. Thus the political battle in Washington took on a more than American significance. Every American presidential election now mattered to those outside the United States as well as to those within her borders.

Ultimately, indeed, it was a matter of national survival. From the time of Franklin Roosevelt, the calibre of the man Americans chose as their chief executive mattered inordinately to other nations. Washington was the focus of the free world. Nor was this simply a matter of military power. It was also an issue of moral force. The American president stood at the apex of the American system of government; rightly or wrongly that position had come about by constitutional development occasioned by events. Now he spoke for the United States and, in so doing, had the opportunity to speak on behalf of what the free world represented. It was easy to become jaded, even cynical, but the power of ideas coming out of the American experience meant that the political development of the United States had world implications. How well did American presidents serve their own people in the modern era? How well did they serve others?

It is salutary to recall that of the pre-eminent figures in twentieth-century world history, most were evil: murderers whose political philosophy wreaked untold misery on their contemporaries – Lenin, Stalin, Hitler, Mao Zedong. It was an American president, together with the system of government he represented, who was the shining exception. For Franklin Roosevelt, looking back on the crisis year of 1933, it was to furnish proof that 'democracy can find within itself the elements necessary to its own salvation'.[14]

1

The Development of Modern America

1 The Rise of Theodore Roosevelt

Modern America can be said to have begun in September 1901 when Vice-President Theodore Roosevelt succeeded to the presidency on the assassination of William McKinley. Yet this apparent accident of fate concealed a deeper set of circumstances. For 'Teddy' Roosevelt's automatic elevation only occurred because the year before he had accepted the Republican Party's nomination to the second place on the ticket that it was hoped would repeat McKinley's presidential election victory of 1896. And while it certainly suited New York State's political boss to remove a governor who had shown a distressing tendency to reform and independence, it is too simplistic merely to see the manoeuvre to make Roosevelt vice-president as a plot that backfired on its authors. Senator Mark Hanna of Ohio's famous comment, 'Don't any of you realize that there's only one life between this madman and the Presidency', was true but incomplete.[1]

Certainly, three vice-presidents had succeeded to the presidency as a result of the death of the incumbent, the last only twenty years previously. But Roosevelt, ambitious, shrewd and purposeful was surely playing a more calculating game. Even if many saw the vice-presidency as a shelf and not a stepping stone, and no vice-president had succeeded naturally since 1836, it is inconceivable that Roosevelt was fool enough to be manoeuvred unwillingly into a political cul-de-sac. He might protest that he wished to remain in New York and complete his agenda; he protested too much: here loyalty to party and its call might be both the excuse and the face-saver. In his early forties, dynamic, well known and restlessly energetic, his eyes were on 1904. McKinley's death merely brought forward the fulfilment of Roosevelt's ambition by three years. A contemporary noted: 'He was not nominated to satisfy or placate, but to succeed. The unspeakably cruel and cowardly assassin has anticipated the slow and orderly processes of law.'[2]

Of course, Roosevelt had some obvious attractions in 1900. He was young, and this would help match the 40-year-old Democratic candidate William Jennings Bryan as he made a second attempt on the White House that had eluded him four years previously. He came from New York and that would fit neatly with McKinley's home state of Ohio: both states were powerful and electorally important. And if it was expedient to the bosses to engineer his promotion and removal, this would not have been possible if Roosevelt had not been personally popular, the hero of the West and a figure of national fame before he had achieved national office. And his tentative steps to reform were just promising enough, without being dangerous, to indicate that readiness to change which reflected the deep, maturing processes of American life and politics. Roosevelt was made for the America of the opening years of the twentieth century and many Americans intuitively recognized it.

Partly, it was generational. Although McKinley was only fifteen years older than Roosevelt was, those fifteen years concealed a deep and unbridgeable gulf between them. For McKinley was the last of that succession of Republican presidents since the Civil War who had validated their credentials in national politics by a prior willingness to enlist and fight in the Union Army. There, in that terrible war that had killed some 620,000 Americans, 2 per cent of the entire population, he had come of age. No man of that generation could escape the war's shadow; it was the central determining experience of their lives. Roosevelt, not yet 3 years old when the war had started, grew to maturity in its aftermath. Private tragedy formed him. When he was 25 his wife died in childbirth (the baby daughter lived); a few hours previously his mother, too, had died. Total immersion in his work, and an escape to the Bad Lands of the Dakotas for a couple of years of ranching, alone helped him to come to terms with the trauma. The war that later catapulted him to public fame and subsequent fortune was the Spanish–American War of 1898 – that 'splendid little war', of which one commentator later noted: 'a good Labour Day weekend kills nearly as many people on the roads.'[3] True, the Spanish–American War was a turning point; but not so much for what it was as for what it represented. It was 50 years since America had fought a foreign power, and then only her neighbour Mexico; 75 years since the

Monroe Doctrine had proclaimed the inviolable integrity of the Americas from foreign penetration; over 80 years since she had concluded the War of 1812 and peace with Britain. Now America was coming of age; a great power had begun to flex her muscles. McKinley, ever the businessman, had been reluctant to go to war. One critic complained: 'McKinley has his ear so close to the ground it's always full of grasshoppers.'[4]

Perhaps, too, having fought in one war McKinley had no eagerness to take his country into another, but in the end, following the mysterious sinking of the US battleship *Maine* in Havana harbour, he succumbed to public opinion and decided to aid the Cubans in their fight for independence. It was a popular war. Roosevelt, more adroitly, both stirred up the clamour for war and responded to it. Assistant secretary of the navy at the war's outset, he was to be in quick succession governor of New York, vice-president and president of the United States.

Roosevelt's active encouragement and involvement in the war furnished a persona that made him immensely electable for public office. It was Roosevelt who prepared Commodore Dewey to sink the Spanish fleet in Manila Bay, a notable triumph that ensured the safety of the American Pacific Coast. It was Roosevelt who then resigned his Washington post to help form a volunteer regiment, 'the Rough Riders'. It was Roosevelt who led them in a much publicized cavalry charge. Memoirs of his war experiences, a wag noted, should have been called 'Alone in Cubia!'[5] Still, behind the self-advertisement there lurked an awareness that the beginning of the next century called for a reappraisal of the nation's outlook and institutions. It had really been needed from the time Roosevelt had first entered politics in 1880; political developments had failed to keep pace with economic developments; now twenty years on, the need was urgent. The Spanish–American War might furnish the occasion for his entry into elective national politics; it was not, however, the cause.

2 The Nineteenth-century Background

To understand why Roosevelt's succession to the presidency was so critical, it is necessary to look more closely at the closing decades of the nineteenth century. Initially, one might well think America had much to be thankful for. Had not the nineteenth century been, but for the Civil War, one long century of stupendous national achievement that had brought her to the pinnacle of economic power and national self-assertion since the perilous enterprise of independence? Did not her achievement amply vindicate the famous letter Thomas Jefferson had written in 1812 to his great antagonist John Adams? Looking back over a long life and the troubles both presidents had faced in establishing the new republic, it seemed to Jefferson how Providence had indeed favoured them: 'Laboring always at the same oar, with some wave ever ahead threatening to overwhelm us and yet passing harmless under our bark, we knew not how, we rode through the storm with heart and hand and made a happy port...and so we have gone on and so we shall go on, puzzled and prospering beyond example in the history of man.'[6]

If this was the official version of American history, by the closing decade of the nineteenth century too many Americans had the uneasy feeling there had been a fall from grace. At first glance one might have surmised that the Civil War had ended for ever the innocent optimism of the early Republic. Of course one cannot overstate the traumatizing effect of this most terrible of wars, not least because it represented a failure of politics as a means of accommodation between starkly different viewpoints. Indeed, even so odious an institution as slavery would have remained intact had the South not seceded from the Union and put the issue to the test. Yet the very breadth and intensity of the war and its all-consuming nature had an almost cathartic effect on American society. In a sense it paved the way for later achievements. It settled once and for all, with the Confederacy's surrender, the indivisibility of the Union as a political federation: secession was henceforth not an option; the United States was precisely that even if the South would nurse its wounds well into the twentieth century.

Indeed, it is the very surge of energy released by the resolution, albeit on the battlefield, of that most intractable of issues, slavery and its extension, that was to generate the problems with which Theodore Roosevelt and his contemporaries would have to wrestle. To move from a society that was rent asunder by war and where involuntary servitude was legally sanctioned, to being the leading economic and industrial power in the world in one generation was bound to create pressures that would threaten its stability. For what strikes the observer of late nineteenth-century America so forcibly, in retrospect, is the disjointed nature of its social structure and the tension between its advanced industrial civilization on the one hand

and the untamed, even raw features of vast areas of the country on the other. America was not a society entirely secure in its self-image, even if it was brashly self-confident and determinedly enterprising. Mark Twain's and Charles Dudley Warner's delineation of it in *The Gilded Age* conveys something of the vulgarity, get-rich-quick mentality that was one of its most instantly recognizable characteristics, but the flaws lay deeper than this surface evaluation, however apposite.[7]

For a start the United States was still not yet a geographically completed nation. Even if its boundaries had now been settled, the American landmass itself between Canada and Mexico was not fully incorporated into the Union of States until the twentieth century. When the Civil War ended in 1865 there were but thirty-six states. Just two more states were added by 1876, the year the United States was beginning her second century. And indeed that anniversary year was to be marred by one of those dreadful happenings that, though subsequently romanticized in the telling, serve to underscore the strangely paradoxical nature of American society in the period of its most brash development. The massacre of the Seventh Cavalry under the command of General Custer at Little Big Horn was a frightening reminder of the rawness of the American frontier experience. Indeed, the last pathetic flicker of Indian resistance to the encroaching white man was to come nearly fifteen years later at the Battle of Wounded Knee in the closing days of 1890. In this respect at least, Sitting Bull's defiance was to occasion the final, unendurable act of insurrection that determined the certain destruction of his people. As one old Indian woman later reflected on its twentieth-century sequel: 'Now the white people claim everything that the Indians used to use in the olden days – If they could do it, they'd take everything – The only thing they'd leave us is our appetites.'[8]

The massacre at Little Big Horn, less than a fortnight before the Fourth of July celebrations for America's one-hundredth birthday, sent a shudder through the nation; but it serves as a reminder that Americans were not yet in full control of the land they claimed as their own. Indeed, it was not until after the census returns of 1890 that the historian Frederick Jackson Turner would argue that the frontier between settlement and wilderness had, in effect, ceased to be. Within a nine-month period, November 1889 to July 1890, a clutch of six new states from west of the Mississippi entered the Union. Finally, Mormon Utah, when the polygamy issue had been resolved, completed Western statehood in 1896. This still left the Southwest. Oklahoma became a state in 1907, New Mexico and Arizona in 1912. Only then were all the contiguous states within the Union. The frontier as such may have gone by 1890, but it was still in many parts of the country a frontier society.

Indeed, one could argue that it was precisely frontier values that manifested themselves in the rapacious pursuit of wealth that characterized the Gilded Age. Of course, the sense of an expanding American nation had been there since the beginning. This was what lay behind Turner's famous thesis that 'The existence of an area of free land, its continuous recession, and the advance of American settlement westward, explain American development.'[9]

Yet Jefferson's belief that there would be sufficient land for 'our descendants to the thousandth and thousandth generation', was proving to be unduly optimistic. This in spite of the fact that such a bold prediction had been made two years prior to the Louisiana Purchase of 1803 which had more than doubled the size of the United States![10]

Turner might sing the praises of the frontier as being 'productive of individualism'.[11] But it seems hard to reconcile his romantic notion with the everyday realities of American life in the closing decade of the nineteenth century. As early as 1871, for example, Walt Whitman could suggest: 'Never was there, perhaps, more hollowness at heart than at present, and here in the United States. Genuine belief seems to have left us.'[12]

Indeed, there seemed an increasing confusion of values. Westward expansion had been so fundamental an element of the American experience, really since the time of the earliest settlements, that it was hard to come to terms with its diminution. As Turner further explained: 'The fall line marked the frontier of the seventeenth century; the Alleghanies that of the eighteenth; the Mississippi that of the first quarter of the nineteenth; the Missouri that of the middle of this century (omitting the California movement); and the belt of the Rocky Mountains and the arid tract, the present frontier.'[13]

But it was precisely the California movement that upset earlier calculations. The discovery of gold in the Sacramento Valley caused an influx of some 80,000 fortune-seekers. By 1850 California's population growth had earned it statehood. But the complicated territorial arrangements that followed the acquisition of Mexican lands after the Mexican–American War of 1846–8, and the attempt to preserve the *status quo* between North and South in the Compromise of 1850, only kept war between free and slave states away for a decade. Indeed, the election of Abraham Lincoln in 1860 as president of the United States marked the victory of the Republican Party as it signalled the division of the nation and the onset of Civil War. Formed in the 1850s from the flotsam and jetsam of older groupings that had shattered on the issue of slavery, it owed its success to a willingness to adhere to the cardinal principle of American politics: that any political party to survive and prosper must represent a coalition of interests. Hence the Republican Party based its mass appeal on a triple programme: to safeguard Northern industries from foreign competition with high protective tariffs; to arrest the extension of slavery; and to grant free land for settlers in the West, a policy enshrined in the Homestead Act of 1862. Of course, the second and third of these policies were mutually supportive; here idealism and self-interest went hand in hand, since had slavery been allowed to spread the amount of land available for free settlement would have diminished. With California already settled, the Western movement now became a filling-in process, the covered wagon giving way to the transcontinental railroad. By 1869 the Union Pacific railroad moving westwards had met the Central Pacific railroad coming eastwards at Promontory Point near Ogden, Utah. A continent was now formally spanned; and thousands of natives augmented by immigrants flooded in to the remaining open spaces, completing in two or three decades a process that had taken two or three centuries.

Here figures tell their own story. In 1840, the last ten-yearly census before the discovery of Californian gold, the Irish famine, and the failure of the 1848 revolutions throughout Europe, the population of the United States stood at a little over 17 million. The decade that had just ended had received almost 600,000 immigrants. The 1840s, however, were a turning point. It was then that there began what was, over the next three-quarters of a century or so, to be the greatest mass migration in human history, with some 35 and more million immigrants arriving in the United States. The numbers exploded and exploded yet again. First the Irish, then the Germans, then Scandinavians, Italians and southern Europeans, Jews from Russia, Poles and other eastern and central Europeans, Chinese and Japanese ensured that every decade immigrants were numbered in millions rather than thousands. The 2, 3 or 4 million mark was reached and passed; in the first decade of the twentieth century immigration climaxed at an incredible 8,800,000. Not until the 1930s, with the earlier passage of restrictive legislation and the Depression taking their toll, would it fall back below what it had been in the 1830s. Meanwhile Americans themselves were reproducing, albeit less so than in earlier decades, as the birth rate in common with most industrialized nations slackened. More significantly, after the Civil War people were dying less quickly. Here better diets, advances in medical knowledge, and improved public health and hygiene more than compensated. Between 1870 and 1900 the population of the United States nearly doubled, the 17 million recorded in 1840 was touching 76 million in 1900.

The problem that population posed was more than one of numbers. True, few would have predicted how soon Jefferson's serene assumption of limitless space would have been invalidated. But it was who the immigrants were and where they went that aggravated the issue. In 1790 the first census in American history showed clearly that the new United States was a White, Anglo-Saxon, Protestant society, of a little under 4 million people, largely confined between the Atlantic and the Appalachian mountains in thirteen seaboard states. Some 95 per cent of this population could be classed as rural; only 5 per cent of Americans could claim to be town-dwellers, in towns of at least 5,000 people. One hundred years later, in 1890, the Superintendent of the Census declared the frontier closed, the year that saw the publication of Jacob Riis's classic exposure of slum living, *How the Other Half Lives*.[14]

Yet had not Thomas Jefferson, that great spokesman for the common man, drawing on his experience of the eighteenth-century European urban proletariat, commented: 'The mobs of great cities add just so much to the support of pure government as sores do to the strength of the human body?'[15] But by 1900 one-third of all Americans would live in cities (by 1920 it would be a majority) and forty American cities would have populations in excess of 100,000, more significantly, almost 30 per cent of the inhabitants of major cities were foreign-born. Now the flow of population towards the city was greater than towards the West and even the Westward movement had an urban dimension: Seattle, San Francisco and Los Angeles were home to a majority of the population on the Pacific coast. Nonetheless, it was back East that the real urban problems festered, in the first cities that the European immigrants made for and encountered once they had passed through Ellis Island off Manhattan. The Statue of Liberty might proclaim: 'Give me your tired, your poor, / Your huddled masses yearning to breathe free / The wretched refuse of your teeming shore.' But it might have added: 'Give me your cheap, economically exploitable labour, ideal as industrial cannon fodder, ignorant of American ways and customs, frightened, alien and confused.'[16]

Certainly the immigrants did not lack for work. Here figures once again tell their own story. In 1870 there were some 12.5 million workers in the United States. Ten years later this number had increased to well over 17 million. By 1890 it had in turn increased to a figure well in excess of 23 million. In 1900 it was more than 29 million, during these three decades male workers outnumbering female workers by more than four to one as a percentage of the total workforce. Their impact could be discerned clearly in the rise of the Gross National Product. Calculated in billions of dollars, it was about 7.4 billion in 1870; by 1880 it was about 11.2 billion, an increase of more than 50 per cent. The rate of advance was a little more subdued in the 1880s; nonetheless, the figure for 1890, 13.1 billion, would ten years later in 1900 be 18.7 billion (that again was almost to double to 35.3 billion by 1910). Foreign trade told a similar story. In 1870 the United States still narrowly imported more than she exported: in millions of dollars, 451 in exports to 462 imports. Thereafter the volume of trade and the balance to her advantage increased and widened. In 1880 the respective figures were 853 million to 761 million; in 1890, 910 to 823; 1900, 1,499 to 930. By the turn of the century the United States was the most productive industrial nation in the world.

The achievement was relentless and overwhelming. Pig-iron production rose from 800,000 tons in 1860, the last full year of peace before the Civil War, to nearly 14 million tons in 1900. In the same period steel production – thanks also to improved methods of removing iron's impurities – which had been a negligible 13,000 tons in 1860, increased to well over 11 million in 1900. Not surprisingly, railroad mileage accelerated. In 1860 it had been 30,000 miles; by 1900 it was getting on for 200,000, more than the whole of Europe and 40 per cent of the world total. An Industrial Revolution that in Britain had taken a century, in America took a generation. By 1900 she was making nearly one-third of the world's manufactured goods.

The value of these manufactures between 1860 and 1900 increased sevenfold; moreover, it was a nationwide phenomenon. Not only in the Northeast, traditionally the home of American industry, but also the Midwest, now one of the greatest industrial centres in the world, and even the rural South. Between 1880 – after the end of Reconstruction and the withdrawal of the last Northern troops when the white South was finally able to manage its own destiny – and 1900, the value of its manufactured products increased about three and a half times. This compared with a national average of less than two and a half. Moreover, the national transformation was achieved with but a 50 per cent increase of establishments producing manufactured goods within the same period; large-scale industry was increasingly the order of the day.

Jefferson had believed almost religiously that 'those who labor in the earth are the chosen people of God'.[17] He had not presumably meant it quite so literally; otherwise, the phenomenal growth of mining might have cheered his heart. This was to develop faster than all other industries; by 1900 the total value of American production was to exceed a billion dollars. If gold and silver never lost their romantic appeal, more prosaically iron, coal, copper, lead, zinc, tin and quartz fuelled the bonanza. Oil, of course, was in a category of its own; in this period its prime use was for heat and light rather than for transport, which would come later. Nonetheless, it was a portent of how the land was changing and the problems that ensued in consequence. America had entered the modern age, but could her institutions cope with such change and expansion? Immigration, industrialization, urbanization all challenged the vision of the Founding Fathers of the American Republic. Jefferson in 1801 could single out the 'absolute acquiescence in the decisions of the majority' or the 'encouragement of agriculture, and of commerce as its handmaid' as essential principles of government. In 1889 Andrew Carnegie would propound a very different agenda: 'We accept and welcome, therefore, as conditions to which we must accommodate ourselves, great inequality of environment, the concentration of business, industrial and commercial, in the hands of a few, and the law of competition between these, as being not only beneficial, but essential for the future progress of the race.'[18]

Yet at least 60 per cent of the American population continued to live in the countryside throughout this period, though the proportion was slowly but ineluctably slipping all the time. Rural America might not have recognized that it was in retreat but it knew that it was threatened. The first stirrings of discontent had, not surprisingly, come from the farmers. They had more than enough of their own problems. Really, from the end of the Civil War agriculture had suffered a consistent depression brought about by overproduction and international competition which together lowered prices. In 1860 American farmers produced 839 million bushels of corn, in 1900 that had tripled to 2,662 but in the interim the price per bushel had dropped two-thirds; the same was true of wheat, even though production has gone from 173 million bushels to 449. In this respect the development of the West and the increasing cultivation of the land was a mixed blessing, as was the increased efficiency brought about by improvements in transportation and farm technology. Looking around for someone to blame, and here human nature combined with a not unreasonable inability to make sense of a number of ill-understood, varying and complex factors, the farmers soon came up with Eastern finance, the railroads and government protectionism for American industry as the source of rural woes. The analysis was not so much wrong as incomplete. However, it was to inspire a series of reform movements that resulted in the formation of a Populist Party which in 1892 ran its own candidate in a third-party bid for president. Given that the two leading parties, Republican and Democrat, are both broad churches, reflecting the inevitable coalition of interests, often indeed united round the lowest common denominator that alone makes an American political party viable in a transcontinental situation, third parties tend to get squeezed into oblivion. That the Populists could get over a million votes and carry four states with twenty-two votes in the electoral college was quite an impressive achievement, and symptomatic of rural discontent and the conviction that the main parties had failed a sizeable section of the population.

Indeed the Populist Party Platform made strange reading to those who still held to a belief in the essential promise of American society:

> We meet in the midst of a nation brought to the verge of moral, political, and material ruin. Corruption dominates the ballot box, the legislatures, the Congress, and touches even ... the bench. The people are demoralized ... newspapers are largely subsidized or muzzled, public opinion silenced, business prostrated, homes covered with mortgages, labor impoverished, and the land concentrated in the hands of capitalists. The urban workmen are denied the right to organize for self-protection ... The fruits of the toil of millions are boldly stolen to build up colossal fortunes for a few ... we breed the two great classes – tramps and millionaires.

Even allowing for political hyperbole, this is a scathing indictment. And it was made worse by the belief that the political process itself had failed. As the Populists further alleged: 'We have witnessed for more than a quarter of a century the struggles of the two great political parties for power and plunder, while grievous wrongs have been inflicted upon the suffering people.[19]

Nor was censure confined only to rural malcontents. That great critic of the period, Henry Adams, a descendant of one of America's foremost families, grandson and great-grandson of presidents, was equally scathing: 'One might search the whole list of Congress, Judiciary, and Executive during the twenty-five years 1870–1895, and find little but damaged reputation. The period was poor in purpose and barren in results.' And the anonymous publication of his novel *Democracy* in March 1880 caused a literary scandal, as it satirized and sought to strip bare the murkier workings of the American political process. And yet what was the alternative? Henry Adams, like many of his class, had eschewed politics. As a refuge he had turned to writing history, seeing in the Jeffersonian era a golden age; after that it had been downhill all the way. Indeed he argued: 'The system of 1789 had broken down, and with it the eighteenth century of a priori, or moral, principles. Politicians had tacitly given it up.'[20]

Acknowledging the system's failings, the equally patrician Roosevelt drew the opposite conclusion to Adams. His entry into politics, shortly after leaving Harvard, was based on a different analysis:

I suppose for one thing ordinary, plain, every-day duty sent me there to begin with. But, more than that, I wanted to belong to the governing class, not to the governed. When I said that I wanted to go to the Republican Association, they told me that I would meet the groom and the salon-keeper there; that politics were low, and that no gentlemen bothered with them. 'Then,' said I, 'if that is so, the groom and the salon-keeper are the governing class and you confess weakness. You have all the chances, the education, the position, and you let them rule you. They must be better men'; and I went.[21]

3 Republicans and Democrats: Hamilton and Jefferson

Twenty years later the consequences of this youthful decision were to be momentous, but it might be asked: how could the Republican

Party serve as a vehicle of reform? For if the political outlook was depressing it was a reflection of its dominance. From the election of Lincoln in 1860 to the election of Franklin Roosevelt in 1932, the Republican Party was the natural majority party of the United States, at least in national politics, and the world of post-Civil War America was very much one of its making. It was the party of the North and the Northern plutocracy; it had won the war; to the victor belonged the spoils. The Democratic Party bore the taint of treason; it was the party of the Confederacy. In 1884 a Republican sympathizer, not entirely inaccurately but unwisely referred to it as the party of 'rum, Romanism and rebellion': the party of the urban poor, immigrants, Catholic Irish and the South. It was to be a costly mistake, helping to elect one of only two Democratic presidents in seventy years, Grover Cleveland of New York. Surely the Democratic Party, as the minority, opposition party was the best hope for the reformers?[22]

Certainly the Populists thought so. The year 1892 had proved their high-water mark. Even though their achievement had been considerable, it was clear that their movement was too narrowly focused to be successful; only in the capture of one of the major parties, and the Democratic Party with its agrarian wing was the obvious contender, was there hope of reform. The election of 1896 was one of the most famous in American history. William Jennings Bryan, only thirty-six years old, virtually captured the Democratic Party nomination with one speech at its Convention and in so doing made the old Populist Party redundant. The campaign that followed was partisan and bitter; Bryan travelled the country, using to the full his much-vaunted eloquence. 'The Boy Orator of the River Platte' (a sobriquet testifying to his youthfulness, rhetoric and origins in Nebraska) was alternatively persuasive and charismatic or facile and dangerous depending on one's viewpoint. To his enemies he was indeed like the River Platte: 'six inches deep and six miles wide at the mouth.'[23] More kindly, he was 'the Great Commoner', a tribute to his identification with the ordinary man.[24]

Even this could be used against him: he was a radical verging on communism threatening the capitalist system! Such tactics helped McKinley and the Republicans amass a huge war chest; and Bryan's panacea for the country's ills of the free and unlimited coinage of silver, as against those who clung to the gold standard, was sufficient to alarm businessmen and urban workingmen alike. Significantly, Bryan did not carry a single state in the industrial Northeast.

It required no great insight to see that an inflationary policy designed to help the farmer would cut the real value of wages, since higher farm prices would have to be paid for by the consumer, and if protectionism helped industrialists, it could also be said to help their employees. The year 1896 confirmed the Republican ascendancy. Indeed it was the first presidential election since the end of Reconstruction in 1876 in which the victor received a majority of the popular vote as opposed to a mere plurality. Grover Cleveland, the outgoing Democratic president, had won a second term in 1892 after a four-year absence from the White House, but had divided his party with conservative policies that caused it to turn to Bryan. Not until 1912 was another Democrat to win the presidency and that, significantly, with a minority of the popular vote, and only when the Republicans, too, were divided. The future for the moment lay with them.

Thus the reform movement would have to make headway inside the majority party; it would be urban not rural; hence the significance of Roosevelt's elevation. The Populists could not command nationwide support; certainly, not on their own; not even in Democratic clothing. Nonetheless, a lot of their prescriptions as to how American politics might be made more accountable, and thus more subservient to the wishes of the people, would help constitute the agenda of reform politics over the next two decades. Populism would fade as Progressivism blossomed, but the former fertilized the latter.

Progressivism was the political buzzword of the opening years of the new century, but its very indefinability and presence in both Republican and Democratic parties is in itself suggestive of the imprecision inherent in the movement. It has been seen as primarily a cause of the middle classes; then again as a reaction to the excesses of the Gilded Age. In other lights it has been defined as an attempt by older established groups to arrest their declining status; alternatively as a catchall banner for political reform. Or was it merely a desire to promote efficient government both at state and city level by the introduction of professionals and their expertise in place of amateur bungling, if not outright corruption? Clearly, however, Progressives of both political parties and none, of differing age, class and political persuasion, scattered across the nation, counted themselves members of the movement. Sometimes they were bound together by a certain common culture, such as readership of the same journals, membership of professions and their associations, or

as college graduates linked through networks of alumni or frater-
nities. Often, however, chance dictated their existence. A charismatic
figure here, a group of earnest-minded citizens there, a corrupt city
hall, a particular scandal or a wave of popular protest somewhere
else fuelled a movement as disparate as it was evidently related. In
many ways Progressivism testified to the importance of grassroots
activism in the American political process and a salutary reminder
that not every political change emanates from Washington. One of its
great causes, indeed, women's suffrage was, of course, supported
and abetted by many who were not even enfranchised.

In Wisconsin, Robert La Follette made the state in Roosevelt's
words, 'an experimental laboratory of wise governmental action in
aid of social and economic justice', with the university there fur-
nishing his experts.[25] In California Hiram Johnson broke the power
of the Southern Pacific Railroad. In Georgia Hoke Smith introduced
business regulation. In New York Charles Evans Hughes and, even
more famously, Woodrow Wilson in New Jersey were to furnish
further examples of one of the most fertile and innovative periods in
American state government. Nor was their example ignored by the
localities. In Ohio, at city level, Samuel M. Jones, cleaned up Toledo,
whilst in neighbouring Cleveland, Tom L. Johnson made it 'the
best-governed city in America' according to one admirer.[26]

In every case the reformers represented a belief in the effectiveness of executive action, at city but more especially at state and
federal level. Here the role of government was less circumscribed
and gave greater scope for legislation; the reforms enacted were
thus more wide-ranging in their impact. Not surprisingly, Roosevelt
both temperamentally and as a former governor of the most populous state in the Union was sympathetic. Yet here one must enter a
caveat. In New York Roosevelt would not have been called a Progressive; he was of very different caste to 'Fighting Bob' La Follette.
Indeed, they were later to become rivals and the latter would
always have something of the suspicion that the true believer has
for the compromiser. Progressivism, though, was not a composite
programme, a creed to each and every one of whose articles one had
to subscribe; it was more a cast of mind. Whilst there were certain
reforms that most Progressives held in common, the desire to establish control – and this, in particular, appealed to Roosevelt – also
bound them together.

The movement was occasioned both by the long-maturing problems of post-Civil War America and by the economic downturn of

the early 1890s that had frustrated Grover Cleveland's second administration. By the end of the decade the economy had picked up; McKinley had no trouble beating Bryan in 1900 more handsomely than he had done four years previously. Thus Progressivism proceeded from strength, not weakness; it was a self-confident movement and, unlike Populism, not narrowly focused. This, too, appealed to Roosevelt. A man of enormous physical self-confidence himself, his adulthood with its emphasis on the cult of manliness, a robust physique, strenuous activity, energetic sports and an extrovert persona was the classic case of over-compensation for a frail childhood. Then small of stature, asthmatic and short-sighted, he had been a natural victim for any street-corner bully. Instead, Roosevelt became something of a bully himself. In fact, it is possible to see his macho posturing as very much in tune with the Social Darwinism, White Man's burden, and Anglo-Saxon ruling attitudes that both reflected and pandered to America's growing sense of her own emerging strength at the turn of the new century. Henry Adams, for one, struck a note of caution. 'Power when wielded by abnormal energy is the most serious of facts, and all Roosevelt's friends know that his restless and combative energy was more than abnormal. Roosevelt, more than any other man living within the range of notoriety, showed the singular primitive quality that belongs to ultimate matter, – the quality that medieval theology assigned to God, – he was pure act.'[27]

Indeed, Roosevelt's general forcefulness, not to say latent aggressiveness, can make him an ambiguous hero for subsequent Americans. It is possible to trace some more disturbing features of the modern American experience to his example. To contemporaries, however, like Henry James, he was that 'wonderful little machine'. More critically, to Mark Twain even after seven and a half years in the presidency, 'He is still only fourteen years old.'[28]

Roosevelt was a member of the majority party; the party, moreover, to which one might reasonably attribute many of the ills of contemporary America. It was a rich, businessmen's party; it identified with wealth. As such, the Republican Party reflected that alliance between government and business that had been urged by Alexander Hamilton, George Washington's Secretary of the Treasury. One of the principal proponents of the new American Constitution, Hamilton had seen in such a relationship the best insurance for the stability and survival of the new Republic. In this respect Hamilton was the direct opposite of Thomas Jefferson; and the tug-of-war

between Hamiltonian and Jeffersonian principles is one of the enduring themes and continuing battles of American history. To Jefferson
'the apostle of liberty', the greatest guarantee of the integrity of the
Republic was a diffusion of power and a reliance on the agrarian
interest. Concentrated wealth would suborn the government to its
own ends. A large number of independent, yeomen farmers who
farmed their own land and had a modest stake in their society in its
most traditional form would be a natural barrier to an unholy alliance
of political power and excessive wealth. Government was to be
viewed with suspicion; it had a tendency to dominate and repress.
Liberty was a delicate plant to be sedulously nurtured. It had many
enemies, especially the rich. To Jefferson, Hamilton was 'honest as a
man, but as a politician, believing in the necessity of either force or
corruption to govern men'.[29] For Hamilton, Jefferson's 'politics are
tinctured with fanaticism . . . He is too much in earnest in his democracy'.[30]

Hamiltonian ideas had been in the ascendant since the Civil War.
Indeed, one might argue that the defeated South with its insistence
on states' rights had taken one particular variant of Jeffersonianism
to its logical conclusion, to the point, indeed, where abstraction flew
in the face of experience. It is interesting to reflect whether, had the
Confederacy broken free, it could ever have endured as a nation,
when at its birth it had sanctified the principle that the minority
could prevail over the majority: a dangerous, double-edged sword
for the future. Its defeat makes this purely speculative, but the North's
victory and the consequent Republican ascendancy were recognition
not only of Northern military might but of its industrial power too,
that had foredoomed the agrarian, rural South.

True, the Republican Party was indeed the party of the plutocracy, the party of the 'robber barons' and thus the party of John D.
Rockefeller, J. P. Morgan, Andrew Carnegie, and E. H. Harriman.
It was the party of men who often operated at the margin of the
law and whose rapacity, ruthlessness and pursuit of profit can only
be justified as a necessary evil in the accelerated development of
the United States inside a generation. But it was also a party of
idealistic principle. This was easy to overlook in the tawdry vulgarity of Gilded Age politics into which Roosevelt made his debut. But
his chosen vehicle was the selfsame party that in part owed its
origins to a detestation of slavery and, in the person of Lincoln,
found a spokesman of unique moral grandeur. Lincoln made of the
preservation of the Union itself a sacred cause, not always apparent

to contemporaries, but one that was subsequently vindicated by events and which, in its turn, entailed the destruction of slavery. Thus the New England conscience that animated the anti-slavery crusade in the 1840s and 1850s might be dormant rather than dead a half century later. It was a potent legacy to party supporters. Given a cause and a champion, undreamed of veins of idealism might be tapped. This time it would not be against involuntary servitude and its possible extension. Instead, it would confront political and economic exploitation that, unless arrested and curtailed, would effect a similar division in the Union, whereby a minority of wealth would frustrate the majority and where, irrespective of law, the many would be in tutelage to the few.

Thus Roosevelt might not be a pure Progressive. But if the movement itself had a moral base and a cast of mind that could be described as almost evangelical in its fervour, it opened up the possibility that it would at the very least find a spokesman. Exhortation, a belief in the power of reason, the promotion of the 'general welfare' of the nation and an optimistic, if sometimes naïve, belief in the perfectibility of man and society through direct action would be their watchwords. And Roosevelt, moreover, was a spokesman who also had at his disposal the practical means to implement Progressive ideas through political programmes, which had the force of a party behind them.

However, one had to ask how far even the office of president would enable such a programme to be fulfilled. The Founding Fathers of 1787 had been wary of a powerful chief executive and the office had been hedged around with restrictions. In the Constitution the carefully contrived system of checks and balances was designed to ensure that no home-grown version of George III would be tolerated. Only in foreign affairs, in those sudden emergencies that might threaten a late eighteenth-century rural society, an Indian uprising perhaps, a naval confrontation on the high seas, was the president to have much latitude for personal initiative. Strictly speaking, he was not even popularly elected but chosen by 'electors' in an electoral college who were themselves voted for by the people. Only the happy chance that George Washington was clearly going to be the first president allowed the office to receive the power it did. He had proved in the struggle against Britain that he could be trusted.

Inevitably, however, the office was sanctified by its holders. Washington himself was perhaps the ideal figure to occupy the post of chief executive in a young republic that had turned its back on monarchy but not yet come to terms with democratic egalitarianism. By the time he retired in 1797 he had invested the presidency with his own dignity and integrity. Thomas Jefferson, elected in 1800, brought intellectual distinction to the office. In the 1830s Andrew Jackson added the popularity of the common man. Above all there was the inspiration of Abraham Lincoln. The nobility of his character and the tragedy of his death would ever after haunt Americans. Indeed, Lincoln's assassination in 1865, at the conclusion of the Civil War, seemed almost martyrdom to the cause of preserving the United States as one nation, free and indivisible. It was a cause that was not merely America's. It ensured, as he sublimely put it, 'that government of the people, by the people, for the people, shall not perish from the earth'.[31]

Moreover, no written prescription of the limitations of the office as enumerated in the Constitution could impede the march of great events. Life demands leaders who can make decisions; as Lincoln himself had warned at the height of the Civil War: 'The occasion is piled high with difficulty, and we must rise with the occasion.'[32] It was America's good fortune that the greatest of her leaders did. Great crises made great presidents. Yet there is no escaping the fact that between the death of Lincoln in 1865 and the accession of Roosevelt in 1901, seven men and eight presidencies were largely unremarkable. The possible exception was Grover Cleveland, whose two split terms of office, from 1885 to 1889 and 1893 to 1897, raised the general standard a little, but nowhere near to greatness. Honest men, honourable men, decent men, perhaps: well-intentioned, hard-working, though the most famous, Ulysses S. Grant the Civil War hero, was a failure. But by 1888 the British commentator James Bryce, in his book *The American Commonwealth*, could actually entitle a chapter 'Why Great Men Are Not Chosen Presidents'. And this less than a quarter of a century after Lincoln's death! Perhaps it is a salutary reminder that greatness does not come to order. The somewhat humdrum politics of this period tended to raise men whose chief virtue was that they did not offend. Anyway, as Bryce explained further: for the really ambitious there were other possibilities.

These railway kings are among the greatest men, perhaps I may say are the greatest men in America. They have wealth, else they could not hold the position ... fame, for everyone has heard of

their achievements; every newspaper chronicles their movements
... power, more power – that is, more opportunity of making their
personal will prevail – than perhaps anyone in political life,
except the President and the Speaker, who after all hold theirs
only for four years and two years, while the railroad monarch
may keep his for life.

In the world of late nineteenth-century America, money not so
much talked as shouted.[33]

4 Theodore Roosevelt in the White House

Still, Roosevelt grasped an essential truth about the office he had
inherited. The president of the United States, with the exception of
the vice-president elected with him, is the only man who is voted
into office by the whole of the American people; no senator, no state
governor, no representative in Congress can claim the same. The
implications in a democratic society were considerable. If the president can claim to be acting on behalf of the American people, if his
policy has their support or he can attract it, he is politically unassailable. Reform politics might yet prevail. Of course, all this would
take time. For a start it came up against the inconvenient reality that
in 1901 Roosevelt was the heir to another man's programme. Not
only did he lack the mandate of popular endorsement, but he also
inherited a party many of whose members, not least in Congress,
were in no way reformers. Roosevelt would not fully be his own
man until he had been nominated by his party and elected by the
people. However, as president in his own right after 1904, he gave a
convincing demonstration of his insight into the potentiality of the
presidency and how it might impact on the Nation. Indeed, his
whole seven and a half years in the White House were significant
for developing those first modern practices that were to be an
increasing feature of the Executive.

At the outset Roosevelt had one powerful attribute: he was no-
ticeable; he enjoyed publicity, indeed revelled in it, recognized it as
a weapon in the political battle. Roosevelt talked to newsmen; he
appealed to the people over the heads of their senators and representatives in Congress; he speechified. The White House was, in
his famous phrase, 'a bully pulpit' and he was happy to deliver
sermons.[34] By his very presence he brought reform to the forefront

of the political agenda. He achieved one of the main objectives of any democratic politician, to make his own concerns those of the public; where he led they should follow. Moreover, he grasped the powers of the office to its fullest. 'I declined to adopt the view,' he later explained, 'that what was imperatively necessary for the Nation could not be done by the President unless he could find some specific authorization to do it. My belief was that it was not only his right but his duty to do anything that the needs of the Nation demanded unless such action was forbidden by the Constitution or the laws.'[35] Inevitably, not all were so enthusiastic. 'Roosevelt's all right,' the Speaker of the House grumbled, 'but he's got no more use for the Constitution than a tomcat has for a marriage license.'[36]

Of course, Roosevelt trod carefully – he had to. One can follow his progress through the years of his presidency and see how he warily evaded head-on confrontation with conservative forces unless he was sure of winning. Still, even if he used the mantle of reformer but in fact often subscribed to and implemented a far more cautious policy, nonetheless ineluctably, reform used him. Partly it was the pressure of events, setting in train the unstoppable process. Perhaps partly it was a tribute to his own capacity for growth: he learnt from experience. But those who not unreasonably question Roosevelt's Progressive credentials have to face up to Roosevelt's conversion from the politics of expedience in 1901 through to the politics of commitment in 1912.

In part, this was because in the final analysis Roosevelt failed to make the Republican Party into the party he believed it should be. Had he done so, the subsequent history of the United States might have been markedly different. Here he harked back to the example of Lincoln, the greatest of his Republican predecessors. Just as Lincoln had stood for the Union, so too did Roosevelt. But whereas the crisis that threatened Lincoln's Union was that of political secession, for Roosevelt it was the internal conflict of classes that he saw as threatening the Republic. 'My business was to take hold of the conservative party and turn it into what it had been under Lincoln, that is a party of *progressive* conservatism, or conservative radicalism,' he later admitted.[37] In this respect, he was clearly disappointed. But it is an important clue as to how he proceeded; if Bryanite Democrats were dangerous radicals, Roosevelt's business was to meet the clamour for change from within the system. This required a delicate balancing act, keeping in with the

Old Guard who often held the power but listing towards the reformers who often made the running. When in the end the Old
Guard won out, Roosevelt threw in his lot with the reformers. That
way he might trim their claws and still preserve class, and hence
national unity. It was to be a forlorn hope and, in any case, an
irrelevant one since he did not win in 1912. Nonetheless, the
White House years of 1901 to 1909 cannot be understood without
reference to the New Nationalism campaign of 1912. They form a
unified whole as America moved further away from the McKinley
era and faced the new pressures of a new century.

Roosevelt first made an impact with the issue of the trusts. Many
of these in fact dated from the time of McKinley. And the growth of
such vast business combinations, though arguably a reflection of
contemporary economic conditions, provided easy ammunition for
reformers who noted their identity of interests with the Republican
Party, their ability to influence political machines, and their apparent independence from normal regulatory restraint. Yet Roosevelt
proceeded carefully. Whilst the problem would not go away if
one ignored it, indeed would worsen, wholesale trust-busting was
far too crude a solution in Roosevelt's judgement. Better, surely,
regulation than some anachronistic attempt to revert to the small-
business model of an earlier era; and, indeed, what to some extent
Roosevelt found most objectionable was not the trusts' size, but
their assumption that they were almost independent equals to
the federal government. Choosing his target with care, Roosevelt
moved against the Northern Securities Company in 1902, a vast
holding company to control the Great Northern and Northern Pacific railroads, hence unpopular with the public and in breach of
the law, as the Supreme Court endorsed two years later. But what
angered him most was the response of J. P. Morgan on a visit to the
White House: 'If we have done anything wrong, send your man to
my man and they can fix it up.' Such insouciance implied a notion
of equality that Roosevelt was determined to rebut.[38]

Much is often made of the fact that Roosevelt's reputation as
a trust-buster is over-generous, that his conservative successor
William Howard Taft in four years initiated twice the trust-busting
suits that Roosevelt did in nearly eight. And it is certainly true that
there was a not-inconsiderable playing to the gallery in Roosevelt's
anti-business manoeuvres. Yet he made the first moves, always
significant, and let the trusts know that they were not laws unto
themselves; in fact, it was as a political rather than as an economic

force that he disliked them. In this sense he was as much a Progressive as those who equally wanted to make the political system fairer by the direct election of senators, the implementation of the legislative initiative, referendum and recall from office, direct primary elections, or indeed votes for women.

Circumscribing the over-mighty subject needed to be matched by concern for the economic underdog if Roosevelt's vision of class cohesion was to be effective. Hence in the same year that he took on the Northern Securities Company, he intervened in the anthracite coal strike between the United Mine Workers and the mine owners then being fought out in the Pennsylvania and West Virginia coalfields. Here the method of resolution of the conflict was more significant than its conclusion. Roosevelt faced the prospect that the mine owners, rather than submit to the miners' demands for a 20 per cent wage increase, a nine-hour day instead of ten, and union recognition, would shut down the mines and leave the nation short of coal. Accordingly, he threatened to take over the mines and run them with the army, a proposal of doubtful constitutional legality. It was enough to end the strike, which a White House conference had failed to do, since the owners recognized that Roosevelt might carry out his threat, backed by public opinion, and the issue was put to a panel of arbitrators appointed by the president. If the miners only secured a partial victory, a nine-hour day, but only a 10 per cent wage increase and no union recognition, the authority of the president and the increasing importance of his role were visibly enhanced.

One must never forget the weight Roosevelt placed on executive action in evaluating his performance. Partly, of course, it appealed to his temperament. But it also allowed him to escape some of the legislative constraints that a conservative Congress might have used to shackle him. It also allowed him to push presidential power to the limit. He would be bound by the Constitution only where it expressly forbade him to act. He openly boasted of his tactics: 'I have used every ounce of power there was in the office and I have not cared a rap for the criticisms of those who spoke of my "usurpation of power"; for I knew that ... there was no usurpation.' It was a portent of the future. Reformers would note the potential of this enhanced role in the relationship between President and Nation. It was a crucial factor in the development of modern America.[39]

Executive power generally was to receive a boost when in 1903 a new Cabinet Department of Commerce and Labor was set up. This included a Bureau of Corporations, which had the power to investigate the activities of such inter-state bodies, and either to guide them in the direction of conforming to the law, or, if they remained obdurate and indulged in malpractices, run the risk of government-initiated antitrust suits. Other measures such as the Elkins Act outlawed the taking as well as the giving of railroad rebates, and an Expedition Act required Federal Circuit Courts to give priority to antitrust suits upon the urging of the attorney-general. Collectively, they signified a further stage in the attempt to extend governmental regulation. It must be conceded that Roosevelt often extracted the maximum publicity from a stance that in point of fact could be of limited effectiveness. Robert La Follette for one, an uncompromising Progressive, was later to complain that '[Roosevelt] acted upon the maxim that half a loaf is better than no bread. I believe that half a loaf is fatal whenever it is accepted at the sacrifice of the basic principle sought to be attained.'[40]

Nonetheless, it was precisely that willingness to compromise or trim, depending on one's point of view that was sufficient to earn Roosevelt re-election in his own right in 1904 under a programme entitled 'the Square Deal'. True, even this might be more for show than action. One disenchanted former admirer later commented: 'His notion of a square deal was to cuff the radical on one ear and the conservative on the other, without enlightening either.'[41]

But this at least represented a desire to strike a balance in society, which to Roosevelt was the most sensible course to forestall radicalism or, even worse, socialism. It was clearly a course with which others sympathized. Two of the defendants in the Northern Securities case, J. P. Morgan and E. H. Harriman, gave $150,000 and $50,000, respectively, to Roosevelt's campaign chest. When it came to the crunch, rich men knew who was their true friend and how limited his trust-busting was in practice. Still, the first two years of his second term were to be the high-water mark of his presidency, where he was bolstered by a huge victory in 1904 which gave the Democrats the worst electoral drubbing a major party had received since 1832. Even congressional conservatives had to bend to the wind of popular opinion. It was in these years that Roosevelt pushed through the Hepburn Act of 1906 that finally gave real teeth to railroad regulation and in the same year the Meat Inspection Act and the Pure Food and Drug Act that imposed public health standards on the food industry. Yet it is also symptomatic of Roosevelt's ambivalent attitude that he criticized the journalists who had exposed some of the abuses of the American food industry in one of his more memorable outbursts. 'The man who never does anything else, who never thinks or speaks or writes, save of his feats with the muck-rake, speedily becomes, not a help to society, not an incitement to good, but one of the most potent forces for evil.' 'Muckraker' thus became a term of opprobrium that later acquired a wholly different status as a hallmark of the best type of investigative journalism.[42]

If Roosevelt's election victory helped propel him through the years of his greatest achievement, it was also to prove his undoing. Overwhelmed by the scale of his triumph, and perhaps also genuinely convinced, like the conservative that at heart he was, that no one should hold excessive power for long, he announced on election night that seven and a half years in the White House was enough for anyone. Accordingly he would not seek another term. The consequence was that he was a lame-duck president as his term drew to an end and the political world looked to his successor. Nor was he helped by a financial panic in 1907 that occasioned a series of banking and industrial failures. In the end he was forced to cooperate with the very business interests he had previously opposed. Conservatives claimed that Roosevelt's own anti-business diatribes had helped bring about the panic. Roosevelt responded by suggesting it was a consequence of the selfish behaviour of those he termed 'malefactors of great wealth'.[43]

In the end the tension between conservatives and reformers in the Republican Party was never satisfactorily resolved, but Roosevelt's increasing reform rhetoric reflected his frustration, that would bear fruit in 1912. Significantly, when Roosevelt came to list his major presidential achievements only one, conservation, related to domestic politics. Here his performance is unquestioned and makes him a topical figure. As early as 1902 he helped the passage of the National Reclamation Act sponsored by Senator Francis Newlands of Nevada, which set aside proceeds from the sale of Western public lands in order to finance irrigation projects in the perennially water-hungry West. Using his executive authority as president, he added some 150 million acres to the national forests, a move further reinforced by the inspired appointment of Gifford Pinchot, one of America's first scientific foresters, to the post of chief forester in the Department of Agriculture. Roosevelt also approved five new national parks, prohibited commercial exploitation of some 85 million acres in Alaska and the Northwest, initiated a scheme to designate certain natural features as national monuments and considerably augmented the number of federal wildlife refuges. In May 1908 the governors of all but five states attended a National Conservation Congress at the White House to consider environmental issues and recommend joint action to their respective legislatures. If little was actually achieved, it did at least give further publicity to the issue.

Roosevelt's disinclination to dwell too long on his domestic achievements was partly, no doubt, a reluctance to emphasize those issues where credit had to be shared with others, of which the passage through Congress of legislation was an example. A case in point is the National Reclamation Act, where he seems to have been mildly jealous of the credit given to Senator Newlands. One might attribute this to the fact that Newlands was a Democrat, were it not that Roosevelt seems equally to have minimized the work of Senator Hanna, an early irrigation enthusiast who was a member of his own party. As one of Roosevelt's sons is supposed to have commented: 'Father always wanted to be the bride at every wedding and the corpse at every funeral.'[44] Partly, however, domestic achievements were not so striking; they usually involved compromise and log-rolling. Roosevelt's diffidence, too, reflected his awareness that his party still had not been made in his own image; a notable bone of contention was the tariff, whose high rates the Old Guard wanted to keep in line with traditional Republican protectionism. Stirrings in the country for lower rates required Roosevelt to tread a delicate path, though the issue was a useful whip to crack over the more recalcitrant conservatives who clung to him for fear of finding something worse. Later, however, it was to break the party apart when William Howard Taft, Roosevelt's secretary of war and hand-picked successor as president, proved less adroit in keeping the warring factions within the Republican ranks happy. Indeed, had Roosevelt been more successful, it might not have been necessary for him to run again for president in 1912.

Still, deep down what inspired Roosevelt was a zest for action; nowhere was this more uniquely presidential than in the field of foreign policy. It could even be enlisted in the cause of Progressivism. '...I too often found,' he wrote in 1912,

that men who were ardent for social and industrial reform would be ignorant of the needs of this nation as a nation,... of what the navy meant to the nation, of what it meant... to have and to fortify and protect the Panama Canal, of what it meant... to get from the other nations of mankind the respect which comes only to the just, and which is denied to the weaker nation far more quickly than it is denied to the stronger ... I feel that the Progressive party owes no small part of its strength to the fact that it not only stands for ... measures of social and industrial reform, but ... also for the right and duty of this nation to take a position of self-respecting strength among the nations of the world ...[45]

Not all, of course, shared this prescription. Here the Bryan and the La Follette Progressives would join hands. Indeed, the speed with which Roosevelt abandoned Progressivism in favour of Preparedness for War by 1916 does raise doubts as to how deep his commitment lay. Perhaps in the last resort Roosevelt was a nationalist, which at home implied a respect for federal authority superior to any other forces, balancing competing interests, and abroad a strong America anxious to take her place in the sun. Here the man and the hour met in happy juxtaposition. True, Roosevelt's foreign policy attracted only modest public support and his celebrated phrase, 'Speak softly, and carry a big stick,' might appropriately have been reversed. For all his loud rhetorical posturing he was actually quite restrained, recognizing that his scope for action was in fact quite limited. Wisely, he only threw his weight around where he would meet no serious opposition.[46]

To be fair, his record did not necessarily match his image. Indeed, he was awarded the Nobel Peace Prize for his role in arbitrating the Peace Conference at Portsmouth, New Hampshire, that ended the Russo-Japanese War of 1904–5; the following year he supported the Algeciras Conference that forestalled a possible European war over Morocco; and in 1907 endorsed the Second Hague Conference. These gave him the international profile that he sought both for himself and for his country, but foreign observers shrewdly noted the latent isolationism of his people and knew that when it came to the crunch America was still not an equal player in world affairs. Here the President was ahead of the Nation: not for the last time in modern America.

Roosevelt, in fact, was at his most forceful in Latin America. Taking the Monroe Doctrine a stage further he moved from excluding European intervention to justifying American intervention by the so-called 'Roosevelt Corollary'. Even more significantly, he helped along a Panamanian revolt against Colombian rule which neatly solved the problem of building the Panama Canal as a reward for American recognition of Panamanian independence. This of course tied in with his increasing commitment to develop American naval power in an age of naval expansion, trade, and colonial acquisition. Nor was a naval building programme bad for business.

It is reasonable to argue that Roosevelt was more prescient than his countrymen were in seeing an equation between domestic and foreign strength, and also in noting the interconnectedness of nations at the opening of the new century. Again, the vulnerability of America, with its two oceans and extensive coastline, and the diminishing value of British naval protection as it faced the threat of an expanding German fleet, were other dangers that he quickly recognized. Meanwhile, on the other side of the world, Japan, too, posed a long-term problem for the United States. Indeed, for years Roosevelt had been a tireless advocate of the geopolitical naval doctrines of Alfred T. Mahan. Not the least attraction of the Spanish–American War had been that it would knock Spain out of the Caribbean, a necessary prelude to a canal across the Panamanian isthmus, which would neatly solve the problem of maximizing the effectiveness of a two-ocean navy. For Roosevelt, talk of a navy sufficient for national defence was to err on the side of caution.

Alternatively, one might see in Roosevelt's exuberant chauvinism a dangerous legacy to a people naive in the ways of foreign policy, insular in outlook, and lacking that sophisticated touch that the management of national interests in balance with resources requires. Roosevelt's insensitive, if not arrogant, admission, 'I don't know the way the people *do* feel – I only know how they *ought* to feel,' seems too often to have been adopted later by his countrymen in their dealings with other peoples.[47]

Even his not unreasonable exhortation to his fellow Americans to encourage the genuine idealism of some of their compatriots could too easily slip into messianism or mask self-interest. 'We who stay at home should as a matter of duty give cordial support to those who in a spirit of devotion to all that is highest in human nature, spend the best part of their lives in trying to carry civilization and Christianity into lands which have hitherto known little or nothing of either.' It was a statement that begged lots of questions.[48]

All in all, it was a mixed legacy, reflecting the ambiguity of American public opinion generally and not necessarily enlightening it. Not for another generation were Americans to come to terms with their world role: until they did so, the problems would increase and multiply both for them and for others. Thus Roosevelt's famous gesture of sending the American fleet on a voyage round the world was a piece of dramatic muscle-flexing, that doubtless raised his profile and enhanced his presidential authority as it was meant to do, but in other respects rather missed its target. It was designed to let the Japanese know what they might have to reckon with should they continue to prove fractious in the Pacific, but the Japanese clearly took the sting out of the ploy by inviting the American fleet to visit Yokohama. This was a request Roosevelt could hardly refuse, and the ships were met with polished courtesy and elaborate displays of peace and goodwill. Meanwhile the American public, having held up their hands in admiration, failed to think beyond the symbolism or show any more sustained commitment to a strengthening of the nation's power as a necessary basis for a realistic foreign policy. Roosevelt regarded it as his greatest accomplishment that he had doubled the size of the United States Navy and sent it on its 46,000-mile voyage. Doubtless, other nations were impressed, yet it is hard to escape the conclusion that for Roosevelt action often served to release his frustrations but did not necessarily achieve much of substance. In foreign policy especially, the dramatic gesture is not always the wisest, and reminds one that Roosevelt had been largely catapulted into public view by the Spanish–American War. Whilst to be fair to Roosevelt it cannot be alleged that he created a drama where none existed, it is perhaps a matter of relief that no great international crisis erupted that led to war during his years in the White House.

5 The Progressive Moment

Surrendering the presidency at the age of fifty would never have been easy for Roosevelt; massacring big game in Africa or being feted in Europe could not compensate for the aching feeling that his best years were now behind him. Thus should his successor Taft get into difficulties, it was on the cards that Roosevelt would be drawn back to the political game. He did not have long to wait. Taft proved temperamentally ill-at-ease in the presidency, with its premium on attention to public opinion, and some of the problems Roosevelt had shelved soon came to a head, notably the tariff and the increasing tension between conservatives and Progressives.

Indeed, in a curious way Taft did reformers a double favour. Firstly by in fact being just that – a reformer himself. He initiated twice the number of trust-busting suits Roosevelt had; continued conservation; established a separate Department of Labor; promoted worker protection; and supported two path-breaking Constitutional Amendments, the Sixteenth authorizing a federal income tax and the Seventeenth mandating direct popular election of United States senators. Perhaps nothing better underlines Progressive effectiveness than to recall that the last Constitutional Amendment had been ratified way back in 1870. Yet now, within a little over half a dozen years, no less than four causes dear to the Progressive heart were to receive formal constitutional recognition. If one might look askance at the Eighteenth that enabled Prohibition and was subsequently repealed by the Twenty-first, the Nineteenth that gave votes to women was the third of that great trinity of reforms that propelled the United States into the modern world. Henceforth, American governments would enjoy a predictable source of revenue that would allow them to expand their field of operations; the people would directly elect their senators; and all the people, irrespective of gender, would select their political masters and, indeed, political mistresses. Alas! For thirteen years they couldn't legally buy a drink to celebrate it.

Secondly, having earned his personal reformer's spurs, Taft then ineptly irritated reformers within his own party by back-tracking on the very Progressive causes that it was assumed he would espouse, thereby determining them to seek an alternative to him for the White House in 1912. Taft's sympathetic overtures to conservatives within the Republican Party over such issues as the tariff and conservation allowed Roosevelt, now a free spirit no longer weighed down by the cares of party management, to develop his ideas further along a Progressive path. Within eighteen months of leaving the White House, on his return from abroad, he was preaching the New Nationalism:

> The Republican party is now facing a great crisis. It is to decide whether it will be as in the days of Lincoln the party of the plain people, ... of progress, ... of social and industrial justice; or whether it will be the party of privilege and of special interest, the heir to ... Lincoln's most bitter opponents, ... that represents the great interests within and without Wall street which desire through their control over the servants of the public to be kept

immune from punishment when they do wrong and to be given privileges to which they are not entitled.[49]

The way was now set for Roosevelt to make a renewed bid for the presidency in 1912 on an avowedly Progressive platform. Of course, it was a mortal blow to the Republican Party's election prospects for that year. Taft, with all the power of an incumbent president, fought off Roosevelt's challenge for the Republican nomination, but the latter's decision to run as a third-party candidate only played into the hands of the Democrats. Independent splinter movements usually benefit the other side.

Rather uncharacteristically, the Democrats did not fluff the opportunity thus presented. Wisely dispensing with Bryan, they turned to the former president of Princeton University, now governor of New Jersey, Woodrow Wilson, who had the additional merit for the Democrats of being a Southerner by birth but a Northerner by adoption, thus linking the Party's two wings. Wilson had the additional advantage of being a relatively fresh face in politics, hence one without a past or a clutch of enemies. Like Roosevelt, he too had disappointed the political bosses who had sought to continue their hold on power, whilst using a front man who turned out to be a genuine reformer. Thus by one of those meteoric transformations that the American political system occasionally allows, a disappointed academic rebuffed by his own university was, within three years, poised to lead the United States in its most critical decade since the 1860s.

In this respect, the election of 1912 that sent Wilson to the White House was crucial. For a start it offered the nation the singular novelty of two Republican presidents: Taft and Roosevelt, running against each other, and two Progressives, Roosevelt and Wilson, locked in combat. Nor should one overlook Eugene Debs the Socialist candidate who knocked up about 900,000 votes or 6 per cent of those cast. Here was the real radical alternative. It is of course because of men like Roosevelt and Wilson, and indeed later Franklin Roosevelt, that it never made greater progress. American politics is fought over the centre. In 1912 the real fight was between Roosevelt and Wilson.

Initially, Roosevelt and Wilson had admired each other; if Roosevelt had all the energy and force of the extrovert and man of action, he had an intellectual side, including several works of history to his name. He was also a voracious reader. Wilson, the classic introvert, self-contained and distant, still had the inflexible will and purpose of the man of action. Wilson, two years Roosevelt's senior, had supported the latter in much of his presidency. Their Progressive prescriptions, however, differed and drove them apart. By 1912 they were opponents and soon to be enemies. Both, however, though they would have loathed to admit it, essentially espoused policies that had a common identity. This was the need to ensure that no other interest, group or faction within the United States should be powerful enough to disrupt or threaten the workings of the political system or suborn constitutional rights to economic gain. Their analysis of how this should be achieved, by contrast, differed profoundly.

Roosevelt's 'New Nationalism' accepted the power of the federal government as the only conceivable regulator among powerful competing interests whom it would ultimately control. Thereby the welfare of the individual would also be safeguarded. If private property had rights, it also had obligations. Only governmental regulation could maintain a cohesive balance between rich and poor. Yet in restraining concentrated economic power to insure social justice one could not turn back the clock. Roosevelt recognized the logic of history, saw in economic concentration the necessary development of the modern industrial state. His programme was a clear-sighted realization that one could not live in the twentieth century by the values of the eighteenth.

Wilson's 'New Freedom', by contrast, sought to diminish by dispersion other potential economic power centres. As a Jeffersonian Democrat, he had a suspicion of concentrated power that was not unreasonable given the prevailing conditions of American society. However, he could be rather woolly in his thinking and seductive though his vision was, it could smack of the politics of nostalgia. 'There has come over the land that un-American set of conditions which enables a small number of men who control the Government to get favours from the Government,' he proclaimed in 1912

by those favors to exclude their fellows from equal business opportunity; ... to extend a network of control that will presently dominate every industry in the country, and so make men forget the ancient time when America lay in every hamlet, ... was to be seen in every fair valley, ... displayed her great forces on the broad prairies, ran her fine fires of enterprise up over the mountain sides and down into the bowels of the earth, and eager men were everywhere captains of industry, not employees.

At one level, of course, Wilson was right in his characterization: 'The Old Order Changeth'; but the choice of verb had more than a taint of unconscious irony.[50] In any case Wilson was to face a dilemma. Even his vision in which economic concentrations of power should be split up could not be achieved except by employing the power of big government, and it flew in the face of political logic to abandon such a tool once his programme had been achieved. Government at the service of reform soon became a reforming government whose scope inexorably widened. Wilson, though he would have been outraged by the charge, was in some ways to become a follower of Roosevelt. The two men may have had different ends but they came to share the same means and the means subtly modified the ends.

6   Woodrow Wilson and Reform

Still, Wilson's victory in 1912 breathed a new spirit into American politics. Though a minority president in terms of the popular vote, he had an overwhelming margin in the Electoral College over Roosevelt, with the luckless Taft in third place. The Democrats had not won a presidential election for twenty years. Now they also had a Democratic Congress with sufficient majorities in both Houses to facilitate their programme. There was a sense of excitement in the air as an avowedly reforming administration got to work in Washington. Wilson 'the professor in politics' brought to his task a lifetime's study of how power operated in the American system, and a determination to harmonize the various branches of government to make them act in unison to effect the popular will. Unlike his predecessor Taft, who had a limited notion of executive responsibility, Wilson would take the lead, as president of the people, as head of the Democratic Party, as party manager of Congress even if not in it. However, he could at least address Congress in person on special occasions, a practice that had been allowed to lapse for a century. Revived by Wilson, it reflected Wilson's love of the spoken word, and endeavoured to promote a sense of a joint working relationship. This was a trick that even a publicity hound like Roosevelt, much to his chagrin, had missed. It would not, could not last and there is perhaps a sense of irony that at the end Wilson was to receive his worst defeat at the hands of Congress. Much as Wilson might have pined for a British parliamentary system, that was not the American way and it was better it should not be so. The modern American president was to receive such large augmentations of power that a pliant and docile Congress would have resulted in executive dictatorship. The Founding Fathers had done their work well. Wisely recognizing that when men get power they tend to behave badly, they had built the American government on the notion of the separation of powers; it is indeed one of America's distinctive contributions to political theory. Hence power was to be divided both vertically and horizontally in a federal structure; the national government was separate from the local state governments, and as the latter already existed they had ceded certain limited powers to the centre. Similarly, the federal government was divided, with the legislative, executive and judicial branches competing with and checking each other. It was a recipe for conservatism in which change would only come when it clearly enjoyed widespread support at all levels in society. In 1913 and 1914 it did. Wilson rightly seized the moment.

As befitted the spokesman of a party with a strong Southern hue, Wilson first moved to reduce the tariff; the agricultural interest would take precedence over the manufacturing one. Here the real battle would be in the Senate where lobbyists were hard at work for special interests, and where but a few years previously, Taft's attempts at tariff revision had foundered and cost the Republican Party dear. This time Wilson took his case to the people. It was enough to show up and shame the lobbyists. The Underwood–Simmons Tariff Act of 1913 reduced import duties on almost 1,000 items, raised them on less than 100, and kept about 300 the same. Another 300 or so were exempt altogether. The general tariff rate was lowered from about 37 to just under 30 per cent. If not an outright free trade measure, it was the most substantial revision since the Civil War, and substituted the principle of competition for that of protection. Loss of revenue would be met by a new graduated income tax levied under the Sixteenth Amendment to the Constitution that had been ratified just before the Democrats came to power.

Wilson kept up the momentum. In some ways these were his happiest years. Having negotiated the thorny issue of the tariff, where his predecessors had failed, he moved on to a reform of the banking system. Here the need was urgent, as the 1907 Panic had demonstrated. Moreover, it was gratifying for the Democratic Party, traditionally the enemy of Wall Street, to take charge of restoring confidence in the nation's financial institutions. Nonetheless, conflicting interests all had their own pet solutions and it required considerable political dexterity – and here Wilson was at his best – to come up with a compromise that would secure congressional support without alienating powerful financial groups whose cooperation would be necessary if the system was to be effective. The issue of the banks could be relied upon to have the more radical factions in Congress and the country spitting blood, and Wilson as Democratic Party leader had to be mindful of the views of his supporters. It took a good six months of bargaining and persuasion to effect the Glass–Owen Federal Reserve Act that was finally passed at the end of 1913. Wilson's greatest legislative monument, the Act cleverly combined central control, with a board of publicly appointed governors, over twelve regional Federal Reserve Banks owned by the constituent members. This pooling of reserves created greater security and helped offset the traditional preponderance of New York's banks. Centralization allowed for greater flexibility in the issuance of currency, and credit was more readily available in all parts of the country.

Next Wilson moved on the trusts. Here again he was running against the record of his predecessors. What was needed, he surmised, was a stronger law than the weak Sherman Antitrust Act of 1890, which had been the only weapon that hitherto could be used against them. This, it turned out, was a fairly easy reform to effect, the Clayton Antitrust Act of 1914 providing more explicit prohibitions against business combinations and more stringent penalties for their violation; it also removed some of the previous antitrust act's provisions that had been used against trade unions. Still, even the law needed enforcement and Wilson believed that it was better achieved through a Federal Trade Commission than reliance on the courts. This was not so easily secured, opposed by both businessmen and those who suspected it showed a less than total commitment to regulation; certainly, in practice the FTC was not perhaps the all-seeing Big Brother that the more radical of its supporters had hoped. Nonetheless, Wilson's antitrust procedures became part of the basic mechanics of American government, vindicating his approach by their durability. Indeed, their establishment concluded a remarkable bout of legislative activity; by the time the European

War broke out in August 1914 no president had achieved so much in so short a period.

Wilson had himself remarked even before he entered office: 'It would be the irony of fate if my administration had to deal chiefly with foreign affairs.'[51] One must never forget this double jeopardy that American liberalism was to have both under Wilson and, indeed, thereafter. Every liberal, reforming president after 1914 was to labour under the necessity of simultaneously pushing forward political change, that inevitably met with opposition since it involved new structures and attitudes, and facing war, potential war or depression. Inevitably the one affected the other. The innocent luxury of a free-spirited wholesale reformation of American society from a position of peace and strength such as Wilson to some extent had enjoyed in his first eighteen months in office was never to be repeated. Perhaps the end of an era was symbolized by the departure of Bryan as secretary of state in June 1915. 'The Great Commoner', naive, provincial, unsophisticated but loyal and generous, had stood by Wilson, often delivering his supporters in Congress when they had questioned Wilson's commitment to more radical policies. In some ways, Bryan had been the conscience of the old rural Democratic Party, but he was also the representative of an era that was passing. Moreover, his going underscored Wilson's own lack of charisma. Even though he dramatized his requests for the support of Congress by addressing it in person, he lacked the human touch or even the rather hearty camaraderie that oils the wheels of democratic politics. Did Wilson even like people? He held news conferences, a partially successful innovation; he could command great loyalty from subordinates; he had a couple of trusted intimates; a devoted family; the death of his wife in August 1914 inevitably inspired sympathy. One could respect him but not identify with him; he was cold, aloof, reserved. He never aroused people like Roosevelt; he was too cerebral, solitary, dependent on his own thought processes. He did not listen to others over-much. Soon he would be misinformed. These faults were over the years to become flaws that could prove fatal.

His Inaugural Address in March 1913 had contained not a single reference to America's relations with foreign nations. Although in practice he had been obliged to continue safeguarding American interests in Latin America, he had salved his conscience by preaching a more idealistic foreign policy than the heavy-handed Roosevelt tactics of furthering American power or Taft's 'dollar diplomacy', geared to American investment. In fact this was easier said than done: Latin American nations could not always see the difference; and in particular Wilson became embroiled in Mexico over the issue of recognition of constitutional government. Still, one's own hemisphere was one thing, Europe was another. Thus to Wilson the great danger of the war across the Atlantic was that Americans might lose 'our self-possession, that we have been thrown off our balance by a war with which we have nothing to do, whose causes cannot touch us, whose very existence affords us opportunities of friendship and disinterested service which should make us ashamed of any thought of hostility or fearful preparation for trouble.'[52] Hence Americans must remain 'impartial in thought as well as in action'.[53]

Both the analysis and the policy prescription were faulty. Whilst like most civilized men Wilson was appalled at the ease with which European nations had slipped into war and barbarism, his mind, admittedly distracted by personal tragedy, was still on domestic issues. A close adviser noted in September 1914: 'I find the president singularly lacking in appreciation of the importance of this European crisis. He seems more interested in domestic affairs, and I find it difficult to get his attention centred upon the one big question.'[54]

This lack of balance was in part a reflection of Wilson's naivety in foreign policy, a failure to discern at once where America's true interests inevitably lay; in part a preoccupation with the wish to concentrate on his liberal programme. He did not wish to be blown off course by events over which he had no control. The best tactics, he surmised, lay in pretending they had not occurred. Slowly, inexorably, reality would intrude.

In fact, the first flood of Wilsonian Progressivism had run its course already; the congressional elections of 1914 were to make inroads into the Democratic majorities. The Republicans were beginning to get their act together; it looked as if in 1916 they might once again be formidable. Moreover, there were increasing social tensions with which Wilson found it hard to cope. Some issues, like women's suffrage, child labour legislation or low interest loans to farmers, failed to win his backing as matters for the federal government and as a Southern white by birth, Wilson was tainted with racist prejudices that spilled over into his administration. Nonetheless, white fundamentalist attitudes were asserting themselves generally: xenophobia, the beginnings of the attack on immigration,

Prohibition, and the first stirrings of the cultural clash between town and country that was to reach its zenith a decade later.

Wilson, always more a political than a social Progressive took a while to get his bearings but, recognizing that more liberalism was his only means of salvation in 1916, decided to press ahead. Already he had been persuaded to support La Follette's Seamen's Act of 1915. A long-overdue measure of social justice regulating the near scandalous safety and working conditions in the merchant marine, it had in fact, under the somewhat old-fashioned habits of the American Constitution, been passed by the Congress that had come to Washington in Wilson's first year. The new Congress did not convene until December 1915. By then foreign pressures made Wilson's job more difficult but also more urgent. The seven major pieces of legislation he pushed through, from a tax hike to limitations on child labour, shipping-rate regulation and a railroad worker eight-hour day law, easier loans and provision of credit to farmers, to federal help for highway construction, confirmed his Progressive credentials. These, along with his inspired nomination of the brilliant reforming lawyer Louis D. Brandeis to the Supreme Court, the first Jew appointed after one of the great Senate battles of the century, proved crucial to his re-election. Whatever doubts Progressives might have had about Wilson, in 1916 they had no really convincing alternative. Admittedly, the Republicans healed their differences and sensibly selected Charles Evans Hughes of the Supreme Court, who had previously been a reform governor of New York, for their presidential candidate. But even if as a Justice he had at least evaded the civil war of 1912, he found himself too often the prisoner of the Old Guard. In California this was to prove fatal to his chances, when through a combination of bad advice and political ineptitude, he appeared to snub the state's progressive forces. With Roosevelt's mind on foreign policy, his supporters too were drawn to Wilson. That, coupled with the peace issue, the culmination of Wilson's efforts since August 1914, proved in the end an unbeatable combination.

7 The United States Goes to War

Wilson had preached neutrality in the European war. This reflected his own preference, common sense and awareness that with different ethnic groupings American loyalties would be divided. Of the so-called hyphenated Americans, some 8 million German-Americans and another 4 million Irish-Americans who cordially loathed the British, comprised a formidable bloc of potential support for the Central Powers. Still there was a deeper Anglo-Saxon culture that would be less strident but more enduring; in the end democratic affinities with Britain, France and later, after the fall of the Tsar, even in a somewhat contrived way with Russia, would count for more. There were also more prosaic factors. The war brought relief to the American economy; indeed, it enjoyed something of a boom. Moreover, the Allies needed money to fight the war, and whatever America's initial good intentions in remaining strictly neutral, she was soon extending credit to the Allies to the tune of 2 billion dollars even before she entered the war herself. Admittedly, British attempts at a naval blockade soon angered the Americans, but this was offset by the Germans' willingness to use submarines to sink without warning merchant ships, heedless of the lives of passengers that entered a 'war zone' defined by themselves. In truth, the Germans, even without skilful British propaganda, had been their own worst enemy in presenting a callous front to the rest of the world. Hunnish beastliness, skewering babies on bayonets and other unspeakable atrocities apart, they had, after all, invaded neutral Belgium. That at least was incontestable. It soon became evident that constant British pinpricks were an irritant, whilst one incident like the sinking of the *Lusitania* in May 1915 with the loss of 1,198 lives, 128 of them Americans, would be a German public relations catastrophe.

The real problem for Wilson was that whilst diplomacy would be an ever-diminishing asset in keeping out of war – even when the Germans pledged to suspend unrestricted submarine warfare, they could soon go back on their promise – it was also of ever-diminishing wisdom. Wilson had privately conceded early in the war that 'England is fighting our fight' and America's interests clearly lay in an Allied victory.[55] Yet perhaps initially for entirely laudable reasons, but later with more than a touch of egocentricity, Wilson saw himself as independent peacemaker. Siren voices seduced him. 'You have an opportunity,' wrote Bertrand Russell in an open letter, 'of performing a signal service to mankind, surpassing even the service of Abraham Lincoln ... It is in your power to bring the war to an end by a just peace ... It is not yet too late to save European civilisation from destruction.'[56]

This fruitless task distracted him from his prime responsibility, to prepare his country should war occur and educate his countrymen on the issues that were at stake. Here Roosevelt, who by now had come to despise Wilson, was more clear-sighted. Unfortunately, an American public that had built its conception of foreign policy on considerable ignorance and half-understood slogans proved remarkably unreceptive to his warnings. Wilson, by contrast, found a ready audience.

To be fair it was not entirely Wilson's fault. Here he was the heir to a century of isolationism. George Washington, in his Farewell Address of 1796 on laying down the presidency, had wisely observed that 'Europe has a set of primary interests which to us have none or a very remote relation... Our detached and present situation invites and enables us to pursue a different course... It is our true policy to steer clear of permanent alliances with any portion of the foreign world.'[57]

Jefferson's First Inaugural of 1801 had also noted the advantages of geography when Europe was in turmoil from the wars of the French Revolution and Napoleon, 'Kindly separated by nature and a wide ocean from the exterminating havoc of one quarter of the globe', and thus advocated 'peace, commerce, and honest friendship with all nations, entangling alliances with none.'[58]

Their countrymen, whose very independence, as Washington and Jefferson were acutely aware, had been secured through an alliance, came to forget the qualifying adjectives 'permanent' and 'entangling'. And this misunderstanding had been cemented by the greatest shibboleth of American foreign policy, the Monroe Doctrine of 1823:

> In the wars of the European powers in matters relating to themselves we have never taken any part, nor does it comport with our policy so to do... With the movements in this hemisphere we are of necessity more immediately connected... We owe it, therefore, to candor and to the amicable relations existing between the United States and those powers to declare that we should consider any attempt on their part to extend their system to any portion of this hemisphere as dangerous to our peace and safety.[59]

It was a position the new republic, that a decade earlier in the War of 1812 had witnessed British troops ransacking Washington and setting fire to the White House, could in no way maintain. The effectiveness of the statement rested not on American strength that was quite incapable of underwriting so wide-ranging a commitment, but on British willingness as the greatest maritime power of the nineteenth century to exclude other European nations from the New World. But to the average American who saw the outward manifestations and not its hidden, tacit substructure, the effect was apparently to furnish three-quarters of a century of a charmed existence not breached until the war with Spain over Cuba in 1898. In fact, the highly nationalistic foreign policy America pursued, with successive augmentations of territory, had only been possible through British benevolence.

In American history those seventy-five years were tumultuous; at the end of them the nation had acquired an overseas empire and was on the brink of world power, yet public recognition of this fact and acceptance of its implications lay in the future. Theodore Roosevelt might note that the expansion of the German fleet would inevitably limit the role of the British and determine that an enlarged American navy would henceforth guarantee her own security and make good the British strategic withdrawal to home waters. Later he deduced that German power as such threatened America. But most of his countrymen's thinking was conditioned by the legacy of isolationism. Here Wilson was in tune with public opinion. As president, however, he ought to have seen its limitations. Moreover, the latent idealism of Americans, their belief in their own power of example to others, made them suspicious of what was represented as power politics. Wilson, in the search for a policy based on the right, too readily dismissed the notion that there are legitimate national interests, secured if necessary by power, that are in no way wrong. Idealism does not necessarily exclude realism.

Thus in 1916 Wilson's re-election campaign slogan 'He Kept Us Out of War' tipped the balance in a desperately close contest.[60] True, it made no explicit promises for the future but the implications were clear. Wilson himself was privately uneasy with the claim, recognizing its hostages to fortune. And so it proved. The German decision, shortly thereafter, to resume unrestricted submarine warfare, together with the discovery of a German offer of an offensive alliance with Mexico in the event of war with the United States, amply vindicated his caution. Still, it came as something of a surprise for many Americans when Wilson now argued that 'The world must be made safe for democracy': to be effected by an American declaration of war.[61]

In fact, Wilson was asserting the rights of neutrals and acknowledging the constant threat that would hang over the United States
should Germany dominate the European continent, not least if it
involved the destruction of the British navy: all legitimate American
interests that had been present since 1914. A more hard-headed
policy earlier on might have led Wilson to confront his fellow countrymen with some unpalatable truths and caused them to react
accordingly. The slow process of the education of the American
public to the realities of Great Power politics might have made it
readier to accept more modest but more attainable objectives. As it
was, the sudden volte-face of war now had to be sold as a priceless
opportunity. In this respect the toppling of the Tsar conveniently
made his claims more credible. Now Americans were to fight
for 'the things which we have always carried nearest our hearts –
for democracy, for the right of those who submit to authority to
have a voice in their own governments, for the rights and liberties
of small nations, for a universal dominion of right by such a concert
of free people as shall bring peace and safety to all nations and
make the world itself at last free'. They were to be sadly disappointed.[62]

The purity of American intentions was indicated by her status as
'an Associated Power', fighting with the Allies but not necessarily
for the same reasons.[63] As Wilson argued: 'England and France
have not the same views with regard to peace that we have by
any means. When the war is over we can force them to our way of
thinking...'[64]

Wishful thinking! The Allies, who were exhausted and desperate
in the fourth year of the war, with Britain but a few weeks from
starvation, were not disposed to violate the precept, 'When a horse
drops from heaven, don't examine its teeth.' True, in the initial
stages the effect of American intervention was largely psychological
in terms of fighting troops; the American peacetime army had to be
multiplied by a factor of ten. Then the soldiers had to be trained and
did not really make their presence felt until the spring of 1918. Still,
it allowed the Allies to bolster their economies with American aid
and naval convoys that drastically reduced their shipping losses
from the perfidious German U-boats. Suddenly it became conceivable that German defeat would only be a matter of time, but only
just, because with Russian withdrawal from the war in the wake of
the October Revolution and the ensuing Treaty of Brest-Litovsk,
the Germans were poised in March 1918 for their last great offen-

sive. They almost broke through the Allied defences, indeed pushed them back, but fresh American troops, 2 million of whom crossed the Atlantic with almost three-quarters of them seeing action, held the front. It was a magnificent achievement, reflecting the ingenuity and resourcefulness of a nation that could in a few months move from peace to war; mobilizing its economy for one over-riding purpose. A War Industries Board was set up to coordinate industrial production. Under Herbert Hoover the accumulation and distribution of food was organized both for domestic and Allied consumption. And national planning was set in place, geared to harnessing the workforce, conserving resources and directing their use in the pursuit of victory.

The war provided a focus for American idealism abroad just as, inevitably, it killed off Progressivism at home. Wilson, forced to accept a new role, sought to give expression to that idealism and make American participation evidence of a determination to bring a new spirit into world affairs. He had failed in his endeavour to arbitrate between the warring parties; now he would fix an agenda for peace. In January 1918, Wilson set out his war aims to Congress under Fourteen Points. Here he detailed general principles of conduct that he believed should govern relations between nations and listed specific territorial settlements to which America was committed at the peace. Famously, Wilson advocated the setting up of a League of Nations to negotiate and resolve future disputes.[65]

A subsequent president, Herbert Hoover, later commented:

> For a moment...Mr Wilson rose to intellectual domination of most of the civilized world...he carried a message of hope for the independence of nations the freedom of men and lasting peace. Never since...has any man risen to the political and spiritual heights that came to him. His proclaimed principles of self-government and independence aided the spread of freedom to twenty-two races...But...European statesmen were dominated by the forces of hate and revenge of their peoples for grievous wrongs...Mr Wilson was forced to compromise with their demands in order to save the League, confident that it would in time right the wrongs that had been done.[66]

Whilst this is a flattering picture of Wilson and certainly reflects his own self-image, it also points up the fatal flaw in Wilson's makeup. No one man could alone solve the world's problems and there was more than a touch of messianism in Wilson's efforts so to do. Even his decision to leave the United States and travel to Europe for the peace-making placed his prestige on the line that the inevitable compromises in human affairs were bound to erode. Wilson could hardly expect Allies with whom he had not consulted, to share his war aims when they had been fighting for longer and more desperately; moreover, Wilson's greatest failure was his own. Firstly he had unwisely appealed to the American electorate to return a Democratic Congress in November 1918. This was partisan politics when unity should have been his watchword. Worse, when they failed to do so, itself a blow to his prestige and future influence, he weakened his position still further by going to Paris with an American delegation that included only one, relatively unimportant, Republican member. Since the Senate, now Republican-controlled, would have to approve by a two-thirds majority any treaty submitted, it was a culpable political miscalculation. Moreover, Wilson did compromise. His principles, however noble, broke on the hard realities of European power politics, deals and bargains that had been made in secret, and victors avid for spoils. Still, it was the League that lay closest to his heart and both would be broken by his intransigence. The problem was Article X of its Covenant: 'The Members of the League undertake to respect and preserve as against external aggression the territorial integrity and existing political independence of all Members of the League.'[67] This conflicted with traditional American isolationism; some argued, not unshrewdly, that the Covenant would be the stronger without it. In any case, even if some thirty-nine senators had indicated their opposition, only sixteen 'irreconcilables' opposed League membership in its entirety. A compromise should have been possible. Wilson, faced with deft parliamentary manoeuvres by Republican opponents, took his case to the people on a strenuous speaking tour across America. Once again he found relief in words and hoped that grassroots pressure might influence wavering senators. It was too much. A stroke ensued, and Wilson's last eighteen months in office saw an invalid president, increasingly divorced from political reality, resolute in his refusal to brook concessions, impervious to reason. Relying on his wife and secretary who disguised the seriousness of his condition and acted in his name, Wilson watched helplessly as his cherished League was defeated by an alliance of those who at his insistence would have Wilson's League and no other, and those who would have none.

Yet public opinion and a majority of the Senate had been initially favourable; Wilson hardened opposition when he might have melted it. In consequence he knew the bitterness of failure. Wilson's administration had begun with high hopes for domestic reform; later, as foreign affairs came to the fore, he had brought the presidency to unprecedented heights; yet it ended in frustration and defeat, brought low by lesser men whose limited vision was more immediately realistic. The successful use of power depends on restraint and compromise, and Wilson made too many enemies with whom he would not negotiate. Later he tried to be philosophical. 'I think it was best after all,' he commented shortly before his death in 1924, 'that the United States did not join... Because our entrance ...at the time I returned from Europe might have been only a personal victory. Now, when the American people join the League it will be because they are convinced it is the only right time for them to do it.' Perhaps; but the world could have done with an American commitment in the interwar years.[68]

The political tide was ebbing fast: reaction at home, disillusionment abroad. Reform had run its course and fear of Bolshevism in the wake of the Russian Revolution induced a conservative panic reaction. In any case, America was tired: tired of the Progressive clamour, tired of a war that had not brought about a brave new world, tired of pretending otherwise. The war killed Progressivism; the peace killed Wilson. He left office a broken man. 'It is only once in a generation,' he sadly noted 'that a people can be lifted above material things. That is why conservative government is in the saddle two thirds of the time.'[69]

8 Normalcy in the Jazz Age

In March 1921 Wilson's successor Warren Harding took the oath of office. The most conservative president since McKinley, his landslide election victory in 1920 seemingly negated twenty years of American political development. The Republican Party bosses who had engineered his nomination wanted a cypher in the White House. Their wishes were amply fulfilled. They had chosen, very possibly, the least competent president in American history. The forces that challenged Roosevelt and captured Taft had reasserted themselves. Was the Progressive period to become an interlude in the normal accommodation between business and politics that had marked the entire post-Civil War era or was it to prove a fertile resource for still further achievement in the future?

For the period of Republican administrations which Harding's election ushered in raises questions both about the evolution of the American presidency, party politics and indeed the United States itself in the wake of the Progressive presidencies of Roosevelt, Wilson and even in a limited sense of Taft. For whilst the 1920s are generally seen as a somewhat aberrant period in American history, a classic case of a postwar era anxious to make up for lost time, they also serve as an example of a cul-de-sac in American political development. The lessons then painfully learned would profoundly influence how thereafter Americans would see the role of government in their society and the part that the respective political parties would play in that vision. In the previous twenty years the presidency had been brought to new heights; Roosevelt's accession to the office in 1901 had inaugurated that burst of creative government that continued until Wilson's departure from the White House, and had placed the president at the centre of events. Moreover, there was now the added dimension of foreign affairs. This in turn involved national defence. Here a president could act with the express sanction of the Constitution. 'The President shall be Commander in Chief of the Army and Navy of the United States...' These few words were to prove a virtual blank cheque for the enhancement of the modern presidency.[70]

Of course, Roosevelt was not the first president to realize his power as commander-in-chief. Here, above all, there was the precedent of Lincoln. He had emancipated the slaves as a war measure; he had saved the American Constitution overall by very possibly breaking it in part. Even if the Civil War was mercifully an aberration and the powers of the late nineteenth-century presidency had become increasingly lethargic, the potential was there, and if ever events should conspire to produce a crisis, the potential could be reactivated. Here Wilson far exceeded Roosevelt. He had had to face a World War. Observers later noted that war was always the health of the presidency. Could one, now that peace had returned, expect the presidency to revert to the limited role to which Roosevelt's predecessors had been accustomed?

The second issue, closely connected with the presidency, was the role of party, reflecting the obvious fact that the president besides being the chief executive is also a party leader; he owes his position as the former to the support he attracts as the latter. Notwithstanding the Founding Fathers' suspicion of 'faction' and Washington's distaste for 'party', party politics had soon become a feature of the new republic. The Civil War had ushered in a period of Republican dominance in national politics: it became the natural governing party of the United States. In congressional elections the Democrats did rather better, owing to their hold on the Southern states of the Old Confederacy, the rural bias of their congressional districts and the political machines of the big cities. Yet the analogy best suited to understanding American politics, it has been suggested, is not of two equally opposing forces but of a sun and a moon in which the latter, in this period the Democrats, is a pale reflection of the former, against whom it marks out its identity. Thus the Democrats had been slaughtered when in 1904 they had run a conservative candidate for president against Theodore Roosevelt when he was endeavouring to cast the Republican Party in a reforming mould. Eight years later they did much better with Woodrow Wilson when reform was the political watchword of the day. Yet the Democrats remained the minority party. In that sense 1920 restored the natural balance of American politics.

Moreover, neither party seemed quite to have found its soul. The Republicans appeared to have turned their back on Progressivism: as the 1920s were to show clearly, they were not a reform party. The spirit of Hamilton lived on and indeed flourished in that era. But the Democrats, too, could also be ambivalent. How did one interpret the many-faceted legacy of Jefferson? This confusion of identity reflected the third and ultimate issue of the day: in which direction was the United States to develop? And here one needs to look back not just to 1901 but to 1865. For the 1920s were the swansong of that raw individualism and laissez-faire capitalism that was the prevailing ethos of the post-Civil War era: if its values had been tempered by Progressivism they had not been fundamentally questioned. Should a situation occur where they might be put to the test, then it was conceivable that one might witness a situation in which a dynamic president, using his party as his instrument, would endeavour to reshape the prevailing public philosophy. This would be a seismic revolution in American politics. Were, at the same time, foreign affairs once again to become a major factor, the whole nature of the American presidency, politics and society would be transformed. Few would have imagined in March 1921, as they watched Harding riding to the presidential Inaugural alongside his discredited predecessor Wilson that within a dozen years so mighty a reversal would begin to occur.

Such a transformation, however, for the moment lay undreamed of in the future. In 1921 Americans wanted only a good time and in the next few years they were apparently to have it. True, as the phrase 'the Jazz Age' might suggest, the rhythm of history was to be suspiciously fast, but to others it was no more than yet another of those energetic surges that are characteristic of postwar eras. Indeed it was an apt sobriquet for so disturbed and restless a period.[71] American society was divided. Already there had been some unpleasant portents as to what the 1920s might throw up by way of social dislocation. The anti-Bolshevik raids initiated at the end of Wilson's presidency which soon became a shameless violation of civil rights and supposed constitutional liberties, a sad end to a great reforming administration, suggested an intolerance that might find other forms of difference from traditional norms difficult to accommodate. They hinted at a fear, never far below the surface of American life, of minorities that could turn ugly should a hitherto dominant group sense a threat to its position.

When the census of 1920 proclaimed that finally America was an urban nation, the scene was set for a confrontation between urban and rural values that neatly encapsulated the tension between those who looked to the future and those rooted in the past. By the time the Republicans had taken over, this cultural cleavage was receiving de facto political blessing. Republican protectionist policies – the Old Guard that had stymied Teddy Roosevelt and captured Taft was now in undisputed control – inevitably squeezed countryside interests. The American farmer never shared in 1920s prosperity. The Fordney–McCumber Tariff Act of 1922 was to raise tariff rates to an all-time high; in 1930 the Smoot–Hawley Tariff Act in a colossal economic blunder was to raise them yet again. Inevitably, foreign nations retaliated; and the American farmer was denied his traditional outlet for the disposal of crop surpluses that evermore efficient scientific farming, additional acreage under cultivation, and the urge to produce more during the war years only made worse. Hence farm prices plummeted, and farm indebtedness, incurred in the good years to meet greater demand, cripplingly increased. This was not the least of the farmers' miseries. With economic adversity came a sense of alienation: the urban, business, industrial ethos of the 1920s seemed a direct assault on traditional rural values.

In any case 'the War to End All Wars' had inevitably acted as a social catalyst; thousands of Americans had been uprooted from their traditional surroundings and exposed to the challenges of un-familiar and sometimes threatening perspectives. Much is rightly made of the impact of Europe upon millions of American troops who never dreamt they would cross the Atlantic. Equally significant was their passage through New York or Boston, their preliminary training in army camps across the country and their meeting with their fellow countrymen from its disparate parts. Add to this a post-war desire to make up for time lost, an exhilarating sense of the potentialities of modern life as evidenced by its technological inven-tions and industrial achievements and the way was open for a cul-tural clash of seismic proportions. Americans – or at least the most vociferous of them – went giddy. Of course one can make too much of the stereotypical images of the twenties; the new-style dances, flap-pers, contemporary fashion, the disregard if not outright flouting of convention. Millions of Americans lived lives of prosaic ordinariness bent on the struggle for economic survival that has been the lot of the overwhelming majority of mankind throughout recorded human history. Still, how the goals of economic betterment were formulated was a telling comment on the period. Thus there was one motor car for every four and a half Americans and a radio in 40 per cent of American households. Some 90 to 100 million Americans went to the cinema each week as the decade was ending. Some 155 Americans in every thousand had a telephone. All this suggested a widespread pursuit of consumer affluence. Such a pursuit had other consequences, both in increasing cultural homogenization and breaking down geo-graphic and social barriers that mail-order catalogue merchandising with its emphasis on uniformity and mass marketing, another char-acteristic of the era, only accentuated.

More and more Americans seemed to be taking charge of their own lives. The movement from the countryside to the city inevit-ably eroded the social controls that small communities can exert on their members. In the city lay both the pleasures and the pains of anonymity. The greater – to some shocking – sexual freedom that the 1920s witnessed, betokened an assault on the social fabric that seemed only the worst manifestation of a general tendency to-wards personal licence. Hence the urge to reinforce private morality with the force of law, always a dangerous notion, of which Prohib-ition is the best example. Enshrined in the Eighteenth Amendment to the Constitution no less, and ratified in January 1919, it stands as a symbol of a society uneasily confronting sudden change and find-ing in repression a neurotic response to which to cling.

Still, Prohibition had at least been motivated by good, albeit misguided, intentions, as Herbert Hoover's much-quoted comment on it in the 1928 election – or possibly misquoted – '... a great social and economic experiment, noble in motive and far-reaching in purpose' acknowledged.[72] Other symbols of the era were much more ugly. The revival of the Ku Klux Klan marked a surge of intolerance that now extended from African-Americans to Jews to Catholics to foreigners in general. For example, in the very campaign where Hoover defended Prohibition, his Irish-American Democratic opponent Al Smith was to face a nasty undercurrent of anti-Catholicism. To further preserve the American nation from alien influences, immigration was drastically curtailed; the halcyon days of open access to all comers, at least from Europe, was replaced by a restrictive quota system based on existing national population percentages that inevitably favoured Anglo-Saxons. Such xenophobia, often coupled with a suspicion of political radicalism, was to climax in the execution of Sacco and Vanzetti in 1927. Two poor Italian immigrants caught distributing anarchist literature, they were charged with a murder of which they resolutely protested their innocence. Their whole long-drawn-out judicial process with its grim denouement attracted international attention, possibly the most celebrated criminal case in American history.

At other times tragedy could turn to farce as when a Tennessee biology teacher, John T. Scopes, was prosecuted under a recently enacted state law for teaching Darwinian evolution and thereby compromising the literal truth of the Creation as detailed in the Book of Genesis. Nor was the merriment lessened by the appearance of William Jennings Bryan, three times Democratic presidential candidate and former secretary of state, as lawyer for the prosecution. Whilst Bryan apparently objected to the notion that an ape could turn into a man, to the irreverent he appeared to be living proof of the reverse process. Indeed, what makes the 1920s so deeply disturbed an era is the buffeting it received in so many directions, the insecurity thus engendered, and the bombastic claims that substituted for quiet conviction. There is a sense in which the overheated economic policies of the period are a reflection of social excitability; to make them palatable, Americans needed to believe that they could be both daring and innovative, yet somehow preserve the traditional myths of the American inheritance.

In fact, Harding had brilliantly caught the public mood. What America wanted, he argued, was 'not heroism but healing, not nostrums but normalcy, not revolution but restoration, not agitation but adjustment, not surgery but serenity, not the dramatic but the dispassionate, not experiment but equipoise, not submergence in internationality but sustainment in triumphant nationality'. It is his most memorable sentence, arguably the only one.[73]

If the language was opaque, the sentiment was clear. Lassitude would descend on the White House. It could hardly be otherwise. A hack politician from Midwestern Ohio, Harding had achieved his wildest ambitions in getting to the Senate; there, but for a pushy wife nicknamed 'the Duchess', he might have died a happy man, enjoying the camaraderie, the poker-playing, the golf that passed the easy-going legislator's day. But this amiable ordinariness, a 'folksiness', was the source of his popularity and fitted superbly a tired nation disillusioned with Wilsonian idealism and international crusades. Harding's one presidential attribute was that he looked like a president: a firm profile, a square jaw, with a magnificent head of silvery hair. He himself knew his limitations, knew that the job of president was beyond him. His self-knowledge was to be amply vindicated over the next three years. Weak rather than personally dishonest, indeed quite a kindly man, he was soon to find out that he was presiding over the most corrupt administration in half a century. 'The Teapot Dome' affair whereby naval oil reserves in Wyoming, having been transferred to the Interior Department, were then leased by its secretary for private development in exchange for a bribe, was only the worst of several examples of venality. Almost as if fleeing from Washington to escape the realization of how some of his cronies had exploited him, Harding embarked on a transcontinental train journey. As his vice-president pithily and characteristically noted: 'In June he started for Alaska and – eternity.'[74] Harding's death at San Francisco in August 1923 in the midst of the impending scandal alone salvaged his reputation from outright disgrace.

His successor, Calvin Coolidge, had not been Harding's personal choice for vice-president but had been forced on him by an infuriated Republican Convention that had seen the presidential nomination slip from them to the wheeler-dealers of the smoke-filled room where the power brokers gathered. A tight-lipped governor of Massachusetts, Coolidge had briefly caught the public imagination with a timely condemnation of a police strike in Boston: 'There is no right to strike against the public safety by any body, any time, any where.'[75] Stories about his taciturnity and stinginess abounded. The triviality of the anecdotes about him was revealing of a lack of weightier purpose. Almost the caricature of the laconic New Englander, he apparently never asked himself what he might actually do as president and seemed to have no conception of the creativity of government. The president, if not quite a passive observer of American society, was at best a routine administrator; it was for others, notably businessmen, to provide a sense of direction and leadership.

9 Herbert Hoover and the American System

This, one businessman in particular, Herbert Hoover, was happy to do. The embodiment of the American dream, Hoover seemed to symbolize the opportunities of American society A country boy from Iowa, orphaned as a youngster, he was a millionaire by thirty. As a mining engineer, his profession exemplified the practical skills so admired by his countrymen. A Quaker by religion, a particularly attractive form of Christianity, worldly success and idealism seemed happily united. It was a combination put to good effect when he helped rescue American citizens stranded in war-torn Europe in 1914, organized relief for Belgium and supervised American aid to starving Europeans when the terrible conflict was finally over. In Paris in 1919 he was to stand head and shoulders above European politicians in the clarity and disinterestedness of his perceptions as to what the situation needed. During the war Hoover had brought his immense skills to Washington as Food Administrator and so great was his reputation by 1920 that both parties, Democrats as well as Republicans, thought of him as a possible presidential candidate. When it was clear where his political sympathies lay, the Democrats could not select him and the Republicans need not. Harding, however, chose him to serve as secretary of commerce in that curious Cabinet of which it is only an exaggeration to say, one half were outstanding men and the other half were crooks. He continued in that post throughout the twenties, the self-proclaimed architect of that spurious Republican prosperity that deceived a decade. It was, of course, as one can see so clearly in retrospect, an era riding for a fall; and one cannot ever look at it without remembering the shadow of the Great Depression that finally overwhelmed it. And Hoover reflects this self-confidence, walking heedlessly, if not indeed running, to disaster. It is perhaps significant that Hoover had never been elected to a public office prior to running for the presidency in 1928. And it is a curious irony that ultimately reflects well on the rough ways of democracy that if at times he seems the sort of chief executive one might select at an interview in response to an advertisement, it was precisely this apparent appeal that was also his greatest limitation. Hoover impressed contemporaries who knew him by reputation, but that reputation was made as the organizer of men, not as their leader.

Born in 1874, Hoover had succumbed to the individualist self-help philosophy that appealed so strongly to the America of his generation. Although he had voted for Theodore Roosevelt in 1912, the aspect of Progressivism that most appealed to him was its accent on efficiency. Hoover's Progressivism was not the moral tub-thumping of a Roosevelt or a Wilson, still less the fierce integrity or burning sense of injustice of a La Follette, but the respect for expertise and professionalism that came naturally to the successful businessman. In 1922 he published a little book entitled *American Individualism*, where he extolled what he saw as 'the primary force of American civilization for three centuries'. It was a doctrine that he applied as much to politics as to business. 'It is our sort of individualism that has supplied the motivation of America's political, economic, and spiritual institutions in all these years...Our very form of government is the product of the individualism of our people, the demand for an equal opportunity, for a fair chance.'[76]

Indeed, the whole book was very much intended to be a message for the times, and Hoover made clear that the American form of individualism which he advocated both softened the edges of raw, uncaring competition and liberated the creative energies of people. More than any other, Hoover made himself the spokesman of the era. He was passionate in defence of his philosophy. In 1928 he concluded his campaign for the presidency by warning:

> It is a false liberalism that interprets itself into the government operation of commercial business. Every step of bureaucratizing of the business of our country poisons the very roots of liberal-ism...political equality, free speech, free assembly, free press, and equality of opportunity...True liberalism seeks all legitimate freedom...without such freedom the pursuit of all other blessings and benefits is vain. That belief is the foundation of all American progress, political as well as economic. Liberalism is a force truly of the spirit...economic freedom cannot be sacrificed

if political freedom is to be preserved. Even if governmental conduct of business could give us more efficiency... the fundamental objection... would remain... It would destroy political equality... It would stifle initiative and invention. It would undermine the development of leadership. It would cramp and cripple the mental and spiritual energies of our people. It would extinguish equality of opportunity... For a hundred and fifty years liberalism has found its true spirit in the American system, not in the European systems.[77]

Big government, then, was the enemy, and what Hoover termed 'the American system' was a unique and precious development that had to be preserved from alien ideas from abroad. If Hoover was a 'liberal' then it was in the classic nineteenth-century sense of the term in which individual freedom had to be safeguarded against state authority. Equally, it had to take precedence over collectivist schemes for social betterment. In any case, the liberalism Hoover practised did not give rise to the contradictions found elsewhere. Unlike in Europe where there was a class struggle between capital and labour, in America, so Hoover believed, capital and labour worked hand in hand. Accordingly, the job of the federal government was to preserve the system, but this required self-restraint. Any unnecessary encroachment by central authority upon individual liberty was to be deplored. Bureaucracy had an innate tendency to self-perpetuate and thus to stifle individual initiative. It was a philosophy that had served Hoover personally very well. Yet his views had been moulded at too early an age; perhaps success had come to him, if not too easily, at least too soon, and he learned little by experience. That experience, too, was essentially that of the businessman, even when he entered government. He had little sense of that give-and-take of democratic politics, even the slightly bogus camaraderie which elective politicians acquire as a means to vote-getting, that, for example, his successor Franklin Roosevelt practised to perfection. He was a shy man, stiff to the point of pomposity; as a president he did himself no good with no-nonsense journalists by showing an over-awareness of the dignity of the presidential office that was transferred by observers to his own person. No president worked harder; an eighteen-hour day was commonplace. But he endeavoured to run America like the managing director of a great corporation, from his desk, and found that the necessary mental rigidity and respect for formulae of the engineer bore little relation to the exigencies of democratic politics. In the last resort, Hoover was an administrator, not an executive, still less a leader.

True, Hoover was the most gifted of the Republican presidents of the 1920s, if not necessarily the canniest. Coolidge wins that accolade by a wide margin. Even his ambiguous refusal to seek re-election in 1928, 'I do not choose to run', may have been inspired by an inner sense that he should not push his luck, and that the apparent good times were indeed too good to last.[78] And Hoover may have been unlucky. What might his reputation be, had he in fact been chosen by the Republicans in 1920 and served a conventional two-term presidency? Such speculation is perhaps unfruitful. Yet it is a valid point if only to underline that the times as much as the man make or break a reputation. And Hoover in 1928 had faced the times with confidence; they were his achievement: 'We in America today are nearer to the final triumph over poverty than ever before in the history of any land. The poorhouse is vanishing from among us . . . given a chance to go forward with the policies of the last eight years, we shall soon with the help of God be in sight of the day when poverty will be banished from this nation.'[79]

Hoover, however, could never make the mental leap to the idea that this desirable objective might be more the province of government than of business. That his own role as president might be more directly interventionist conflicted with his deeply held philosophy of laissez-faire that had characterized his own career. Hoover had actually lived out his beliefs and saw no reason why what had worked for him should not work for all. What a later generation would endeavour to secure by 'supply side economics' or the 'trickle-down theory' basically could be said to constitute a form of economic Darwinism, that believed that society as a whole benefits from the exertion of its leaders. In this, government was a passive observer, at best no more than a regulator ensuring reasonable fair play and averting manifest malpractice. The fallacy of the assumptions underlying this philosophy seem obvious; but it was a reflection of the deep-seated trust in businessmen, and more especially business leaders, that grew out of the experiences of American history. Government, for example, could have played only a minimal part in the expansion of the post-Civil War economy. What was needed was for government to give businessmen their head; there was no way, for instance, that the development of the trans-Mississippi West, the part of the country Hoover grew up in, could have been controlled and regulated by Washington, DC. In this respect Hoover seemed to enshrine the very values that had worked for the success of modern America and, one could argue, continued to work.

In the 1920s the nation, at least on the surface, enjoyed unparalleled prosperity. It was an era of business triumph. Many business leaders were seen as veritable gurus whose views were eagerly sought on a whole range of issues. They exemplified the promise of American life and testified to the wisdom of Republican policies. In a notable address Coolidge had applauded their calling.

True business represents the mutual organized effort of society to minister to the economic requirements of civilization... While it is not an end in itself, it is the important means for the attainment of a supreme end. It rests squarely on the law of service. It has for its main reliance truth and faith and justice... it is one of the greatest contributing forces to the moral and spiritual advancement of the race.[80]

At one level at least, the facts would seem to bear him out. The number of income millionaires rose from 65 persons in 1919 to 513 in 1929. The gross national product in the same period rose from 72 billion dollars to 104 billion. From 1922 to 1929 the economy grew at 5 per cent a year; at the height of the Coolidge boom, 1923 to 1926, the growth rate was no less than 7 per cent per annum. Notwithstanding regular reductions in taxation throughout the period, especially advantageous to the wealthy, government expenditure dropped so markedly that it proved possible to pay off a quarter of the National Debt between 1923 and 1929.

More acute observers might have noted that the distribution of wealth was worryingly lopsided. In the very year of the Great Crash, a survey ominously entitled *America's Capacity to Consume* recorded that just one-tenth of 1 per cent of American families had an aggregate income equal to that of the bottom 42 per cent. Moreover, the same minuscule group had a third of all savings; just 3 per cent of families in fact, had two-thirds.[81]

The scene was set for what was to be one of the great ironies of the Depression, poverty in the midst of plenty. Instead of underproduction and over-consumption, the normal state of affairs when an economy is in crisis, with too many people chasing too few goods, the reverse was happening. There were goods aplenty; the problem was that there were not enough purchasers to pay for them. The market that had sourced the Coolidge boom was drying up. And yet there is a certain irony in the fact that Coolidge, Hoover and his colleagues had no difficulty accepting what in effect was private deficit funding to fuel this economic boom. In fact the rapid rise in consumption and the sale of consumer goods was largely paid for by hire purchase. But they would have steadfastly refused to countenance the notion that, should difficult times occur and people suffer, it might be possible for government to practise comparable public deficit financing: to support, say, a public works programme to provide jobs, alleviate hardship and put money back into circulation to allow the economy to revive. Indeed, much of the 1920s prosperity was based on the assumption that the economy could expand endlessly by stimulating demand that would be paid for in the future. It was too good to be true. Businessmen might be the leaders of American society. They succeeded by success. But what if they should fail? Power, like nature, deplores a vacuum. Somewhere in American society decisions would have to be taken to rescue it. Logically, inevitably, as Roosevelt and Wilson had discovered, that could only be the federal government, more precisely the president.

When Depression struck in 1929 and gradually worsened, the contradictions of Hoover's position became manifest. With business failure, somebody had to give a lead. Hoover resorted to exhortations, not in itself a bad thing, but insufficient and certainly dangerous when they convinced no one but Hoover. Moral leadership depends on more than words, and encouragement, if merely verbal, is an investment of diminishing returns. Moreover, Hoover believed passionately in voluntarism: it might be a president's job to give a lead, to encourage and exhort; it was for others to do the work. Self-help, self-reliance, private charity were his watchwords; anything else would sap Americans' spirit and depress their morale. Perhaps initially Hoover's policies had something to recommend them. In his period as secretary of commerce Hoover had encouraged voluntary trade associations on the principle that self-regulation pre-empted the need for governmental oversight, and that businessmen, not bureaucrats, knew best. Thus it was natural to turn to them again in a crisis. Nor, given the then distribution of power in America, was it unreasonable. Businessmen were respected; they were society's leaders; moreover, they had a far greater input into the economy than government, national or local. Even here there was an imbalance. Whilst the federal government spent about 3 per cent of the GNP in 1929, state and local governments spent five times as much. And if the economy needed stimulus, private industry that spent as much as 9 billion dollars on construction projects that year was surely a safer bet than the states that did not exceed 2 billion, whilst the federal government itself could only manage a paltry 200 million. The instruments of interventionist government were simply not at hand.

Moreover, the stock market crash that Hoover among others had warned about was not necessarily what it appeared in retrospect. Did this in itself inevitably mean depression? It might have been a release of pressure entailing misery for some, but arguably America had been through this before. Of course 'Black Thursday', 24 October 1929, when just under 13 million shares changed hands following on the previous day's loss of 4 billion dollars' worth in value was dramatic enough by anybody's standard. Yet fear is a bad counsellor; and Hoover's reassurance on the Friday that 'the fundamental business of the country, that is, production and distribution of commodities, is on a sound and prosperous basis' was not so far-fetched as it has subsequently come to seem.[82]

True, 'Black Tuesday', 29 October, a bare five days later, that saw another outburst of panic selling in which over 16 million shares were traded, turned a fall into a collapse. The speculative mania had got its come-uppance with a vengeance; Wall Street was rocked to its foundations. This clearly was a watershed. From the late 1890s when McKinley sat in the White House to the early 1920s under Harding, albeit with wide fluctuations, the United States stock market had sustained a growth rate of about 6 per cent. In the last eight years, from 1921 to 1929, it had risen by an incredible 340 per cent, a compound growth rate of 20 per cent. The 'boom' psychology would be followed by one of 'bust'. But when less than three Americans in a hundred owned shares anyway, it is arguable that the collapse might have been contained from becoming a general economic contagion. This, however, required an Executive exertion that Hoover simply would not make.

The banks are a case in point. These were the very arteries of American capitalism, and there were some 25,000 of them in 1929. Historically, American banks had always been an individualistic and motley collection; here populist railings against Eastern finance had produced a situation where only some 750 operated a branch system and the vast majority were effectively single institutions.

This inevitably made for weakness and throughout the 1920s bank failures averaged some 600 a year. Moreover, for every national bank there were at least two state banks so that in practice there were some 50 differing sets of laws whereby they were regulated. Given that 90 per cent of American currency was in the form of bank cheques, these were no better than the bank on which they were drawn. The latter in turn depended on the reliability of the collateral they held to guarantee the loans they made with depositors' money; rural banks with land that plummeted in value as the agricultural crisis worsened were the first to suffer. Then urban institutions, those with securities sent reeling by the Crash, were forced to sell large amounts at an unpropitious time to recoup whatever they could; by 1930 bank failures were double the annual average. In 1931 failures would exceed the previous two years combined. When in December 1930 the Bank of the United States, a large New York City institution, folded, the sickness had assumed epidemic form. The old joke became for many Americans a grim reality: if the bank has my money I don't want it; if it doesn't I do.

When Hoover did move, characteristically he went to the bankers. In October 1931 he met privately with forty leading figures in the banking and insurance world. It is what Teddy Roosevelt had done in 1907; 'the malefactors of great wealth' had, in effect, bailed him out. Here the very individualism that Hoover so lauded proved his undoing; the National Credit Corporation set up by the New York banks was vitiated by individual caution and shortsightedness that put private interest before national need. Besides, it was no longer 1907: there was now a Federal Reserve System; this, surely, let the bankers off the hook. By 1932 even Hoover was forced to compromise his principles. On 22 January he signed into law the Reconstruction Finance Corporation that was authorized to loan $500 million to railroads, banks and other financial institutions; the next day another Act provided an extra $125 million for Federal Land banks. It was too little, too late.

The inertia was replicated elsewhere. Even before the Crash Hoover had recognized the seriousness of the farm problem and called Congress into special session to enact an Agricultural Marketing Act, establishing a Federal Farm Board to support farm prices. This had initially some limited success. But when the crisis deepened, he drew back from the increased governmental intervention that was the only hope for a solution. Unless a majority of farmers could be induced to cut production, and a processing tax were to be levied to support prices and help even out the imbalances between the return on domestic and overseas sales, the situation would only worsen. In any case Hoover seemed to be paddling in opposite directions. When he ignored the pleas of a thousand economists – and they almost begged him on bended knees – to veto the Smoot–Hawley Tariff Act that paralysed international trade just when it was most sorely needed, yet another narrowing opportunity for the American farmer to cut crop surpluses was closed.

Unemployment highlighted Hoover's passivity still further. Once again, though he was much more active than his two predecessors, it was action that was needed. This Hoover's philosophy precluded. Private industry and labour unions between them could work out ways to mitigate the problem and private charity could alleviate distress. The president's Emergency Committee for Employment was at best a facilitator, processing information as to where the need was greatest. Federal aid was unnecessary and undesirable; nothing was to be deplored more than the European recourse to the dole that sapped individual self-respect and created spineless dependency.

It is possible that only towards the end did Hoover really grasp the scale of the problem. At first the situation, though severe, was not proportionately as bad as it had been in the postwar slump when he had first joined the Cabinet; then unemployment had been almost 12 per cent, now it was initially less than 9. Secondly, local officials were slow to concede that the crisis was beyond their resources, until it became evident that such was the scale of the disaster that they were not to blame. No politician readily admits to helplessness. And Hoover came to believe his own reassurances. Partly, no doubt, he wanted to; partly, it seemed they could be sustained. Hoover himself had been the victim of Depression: that of 1893 which had forced him on graduation from Stanford to take a backbreaking labouring job at derisory wages. He, and the nation, had pulled through. Once again the capitalist cycle was going through a rough time as it did periodically; once again it would right itself as it always had. Meanwhile, sit tight and above all don't panic. The test of the American System was that one stuck with it in bad times as well as good. Only the First World War had justified its abandonment. In 1928 Hoover had warned his countrymen:

During the war we necessarily turned to the government to solve every difficult economic problem ... For the preservation of the state the Federal Government became a centralized despotism which undertook unprecedented responsibilities, assumed autocratic powers, and took over the business of citizens. To a large degree we regimented our whole people temporarily into a socialistic state. However justified in time of war if continued in peace-time it would destroy not only our American system but with it our progress and freedom as well.[83]

Thus Hoover's failure was due not just to ineffectual policies but to clinging grimly to a philosophy that had long outlived its usefulness. While he remained in power he was an obstacle to fresh thinking. It was a sad denouement for a man who had at various times fed 150 million of his fellow human beings. Now in the most advanced nation in the world, gaunt, hungry people scavenged among garbage cans. Across the land malnutrition was rife and actual starvation clearly documented. Meanwhile, in the countryside crops rotted in the fields because farmers had no markets. In the towns industrial production was less than half what it had been in 1929 and one in four of the American labour force was out of work, whilst once-busy factories stood idle. Those unfortunate enough to be made homeless lived wretchedly in cardboard boxes. Manifestly, the resources of private charity were pathetically inadequate even to mitigate the catastrophe, let alone to master it. It was surely terrifyingly obvious that there were greater dangers than that of excessive government. Self-help was not enough. The price of individualism, apparently, was collective misery. America had reached a turning point.

2
The Achievement of Liberalism

1 The Emergence of Franklin Roosevelt

In January 1932 Franklin Roosevelt, the amiable, extrovert, yet privately enigmatic governor of New York, announced his candidacy for the presidency. Roosevelt was the only presidential candidate in either major political party who consistently criticized business leadership, a novelty that bordered on the radical; who called for drastic, if unspecified, changes in the economic system, a demand made the more potent by its imprecision; and who promised 'bold, persistent experimentation' and a commitment to 'the forgotten man at the bottom of the economic pyramid', brilliant phraseology that did much to win him his party's nomination.[1] Faced with so powerful a Democratic challenge, the luckless Republican President Herbert Hoover was not in doubt as to its implication.

This campaign is more than a contest between two men...more than a contest between two parties. It is a contest between two philosophies of government. We are told by the opposition that we must have a change, that we must have a new deal. It is not the change that comes from normal development of national life to which I object, but the proposal to alter the whole foundations of our national life,...They are proposing changes and so-called new deals which would destroy the very foundations of our American system...Dominantly in their spirit they represent a radical departure from the foundations of 150 years which have made this the greatest nation in the world. This election is not a mere shift from the ins to the outs. It means deciding the direction our Nation will take over a century to come.[2]

73

In 1932, the overwhelming political question of the day was the dire situation of the economy and how best it could be remedied. Did one adopt a static approach and wait for the economic cycle to renew itself, the solution apparently favoured by President Hoover with less and less conviction? Or did one rethink the assumptions of American society, recognizing the interrelationship between politics and economics, in other words adopt the 'New Deal' of Franklin Roosevelt, however generalized a concept that might be?[3] Roosevelt was to reorder American politics but it would have taken an unusually perceptive observer to foretell this in 1932. Yet genius, or one definition of it, is the ability to bring order out of chaos. By this definition, Roosevelt was a political genius of the first magnitude. He was also one of the half dozen most significant figures of modern history for good or ill, and one of the three greatest of American presidents. Both what Roosevelt did and how he achieved it deserve close examination. They are an essential component of modern American history. So profound was Roosevelt's influence that his years in the White House mark a break between an older and a newer America every bit as fundamental as the ones that preceded and followed the Civil War.

Roosevelt, born in 1882, was just fifty years old when he announced his bid for the presidency. A distant cousin of Teddy Roosevelt, whom he always admired and sought to emulate, he had married Teddy's niece Eleanor, later entering politics in New York State. However, he had first achieved a public profile as assistant secretary of the navy in Wilson's administration, the self-same job that Teddy had used to gain national prominence. Franklin Roosevelt had been even luckier in that the advent of the First World War had inevitably made the position an important one, and on the strength of his performance and famous name he had been chosen by the Democrats to be their vice-presidential candidate in 1920. Handsome, convivial, enthusiastic and energetic, Roosevelt had acquired valuable experience of a national campaign in second place on the ticket, without bearing the stigma of a loser. Indeed, in the wake of their crushing defeat Roosevelt had shrewdly predicted that it would take a Depression to elect a Democratic president. That remark was itself an indication of the momentous sea change in American politics that would be required. The transformation of the Democratic Party from minority to majority status and the change in its character from a party centred on rural conservatism to one based on urban liberalism is the central feature of American politics in the second third of the twentieth century; the one required the other. In so doing it also profoundly altered the role of the federal government and in particular the Presidency and its impact on the Nation.

In the 1920s this might have seemed unlikely. The Democrats were not even the unalloyed party of reform. Indeed, Roosevelt's analysis indicated the weakness of the Democrats' attractiveness. It implied a weary acceptance that Republican administrations were the norm and that only when things went wrong would the Democrats' turn come. It was negative politics at best and hinted at the flaws in the party's philosophy. This had been brutally revealed at the Democratic Convention in New York in 1924. It was a near fiasco. The urban and rural wings of the party fought each other to exhaustion for the presidential nomination. Neither, predictably, triumphed. After 103 ballots, a colourless lawyer John W. Davis, a former ambassador to Britain, emerged as a compromise candidate, showing the depth of the rift between the two factions. Hence their inability to define what the Democratic Party stood for; their unwillingness to face up to the realities of contemporary politics by evolving a coherent, mutually agreed programme, condemned it to defeat. Nor was the division merely between urban liberals and rural conservatives. Many financiers, bankers and industrialists called themselves Democrats, whilst the old Populist spirit still lived among rural farmers. The 1920s exemplified the sun and moon theory of American politics: the Democrats seemed to offer a pale reflection of Republicanism. And indeed in many ways, the most reform-minded group of politicians was nominally to be found in the ranks of the Republican Party itself. That group of Progressive Republican senators, such as Robert La Follette, who even ran as a Third Party candidate in 1924. In the era of conservative domination presided over by Harding, Coolidge and Hoover, they remained a constant thorn in the side of the official party leadership and kept alive the hopes of liberal reformers. Too independent-minded to act in unison, prima donnas some of them who deferred to no one, they nonetheless comprised the most interesting ginger group in American politics in an age of dull conformity.

Two events, however, in 1920 suggested that the political landscape might be changing. The first was the recognition by the census of that year, that, for the first time in its history, America had become an urban nation. The implications for politics that more Americans now lived in towns than in the country suggested that the balance of power might at last be shifting. It took time for this change to register, yet as early as 1922, recovering from the debacle of 1920, the Democrats picked up 73 seats in the House of Representatives in the off-year elections. More significantly, for presidential politics, the twelve largest cities of the country that had given Harding a plurality in 1920, by 1928 were doing the same, albeit narrowly, for the Democratic presidential candidate Al Smith.

The second event of 1920 effecting a change in the pattern of voting was initially harder to call but intriguing in its possibilities. This was the enlargement of the electorate by the ratification of the Nineteenth Amendment to the Constitution, which gave women the right to vote. Nor must one construe this narrowly as merely releasing large numbers of hitherto disenfranchised voters into the polling booths. It also increased the number of potential party workers and political activists and subtly influenced voter perception of what were the crucial electoral issues. Presumably, the importance of welfare issues did not actually diminish as a consequence of women's participation in the political process, whilst practical bread-and-butter issues might well attract additional voter interest. When the politics of compassion were to be invoked to replace the politics of competition, the new female electorate may have been not unwilling to lend a sympathetic ear.

Yet three Republican presidents, Harding, Coolidge and Hoover, won striking victories in three successive elections throughout the 1920s. Republican prosperity was clearly a vote winner; even New York, Smith's own state, where he had been an able and reform-minded governor, went into the Republican column. Indeed, it was Smith's weakness, even on his home ground, that had led him to persuade Roosevelt to return to active politics and run for governor, thereby strengthening the Democratic ticket. It was a manoeuvre that failed as far as Smith's presidential aspirations were concerned, but it made Roosevelt chief executive of the most influential state in the country, ideally positioned to make a bid for the presidency should the times prove propitious.

If every public man needs a period of withdrawal and reflection, then the 1920s were undoubtedly Roosevelt's. Forced by tragic circumstance to be an observer of the political battles of the period, the enforced inactivity in fact worked to his advantage. In the summer of 1921, cruelly crippled by the sudden onset of polio that left him bedridden and immobile, Roosevelt with awesome moral and physical courage, had resolved to once again walk unaided. It was to prove an unrealizable ambition and though some improvement was effected, always thereafter he would be physically dependent on others. Characteristically, Roosevelt made light of his illness. In fact the greatest statesman of the twentieth century in its most turbulent era was seriously disabled. The tragedy, however, had the immediate, unforeseen benefit of removing him from active politics when to go forward would have in all likelihood incurred defeat in the triumphant Republican years, and thus ended his political career. It gave him time to think, to take stock, to watch the movements of the political tide and determine how his own career and the future of the Democratic Party would take shape as changed circumstances allowed. Here his illness conferred another advantage. Bent on restoring movement to his crippled legs, he found a hydro-therapeutic pool at Warm Springs, Georgia, where increasingly he rested; soon he could claim to be a Southerner by adoption, which coupled with his office as a Northern governor happily combined two Democratic Party bases. Furthermore, New York State was as much a rural as an urban centre; and in its mixture of ethnic and religious groupings, social classes and domestic problems, it served as a microcosm of the nation. Some have seen in Roosevelt's programme as governor in the wake of the Depression, the genesis of the New Deal. How far there is a direct relationship is not always a matter of precise imitation. But at just that historic moment when a party of Southern rural bias was about to be transformed into a party of Northern urban emphasis, it had, uniquely, a leader who found no difficulty in embracing the two.

The change was not immediate; indeed, the culmination of the process was not to occur until the 1960s; moreover, it is arguable that the change itself was, at least initially, unintended and the consequences certainly unforeseen. Roosevelt was not even the urban Democrats' leading champion, a role still filled by Al Smith, who hoped for another shot at the presidency. In fact, the first person to call publicly for Roosevelt's nomination for the presidency was Senator Burton K. Wheeler of Montana, a Western Progressive from a rural state. But if Roosevelt attracted reformers in the Democratic Party, to more conservative groups he also appeared as a candidate who understood the party's historic lineage. Perhaps style had something to do with it; Roosevelt was undoubtedly a patrician. But it also reflected a belief that Roosevelt, even if he came from New York and had Progressive tendencies, had a conservative disposition that would prevent him from espousing overtly radical policies. What this calculation overlooked is that the most effective reformer is often the self-assured one who comes from within the establishment and is neither in awe of it nor resentful of it. It would not be long before it was being said that Roosevelt had betrayed his class. For the moment, however, Roosevelt garnered support because he looked like a winner, and after twelve hungry years in the political wilderness this was a calculation of considerable weight inside Democratic Party councils. Pragmatically, he was also a candidate who enjoyed a wide measure of Southern support. This last was to prove crucial in 1932 when the Speaker of the House of Representatives, John Nance Garner of Texas, another candidate, sensing he could not win, released his delegates to Roosevelt in exchange for the vice-presidency. Accordingly, Roosevelt became the nominee; a nomination that was never made unanimous as the Smith forces refused to accept that their moment had passed. Thus the man who would later come to pile up huge majorities in the big cities was denied the endorsement of their most famous spokesman. It would not be the last of Roosevelt's troubles with his party.

2 The Democrats Win Power

The party that Roosevelt thereby inherited was, as all successful American political parties must be, a coalition of divergent interests. The bedrock of its strength lay in the South and hence in Congress. One-party rule was the norm for the states of the Old Confederacy and Democrats were regularly returned to represent them in Washington. Under the strict seniority rules that then prevailed, the longest-serving legislators filled the most influential congressional committees and, if their party was in the majority, occupied the chairmanships. Such a system clearly favoured unbroken service and unless a Southern Democratic politician fell out with his party or manifestly lost his grip over his constituency, he was assured of a job for life with all the prerogatives of safe incumbency. This secure congressional base was not an unmixed blessing for the Democratic Party as inevitably it gave it a rural, conservative, even fundamentalist bias just at the time when the nation was moving steadfastly in an urban, liberal, somewhat progressive direction. Moreover, the cause of the South was not the cause of the nation; indeed, that region was separate from and even in some ways opposed to mainstream America. The tension between North and South was real, as the exodus of disenfranchised African-Americans from the Southern states to Northern cities indicated; it suggested a future source of trouble when they came to exercise their civic rights as Democratic Party voters. This conversion was still in the future; those African-Americans who voted were still loyal to the party of Lincoln from whom they had received their freedom, yet, logically, American politics required a realignment of voting interests. Other ethnic groupings in the big cities were now usually in the Democratic column and their numbers would be augmented by New Deal policies.

The realignment that did take place did so without its significance being immediately comprehended. In 1932 Roosevelt ran a campaign to maximize potential support in consequence of Republican failures; the overwhelming success of this strategy suddenly presented the Democratic Party with floods of new supporters whose endorsement inevitably influenced its leaders. By 1936 the Democratic Party was the party of government. Yet presidential elections only take place every four years and political parties exist between them. Increasingly, the party that campaigned for the presidency was different from the one that existed on a day-to-day basis in local statehouses and the halls of Congress. Every four years the troops were mobilized for the presidential battle; but they were asked to fight a different war from the one they practised intermittently in the interim. In a sense, this is true of all presidential politics, but in the particular circumstances of the times, the tension was manifest and the consequences discordant.

Illustrative of the tension that would later occur was the apparently happy selection of Speaker of the House John Nance Garner of Texas to be Roosevelt's vice-presidential candidate. It combined a Northern governor and a Southern congressman, a New Yorker and a Texan, an innovative, charismatic professional and an old Democratic Party war horse. It looked like one of those classic political stitch-ups designed to make everybody happy and maximize support from the widest range of the political spectrum. Garner, who had been in Congress since 1903 and had been the perennial Southern candidate for the presidential nomination, represented the congressional bedrock strength of the Democratic Party. As one observer noted: 'His mind was like a field sparingly planted. He never tried to raise too much per acre. What grew there needed the air and sunlight to fill out and nourish itself. His mental life was no aggregate of half-suffocated plants, and there were very few weeds. The principles that guided his votes and his sparing vocal support were few. But they were of the sort which have stood the test of centuries.'[4]

Garner had, as his position of Speaker of the House of Representatives might suggest, formidable political skills, but also an attachment to rural conservatism, that embraced the deflationary, sound-money, budget-balancing, reduction in government expenditure ideals of the New Deal as proclaimed in 1932. When these passed into history, though like most Southerners appreciative of federal aid programmes for agriculture, for instance, he became increasingly uneasy about the huge expenditure on welfare, the liberal reform agenda and the urban interests that increasingly became the hallmark of the New Deal. Yet Garner, like so many of his Southern congressional colleagues, shared one particular trait that overrode ideological disenchantment, namely loyalty to the Democratic Party and in consequence to its elected leader. It would take a very great deal to stretch that loyalty to breaking point and for several years Roosevelt was able to rely on the good will of many who doubted in private but were faithful in public.

The conservatism of the old Democratic Party had been well illustrated by its lack of imagination in offering panaceas for the Depression; in 1931, the chairman of the Party had even suggested that Prohibition was the key political issue of the day! And in 1932 no less than 25 per cent of Roosevelt's campaign fund was to come from bankers, scarcely a radical group of men. With customary myopia, they predictably endorsed the tired nostrums of budget balancing, reduction of federal expenditure and economies in public spending designed to restore business confidence, to which the New Deal in part seemed to subscribe. Indeed, one of Roosevelt's concerns in the opening days of his administration was to affirm his conservative credentials, to shore up that wing of his support, before getting down to the business of reform politics that would come increasingly to dominate his agenda. It is interesting to observe, in the light of subsequent history, that some of Roosevelt's most vociferous critics later on, from within the Democratic Party, affirmed to the end of their days that they were the true New Dealers. That it was Roosevelt's programme, not they, which had been blown off course in the years after 1932.

Roosevelt deliberately adopted an ambiguous stance in the campaign of 1932, for he had no desire to alienate potential supporters by too explicit a series of campaign promises and could rely on Hoover to defeat himself. At times his refusal to take precise positions bordered on the deceitful. When faced with alternative drafts of speeches, one advocating a reduction of tariff rates, the other more cautiously promising no more than bilateral negotiations, Roosevelt astounded his speechwriter by asking him to 'weave the two together'.[5]

On another occasion, in a rare hostage to fortune, he committed himself to balancing the budget and cutting federal expenditure by 25 per cent. He honoured neither goal. By and large, Roosevelt stuck to generalities. Thus while it can be argued that it is possible to trace the genesis of the New Deal in his campaign speeches, this was only accurate in so far as any incoming president would have to deal with the crisis in collapsed agricultural prices, prostrate manufacturing industries and mass unemployment. Other than that, the connection between his campaign speeches and subsequent policies was often as tenuous as that between the prophecies of the oracle at Delphi and their subsequent vindication: a tribute less to foresight than to the hedging of bets. To some this was merely common prudence, a desire not to alienate potential supporters. To others, not least President Hoover, who did see the implications clearly and what a Roosevelt victory portended, the refusal to cite facts and figures and enter into meaningful debate – Hoover, in effect, was ignored for most of the campaign – suggested a dishonesty of purpose. Few historians have criticized Roosevelt for this and perhaps one should judge by results.

In some ways Roosevelt did himself an injustice, for he had it within him to elevate political debate. Reading his speeches, one is struck by how reflective and thoughtful they could be; he had a philosophy of government and American history that, on occasions as at the Commonwealth Club in San Francisco in September 1932, could be intellectually impressive.

The issue of Government has always been whether individual men and women will have to serve some system of Government or economics, or whether a system of Government and economics exists to serve individual men and women ... In other times we dealt with the problem of an unduly ambitious central Government by modifying it gradually into a constitutional democratic Government. So today we are modifying and controlling our economic units. As I see it, the task of Government in its relation

to business is to assist the development of an economic declaration of rights, an economic constitutional order. This is the common task of statesman and businessman. It is the minimum
requirement of a more permanently safe order of things...The
Declaration of Independence discusses the problem of Government in terms of a contract. Government is a relation of give
and take, a contract, perforce, if we would follow the thinking
out of which it grew. Under such a contract rulers were accorded
power, and the people consented to that power on consideration
that they be accorded certain rights. The task of statesmanship
has always been the re-definition of these rights in terms of a
changing and growing social order. New conditions impose
new requirements upon Government and those who conduct
Government.[6]

Roosevelt's almost intuitive sense of the mainsprings of American
history comes over clearly, and equally his willingness to adapt to
new circumstances. Roosevelt's pragmatism was one of his greatest
political assets, but such an approach does not require much detailed
logical argument. Perhaps a commitment to a 'New Deal', a folksy
colloquialism suggesting some form of economic redistribution, was
about as far as he could go.

The strategy was triumphantly effective; the American electorate
contrived one of the most astounding political turnarounds in their
history. Hoover, who but four years before had swept into the presidency with 40 of the 48 states supporting him, was now left with 6;
nor did he succeed in carrying a state south or west of Pennsylvania;
geographically, apart from an East Coast fragment, America was
Democrat. Both chambers of Congress, Senate and House of Representatives, also returned heavy Democratic majorities. The way was
cleared for action.

Instead, the nation got paralysis. For the last time in American
history the country faced a four-month interregnum from November until March, itself a hangover from the more leisurely eighteenth century, perhaps symbolic of an era that was now to be laid
to rest. The Twentieth Amendment to the Constitution that would
replace 4 March with 20 January as Presidential Inauguration day
and bring forward the swearing-in of the new Congress to 3 January, though ratified in 1933, was too late to come into immediate
effect. Thus Hoover, although defeated at the polls, tried to exact
from his successor some form of commitment to announce policies

that, he argued, would restore public confidence. Hoover's suggestion seemed uncannily to embrace the very policies that the electorate had just repudiated. Indeed, Hoover himself admitted it would have implied 'the abandonment of 90% of the so-called "new deal" '.[7] The proposal was a non-starter and merely cast Hoover in a bad light, weakening his authority still further. Reasonably, Roosevelt steadfastly refused to accept responsibility without power. For the Roosevelt dynamism to succeed, he required sole executive authority. It was not, as Hoover and other critics have alleged, that Roosevelt lacked a sense of urgency. He had a true appreciation of the gravity of the crisis, and knew that lacklustre measures or a diffident attitude to the powers of his office were insufficient for what was required. Hence Roosevelt's determination to be the president solely and exclusively, for he was about to raise the profile of the chief executive. Roosevelt's success as president lay so often in his true appreciation of what was politically essential.

And Roosevelt intuitively understood the public psychology. Four years of Depression had taken their toll. Contemporary observers noticed that the most frightening aspect of the public mood was not a seething anger with conditions, that would at least have denoted energy, but a passive inertia of defeat and despair that suggested a helplessness in the face of overwhelming disaster. 'The majority of people were hit and hit hard,' one old lady recalled of her days in Oklahoma. 'They were mentally disturbed you're bound to know, 'cause they didn't know when the end of all this was comin'. There was a lot of suicides that I know of. From nothin' else but just they couldn't see any hope for a better tomorrow. I absolutely know some who did. Part of 'em were farmers and part of 'em were businessmen, even. They went flat broke and they committed suicide on the strength of it, nothing else.' 'Another remarkable thing about the Depression,' a Chicago broker recalled, 'it never resulted in revolution. I remember that out in Iowa some place, there was a fellow named Reno, who led a small following. There were some trucks turned over, and sheriffs weren't allowed to foreclose. But when you consider what was going on in the country – the whole country was orderly: they just sat there and took it. In retrospect, it's amazing, just amazing. Either they were in shock, or they thought something would happen to turn it around ... My wife has often discussed it with me. She thinks it's amazing, the lack of violent protest, especially in 1932 and 1933.'[8]

If for farmers' leaders like Milo Reno, the solution lay in a Farmers' Holiday Association to refuse to ship produce to market, for others prayer was the only answer. In 1929 the Catholic National Shrine of St Jude the Patron Saint of Hopeless Causes was inaugurated. The timing could not have been bettered. Soon it was to be swamped with petitions from the desperate victims of economic disaster. 'Letters of thanksgiving for Jude's help during the Depression continued to arrive in Chicago for years afterward, as women recalled with relief the saint's assistance in this desperate time', its historian has noted.[9] The scale of the tragedy was enormous. 'The economic situation is very unfortunate here too', a German immigrant in St Louis reported to his brother back home as the doomed Weimar Republic staggered to its grave. 'We have between 10 and 12 million unemployed here. And the taxes keep going up. Thousands have lost their property because they weren't able to raise the money for the high taxes.'[10]

Was there any reason why American democracy should not go the same way as its German counterpart? It was a frightening situation and one that might prove terminal. Some commentators, by no means alarmist, wondered whether liberal democracy might have had its day: that it was a luxury only to be sustained by economic growth. Was it the end of an era, where the future lay with the contemporary vogue of totalitarianism; either that of the right as practised by Hitler or Mussolini, or that of the left as seen in Stalin's Russia?

3 FDR Enters the White House

That such an eventuality was not to occur owes much to Roosevelt. Indeed, his presence at so critical a juncture seems to reflect an intuitive genius in American democracy in calling forth the man for the hour to meet a threatened society's deepest needs. He appears never to have doubted himself, and his confidence inspired others. In many ways it was a remarkable performance. 'So, first of all, let me assert my firm belief that the only thing we have to fear is fear itself – nameless, unreasoning, unjustified terror which paralyzes needed efforts to convert retreat into advance.'[11] It is the most famous passage in his first Inaugural Address. 'The only thing we have to fear is fear itself': a memorable phrase and, as his closest aide Raymond Moley observed, 'a glittering but inspiring untruth'.[12] Of course, Americans had more to fear – much more. But Roosevelt understood that the nation looked to him for a lead. On the other hand, words alone were not enough. That had been the mistake of Hoover. What makes Roosevelt's first moments in the presidency so significant, and why his speech had such an impact, was that it was all of a part of what subsequently happened. Roosevelt was no mere empty rhetorician. Had actions not followed words, the speech would now be remembered, if at all, as yet another set of bombastic promises that are a monument to the vanity and self-deception of their authors and litter the pages of political history.

This empathy between Roosevelt and the American people was to be an enduring characteristic of his presidency; he had absorbed the lesson of his cousin that no other politician could claim so broad a constituency. Thus Roosevelt personalized the presidency in a unique way. Characteristically, his initials FDR afforded instant recognition. The White House became a family home where public and private demarcations were subtly blurred. This sense of family overlapped his administration; associates became colleagues, colleagues became family friends. His wife Eleanor was an independent political force, and five children tended to enhance the sense of a public family. There was a paternalistic streak in Roosevelt, as some of his critics noted. Visitors were called by their first names; audiences were addressed as 'My friends'.[13] The friendliness could occasionally be misleading; and one or two who worked for him were to be hurt when they took it for friendship and found that once they had served his larger purposes, they were dispensable. On the other hand, he inspired trust; people enjoyed working for him; he was a considerate, indeed kind employer; they felt he was on their side. Many stayed with him for years. He rewarded loyalty even to the extent of keeping on some whose competence might be questioned. When it came to firing people Roosevelt admitted to being 'a complete softy'.[14]

Still, it made for team spirit and often brought the best out in people. And even a slightly misleading camaraderie was what the times demanded. They were all in it together. As he said in his first 'Fireside Chat' when he spoke to the American people about the banking crisis the weekend following his inauguration: 'It is your problem no less than it is mine. Together we cannot fail.'[15] His appeal to partnership was more than a political ploy. Roosevelt liked people and they liked him. Frances Perkins, an acute observer who had known him for years and was to serve in his Cabinet throughout his presidency, could recall only one man, a notorious New Deal critic and misanthrope, leaving his presence 'with an austere, indifferent, even sneering look on his face'. Most, even enemies, 'could not resist his contagious fondness for people – all kinds of people'.[16] Nothing could be a greater contrast than the former President Hoover, sunk in gloom, overwhelmed by his responsibilities, and the ever-cheerful Roosevelt, serenely on top of his job, taking every difficulty in his stride.

The phrase serves to remind one of a fact that many forgot and he ignored: that Roosevelt himself was a cripple. Perhaps this helps explain his pragmatic concern for human want and his willingness to set aside appeals to abstract principles that had so handicapped his predecessor, and offer a programme of action, albeit an imperfect one. There was the imperative to do something. Roosevelt was essentially a humanitarian; indeed, it is possible that he was only able to visualize politics in human terms; that he had neither the cast of intellect, nor the intellectual attraction to abstract thought, to evolve a coherent set of theoretical underpinnings for the measures he took. It is hard to imagine Roosevelt writing a book like Hoover. Instead, in the best tradition of American political theory, his contribution lay in a series of speeches that grew out of specific problems and circumstances. If the contribution, in consequence, appeared piecemeal, it was nonetheless a coherent, unified whole. It was the attitude Roosevelt brought to the problems he found that was deep-seated, even profound and represented a new departure. He was, as he once said, 'a Christian and a Democrat, – that's all'.[17] And this apparent lack of philosophical sophistication in fact represented the mature, reasoned outlook of an integrated personality in whom thought and action cohered. There is a sense in which Roosevelt represented the fundamental forces in American historical development, articulated them and set the parameters for his successors. Roosevelt was a truly creative thinker whose ideas found expression in action. It is interesting to note how throughout his presidency, he consistently set out his programme within the context of American history. As somebody whose family, on both sides, had arrived in America in the first half of the seventeenth century, he had an intuitive understanding of the nation's historical progress, and how old values must be redefined in modern conditions. This was to be a legacy on which his successors were to draw. Roosevelt cast a long shadow over the presidency; none of those who came after him could entirely forget the ideas he had articulated or the programmes he had implemented. They operated in a world that he had made.

Roosevelt's achievement, and the legacy he bequeathed, was the very opposite of totalitarianism; indeed, it was its most effective antidote. It might be described as 'democratic humanism'. At a basic level there was a genuine concern for human distress and the ability to relate to the unfortunate. There are many stories to attest to this, like the economist casually advocating policies that involved an acceptance of periodic hardship to allow a fundamentally sound system to right itself whatever the cost to human beings, and Roosevelt's incredulous response: 'People aren't cattle, you know!'[18] He was the elected representative of the American people and depended on their continued support. Partly out of conviction, partly out of calculation, Roosevelt played broker politics. He genuinely believed that in a democracy, if enough people really wanted something, it was the duty of the government to meet them halfway. The government would arbitrate between conflicting needs, giving a little to everyone; equally, it was the duty of government to call into the political spectrum of concern, disadvantaged groups and neglected minorities, whose voice, hitherto, had not been heard. 'The forgotten man, at the bottom of the economic pyramid' might be an unskilled, Italian immigrant in a city breadline, a black share-cropper in the Deep South, or a drought-stricken small farmer in the Midwest. In other words, there would be a New Deal.

4 The New Deal

Such a programme, speedily executed, all-embracing in its manifestations, needed central coordination. Fifteen major pieces of legislation in the famous 'One Hundred Days' between March and June, which initiated the realignment of the American political landscape, needed a conductor; the legislative orchestra had to play together. One only has to contrast the ill-advised, disparate, uncoordinated, fitful gestures that characterized the legislative programme of the lame-duck Congress of early 1933 with the decisiveness and resolution that followed Roosevelt's inauguration to see the difference. The Seventy-third Congress was the most creative in American history; but the lead came from the White House. As *The Times* of London noted at the time, it left 'Mr. Roosevelt clothed with extraordinary and dictatorial powers undreamed of by any of his predecessors in office. By reason of them the President is now in a position to launch the United States upon a social and economic revolution which will be no less a revolution merely because it has constitutional sanction.'[19]

Commentators do not always appreciate Roosevelt's legislative virtuosity when dealing with a formally separate body, the Congress. 'The President proposes, Congress disposes' is an old truism not entirely without validity: why, then, was Roosevelt so uniquely successful? The answer lay in the nature of the crisis of 1933. Such a situation required the decisive leadership that only one man could give. Having seized the initiative, Roosevelt was loath to let it go.

Nothing better characterizes this sense of presidential leadership than the Emergency Banking legislation of the first week of his administration. Before anything else, Roosevelt was obliged to shore up the nation's banking system that was in a state of virtual collapse when he took the oath of office. Having declared a 'bank holiday' in the small hours of Monday 6 March, a clever misnomer, Roosevelt and his officials worked with the outgoing administration to devise some solution to a crisis that struck at the very basis of American capitalism. The essential issue was one of confidence. Having witnessed 5,000 bank failures in the last three years Americans were more inclined to put their savings under the mattress than risk total loss, inaccessibility through temporary closure, or partial payment. What few banks were open often limited savers to withdrawing as little as 5 per cent of their assets. But restoring trust required understanding human psychology as much as technical expertise. Thus for Roosevelt some solutions were automatically precluded. Reformers might dream of nationalizing the banks, of seizing a unique chance that might never recur to make Wall Street finally subservient to Washington. A Senate committee had recently been turning up a succession of banking scandals. By 1933 the banking community had few friends or admirers. But trust is an elusive quality. As Roosevelt shrewdly appreciated, such schemes would have the drawback of novelty. When it comes to money matters people tend to be conservative. They know what they like and like what they know. What was needed was the safety of a revitalized, but familiar system that would restore public confidence. Thus banks would gradually be reopened when government-appointed regulators declared they were sound; some less stable institutions would be amalgamated or absorbed by others; a few weak sisters would be closed. The president was to have broad discretionary powers to control the export of gold and foreign exchange transactions. Commercial and investment banking would be separated; later, against Roosevelt's earlier inclinations, bank deposits up to a modest level would be federally guaranteed.

By Thursday 9 March, the House of Representatives was passing his bill sight unseen after perfunctory debate; even the Senate only gave it several hours' consideration. It was this pliancy of Congress, called into emergency session, that persuaded Roosevelt to keep it on longer in Washington, striking testimony to his adaptability and the haphazard, improvised nature of his policies. It was an opportunity not to be missed. Of course, close examination shows that cooperation was not necessarily all one-way; the Seventy-third Congress was not a rubber stamp, but whatever historians may prove in fact, in appearance it was Roosevelt who set the agenda. That image of potent presidential leadership was psychologically all-important. A successful president had to give a lead.

The pressure was relentless. Roosevelt had proved his conservative credentials by orthodox banking legislation: 'capitalism was saved in eight days', a colleague noted.[20] Then economy measures designed to show that there was a tight hand on governmental expenditure – some 500 million dollars was slashed from the federal budget – reinforced the message. Now the way was open for that creative mix of measures that dazzled contemporaries. Often thrown together in haste, not always carefully drafted, sometimes trying to do several things at once, they did at least all testify to a willingness to act. Even the earliest proposal legalizing beer and wine, anticipating the repeal of Prohibition by the Twenty-first Amendment to the Constitution making its way through the various state legislatures, helped cheer the nation – or at least all but die-hard Prohibitionists! It also made for a useful source of revenue. The One Hundred Days might throw up a pot-pourri of legislation, but underneath lay a common purpose. Looking back a year later, Roosevelt was to characterize his programme as coming under 'three related steps', 'relief', 'recovery' and 'reform and reconstruction.'[21]

Perhaps, of all the welter of legislation relief was the most innovative, unusual, and represented a new departure in the role of government. At the immediate level the various relief programmes found people work and they became a characteristic feature of the period. Even before the month was out, Roosevelt had set up the Civilian Conservation Corps (CCC), an imaginative scheme that took unemployed young men off the streets and put them to work on conservation projects in the countryside. This last was an issue dear to his heart. Roosevelt was environmentally conscious, indeed ahead of his time. Ultimately, in some ten years over 3 million of the jobless between the ages of 17 and 24 would be recruited. Characteristically, the Agriculture, Labor and War Departments would all be involved. It was a classic New Deal approach.

The ordinary unemployed, too, needed help. Soon a Federal Emergency Relief Administration (FERA) was established. Harry Hopkins, its administrator, had 500 million dollars to spend to fund relief projects: 200 million in cooperation with the states, on the basis of their own expenditure, which made for local variation: 300 million at Hopkins's own discretion. When speed was of the essence, Hopkins's no-nonsense, red-tape-cutting mode of operation made him an ideal appointment. He spent 5 million dollars in his first two hours! As the New Deal continued, he grew increasingly close to Roosevelt, shared his liberal philosophy, and before long became his right-hand man. He understood the imperative to act. Of one relief proposal that Hopkins was assured would work 'in the long run' he noted: 'People don't eat in the long run – they eat every day.'[22]

Later he would be in charge of the Civil Works Administration (CWA) that tided the unemployed and those on relief over the vicious winter of 1933–4 and provided work for some 4 million people. In three and a half months they built or improved 40,000 schools, 3,700 playgrounds or athletic fields, and 255,000 miles of road, they laid 12 million feet of sewer pipe, built 469 airports and improved another 529. In addition, 50,000 teachers were employed to teach adults or keep open rural schools that would otherwise have been closed. By 1935 Hopkins would head the Works Progress Administration (WPA) with a massive budget of almost 5 billion dollars. Its record was astounding. WPA workers improved 572,000 miles of rural roads; built 78,000 new bridges and viaducts; laid 67,000 miles of city streets; and 24,000 miles of sidewalks. They repaired 85,000 public buildings and constructed 40,000 new ones, created 8,000 parks and built 350 airports. Although the intensity of WPA varied on a yearly basis depending on its appropriations, it is reckoned that altogether it put some 10 billion dollars into the economy when it was sorely needed and found jobs sometimes only for short intervals, sometimes for longer ones, for 8 million Americans.

It would doubtless have surprised Roosevelt had he known that WPA, the largest of the relief schemes, would not be wound down until 1943. Partly this was a tribute to how necessary they were: partly that 'recovery', the great, elusive goal of the 1930s that would have made such schemes superfluous, was never fully achieved until the war. At a deeper level, one of the greatest of Roosevelt's contributions came in the changed public attitude to government as the result of his presidency. Instead of the old Jeffersonian suspicion that government governs best which governs least, a cast of mind that died hard, it became a factor to be positively welcomed. Previously, it could be said with pardonable exaggeration, that the average American citizen only came into contact with the federal government when they went into a post office.[23] Yet the statement reflected the distance between the federal government in Washington and the day-to-day activities of its citizens. Government was often seen as intrusive at best, oppressive at worst. After Roosevelt the perception changed. For many American citizens, perhaps for a majority, government became a supporter and protector. During the 1930s, it has been estimated, something like 46 million people, or over one-third of the population, received some form of public and/or social insurance at one time or another. In 1929 the funding for these programmes was virtually non-existent; ten years later, it totalled 5 billion dollars. The federal government, sometimes literally, kept people alive.

Conservatives might rail against handouts, that the spirit of the nation was being sapped, that self-help and independence were giving way to dependency. Nor would Roosevelt necessarily have disagreed. 'The Federal Government must and shall quit this business of relief', he had vowed, as early as January 1935.[24] Relief, yes, that the government would try to limit; but it was willing to provide opportunities for self-help in the short term. In a longer perspective, relief would be unnecessary when the American people achieved economic security. Roosevelt deemed it his duty to work towards this on three broad fronts: '1. The security of a livelihood through the better use of the national resources of the land in which we live. 2. The security against the major hazards and vicissitudes of life. 3. The security of decent homes.' It was, he conceded, 'a program which because of many lost years will take many future years to fulfill'.[25]

It took the disaster of the Depression to move Americans to this way of thinking. If hands-off government led to this; if government must not interfere even when the very livelihood and welfare of its citizens was threatened and millions seemed doomed to destitution, perhaps an activist government might not be such a bad thing after all. It is hard to sustain any philosophy for long if it leads one to be hungry.

The election of 1932 was indeed a watershed. For the first time an American president enunciated the principle that the welfare of the American people was a direct responsibility of government. In retrospect it is surprising how modest were these claims; in the 1960s it was fashionable for New Left historians to berate the New Deal for its minimal achievements. This is to be unhistorical. In 1933 the principle alone was important; what strikes an observer of the United States is how backward were its social security provisions, using the phrase in the broadest sense. The welfare state simply did not exist. One could hardly construct Utopia in five years; what is remarkable is how much Roosevelt and the New Deal did achieve, and in a time of poverty not of plenty. The circumstances for a new beginning could scarcely have been less auspicious.

Meanwhile there was much hard work to be done. The agricultural crisis was deep and of long standing. By 1933, farm mortgages foreclosed at a terrifying 20,000 a month. If revolution ever came to America, it might well start in the countryside. The Farm Credit Administration (FCA) would consolidate all federal agricultural credit agencies and provide funds to enable farmers to renegotiate their mortgages and thereby keep their farms.

Meanwhile, in the South spring planting had already started even before Roosevelt took the oath of office. Another bumper cotton crop threatened a further slump in prices. It was symptomatic of a range of agricultural produce. The Agricultural Adjustment Act, that set up the Agricultural Adjustment Administration (AAA), aimed to reward farmers who grew less by cleverly calculated government subsidies; reduced output would raise prices and restore farm income. It would also consequently improve purchasing power for industrial products. At long last the balance between city and countryside would be restored. As usual, Roosevelt relied on voluntarism not coercion, but notwithstanding initial teething troubles, which involved ploughing up growing cotton or slaughtering piglets and which occasioned the predictable outcry, he found the key to an effective farm policy that has relied on subsidies ever since. Perhaps the greatest tribute to Roosevelt is that in ten weeks he came up with a solution that had eluded his predecessors in ten years.

Of course, as always, there were winners and losers: one reason why in retrospect the New Deal has had its critics. What could be done then was often less than what reformers have deemed acceptable later. Here one must never forget the context in which Roosevelt operated. Clearly a scheme run by farmers themselves would benefit the more prosperous and powerful. Indeed, federal subsidies even went to large corporations and insurance companies that happened to own land but did not work on it. And if the government was going to pay farmers to cut back production, the first land the wealthier ones took out of cultivation would be that leased to tenants. Some of the most wretched groups in American agriculture, such as sharecroppers who paid rent for their land not in cash but in produce, would be pushed down even further. True, later measures such as the Resettlement Administration (RA) in 1935 aimed to improve land use practices, whilst the Farm Security Administration (FSA) in 1937 sought to assist poor farmers who either owned small farms or were merely tenants. Nonetheless, critics of the AAA had a fair point when they drew attention to the consequences for the most vulnerable rural inhabitants, among whom African-Americans were especially numerous.

On the other hand the Rural Electrification Administration (REA) of 1935 would transform the countryside. In 1933 it was reckoned that only one in ten American farms had electricity. Life in the American countryside was primitive in the extreme. Nor were the power companies anxious to pay the high capital costs that bringing electric power to the countryside entailed. For the REA and regional development schemes like the Tennessee Valley Authority (TVA), this was no problem when the profit motive was irrelevant. In 1950 nine in ten American farms had electric power. By then, of course, there were fewer of them. Critics noted that the farms that remained grew bigger, small farms were consolidated into larger units; the family farm virtually disappeared. Here nature had also played its part. The Dust Bowl storms of the 1930s that ripped off the rich agricultural topsoil loosened by drought, making the land unfit for cultivation, as immortalized in John Steinbeck's *The Grapes of Wrath*, helped finish the process that the AAA had started. Land was involuntarily taken out of production. The 1933 wheat harvest, for example, was the smallest since 1896.[26]

One could mourn the passing of a way of life that had endured for three centuries where man and the land were bound together in an almost religious partnership that, if it scarcely rose above survival level, still ministered to the deepest human instincts. One might argue that even a barter system that insured its continuance would have been preferable to the relocation of thousands from the intimate community life of the countryside to the anonymity of the city, the price of profit-induced farm amalgamation. What the New Deal started, the Second World War and technological change completed in a generation, particularly in the emergence of 'the New South', which before had been described by Roosevelt as 'the Nation's No. 1 economic problem'.[27]

Of course, the New Deal had its failures and it should not be idealized; it was a pragmatic response to an urgent need, using whatever tools were available, and it was bound to have its limitations. But no one reading James Agee and Walker Evans's *Let Us Now Praise Famous Men*, a famous contemporary record of the lives of typical Southern sharecroppers with its searing photographs, can fail to question whether some historians have not fallen into the opposite trap. They idealize an existence they themselves could never endure, of human misery, degradation and squalor, which many of its victims did, because they could do no other. It is highly speculative whether a viable alternative to that adopted by the New Deal, however attractive in theory, realistically existed. One might equally ask what would have happened had Roosevelt done nothing? In the long run the American countryside was in inexorable retreat before the city. Nonetheless, over the Roosevelt years farm income rose some 400 per cent.[28]

With industry he was less immediately effective. Here, to some extent, his hands were tied by the corporate nature of his solution, perhaps the only way forward in the circumstances. The National Industrial Recovery Act, which set up the National Recovery Administration (NRA), aimed to stimulate economic recovery through meeting the needs of both manufacturers and workers. Another component, the Public Works Administration (PWA), with a budget of nearly 3.5 billion dollars, sought economic stimulus through permanent and socially useful public works projects that would also provide jobs and increase purchasing power. Certainly, if rather slow off the mark in construction – the immediate relief benefits were much less than they might have been due to excessive caution in their selection – the public works themselves proved remarkably durable. Ultimately over 6 billion dollars would be expended on projects that ranged from bridges to courthouses, dams, hospitals, jails, power plants, roads, schools and sewage works. PWA even built two aircraft carriers for the Navy, plus a collection of smaller craft.

In 1933, however, it was the NRA that attracted most attention. For Roosevelt it represented an important exercise in government–business cooperation. Again, he tried to give a little to everyone – a characteristic hallmark – and a friendly critic said that he succeeded in his aim of giving 'a shot in the arm for industry'. Psychologically, too, it was important. Even some of the ballyhoo that accompanied it at least gave a sense that action now substituted for inertia. Perhaps the NRA was, as Frances Perkins the secretary of labor further noted, 'One of the most vital causes of the revival of the American spirit, and signalized emergence from the industrial depression.'[29]

Nonetheless, the suspension of antitrust laws against businessmen anxious to avoid wasteful competition in exchange for their agreeing minimum wages, maximum hours and union rights for workers, partly foundered on excessive red tape. Sometimes in its enthusiasm to get agreement the NRA lacked a sense of proportion. It seemed a bit silly to regulate quite marginal industries such as the dog food or the shoulder-pad manufacturing industry when a major employer like Henry Ford stood aloof. Even striptease artistes came under NRA regulation of the burlesque theatrical industry. One hopes this was not too vital to the restoration of the American economy. Moreover, as an added come-on, compliant manufacturers were promised government exhortations to the public to buy only the products of those who had signed up to the relevant codes for their industries, indicated by the symbol of a blue American eagle. Thus equally damaging was the often cynical readiness to subscribe, but laxity in observing the obligations whilst enjoying all the benefits, and perhaps a general incompatibility of aim between businessmen and a reforming government.

Yet NRA was extremely important for what it represented. Even if it was over-ambitious and not always well directed, it made a statement as to what should be the relationship between the government and its people. Thus in one of Roosevelt's most memorable press conferences, he took to task the Supreme Court when it ruled that the NRA was unconstitutional. In May 1935 the Court invalidated it, and based its decision on an interpretation of the interstate commerce clause of the Constitution that seemed to accord ill with modern developments. The Schechter brothers of Brooklyn had been found guilty of violating the NRA's Live Poultry Code, including selling diseased chickens; the case was immortalized thereafter as the 'sick chicken' case. According to the Court, irrespective of the fact that the chickens may have come from outside New York State, the Schechters themselves were only involved in intrastate not interstate commerce, and thus were exempt from federal government regulation. As Roosevelt argued:

> The whole tendency over these years has been to view the interstate commerce clause in the light of present day civilization. The country was in the horse-and-buggy age when that clause was written and if you go back to the debates on the Federal Constitution you will find in 1787 that one of the impelling motives for putting in that clause was this: There was not much interstate commerce at all – probably 80 or 90 per cent of the human beings in the thirteen original States were completely self-supporting within their own communities.[30]

Roosevelt's exasperation was the understandable reaction of a man watching one of his major legislative achievements buried without trace. As a British newspaper put it: 'America Stunned; Roosevelt's Two Years' Work Killed In Twenty Minutes.'[31] Yet the Court's decision symbolized the problem that went to the heart of reform politics; before one could achieve liberalism one had to redefine what was thought appropriate to the actions of government. In the same press conference, Roosevelt put it succinctly:

> They had in those days no problems relating to employment... to the earning capacity of people – what the man in Massachusetts earned, what his buying power was. Nobody had ever thought of what the wages were or the buying capacity in the slave-holding States of the South. There were no social questions in those days ... health on a national basis had never been discussed. The word was unknown in the vocabulary of the Founding Fathers. The ethics of the period were very different from what they are today. If one man could skin a fellow and get away with it, why, that was all right.[32]

In other words, the whole apparatus of modern interventionist government not only did not exist; more importantly, it even went unthought.

It is sometimes easy to believe that this struggle for liberalism was a battle between progressive and conservative forces with the latter fighting a rearguard action ultimately doomed to failure. But this misrepresents popular conceptions as to the nature of government itself. The nineteenth century had witnessed an increasing realization of the need to enlarge the role of government. But it was a slow, limited awakening; even the notion that a government might institute a graduated income tax or legislate against child labour could be seen as a gross violation of individual freedom. The Constitution had been devised for a society of 13 seaboard states, 95 per cent of whose population lived in the countryside; the first census in 1790 put their number at just under 4 million. Now the same Constitution had to serve a nation of 130 million, predominantly urban as the census of 1920 had first indicated, living in 48 states that stretched from the Atlantic to the Pacific. Obviously, the Constitution of 1787 was not the Constitution of 1933. There had been developments in attitudes: one of the reasons why Roosevelt was genuinely shocked by the abrupt reversal by the nine Justices of the Supreme Court of what had appeared to be a increasing tendency towards a more liberal interpretation. Yet in the late nineteenth century, when this tendency had slowly begun to operate, it was clear that the political, constitutional revolution had not kept pace with the economic revolution. Only an enlarged role for government could synchronize the two.

This was a departure that violated considerable taboos in American thinking. There was ancestral suspicion of government; the memories of George III had sunk deep into the national consciousness. Federalism fragmented government even while it united it, limiting the role of the centre. Yet the suspicion ran against the tide of history. It seemed odd to accept economic concentration that wielded great power often at the expense of individuals, but to reject concentrated political power that at least was answerable to the voters. Teddy Roosevelt and Woodrow Wilson had both grappled with this problem, whilst the First World War did at least illustrate how, in a time of crisis, the resources of the government and the economy might be coordinated and organized in the pursuit of victory. It was this memory that was to prompt Roosevelt's assertion in his first Inaugural that he would, if necessary, ask Congress for 'broad Executive power to wage a war against the emergency, as great as the power that would be given to me if we were in fact invaded by a foreign foe'.[33]

Thus the War Industries Board of 1917 had provided the inspiration for the National Recovery Administration of 1933 that, two years later, the Supreme Court declared unconstitutional. No wonder Roosevelt's exasperation that the Court could not or would not see the emergency of 1933 as serious in its own way as that of 1917. The problem lay in the field of political philosophy. Government was a necessary evil; at times, as in the First World War the evil had to be augmented. But this was a temporary aberration to be dispensed with as soon as possible. Otherwise it would stifle the individual. It was the creed of Herbert Hoover. The issue, however, was not as simple as it was made to appear. As Roosevelt himself put it in a campaign address in 1936: 'I believe in individualism. I believe in it in the arts, the sciences and professions... in business... up to the point where the individualist starts to operate at the expense of society.'[34]

This respect for individualism was deep-seated in American society; in a sense it was what America was about. 'Life, liberty and the pursuit of happiness' were not the watchwords of automatons. Individualism had secured independence and made a nation, tamed a frontier and developed a continent. Jefferson was its patron saint; he was also a Democratic Party hero. How could the party of Jefferson abandon his philosophy? The answer, as postulated by Roosevelt, was quite simple: it was not to try. Jefferson would remain the Democratic Party hero; his legend, indeed, would be sedulously cultivated. Yet his name would be invoked as the patron of causes he would have viewed with bewilderment if not outright loathing. Or would he? Certainly, at one level, it is difficult to see the aristocratic, rural democrat of the eighteenth century in such a role. The selfsame Jefferson who roundly condemned the urban proletariat of his day: 'the mobs of great cities add just so much to the support of pure government, as sores do to the strength of the human body'.[35] Was he really a champion of the New Deal democracy that returned Roosevelt regularly to the White House as a result of huge majorities built up in the great cities, by coalitions of urban immigrants and blue-collar workers?

Yet Roosevelt positively identified with his great predecessor, invoking his name wherever possible. A man of greater intellectual consistency might have found this difficult; here Roosevelt's famed flexibility and pragmatism worked to his advantage. It is easy to be sceptical. Raymond Moley alleged that 'his knowledge of political and constitutional history and theory was distinctly limited'.[36] Roosevelt was certainly no scholar; his mind was far too flexible and, in an academic sense, undisciplined. But he reviewed Claude G. Bowers's *Jefferson and Hamilton: The Struggle for Democracy in America*, a milestone in Jefferson studies when it appeared in 1925. Still recovering from his illness and not yet returned to active politics, Roosevelt had time to ponder the significance of Jefferson at a time when Hamiltonian ideas seemed to be in the ascendant. 'I have a breathless feeling as I lay down this book... of what might have been if the Republic had been finally organized as Alexander Hamilton sought... I wonder if, a century and a quarter later, the same contending forces are not again mobilizing. Hamiltons we have today. Is a Jefferson on the horizon?'[37]

Thus Roosevelt would refashion Jefferson in a twentieth-century image, taking those parts of his philosophy he found most useful. Who is to say he was wrong? Perhaps the spirit of Jefferson was best preserved by insuring a new lease of life for the America he had done so much to father. 'Thomas Jefferson survives', his great rival John Adams had said on his deathbed.[38] Possibly, the words had a greater significance than Adams had intended. Ideologically, Roosevelt at least would not live in the 'horse-and-buggy age'. He would update, revise, replenish, borrowing what he needed to fashion a new philosophy that gave to the common man in an industrial society the rights that had first been adumbrated in 1776. Had not Jefferson himself, as Roosevelt reminded his hearers when he spoke of individualism, warned that 'widespread poverty and concentrated wealth cannot long endure side by side in a democracy'.[39]

There is something distinctly appealing about the patrician Roosevelt, born with a silver spoon in his mouth, making himself the spokesman for twentieth-century, common-man democracy. It was one of his greatest acts of creativity, and if there was an element of *noblesse oblige* in his make-up, not always his most attractive trait, his heart at least was in the right place. Seen in this light, government was a patron to be looked up to; it would do, only it could do what the local landowner, squire or planter might have done in a very limited sense in the eighteenth century. Democratic government was not oppressive; it liberated; it acted as a protector; it insured justice; it served its citizens; it gave meaning to their lives and enriched them. It was, in retrospect, the most powerful antidote to all forms of totalitarianism, the great scourge of the modern world. Like a company beholden to its shareholders, the American government would be beholden to its citizens; voluntarism, indeed, lay at the heart of the New Deal. Government would be creative; its ramifications went indeed even beyond the immediate issues of practical politics; it had almost a spiritual role. The religious side of Roosevelt was deep, if often unstated. Like Lincoln, his religious sense was too wide and all-embracing to be trapped in the narrow grooves of sectarianism. It was all the more powerful for that. Just occasionally, he revealed his hand. 'We can, if we will,' he told Congress,

> make 1935 a genuine period of good feeling, sustained by a sense of purposeful progress. Beyond the material recovery, I sense a spiritual recovery as well. The people of America are turning as never before to those permanent values that are not limited to the physical objectives of life. There are growing signs of this on every hand. In the face of these spiritual impulses we are sensible of the Divine Providence to which Nations turn now, as always, for guidance and fostering care.[40]

Thus there is a sense in which the New Deal was much more than the sum of its parts. Whilst it mitigated distress with relief, sought recovery with various schemes of varying success and pushed through reform measures to curtail the abuses of the 1920s, its overall aim was to build a more inclusive America. For a start, it would ensure that the malpractices that had too often benefited the unscrupulous few, at the expense of the naïve and sometimes gullible many, would not recur. This was clearly socially divisive. It is odd to recall that Roosevelt was accused by the more virulent of his enemies of fomenting class war and setting rich against poor. Actually all he wanted was for the rich to behave a bit more responsibly. Although reform legislation was often the least dramatic of the New Deal measures it had long-term consequences. The Securities Act of 1933 and the Securities and Exchange Act of 1934 which set up the Securities and Exchange Commission (SEC) outlawed many of the irregularities on Wall Street of the previous decade and provided for governmental supervision. They still operate today.

Sometimes, as with the TVA that built dams and hydroelectric power plants in the Tennessee Valley, to produce and sell cheap electricity and nitrate fertilizer and develop one of the poorest parts of the Southern United States, there was a manifest visionary social utopianism. Then, it might aim to mix employment with conservation, as with the CCC using young men to work in the countryside. At its most practical, it could set up the Home Owners Loan Corporation (HOLC) to enable people with mortgaging difficulties to keep their homes. In the end it would purchase or insure one in five of non-farm dwellings. At its zaniest, it could come up with the Shelterbelt project to reduce the winds sweeping across the drought-ridden Great Plains and eroding the rich agricultural topsoil by their force, through planting thousands of trees. Critics scoffed, but it worked as Roosevelt and any other keen gardener like him could have predicted. If the scale was infinitely larger, the principle that trees serve as a windbreak remains the same. Hopefully, farm dispossession occasioned by soil exhaustion would lessen. Thus the New Deal would cast its net widely: no group or section of American society would be excluded from participation.

5 The Expansion of the Presidency

At the outset Roosevelt genuinely hoped that there might be a new era of government–business partnership, reflecting his belief that the New Deal could be successful if it engendered a spirit of cooperation among previously competing groups. Perhaps briefly in the spring and early summer of 1933 with a new president, a national emergency and a renewed sense of activity, the hope had substance. Certainly Roosevelt believed that his arrival in Washington betokened more than a routine change of administration; indeed, it would be impossible to deal with the crisis if it was merely seen as a case for new men and new measures. This time the American government required a fundamental overhaul; six years later, he reflected: 'The tools of government which we had in 1933 are outmoded. We have had to forge new tools for a new rôle of government operating in a democracy – a rôle of new responsibility for new needs and increased responsibility for old needs, long neglected.'[41]

'Tools of government' is a practical phrase and reflects the pragmatic approach that Roosevelt adopted, always one of his greatest strengths. As its greatest modern innovator, the presidency was in Roosevelt's blood; in addition to his distant cousin Teddy, he could claim at least a kinship with ten other presidents. More significantly, he had a deep-seated, genuine respect for democratic forms, but flexibility over the means he employed to secure democratic ends. Similarly, he had a profound sense of right and wrong and inherent commitment to moral values; there were various ways, however, in which these might be implemented in a social context. He was a Christian and a Democrat. These beliefs explain the inspiration for his policies and their extent. He was a Democrat by party but he was president of all the people; like all great democratic politicians he never forgot his ultimate paymaster. This bond between Roosevelt and the American people gave him the underlying certainty that he was acting on their behalf; hence, constitutionally sanctioned incremental increases of his power were for their good. Just as he had grasped that the crisis of 1933 was as grave as war, so he grasped that he must act as war leader, explaining, cajoling, encouraging. He had explicitly recognized this in his Inaugural address: 'We do not distrust the future of essential democracy. The people of the United States have not failed. In their need they have registered a mandate that they want direct, vigorous action. They have asked for discipline and direction under leadership. They have made me the present instrument of their wishes. In the spirit of the gift I take it.'[42]

'Leadership' is an elusive quality. It is difficult to define, easier to recognize. It requires an empathy with one's followers; there must be a sense of shared purpose. This, in its turn, requires communication. Roosevelt had been one of the earliest politicians to understand the importance of radio in democratic politics. Coolidge had been the first American president to speak over it and by the beginning of Hoover's presidency over 40 per cent of American families had one. Interestingly, even in the depths of the Depression this was one 'luxury' item where sales increased. Roosevelt set out to master the new invention; perhaps as a cripple he welcomed a form of direct communication that required no physical mobility. Or, shrewd as ever, he saw the irresistibility of carrying his policies directly to the people. Certainly, Roosevelt was an accomplished performer. In his set speeches, when he was addressing large audiences, he came over as strong and confident. Alternatively, in his 'Fireside Chats' a characteristic innovation, he would explain his policies, informally, non-technically, seemingly on a one-to-one basis, seeking to establish a rapport with a family listening by their fireside. So successful was Roosevelt in his first talk, explaining the banking legislation that the next day when the banks reopened after an eight-day closure, deposits exceeded withdrawals – striking testimony to his persuasiveness. It is one thing to tell an opinion pollster you approve of the president's policies, quite another to entrust your money to hitherto suspect institutions. The people clearly believed his assurances that the banks were now safe. Suddenly, the president was no longer a remote figure in Washington; he became a ubiquitous presence in American life. Actually, Roosevelt was quite sparing in his use of this new medium; he gave just over thirty such broadcasts in twelve years, recognizing the dangers in over-exposure. Yet many recalled a much greater frequency. Perhaps it was the novelty or the seriousness of the times. However, it is clear that many Americans, thousands upon thousands, identified with Roosevelt personally and saw him as a friend and confidant that they could turn to in difficulties. A White House aide noted that Roosevelt received as many letters in a day as Hoover had in a week. His personality was pervasive. No other politician could compete.

With the ability to spread the news came the ability to manage the news. Roosevelt had already endeavoured to do this in his days as governor of New York when he would speak informally, off the record, to newsmen. He did the same thing in Washington. The press was in competition with the radio; if the president spoke directly to the people, it was all the more important for newsmen that he spoke directly to them. They were working reporters with a job to do. They were also, as Roosevelt shrewdly appreciated, largely employed by Republican newspapers. His willingness to confide in them gave them privileged information that helped offset partisan editorials. Facts carry greater weight than opinions. Such favours had to be paid for. Access to news is also vulnerability to it. The institutionalized press conference was not in itself a novelty; Teddy Roosevelt had spoken to reporters; Wilson, too, had met with them; Hoover had dealt with written questions submitted in advance. Roosevelt, however, took the procedure much further; indeed, in his twelve years in the presidency he was to give almost a thousand press conferences. Moreover, Roosevelt's willingness to talk informally, off the record at his desk, gave the impression of intimacy whilst insuring that the presidential viewpoint made an immediate impact. Where did objective news and partisan comment begin and end? Propaganda is always most effective when it is most subtle; by taking the initiative in disseminating news, comment and opinion to the assembled newsmen, Roosevelt set out to create a climate of opinion that was at best his version of the truth.

Reporters who did not play along could be frozen out. It was to be a powerful weapon in the hands of both Roosevelt and his successors.

Newspapers did not only disseminate news; they also published photographs. Newsreels, too, played in cinemas across America, which attracted audiences of nearly 100 million each week. Inevitably, the visibility of the presidency increased. The White House became much more the focus of the nation. 'Many years ago it had become clear to me,' Roosevelt recalled in 1940, 'that, properly availed of, the Governorship and the Presidency, instead of being merely a party headquarters, could become the most important clearing house for exchange of information and ideas, of facts and ideals, affecting the general welfare.'[43]

What Roosevelt began in Albany, he continued in Washington. Much has been made of his group of advisers or Brain Trust, the private coterie of experts who fed him ideas and assisted with his speeches. This was certainly an innovation and a welcome one. The most influential of the group, Raymond Moley, who was closest to Roosevelt when he was seeking the presidency and first exercising it, claimed that he 'never knew him to read a serious book'. To be fair this was when he was once again immersed in politics. Still the pace of campaigning and governing allows little time for solitary study. 'Like most political figures, he learned by listening.'[44] Ideas men who can feed and sift information are an essential adjunct to the modern chief executive.

More significant was the institutionalization of the White House, virtually as a separate government department. Ironically, it was under the incompetent Harding that the Bureau of the Budget had been set up in 1921, that in itself marked a decisive step forward in increasing Executive control, though huge federal budgets and massive government spending lay undreamed of in the future. But it was during Roosevelt's presidency that the Executive Office of the President was created on the simple premise that 'The President needs help.'[45]

Roosevelt was not the first president to complain of overwork, but the New Deal, the vast extension of governmental operations that it entailed and the constantly increasing personnel and bureaucracy thus demanded, stretched presidential capacities to breaking point. The job was simply too big for one man – any man. New procedures were urgently required. Henceforth, the president would have to be kept fully informed and alerted in advance to possible problems. He had to be able to reach prompt, but not hasty, decisions. It was essential that he be protected from secondary issues that could be resolved at a lower level. He needed to be guarded in his time and assured that his orders would be implemented. Only then could the job be made manageable. Thus it was Roosevelt who set up the commission that proposed the recommendations that finally, after much congressional obstruction, resulted in the Executive Order of September 1939 that institutionalized the role the White House played in the mechanics of government. It was possibly Roosevelt's greatest administrative legacy to his successors.

It made the presidency formidable, not just as the Executive branch of government, but in relation to the other parts within that branch. Cabinet government, for example, had always been something of a fiction within the United States. Cabinet officers usually have no independent power base apart from the support of the president unless they are particularly beloved by the Congress, their party or the public; if they cannot all be sacked they can easily be sidelined or frozen out of influence. Increasingly, their collective significance diminished further, even if, on an individual basis, some members of Roosevelt's Cabinets were clearly key advisers. Cabinet meetings were hand-stroking sessions, good for a bit of mutual camaraderie and, significantly, when the pressure of events increased, as for example, during the war, their frequency lapsed. The members mainly prized them for getting access to the president after their meetings had formally ended. Roosevelt preferred to deal directly with his officials; so did they. And when various White House assistants had as much power, if not more, than many a secretary of a government department formal rank had little meaning. Inevitably, power accrued to the one man who had the overall picture and negotiated with all. The Cabinet, the Executive Office of the President, was there to do his bidding. One man, in effect, was one of three branches of the American government. The president was its Executive.

Of course the change did not come immediately. Inevitably, however, Roosevelt's twelve years in the presidency, the formidable experience it gave him, the gravity of the decisions he alone could take, enhanced his position. It was a tribute to his strength that so many of the men around him were themselves outstanding figures. As Roosevelt grew, they grew with him. As Dean Acheson, no great friend of Roosevelt, acutely noted, the legend that he liked organizational confusion, which permitted him to keep power in his own hands by playing off his colleagues one against the other, 'is nonsense. Such is a policy of weakness, and Roosevelt was not a weak man.'[46] In fact, the roll-call of Roosevelt's colleagues is one of the most glittering in the history of the American presidency.

What gave rise to the suspicion of divide-and-rule was Roosevelt's tendency to throw a problem at different parties and see what they came up with. No doubt this did play on the departmental jealousies of more suspicious colleagues. Some thought it reflected unorthodox, even erratic administrative procedures that bordered on the slipshod. The acid test was, did it work? One official who worked closely with him for several years concluded: 'Roosevelt must have been one of the greatest geniuses as an administrator that ever lived. What we couldn't appreciate at the time was the fact that he was a real *artist* in government.'[47]

This enhancement of the presidential role similarly affected relations with the Congress. Initially, many congressmen were vastly more experienced in the ways of Washington than Roosevelt; indeed, he even seems to have been ill at ease with them, a hint that the bonhomie for which he was so famous could at times be forced. Inevitably, however, the sheer volume of legislation and the growth of the federal bureaucracy to effect it, pulled power away from Congress; once again, attention switched to the president who conducted the legislative orchestra.

There were those who found this development disturbing. Were the instruments of the demagogue at hand? There were the contemporary examples of Germany and Italy. It might seem absurd to compare Roosevelt with Hitler or Mussolini, and only the unworthiest of his political opponents did so. Yet there was a lurking danger. Senator Huey Long, whom Roosevelt himself described as one of the two most dangerous men in the United States, cast covetous eyes on the presidency. As governor of Louisiana, Long had turned that exotic Southern state into a virtual dictatorship to provide himself with a power base for national politics. What might a man like that do with the office? The example is not reassuring. Paradoxically, however, the popularity of Roosevelt strengthened the presidency. Even if Raymond Moley, his closest adviser in 1932, became increasingly disenchanted, comparing the humility of that year to the stridency, even demagoguery of his mass appeal in 1936, Roosevelt was self-evidently the people's choice. No one could question the legitimacy of his rule.

This was to be a priceless asset in the age of the dictators, and indeed thereafter. It must be remembered that even in wartime the normal constitutional processes continued: presidential elections every four years, congressional elections every two. It serves to underline the vitality and self-confidence of American democracy, which had observed the normal constitutional processes even at the height of the Civil War. Similarly, it has often been noted that Roosevelt seemed a natural in the presidency, enjoyed the job, did not let it get him down. Partly, this was a matter of personality, 'A second class intellect, but a first class temperament,' one experienced witness famously remarked.[48] The second half of this thumbnail sketch, at least, is accurate. But it was also recognition of his indispensability and effectiveness; success throve on action. He was at the centre of events.

To anyone charting the drifts and tides of Roosevelt's presidency in detail, it is clear that inevitably the pressure could not be sustained continuously. Roosevelt's period in office had its doldrums, its indecisions, its slowness in confronting certain challenges, its lethargy and missed opportunities. At times, as in the recession months of 1937–8 when he heeded his conservative critics and cut back on relief and governmental spending, it even seemed to put the clock back. But this is a day-to-day or week-to-week observation. The overall effect was very different. Here first impressions were all important. Arguably, the apparent momentum of his presidency was not questioned until his fruitless fight over the Supreme Court in the spring and early summer of 1937. That very year the editors of *The Economist* commented: 'Mr Roosevelt may have given the wrong answers to many of his problems. But he is at least the first President of modern America who has asked the right questions.'[49]

Roosevelt was in command. That is why people voted for him. They could forgive his mistakes, if mistakes were the price of action. He admitted as much himself. 'Governments can err, Presidents do make mistakes, but the immortal Dante tells us that divine justice weighs the sins of the cold-blooded and the sins of the warm-hearted in different scales. Better the occasional faults of a Government that lives in a spirit of charity than the consistent omissions of a Government frozen in the ice of its own indifference.' There are worse definitions of liberal activism.[50]

Inevitably, therefore, as the Executive branch of government expanded, the American people would be active, not passive, players in this expansion. Their stake in government, too, would increase. If Roosevelt played 'broker politics', they would become the client investors. Cooperation, not dependency, would be the model.

Nothing better exemplifies this than the Social Security Act of 1935; Roosevelt's proudest legislative accomplishment; and the measure that gave him, more than all others, the greatest personal satisfaction. For the first time in American history there would be some limited attempt to provide certain categories of Americans with security in their old age, a situation long established in Britain and Germany. The security given, however, would be a right not a favour, to be effected by making recipients pay contributions in advance. There were strong economic arguments against this; it was deflationary, particularly in a Depression, when the more money available to go into circulation and boost consumer spending was at a premium. It locked money away just when it needed to be loosed. Roosevelt, however, saw the political reality. Once people financed their own old age pensions, no future conservative administration would be able to dismantle them as a budget-trimming expedient. Government defined the ends; the people furnished the means.

Even if under Roosevelt the presidency did take on an element of paternalism, it was the inevitable consequence of so many people being personally indebted to his policies. In the campaign of 1936 he was to be met with vast, excited crowds, calling out that he had saved their homes, their jobs, their farms, etc. Possibly, it was a facet of his character and upbringing; he was descended from the old Hudson River Valley aristocracy and perhaps democrat though he was, never quite lost a paternalistic streak. Partly, it was the slow acceptance of people unused to government assistance, that what was first seen as a favour, was in fact a right. It takes time to change attitudes. Sadly this was also true for his opponents.

6 Liberals and Conservatives

Roosevelt had endeavoured to maximize his support both before and after the election by rising above party politics and preaching government–business cooperation. Doubtless, he was sincere, but as the outlines of his programme became clearer, conservatives became increasingly disenchanted. As early as August 1934, the American Liberty League was set up, an organization of conservative Democrats that included ex-presidential candidates John W. Davis and Al Smith, the latter of whom went so far as to denounce Roosevelt for preaching class war. The charge would sound ridiculous to the ears of a subsequent generation that would condemn the New Deal for its moderation, even timidity, in grappling with the forces of capitalism. But its foundation, though the League never came to much, is at least an indication of how members of the Democratic Party establishment soon wondered where their president was taking them. This puzzlement was duplicated in Congress. Once the emergency of 1933 was over, critical voices, though muted, were beginning to be heard, if not on the floors of the debating chambers, then certainly in the corridors and cloakrooms. By 1934 it was possible to identify conservative New Deal critics within the Democratic Party who were kept in line partly by political prudence, partly by the example of the Southern leadership, and partly by the lack of any viable alternative to the policies of the administration. Yet they sensed, and sensed rightly, that the old Democratic Party that they had grown up in was changing, and there would come a time when they would endeavour to arrest the change.

Roosevelt, in appealing to 'the forgotten man', had inevitably widened the sources of his support. Now New Deal programmes confirmed this support by creating whole classes of dependants who knew to whom they owed their homes, their farms, their jobs, their welfare. Harry Hopkins's alleged comment, 'We shall tax and tax, and spend and spend, and elect and elect', was an honest if cynical assessment by the New Deal's leading welfare and relief administrator of the power of patronage in enlisting support, and the popularity with the voter of federal benefits. That he apparently never said it, did nothing to assuage the fears of political opponents that he perhaps ought to have said it and come clean about what he was up to.[51]

Yet though these benefits were as welcome in rural as in urban areas, it was particularly in the latter that they translated into increased political support that subtly altered the power relationships inside the Democratic Party. As the cities grew in size, their political clout increased in relation to their surrounding areas. New York City, for example, could balance and offset Republican votes in the rural New York State hinterland; Chicago could do the same for Illinois; Philadelphia or Pittsburgh for Pennsylvania. Under a winner-take-all system, a theoretical one-vote popular majority could deliver all a state's electoral votes to a presidential candidate, and certain populous, key states had a disproportionate significance in the Electoral College. Thus the wooing of blue-collar workers, lower socio-economic groups of ethnics and immigrants, could ensure sizeable Democratic majorities. The strength of the old-style city machines was that they had always got out the vote. 'Vote early, and vote often' was a catchphrase that paid tribute both to their cynicism and to their efficiency.

But this was now reinforced by another form of machine that came to maturity in the 1930s and transformed the power base of the Democratic Party. It is an ironic commentary on the political changes of those years that if contemporaries sometimes misread the portents, so too did the professionals, even the greatest professional of them all. In retrospect, Roosevelt's failure to see the significance of the political mobilization of labour in consequence of New Deal legislation is all the more surprising because it seems so obvious; here Roosevelt's remarkable political sensitivity for once deserted him. Yet by 1936 unions were raising campaign funds and disseminating propaganda to their members, that gave the Democratic Party a political power base that was both integrated and nationwide. Inevitably, there was a price to pay and though it was paid happily by those who saw the future of the Democratic Party and, indeed, its *raison d'être*, as the party of urban liberalism, it was one that was bound to cause disquiet in more conservative Democratic circles. Southerners, in particular, were no friends of organized labour. While the Depression was at its most savage, this tension was not a problem. There were too many other worries to permit the luxury of internal party bickering. Moreover, the Democratic Party required a collective effort, but as the situation eased the grand Roosevelt coalition that apparently swept all before it, might be shown to be less monolithic and united than a cursory examination might suggest.

Roosevelt himself had accurately divined these tensions even amidst his greatest triumphs. Although appreciative of the loyalty of some of the conservative Democrats in Congress, he knew that deep down they did not like the direction in which the party was moving. What he was bent on fashioning was a Democratic Party that was truly liberal. In July 1935, he had confided to a couple of intimates how one or two of the leading Southerners really viewed the situation.

Moreover, at bottom, the leaders ... are troubled about the whole New Deal. They just wonder where the man in the White House is taking the old Democratic party. During their long public life, forty years or so, they knew it was the old Democratic party. They were safe and when the Republicans got into trouble, the old Democratic party won nationally. But in any event they, and in the South without opposition, were all right and old-fashioned ... They are afraid there is going to be a new Democratic party which they will not like ... and that explains why I will have trouble ... from this time on in trying to carry out further programs of reform and recovery. I know the problem inside my party but I intend to appeal from it to the American people and to go steadily forward with all I have.[52]

That Roosevelt should have divested himself of this analysis when he had been president a little more than two years suggests how deep a cleavage was opening up inside the ranks of his own party. For, clearly, by the time of the Second New Deal then in the process of enactment, Roosevelt's intention to adopt a political stance 'a little left of center' was causing grave misgivings within more conservative circles.[53]

Fearful of the increasing criticism from the left, led by such figures as Huey Long, that much more needed to be done, and divining that business was at bottom antithetical to real reform, Roosevelt, stung into action by the invalidation of NRA, pushed for further liberal legislation. Apart from the Social Security Act, the Wagner Labour Relations Act gave workers the right to unionize and sanctioned collective bargaining, gains that had been lost when the Supreme Court struck down NRA. Meanwhile, the Banking Act further extended the Federal Reserve System's control of the monetary structure. The administration nailed its colours to the mast with the Public Utility Holding Company Act that put an end to the practice of 'pyramiding' of companies in the utilities industry, in effect evading responsibility by the creation of artificial layers of management fronts behind which unscrupulous businessmen could hide. And the leftwards stance was confirmed by the Revenue Act, popularly known as the 'Soak the Rich Tax', which aimed at modest redistributive taxation. Whatever private doubts there may have been, publicly the party presented a united face, a self-control that paid off handsomely in 1936 when Roosevelt swept the nation, carrying all but two of the forty-eight states in the presidential election. It was a landslide endorsement.

Yet it was a verdict on what had been achieved, rather than an encouragement to proceed still further. And even colourless Alf

Landon, the Republican candidate, persuaded 16.5 million of his countrymen to vote for him (against Roosevelt's 27.75 million). They were not all wealthy and privileged. It was clear that even in the Depression this core of Republican votes reflected a suspicion of Roosevelt and what he stood for. And as the very worst effects of the Depression receded, its harshest features mitigated by New Deal legislation, so the impetus for further reform subtly waned. Roosevelt might well see 'one third of a nation ill-housed, ill-clad, ill-nourished', as he memorably proclaimed in his Second Inaugural Address in January 1937, but by definition they were not the middle class who, as their lot improved, reverted to their traditional conservatism.[54]

Similarly, those groups who had for the first time begun to find their political wings, who wanted to capitalize on the achievements so far, labour for example, would only progress at the price of further undermining Roosevelt's more conservative supporters. Just as businessmen, once the crisis of 1933 had passed, began to show their true colours, equally the more comfortably off, or at least less economically insecure sections of the nation, as their prosperity returned could cool in their support. Hence the wave of sit-down strikes that engulfed the nation in 1937, which confirmed workers' benefits and trade union rights, did so at the risk of further alienating those middle-class voters who had recently been in the Democratic Party column.

Roosevelt had foreseen the rupture but had thought he could appeal to the American people. Yet their innate conservatism rendered this difficult in practice; hence the debacle over the reform of the judiciary in the spring and summer of 1937 which is generally taken as the turning point in Roosevelt's domestic political fortunes. That year the American Constitution was 150 years old. Such an event might have been an occasion for rejoicing, but it coincided with one of the more traumatic moments of Roosevelt's presidency. Emboldened by his landslide election victory and frustrated by what appeared to be a judicial veto over much of his New Deal legislative programme, Roosevelt determined to take on the Supreme Court which seemed to be the last bastion of conservative Republicanism left in Washington. This was not an entirely unfair characterization; indeed, the famous 'horse-and-buggy' press conference in May 1935 had been an explicit condemnation and if, thereafter, Roosevelt had wisely kept his counsel, it was clear that judicial intransigence was an issue that could not be left untackled. To some extent, Roosevelt had merely been unlucky. After twelve years of Republican rule, the Court's personnel were largely of Republican presidents' making, while somewhat unexpectedly Roosevelt had had no opportunity to make even one appointment throughout his first four years in office. Not that party appointments told the whole story; McReynolds, the most embittered conservative who seemed to personalize his conflict with the New Deal, was a Wilson appointment, whilst the liberal Stone had been Coolidge's attorney-general. Yet seven of the nine judges had been Republican appointees and the chief justice, Hughes, a former Republican presidential candidate in 1916 and later Harding's secretary of state. More tellingly, their collective viewpoint largely represented an earlier judicial philosophy, unhappy with excessive governmental regulation and inclined to the defence of individual and business rights more in keeping with the age of laissez-faire.

Although the battle between Executive and Judiciary culminated in 1937, it had gone on throughout the years since Roosevelt's entry to the White House. Indeed, it was latent in Roosevelt's assertion during his first Inaugural that 'Our Constitution is so simple and practical that it is possible always to meet extraordinary needs by changes in emphasis and arrangement without loss of essential form. That is why our constitutional system has proved itself the most superbly enduring political mechanism the modern world has produced.' But was past experience necessarily a guarantee of future flexibility? One could, of course, hope so. Roosevelt did: 'It is to be hoped that the normal balance of executive and legislative authority may be wholly adequate to meet the unprecedented task before us. But,' he conceded, 'it may be that an unprecedented demand and need for undelayed action may call for temporary departure from that normal balance of public procedure.' Herein, however, lay a considerable hostage to fortune. For, in the last resort, it was not for Roosevelt or, indeed, the Congress to determine what 'temporary departure from that normal balance of public procedure' was allowable. Though Roosevelt might look to Congress to grant him, if necessary, 'broad executive power', that grant would ultimately be subject to the approval of the Supreme Court. Nine judges would decide how far the Constitution might be stretched to accommodate unusual circumstances. Hence the debacle over the NRA.[55]

It is a pleasing myth of American history, perhaps necessary for a free people, that the Constitution is set in stone. In fact, to understand the law, one has to understand the lawmakers. Not only does the Constitution have formalized procedures for amendment; the way it is interpreted may itself be a form of amendment. The Constitution, inevitably, reflects the will of those who hold power: when the power bloc that made it is challenged by another grouping, some concession and compromise has to take place. Thus the Federalist makers of the original document in 1787 were obliged to concede to Southern agrarian criticisms that found expression in the first twelve amendments to the Constitution. The North, in turn, in the aftermath of the Civil War, consolidated its victory with the passage of the Thirteenth, Fourteenth and Fifteenth amendments. Later the increasing power of the trans-Mississippi West and the legitimacy of its concerns was encapsulated in the Sixteenth to Nineteenth amendments, the so-called Progressive amendments, adopted between 1913 and 1920. Later amendments indeed, from Roosevelt onwards, were to reflect the expanded role of the Executive and the need to define it or, in certain cases, balance or restrict it. All these amendments represented a shift in power and status of the ruling groups in American society, but they were only the most obvious indicators of a more subtle process of evolution. The Supreme Court, in effect, acted as a continuous Constitutional Convention; its decisions were themselves indicative of the prevailing mores of American society and the groups thus represented.

There was nothing heretical about this. The greatest of the Court's Chief Justices, John Marshall, back in the early nineteenth century had remarked that the Constitution was 'intended to endure for ages to come and consequently to be adapted to the various *crises* of human affairs'.[56]

And indeed, the language in which the Constitution was couched both encouraged and deliberately enabled adaptation by its very generality. It was another chief justice, the man Roosevelt faced in the 1930s, Charles Evans Hughes, who had said that 'the Constitution is what the judges say it is'.[57]

There could be no doubt that for all the apparent definitiveness that a written Constitution might seem to supply, in practice all that it did was to lay down parameters within which flexible interpretation might take place. Yet it suited Americans to believe that this interpretation was of almost abstract purity. It removed the Constitution from the political battle, made it the veritable 'Ark of the Covenant' of the American polity. And since the Supreme Court judges had no way of enforcing their decisions, they relied on popular acceptance of their verdicts to be inspired by respect bordering on reverence for the Constitution in whose name they acted. Partly, this respect came from what in effect was tantamount to ignorance. Since legal interpretation is necessarily an arcane calling, the average American might rest content that issues were resolved by recourse to legal metaphysics unsullied by judicial bias. Indeed, not the least interesting aspect of constitutional evolution since Roosevelt is how this assumption has come to be popularly discarded. Increased public knowledge has come from a closer examination of the Court and its workings. There has been greater education and insight into the nature of judicial interpretation. Above all, the contentiousness of the issues the Court has been asked to resolve and their perceived relevance to people's lives have all tended to bring the Constitution and the Court back into politics: which in truth is where in practice they have always been located. Indeed, as a rule of thumb it might be argued that throughout its history, those who have been happy with Supreme Court decisions have assumed that the Court in its interpretation of the Constitution was above politics. In contrast, those who disliked its decisions and wanted to change them have seen the Court as indulging in politics.

In retrospect, it is clear that one might have anticipated a constitutional renewal some time in the 1930s. Just as the Depression had dissolved the old parameters of politics and the assumptions on which they had been enacted, so the effect of this political realignment would inevitably make itself felt in the area of constitutional interpretation. Politics was changing because the focus of power was changing; new forces were coming into play that would expect due recognition, in time, of their place not only in American politics, but also in the American polity. It was always thus. Yet that human tendency to see what was immediate as what had always been made natural evolution seem like revolutionary change. And because the pace of constitutional evolution is not always a constant, those periods of sudden acceleration, often occasioned by unyielding conservative intransigence, seem more dramatic and disturbing at the time than in retrospect.

Perhaps inevitably the Supreme Court has to have a conservative bias, otherwise one would have a government of lawyers, not of politicians. It is for the executive and legislative branches of government to initiate; for the judicial branch to sift carefully such proposals and see how far they are in accord with the Constitution, which ultimately is the depository of the people's wishes. There will always be a tension between innovation and tradition. But if the innovations are insistent, if they seem to have consistent popular backing, if they appear to speak with an authority that transcends a passing political majority, then the Court must needs bow gracefully to changing needs and concepts. The Court may drag its feet; it cannot afford to stand and fight in the last ditch. Perhaps only once in its history has it done this, in the decade before the Civil War when the Court with a Southern majority on it, failed to read aright the temper of the times and found itself defending a cause that was politically doomed and morally indefensible. The ineptitude of the Court's ruling in the notorious Dred Scott decision of 1857, and its apparent legitimization of slavery and even its extension to parts of the country hitherto denied it, served as a dreadful reminder to subsequent Supreme Court justices. Legal abstractions divorced from popular consensus are a recipe for disaster.

Since the judges hold lifetime appointments and only death, retirement or, theoretically, impeachment can remove them from the bench, inevitably they reflect the dominant political majority at the time of their elevation to America's highest court. And as there are only nine such judges, whose tenure of office might well run to twenty or thirty years, there will be an inevitable hiatus between current political concerns and earlier judicial philosophies. Of course, judges themselves, at least the better ones, are not intellectually static; they, too, are aware of contemporary developments; the Court at periodic intervals loses and gains members; and caution rather than obstruction is the characteristic judicial reaction. Not that to critics of the Court's behaviour the two are always easily distinguished. Thus one can sympathize with Roosevelt's frustration over what was to him, at least, the Supreme Court's obstructionism. A core of conservative judges augmented by others at periodic intervals had managed to find no less than twelve major pieces of New Deal legislation unconstitutional; they, it was clear, were more than happy to go on living in 'the horse-and-buggy age'. And the stratagem of enlarging the Court in order to get more liberal judges seemed the only way forward. Thus Roosevelt suggested that whenever a judge who had served ten years and reached his seventieth birthday did not retire within six months, the president might appoint an additional judge, up to six in number; thus, theoretically, the Supreme Court might have had as many as fifteen members. Still Roosevelt would have been wiser to admit openly that was what he wanted than to talk cant about the Court being behind with its work, elderly judges needing assistance, and erecting a smoke-screen by throwing in additional judges for the lower federal courts for good measure. Yet for all those with doubts about the New Deal and the direction Roosevelt was taking the Democratic Party, the proposal was both an opportunity and a watershed. As Hatton Sumners, the Texan chairman of the House Judiciary Committee, put it when hearing of the plan: 'Boys, here's where I cash in my chips.'[58]

Some of Roosevelt's opponents were genuinely outraged by what appeared to be a self-interested tinkering with the Constitution; some, more maliciously inclined, relished the opportunity to fight on an issue that did not involve New Deal reforms as such. What is noteworthy is that the congressional opposition in general came from within the ranks of the Democratic Party. Indeed, the Republicans wisely kept their heads down and let the Democrats fight it out amongst themselves. They had no desire to distract Roosevelt's opponents from the issue in hand or let the president off the hook by allowing him to appeal to party unity. When Herbert Hoover entered the fray he was very quickly silenced by members of his own party.

In retrospect, Roosevelt's subsequent claim that if he lost the battle, he won the war seems justified. The Court did change. It did take note of the prevailing public mood as evidenced by successive Democratic election victories. It did adopt a far more liberal stance as, one by one, the conservative judges departed from the bench – there was a veritable exodus in the next two years – to be replaced by Roosevelt appointees. By the time of his death eight of the nine judges had been put there by Roosevelt, and Stone, the liberal, got his reward with promotion to Chief Justice. The year 1937 saw the start of a constitutional revolution whereby the Court endorsed the notion of the enlargement of federal power. This, coupled with Roosevelt's own activism, his liberal New Deal programmes and later enlargement of his presidential role with the coming of war, collectively transformed the content and contours of American politics. But the immediate price was a humiliating long-drawn-out battle in the Senate that squandered a good deal of presidential political capital.

The subsequent defeat of the proposal hurt Roosevelt more than he cared to show and strengthened his resolve to make the Democratic Party a genuinely liberal one; he would separate the liberal sheep from the conservative goats. Hence his decision to intervene in the primary elections of 1938 to ensure that candidates who were genuine supporters of the New Deal received the Democratic Party nomination for their respective Senate and House contests. As he reasoned:

> As President of the United States, I am not asking the voters ... to vote for Democrats ... as opposed to Republicans ... Nor am I ... taking part in Democratic primaries. As the head of the Democratic Party, however, charged with the responsibility of carrying out the definitely liberal declaration of principles set forth in the 1936 Democratic platform, I feel that I have every right to speak in those few instances where there may be a clear issue between candidates for a Democratic nomination involving these principles, or involving a clear misuse of my own name.[59]

The reasoning was as impeccable as the strategy was flawed. Congressional elections are local elections and presidents intervene at their peril, as Wilson had found to his cost in 1918. In any case, the last two years had been difficult. Though Roosevelt had targeted several opponents within his own party for defeat, in only one case was his advice heeded. His enemies returned to Congress emboldened, and the sweeping Republican gains of that year foretold the end of the New Deal.

The jostling for what might happen in 1940 serves to underline how much a half-way house the Democratic Party had become. Roosevelt determined to ensure that he left a liberal legacy seems to have flirted with the notion that Harry Hopkins might be his successor. Certainly, the building-up of this archetypal New Dealer and his appointment as secretary of commerce to make him more acceptable to the business community suggests that Roosevelt saw him as a possible candidate in 1940 if he himself chose not to seek re-election. And the general assumption was that the traditional two terms would be his lot before he retired from the presidency. Against Hopkins were ranged less acceptable, more conservative possibilities, such as Garner the vice-president who had, after years of strained loyalty, publicly broken with Roosevelt, or Millard Tydings, senator from Maryland whom Roosevelt had unsuccessfully tried to defeat in 1938. Indeed, had not foreign affairs come to the fore and Roosevelt signalled an end to reform legislation, the bloodletting inside the Democratic Party might well have ensured a Republican victory in 1940. One of the reasons that Roosevelt resolved to run again was the findings of opinion polls that showed he was the one Democratic candidate who would be assured of defeating any named Republican challenger. And this was in the context of 1940, Europe at war, Japan threatening, when clearly Roosevelt's experience and reputation added significantly to his attractiveness. Had the world been at peace, it is surely unlikely that Roosevelt would have run again and the latent conservatism indicated by the widespread Republican gains of 1938 might have been replicated nationally. The attention focused on foreign affairs also helped to mask the domestic political deadlock.

Issues of war and peace, moreover, transcended ideological loyalties. Some liberals, fearful that war would kill reform as it had Progressivism twenty years previously, favoured isolationism. Conservative Southerners, by contrast, with their ancestral memories of what invasion had meant to the South in the 1860s, were happy to back Roosevelt's militancy; old friendships were broken, new alliances formed. Still there was no getting away from the ideological divide within the Democratic Party that as often as not meant that a Republican from New York might be more in sympathy with Roosevelt than a member of his own party from Alabama or Virginia. And when Republicans and conservative Democrats did make common cause, the congressional arithmetic was with them. The Democrats were the majority party; the conservatives were the majority cause.

Conservative Democrats predominantly from the South allied with Republicans could usually block liberal legislation. It served to emphasize the contrast between an activist presidency and a recalcitrant Congress. A president elected by all the people battled with congressmen, often from sparsely populated rural areas. Sometimes these were put in office through a system that, by one device or another, effectively disenfranchised a majority of their electorate. In addition, state legislatures drew up congressional district boundaries to favour country as opposed to city voters, as indicated by variations in constituency populations, an imbalance they were only compelled to address by the courts in the 1960s. The hidden conservative bias in the electoral system was clearly out of kilter with reformist public attitudes. The president was manifestly the spokesman for the latter; he might be checked but he could not be repudiated.

If this made for tension within the Democratic Party where the presidential wing of the party was liberal-leaning, the situation, though less obviously, was replicated within the ranks of the Republicans. Successive Democratic victories throughout the 1930s – they had started two years before Roosevelt was first elected president as the Depression began to bite – had gradually removed the more moderate Republicans from the more marginal seats where a genuine party battle took place. Those that remained were entrenched in rock-ribbed Republican areas and tended in consequence to be more politically extreme; they had no need to trim their opinions to opposing political winds. Such figures might appeal to the party faithful but they had little chance of making a favourable impact on the national stage; hence the Republican Party, too, found it expedient to move to more liberal figures when it competed in presidential elections. It is ironic how again and again the upholders of Republican ideological purity, the leading spokesmen of their party in Congress, were passed over when it came to the presidential nomination. It was recognition of the fact that the nation had moved leftwards: the Roosevelt years could not be undone. And to make any realistic attempt to capture the White House required a Republican nominee who would appeal not only to the party faithful but reach out to the uncommitted voter. This moderation of presidential politics every fourth year often contrasted strongly with congressional politics in the interim. Once again, the sun and moon theory of American politics was repeated, except that the Roosevelt victories had now made the Democrats the natural majority party, of which the Republicans were a pale imitation. It was also a recognition of the growth in the power of the presidency and how capture of the office required a figure of national appeal who could transcend partisan loyalties; for a minority party this could lead to extraordinary expedients.

In 1940, for example, the decimation of potential Republican leaders in the wake of the Roosevelt victories even caused the party to turn to a complete outsider who had, but a short time previously, actually been a registered Democrat. Wendell Willkie was, all things considered, probably as good a candidate as the Republicans could have come up with at such a time. His freshness on the political scene, his apparent simplicity of background compared to Roosevelt's sophistication, the army of amateur volunteers he mobilized to launch his bid for the nomination, made him an interesting figure who might attract support where more conventional figures would fail. But his selection underlined the limitations of the official Republican leadership and suggested how far the party had declined from the days when it had enjoyed a natural national dominance.

Willkie had first come to public notice as the president and chief executive officer of a public utilities holding company that was doing battle with the Tennessee Valley Authority as a direct competitor, with which he fought an ultimately losing battle both in Congress and the courts. And if anti-New Deal, he was at least a doughty fighter. Moreover, he symbolized the political reality for which Roosevelt was groping, as the disenchantment between the liberal and conservative wings of the Democratic Party became ever more intense. Willkie was an unorthodox figure and not loved by his own party regulars – reasonably, as he was the outsider who had taken the crown. As one Republican commented: 'I don't mind the church converting a whore but I don't like her to lead the choir the first night!'[60]

Still, this novelty and absence of obligation to the regulars made Willkie a freer spirit, and suggested to Roosevelt that this brand of Republicanism might combine with the Democrats to make a truly liberal party. This would then leave the conservatives of both parties to declare themselves and reconstitute as a revised Republican Party. Not that this was a line that could be pursued in 1940, but the speed with which the Republican Party turned its back on their candidate after his defeat and, to tell the truth, vice versa, suggested the possibility might be worth exploring. Had foreign affairs and American involvement in the war not put domestic politics inevitably in the shade, the process might have gone still further, but Roosevelt thought it sufficiently worthwhile to send one of his closest advisers to meet with Willkie to discuss possibilities. His early death in 1944 ended any further consultation and it remains one of the might-have-beens of American politics. It also calls into question how far any individual can effect political realignment especially when, as with Willkie, he was now merely the previous presidential nominee of his party, a status that gives little power. Yet it highlighted the anomalies of American politics that seemed often to owe more to history than to present-day reality, a fact underlined by the acceptance in 1944 by the Republican Party of the achievements of the New Deal. It was a recognition that politics had, inevitably, moved on: that the era of Herbert Hoover was dead and buried. And there was no sadder spectre at the political feast than Hoover, who was to live on more than thirty years after he left the White House. An albatross around the neck of the Republicans that had to be jettisoned not only by them but, more importantly, from the minds of the public, if they were ever to make a comeback. The equation between Republicans and the Depression delivered Democratic majorities for twenty years.

Yet the rhetoric of presidential campaigns obscured the reality of the day-to-day grassroots structure of the party. And Roosevelt's attempts to make his party a liberal and internationalist one needed a closer fusion between the two. In one sense, he was only developing what had long been accepted within its ranks. The Democratic Party was the party of Woodrow Wilson; the Democrats had long advocated tariff reduction and free trade; and Southern conservatives from agricultural states needed the freedom to penetrate overseas markets to safeguard the interests of their constituents. Yet this economic internationalism accorded ill with a scepticism about big government, a desire to leave as much power as possible to the localities, a rallying cry of states' rights whenever their particular interests seemed threatened by Washington, and a reluctance to embrace wholeheartedly a progressive reform programme.

A further complication now entered the scene. The issue of race had always been a potential source of embarrassment for the Democratic Party, save that white supremacy in the South had ensured that the African-Americans were largely disenfranchised. The relatively few African-Americans that did vote supported the Republicans as an act of piety to the memory of Lincoln, but their power was negligible. In the 1930s, for example, Roosevelt would not support an anti-lynching bill for fear of alienating Southern congressmen, risking a dreaded filibuster and jeopardizing sorely needed New Deal legislation. Yet other forces were at work. Some influential New Dealers and notably Eleanor Roosevelt, the president's wife, took up the cause of black Americans; more were found jobs in the government, and at higher levels, than ever before. And New Deal policies that benefited the poorer sections of the community manifestly benefited African-Americans. One comment said it all: 'My friends, go turn Lincoln's picture to the wall. That debt has been paid in full.'[61]

The war accelerated the process of inclusion that had been going on since the 1920s. African-Americans migrating northwards had begun to find their political freedom; now service in the armed forces and their general contribution to the war effort served only to underline the injustice, and indeed the inefficiency, of racial discrimination. The first steps were being taken in what would ultimately become a nationwide campaign for civil rights. It posed problems for the Democratic Party, problems so intense that they would never satisfactorily be resolved within its ranks. The first rumblings of what would become a political earthquake were now being heard.

Still, the war inevitably placed something of a brake on normal political development. However, in one respect it gave liberalism a push. The welfare state of the 1930s, limited though it may have been, was conjoined with the 'warfare-state' of the 1940s; together they insured prosperity. Indeed, that government–business cooperation that had earlier eluded Roosevelt made something of a comeback. He had recognized the force of his secretary of war's advice: 'If you are going to try to go to war, or prepare for war in a capitalist country, you have got to let business make money out of the process or business won't work.'[62]

But the price was an acceptance by business of changes they had hitherto resisted. For a start there had to be government direction of the economy and an enlargement of federal income tax; in the last full year of the war government revenue exceeded 50 billion dollars. Then deficit spending way beyond anything occasioned by the New Deal was vindicated by a massive increase in the GNP, more than 200 billion dollars in 1945, which virtually eliminated unemployment. Consequently, corporation profits escalated, for which expanding union membership seemed a small price to pay. Indeed the war rounded off what had been a spectacular increase in their recruitment since the 1930s; by its end one in four of the labour force had union representation. In many respects the unions became the guardians of the New Deal legacy, ensuring the extension of its social welfare benefits – the bread-and-butter issues that concerned their members above all else. Workers' incomes doubled and thus spending increased. Both business and labour seemed to have come to a *modus vivendi* in a corporate liberalism, which benefited each. If this renewed prosperity dulled the edge of New Deal reform, it sharpened its interventionist techniques.

Of course, the straight political party battle itself still continued, and Roosevelt in 1944 had to squash a Republican whispering campaign against his health in seeking re-election. Indeed, it was an issue that might conceivably have sunk him had he not taken energetic steps to disprove it by some high-profile campaigning that included a considerable element of subterfuge. In retrospect it is clear that the rumours had substance. Six months later he was dead. On 12 April 1945, at the comparatively early age of sixty-three, while resting at Warm Springs, Georgia, Roosevelt suffered a massive cerebral haemorrhage. His death was a reflection of the terrible pounding his body must have taken throughout twelve traumatic years in the presidency, and of how far his deteriorating health had been concealed from the nation. In a very real sense, Roosevelt had given his life for his country.

7 Harry Truman Continues the Struggle

Once Roosevelt departed the scene, the political pendulum began to swing back towards the Republicans. And his successor Harry Truman was manifestly no Roosevelt. A vice-president of only three months' experience, largely ignored by his predecessor, he had to face the criticisms that come easily from an opposition party able to exploit war weariness and the feeling that peacetime had not delivered the utopia that everyone romantically expected. Hence the Republican gains in the off-year elections of 1946 that gave them control of both the Senate and House of Representatives and seemed to augur Republican capture of the presidency in 1948. Yet in an odd way this victory worked to the Democrats' advantage. For if the Republican Party was no longer the party of Hoover the speeches and actions of some of its members in Congress might allow one to think so. It emphasized what the Democratic Party under Roosevelt had achieved and what might be lost if his legacy was not consolidated and renewed. Conservatism might have developed inside the ranks of the Democratic Party almost, as it were, by sleight of hand – the Southerners combining with the Republicans to thwart the wishes of the urban, liberal wing of the party. There was clearly only room for one conservative party in America; and the Republican Eightieth Congress elected in 1946 showed clearly which party this should be. Nationally, if not always regionally, the Democratic Party was now a liberal, Progressive party or it was nothing. Its postwar defeat helped it to find its soul.

Significantly, the most famous legislative initiative sponsored by the Republicans' leading spokesman Senator Robert Taft of Ohio during their brief ascendancy, the Taft–Hartley Act of 1947, limited organized labour. Whilst basic union rights as enshrined in the landmark Wagner Act of 1935 remained in place, the closed shop and secondary boycotts were outlawed. States were allowed to pass 'right to work' laws which no longer required all the workers on site to join a union if a majority voted to do so, whilst the system was ended by which employers deducted union dues from wages. Nor could labour contribute to campaign funds. Unions could be held liable for breach of contract both directly and for losses sustained by third parties. The president might request a court injunction granting an eighty-day cooling-off period for projected strikes he thought threatened national welfare. And, symptomatic of the times, before engaging in collective bargaining union officials were required to sign non-communist affidavits.

The Act certainly generated much middle-class support. Strikes had clearly got out of hand in the immediate postwar years; there was a veritable epidemic of them in 1945–6, as workers sought to make up lost time in the dislocations inevitably imposed on the economy in the war years, and its peacetime conversion. But it was not a piece of legislation that would appeal to the swelling ranks of blue-collar workers who every four years made up the Democratic Party presidential candidates' majorities. Significantly, Truman vetoed the bill. Equally significantly, it was passed over his veto, which requires a two-thirds' majority of each Chamber of Congress. Clearly conservative Democratic votes were needed for the bill to be enacted into law but the mud stuck to Taft and the Republicans, whose 'vicious' Act Truman made good use of when campaigning for election in 1948.[63]

Thus the Democratic Party did not waver in its liberal commitments. Spurred on by such ginger groups as the Americans for Democratic Action (ADA), it even nailed its colours firmly to the mast of civil rights. The 1948 Democratic Convention was in turmoil, as the mayor of Minneapolis, Hubert Humphrey, refused to allow a weak party platform on the issue and took the fight to the floor of the convention hall. Courageously, it did not balk even at the cost of its embattled president suffering further electoral hazards when Southern Democrats reneged from their ancestral party and ran a separate Dixiecrat presidential candidate committed to states' rights. Coupled with the defection of former vice-president Henry Wallace, running as an independent third-party Progressive candidate, Truman's defeat seemed certain. Defiantly he ran a brilliant, gutsy campaign against a too self-confident, complacent and not very likeable Republican candidate, notwithstanding a series of misinformed opinion polls, misled by a public too embarrassed to admit publicly that privately they were going to vote for a man seen as a certain loser. It produced the political upset of the century. Truman's 'Fair Deal' would continue the work of the 'New Deal'. Once again the Democrats controlled the presidency and the Congress. The year 1946, it seemed, was an interlude, not a turning point. Roosevelt's legacy would continue.

Yet the defection of Southerners in 1948 over the party's commitment to civil rights, even if it was unavailing, presaged real trouble for the Democrats. Matters were being brought to a head when in politics letting sleeping dogs lie is often the wiser policy. The issue, however, was more than simply one of tactics; it had the transcendent moral quality to it that, like the manoeuvrings in the 1850s over the issue of slavery, showed up the limitations of mere politics. With the Cold War at its height and becoming a shooting war in Korea in the summer of 1950, attention was fixed elsewhere, but it was an issue that would increase not decrease in its contentiousness. Coupled with Southern conservative disenchantment with the Rooseveltian liberalism continued by his successor, Truman's 'Fair Deal' was largely mauled to pieces with only modest extensions of social security, the raising of the minimum wage, and some provision for slum clearance and low-cost housing getting Congressional approval. There would come a time when different wings of the Democratic Party were no longer speaking the same language. Had it not been for the fluke of Eisenhower's election to the presidency, a re-alignment might have begun in the 1950s.

8 Eisenhower Republicanism

It is interesting to speculate on what might have been had the Republicans run an avowed conservative in the 1952 election. Perhaps he would have gone down to defeat and handed Adlai Stevenson the presidency. Perhaps in an overt appeal to conservative votes, he would have started that weaning of the South away from the Democratic Party that was not to come until more than a decade later. As it was, the Democratic candidate, the governor of Illinois, adopted the old Roosevelt strategy and took Southern Senator Sparkman of Alabama on the ticket to shore up his Southern base. The Republicans, more concerned with winning than with defining their principles, ran the most non-political candidate of the twentieth century, Dwight D. Eisenhower. Indeed, Eisenhower had never held an elective job in his life; even his politics were in doubt prior to 1952. It was an inspired choice but one that obscured the contours of the political landscape.

The attractions of Eisenhower, not least to a perennially losing party, were obvious. A famous soldier, he seemed to transcend the pettiness of party politics. In all conscience these had sunk to a new low, in the wake of twenty years of Democratic rule, some pretty insalubrious administration corruption, Republican bitterness at their political exclusion and the over-heated atmosphere of the postwar years. Had Eisenhower had his way, he would no doubt have liked to have the Republican nomination offered to him on a plate. A selection by acclamation would have accorded well with his chosen image; the reluctant general prevailed upon to give up his hopes of peaceful retirement, to accept an office he had not sought, to serve his country in its hour of need. In fact, he had to indulge in a bruising fight with Senator Taft: 'Mr Republican', son of a president, who all but had the nomination sewn up, beloved as he was by the party regulars. This affection, however, did not make for electability, a truth the more prescient liberal members acutely discerned. And having watched Republicans snatch defeat from the jaws of victory in 1948, they did not intend to spend another four years staring longingly at the White House from the outside. It meant, however, Eisenhower coming off his pedestal and some fast-moving shenanigans at the Republican Convention to deny Taft some of his pledged votes and secure the nomination. But it gave the Republicans a candidate who appealed to middle-of-the-road voters, an essential prerequisite for office of the minority party it had now become, and one who softened its starker features.

As an older man who had lived through the domestic changes in his country, and watched how America had altered since his birth in 1890 and up-bringing in rural Midwestern Kansas, Eisenhower sensed intuitively that the decade of the 1950s was a period of social consolidation. For the majority of Americans with whom he identified, the traumatic events of the 1930s and 1940s now required a time to take stock and enjoy some of the benefits of their new-found prosperity. That there were forces under the surface, notably in the field of civil rights that he did not fully comprehend, is perhaps symptomatic of that generational theory of American history that sees one period of change harden into orthodoxy before itself succumbing to new pressures. And Eisenhower was ideally suited to conserve rather than to innovate. Change was the prerogative of the 1960s but Eisenhower demonstrated an important lesson for the modern presidency: that it was the office of the unifier and healer. Some of the problems faced by his successors were in part due to the fact that they failed to live up to that standard. 'I like Ike' was the most effective political slogan in a generation.[64]

The electorate liked Ike a lot, so much so that they twice elected him president over the same opponent. More importantly they liked him a lot more than they liked his party, whom he consistently outperformed. It was one of his greatest sources of strength that, wisely, he did nothing to impair. In 1952 he pulled into office enough of his supporters to give the Republicans control of Congress, but this was lost two years later. And the Eisenhower years witnessed a gradual diminution of their numbers, culminating in the Republican massacre of 1958 which reduced the party to a size not seen since the 1930s. The lesson was clear enough; Eisenhower the man was more popular than was Eisenhower the Republican. The more the electorate thought of the former and the less of the latter, the better he did.

Eisenhower, a very canny operator, much more than his carefully contrived bumbling grandfather image suggested, realized that for him partisan politics paid no dividends. Moreover, he was genuinely bored with them, having little respect for professional politicians as such, much preferring to surround himself with men who had achieved distinction in other fields, who then entered politics with a reputation already to their credit. In particular, he seemed to have a penchant for businessmen of independent means. Indeed, having lived off an army salary most of his working life, it has to be said that Eisenhower was not averse to the company of the wealthy. It was not a habit that made for radicalism. This temperamental disdain for the practice of politics as such was reinforced by the behaviour of some of the leading Republicans in Congress; partisan figures whose Republicanism appealed mainly to the party faithful. Perhaps only Eisenhower's army training, his ability to work with anybody who was one of the team, and his reluctance to indulge in personalities, enabled him to achieve the working relationship he did with some of the more difficult members of his party.

This was not always an unalloyed advantage; Eisenhower had the defects of his virtues. When it came to dealing with the phenomenon of Senator Joe McCarthy, Eisenhower found discretion the better part of valour. Firstly, it has to be said that McCarthy had had his uses; clearly, his indiscriminate and irresponsible allegations of communist subversion had contributed to a weakening of the Democratic administration and paved the way for the Republican victory. Moreover, he clearly enjoyed widespread support – a tribute both to his own effectiveness, the climate of the times, and the fearful gullibility, not to say sporadic ugliness of soul, of a sizeable portion of the American public. Also, as Eisenhower rightly noted, 'McCarthyism antedated the appearance of Joseph McCarthy of Wisconsin and would last longer than the man's power or publicity.'[65]

But Eisenhower never seemed to think that it might be his duty to elevate the public political discourse and confront the man, his malice and his movement, head on. True, there were arguments against this. Eisenhower saw that McCarthy craved publicity and was not inclined to feed his habit by allowing him the satisfaction of presidential notice: 'I'm not going to get down in the gutter with that guy.'[66]

One might argue – in a strained sort of way – that free speech applied equally to red-baiters, whatever their capacity for slander and detraction and its consequent damage to the innocent. Or, give enough rope and a hanging would surely follow. Which, in the end, it did. But there was also the shrewd realization that an Executive assault on a senator, any senator would immediately invite a closing of legislative ranks and that the best way to dispose of the nuisance was for the senators to do it themselves. Perhaps all in all it was clever generalship: wait for the right moment, ensure weight of numbers, and make sure of your ground. When McCarthy turned on the American Army and television showed up his nastiness, he dug his own grave. But it was victory at the price of some seeming loss of moral integrity; it made Eisenhower look powerless or complacent, even if it stopped Republicans fighting among themselves.

Equally, Eisenhower never forgot that he owed his position to large numbers of uncommitted voters and even registered Democrats who had temporarily absconded. And their support had not necessarily prevented them from staying loyal to the Democratic Party at state and local level. Thus there can be little doubt that Eisenhower actually preferred to work with the Democrats when they recaptured control of Congress in 1954. Men such as Speaker of the House Sam Rayburn and Senate Majority Leader Lyndon Johnson, both from conservative Texas, were more in tune with Eisenhower's middle-of-the-road politics than the Leader of his own party in the Senate, William Knowland of California or some of his strident henchmen. Moreover, it suited Eisenhower to disdain some of the cruder political aspects of his office: to appear to be above politics was the most effective politics of all.

Thus Eisenhower wisely resisted calls from Republican extremists to scrap social security; indeed, he greatly extended its coverage and enhanced its benefits. He also understood that national security necessitated national planning. In effect, he became a New Dealer when he accepted an enlarged role for the federal government and sponsored the biggest public works in American history with the Federal Highway Act of 1956. Here the need for mobility to evacuate populations from cities and move military forces across the nation in a crisis could be cited as both a reason and a pretext. The Act committed the government to spend more than 33 billion dollars in fourteen years in constructing over 40,000 miles of interstate highways. Every American city with more than 50,000 people would be linked together. That the Act had profound economic and social consequences not necessarily foreseen by its proponent – particularly the growth of suburbia – does not diminish its significance as an example of governmental engineering. Similarly, it is to Eisenhower that the nation owes the opening up of the Great Lakes to Atlantic merchant ships in the St Lawrence Seaway Act of 1954, a project Franklin Roosevelt had supported more than twenty years previously. As in the First World War, as in the Second World War, so the demands of the Cold War made governmental direction and its expansion inescapable.

Although Eisenhower did genuinely believe in a less activist role for the presidency, at least domestically, the Eisenhower years were not as somnolent as has sometimes been maintained. Whilst there was a great deal of social conformity characterized by the enlargement of the middle class which became the most salient feature of American society, change was occurring that was to have profound consequences for the stability of the nation itself. And it is arguable that had these changes been managed more immediately or been anticipated more presciently, the subsequent turmoil of the 1960s might have been lessened if not actually avoided. The comment attributed to Talleyrand that the art of politics is to anticipate the inevitable and facilitate its occurrence has perhaps special relevance to the 1950s. And it is a reflection on the Eisenhower administration's social conservatism that the great impulse for change which was to affect politics so profoundly came from that branch of government generally deemed the most reluctant to initiate, namely the Supreme Court. The landmark decision in 1954 which ruled

separate but equal facilities for black Americans in schools unconstitutional, was the prelude to the great battle for civil rights that
lasted ten years, culminating in the Civil Rights Act of 1964 and the
Voting Rights Act of 1965. Effectively, Northern liberals would
make common cause with Southern blacks against Southern whites,
all nominally inside the same Democratic Party, both sides aided
and abetted by members of the Republican Party depending on
their ideological preference. Clearly, this was an illogical situation
that heralded a substantial realignment within the American party
system. By 1956 Southern congressmen were issuing the 'Southern
Manifesto', nailing their colours to the segregationist, states' rights'
mast. But the old Democratic party trick of balancing a Northerner,
or in this case a Midwesterner Adlai Stevenson, with a Southerner
Senator Estes Kefauver of Tennessee, on the presidential ticket ensured no mass defections. Yet it was clear that instead of writing off
'the solid South' as Republican strategists were wont to do, potentially there were rich pickings to be had. Four former Confederate
states of the outer South had gone Republican as early as 1952. In
1956 Eisenhower even took Louisiana, the first Republican victory
in the Deep South for eighty years. In 1960 Richard Nixon, as
Republican candidate, was to campaign throughout the region; a
year later Texas elected the first Republican to the United States
Senate since the days of Reconstruction.

9   John Kennedy Wins the Presidency

This ambiguity inevitably affected the Democrats. Tied by history,
they were unable to cut loose from their Southern inheritance and
become wholly the liberal party that logic suggested they should be.
No Democratic president could deliver what he promised. Even as
the South was voting him into office – and this was an important
calculation not lightly discarded – it was returning congressmen
who could be relied upon to frustrate his programme.

This was a truth painfully learned by Kennedy when he won
the presidency by a wafer-thin margin in 1960, a dubious mandate
weakened still further by the fact that the Republicans actually made
gains in the congressional elections to offset the staggering losses of
two years previously. Kennedy's capture of the Democratic nomination for the presidency revealed the widespread desire within the
ranks of its supporters for a truly liberal candidate. Indeed, there

was even a chance the prize might have been snatched from him at the Convention by supporters of Adlai Stevenson, the liberal candidate *par excellence*. Kennedy ruthlessness, the tag of twice-time loser and his own indecision frustrated whatever such ambition Stevenson still had. Lyndon Johnson, the leading Democrat in the Senate, was the perennial Southern candidate, yet significantly it was his apparent lack of commitment to liberalism that made him suspect to many Democrats; he was seen as the archetypal Southern wheeler-dealer politician best confined to the halls of Congress. Indeed, there was considerable liberal fury at his selection by Kennedy for the vice-presidency, mitigated only by the hard-eyed realism that had occasioned it. A Northern liberal, and Catholic to boot, in what would be a tight election, desperately needed a Southern Protestant of Johnson's stature to balance the ticket and keep the South in line. This neglect of ideological principle in favour of political expediency was softened by the explanation, true but less than honest, that if anything happened to Kennedy, Johnson was the man best qualified to succeed him. And though the wisdom of this analysis was justified by the assassination of Kennedy in 1963, the decision's immediate vindication was in the closeness of his victory in 1960.

Thus, John Kennedy reached the presidency. Scarcely a strong candidate when he began his quest, he had the good fortune to run against Eisenhower's less than popular vice-president, Richard Nixon, a partisan politician who seemed temperamentally ill-suited to the compromises of democratic politics that need to transcend party loyalties. In 1960 the voters sensed that as a Republican president the accent would be on the Republican and they had shown as the 1950s wore on their increasing disenchantment with this narrow appeal. That Kennedy won the presidency so narrowly, a mere 0.2 per cent of the popular vote, suggests that apart from legitimate doubts about Kennedy's own capacities, had the Republicans found another popular, apolitical figure as their standard bearer they might have been successful. The political parameters laid down by Roosevelt were still in place – either a New Deal Democrat or an unthreatening Republican content to let liberal sleeping dogs lie. Only in foreign affairs might expertise substitute for ideological soundness. The latter was Nixon's greatest strength, but in 1960 an ill-judged television performance probably tipped the balance against him when coupled with other negative factors. It erased the essential advantage that, as a vice-president of eight years' standing, he had over a senator whose major qualifications appeared to be money, ambition and appearance.

It was victory, however, at a price. For all the hullabaloo and self-advertisement that seemed the inevitable concomitant of Kennedy politics, the mandate was indeed precarious; a fact easily perceived by the members of Congress with whom the new president had to work. Doubtless, the resentment that older men felt towards a newcomer, who had been a relative junior in their midst and was now their nominal master, did not help matters, a state of affairs exacerbated by some remarkable administration ineptness. Sheer inexperience compounded by arrogance took a heavy toll. But whatever the cause, the plain fact was that Kennedy's domestic legislative record was remarkable for its non-achievement; the bi-partisan coalition of Republicans and Southern Democrats lay in ambush when they did not openly obstruct.

Thus having, not unfairly, criticized Eisenhower for a certain lethargy that seemed to descend on America during his last years in office, Kennedy committed himself to a 'New Frontier'. This was, grandiloquently, 'the frontier of the 1960s – a frontier of unknown opportunities and perils – a frontier of unfulfilled hopes and threats'.[67] In fact most of Kennedy's legislative initiatives got nowhere. Determined to provide health insurance for the aged, increase federal aid to education and set up a new Cabinet Department of Urban Affairs, Kennedy found that good liberal intentions counted for little. Even successes like raising the minimum wage came about after initial administration defeats that weakened Kennedy's credibility. Meanwhile, his handling of the economy still left him trying to cut unemployment and stimulate growth in his last year in the White House by requesting a 14-billion dollar tax cut that Congress also refused. As he wryly commented: 'When I was a Congressman, I never realized how important Congress was. But now I do.'[68]

So frustrating was the situation that Kennedy was prepared to put his prestige on the line and campaign for increased Democratic representation in Congress in the off-year elections of 1962. The happy coincidence, from the Democrats' points of view, of the Cuban Missile Crisis and the enhancement of the presidential image, did impress the voters sufficiently to effect a marginal improvement in the situation. But it was clear that any substantial progress would have to be left to a second term, itself a commentary on the limitations of Kennedy's first-term record.

Here the Republicans would prove obliging; for if Kennedy experienced frustration in dealing with conservative members of his own party, that frustration was shared by the Republican Party, with liberals within its own ranks. This polarization of American politics suited Kennedy admirably. He looked forward to a genuine contest between a liberal and a conservative, and one he was convinced he would surely win. Ironically, it was in anticipation of that election that he made his ill-fated trip to Dallas. Anxious to bind the wounds of the Texas Democratic Party, split between its liberal and conservative wings, that threatened to jeopardize the presidential election the following year and lose him the electoral votes of a key state, Kennedy died campaigning. Tragic though the outcome was, it catapulted into the presidency the one man uniquely qualified to maximize the opportunity thus presented and finally complete the experiment Franklin Roosevelt himself had launched thirty years previously. The terrible deed done in that most conservative of cities, Dallas, was the worst thing that could have happened from conservatism's point of view. In Lyndon Johnson, the Democratic Party found its elemental unifying force.

10   Lyndon Johnson and the Great Society

The saga of Lyndon Johnson, for it is nothing less, and his transformation into the liberal sachem of modern America, is a unique episode in American history. Yet it is not as unexpected as those who only came to know him when he first dominated the national stage have sometimes suggested. For a start, though he was indeed a Southerner with a pronounced regional identification, which he never lost, the South has, for all its conservatism, had a rich tradition of populism manifested in some of the candidates it has chosen to represent it in Congress. Furthermore, Johnson was from Texas, a maverick state, in the South but not always of it; a state, moreover, that is also part of the Old West. And Johnson's entry on to the national stage coincided with the advent of Franklin Roosevelt, to whom he hitched his wagon; given Johnson's subsequent career it is easy to forget just how liberal he was as he began the climb to national prominence. It was Johnson who, as national youth administrator for Texas, oversaw a prime New Deal agency, a base from which he built the necessary support for a career in Congress. In 1937, when this became a reality, it was due to his unswerving support for Roosevelt, then embroiled in his famous fight over the enlargement of the Supreme Court. Whoever won the Democratic primary election for the vacant congressional district was bound to win the subsequent election; other candidates opposed Roosevelt's proposal, as had the Texas legislature; Johnson supported it. It was a shrewd combination of principle and pragmatism that paid off handsomely; all those many voters who also disliked the apparent tampering with the Supreme Court divided their votes among several like-minded candidates; the voters who agreed with Roosevelt united behind Johnson. He came top of the poll.

In Congress, Johnson was a convinced New Dealer. He sought Roosevelt's approval and endorsement at every turn. When Roosevelt died, he was broken-hearted. Johnson declared that 'he was just like a daddy to me always; he always talked to me just that way . . . I don't know that I'd ever have come to Congress if it hadn't been for him.'[69] This liberal phase, however, was not to last. Statewide election required considerable liberal trimming; having tried unsuccessfully in 1941, he was not going to repeat the mistake. Election to the Senate and rapid promotion – Minority Leader in 1952, Majority Leader in 1954 – depended on the approval of the Southern Old Guard who resolutely strove to defend the conservative values of the Southern cause. Johnson, working in with Northern Liberals as Senate Leader, the greatest Majority Leader in its history it was said, was acutely aware of the variegated mixture of beliefs with which he had to deal. But the exigencies of his own state, the alliance with fellow Texan Sam Rayburn, Speaker of the House of Representatives, the need to work with a Republican president, Eisenhower, and the climate of the times all pulled him in a conservative direction. He was the liberals' least favourite candidate for the Democratic nomination in 1960; some of his Senate allies were distinctly unsavoury in liberal nostrils; and his personal style was far removed from the liberal intelligentsia exemplified by the Americans for Democratic Action.

The years of the vice-presidency did little to improve this reputation. Callously sidelined by many of the New Frontiersmen if not by Kennedy himself, who was punctilious in respecting his deputy's age and experience, Johnson seemed a fish out of water among the smooth sophisticates who made up the best and the brightest of the Kennedy Camelot. Cruel whispers that he would be dumped in 1964, untrue and inconceivable given the need to ensure every possible Democratic vote, did little for his stature. He was widely perceived as a necessary holdover from an earlier age. For Johnson, these were years of frustration and private torment: a man of great gifts watching the legislative blockage that his talents might have circumvented, forced into relative inactivity which no amount of ceremonial functions, foreign trips and formal occasions could assuage.

Hence the assassination of Kennedy in November 1963, perhaps for the first time in American history, witnessed a succession in which, in many respects, the new president was more experienced than his predecessor had been. No previous vice-president who had inherited the office, even Theodore Roosevelt, had so clearly come into his own. All Johnson's shrewdness and sagacity, parliamentary skill and legislative cunning, a quarter of a century in the making, would now be at the service of the liberal causes that had remained deadlocked or impeded for as long. The old president, it transpired, was to be the young New Deal congressman writ large. It would be a staggering performance.

To the hardened veterans of Capitol Hill the death of a president, once a decent interval of mourning was over, might not signify any reason for a departure from business as usual. And though Johnson would certainly wring every last shred of sympathy he could out of the assassination if he might turn it to political advantage, the actual political arithmetic was unchanged. It was also late in the political season, less than a year away from the presidential election, a time when politicians' eyes are on their jobs, and consolidation rather than innovation is the order of the day. Nor do succeeding vice-presidents, at least until they are elected in their own right, customarily see their role as one of dramatic leadership.

Yet three months before Kennedy was assassinated, the campaign for civil rights and the redressing of three centuries of injustice had culminated in a 'March on Washington'. Standing on the steps of the Lincoln memorial, the movement's most famous figure, Martin Luther King, delivered an impassioned address to a crowd of upwards of 250,000 of his supporters, the largest political gathering in American history:

> I have a dream that one day this nation will rise up and live out the true meaning of its creed: 'We hold these truths to be self-evident; that all men are created equal.' I have a dream that one day on the red hills of Georgia the sons of former slaves and the sons of former slaveowners will be able to sit down together at

the table of brotherhood. I have a dream that one day even the state of Mississippi, a desert state sweltering with the heat of injustice and oppression, will be transformed into an oasis of freedom and justice. I have a dream that my four little children will one day live in a nation where they will not be judged by the color of their skin but by the content of their character.[70]

Yet for that dream to become a reality the first requirement was that such a legitimate aspiration should be enshrined in the nation's laws. Kennedy, a somewhat hesitant convert to the cause of civil rights, had finally sensed the urgency and sent a bill to Congress; now Johnson would see it enacted. Moreover, the bill would have to be a strong one, not one that was watered down to effect its passage. Only thus would it be meaningful and establish Johnson's liberal credentials to any who still doubted them. It would ban racial discrimination in public facilities such as cinemas, theatres, hotels and restaurants. The Justice Department would be empowered to eliminate statutory racial segregation in hospitals, playgrounds, libraries, museums and, most importantly, public schools. With the latter, the attorney-general could go to court on behalf of parents protesting discrimination and the government would pay the legal costs: and federal funds would be denied institutions generally that practised segregation. Equally, discrimination on grounds of race, sex, colour, religion and national identity would be outlawed in employment. Even if not all the bill's provisions were immediately enforceable – the capacity for rearguard evasion by those who opposed it was both subtle and stubborn and voting rights, for a start, would require separate legal protection – it was unquestionably a landmark piece of legislation. The Civil Rights Bill would be the nemesis of the Democratic Party's conservative wing; and liberalism's victory would be total. For the scale of victory demanded would permit of no other interpretation.

In order to ensure the bill's passage a simple majority would not suffice: had it been so a Civil Rights Act might have been enacted any time in the previous decade. The bill's approval was assured in the House with its preponderance of sympathetic members, Republican and Democrat. The crux of the issue lay in the lax rules of the Senate, which allowed unlimited debate and hence the opportunity for a Southern filibuster. In the past, the very threat of this, with its potential for wrecking an administration's legislative programme, had been enough to cause proponents to desist. Before any passage of a Civil Rights Act, the Senate would have to vote for closure of debate; and this required, in those days, not just a simple majority but two-thirds. Sixty-seven sympathetic senators willing to remove from their Southern colleagues a weapon any of them might wish to use at a future date was a very different parliamentary obstacle to overcome. Even a moderate commitment, or at least openness to the justice of the legislation itself, might be outweighed by a stronger commitment to the value of unrestricted debate from which each and every senator was a potential beneficiary. Moreover, the larger the majority needed, the easier it was to construct an obstructive minority by appeal to principle, by pressure, by special interest or favour, by promise or cajolery. That it was not until 2 July that the bill was finally signed into law gives some idea of the scale of the parliamentary battle. Even if 'no army can withstand the strength of an idea whose time has come' – and though, as Everett Dirksen, the Republican leader in the Senate whose support was so crucial, reflected, 'In the history of mankind, there is an inexorable moral force that moves us forward' – it took all Johnson's legislative skill to be history's midwife.[71]

True, the civil rights campaign was a broad grassroots movement. The pressure for African-American rights was long in maturing; in the previous decade it had accelerated spectacularly. Many people's individual courage, even heroism, had brought it to fruition. Nonetheless, perhaps only Johnson could have done it; certainly the previous paltry Kennedy legislative record suggests it. The Northern liberals in the Democratic Party had faced down their Southern conservative colleagues; that the man who led them was himself a Southerner compounded their victory. The way lay open for the consequent political realignment. Once again the impact of the President upon the Nation in the making of modern America was decisive and incontestable.

The election of 1964 was a landslide for liberalism. Faced with the stark alternatives of a Johnson–Goldwater contest, the electorate gave a ringing endorsement of the former. Running with Hubert Humphrey as his vice-presidential candidate, the same Humphrey who in 1948 had insisted the Democratic Party first endorse civil rights and thus paved the way for that year's Dixiecrat defections, the now liberal senator for Minnesota reinforced Johnson's message. The Democratic Party's ideological realignment was unquestioned. In the biggest landslide in American history, the conservative cause triumphed only in Arizona, Goldwater's home state and, significantly, in five states of the once-solid Democratic South: Alabama, Georgia, Louisiana, Mississippi and South Carolina. Moreover, in at least another four Southern states – Arkansas, North Carolina, Tennessee and Virginia – only the black vote saved them for the Democratic Party. The white Southerner was now very largely a Republican; thirty years on, Roosevelt's hopes for a political realignment were coming true.

If race was the salient cause in Southern defections, the promise of liberalism was the reason for Johnson's otherwise national endorsement. In March 1964 he had declared the 'War on Poverty'. To Johnson: 'it is not a struggle simply to support people, to make them dependent on the generosity of others. It is a struggle to give people a chance. It is an effort to allow them to develop and use their capacities, as we have been allowed to develop and use ours, so that they can share, as others share, in the promise of this nation. We do this, first of all, because it is right that we should.'[72]

Hence the Economic Opportunity Act costing almost a billion dollars would tackle the problem on five fronts. Firstly, it would give almost half a million young Americans the opportunity to develop skills, continue in education and find employment. Secondly, it would give every American community the chance to develop a comprehensive plan to fight its own poverty. Thirdly, it would recruit and train volunteers to help in the battle. As Johnson noted: 'Thousands of Americans have volunteered to serve the needs of other lands. They should have a chance to serve the needs of their own land.'[73] Fourthly, it would give certain particularly hard-hit groups the opportunity to break out of traditional patterns of poverty. And finally, in order to avoid disparate and uncoordinated attacks on the problem, there would be a new Office of Economic Opportunity with a director who would be the president's personal chief of staff for the war against poverty.

Now Johnson moved on to embrace the whole of the nation, not just its disadvantaged. The 'Great Society' had first been floated in a speech in May 1964. It was an important speech for Johnson, and its enthusiastic reception by an audience of some 80,000 marked the moment in his own mind when finally he broke free from the Kennedy inheritance. It foresaw an America that would be based on 'abundance and liberty for all' and demanded 'an end to poverty and racial injustice'. In its way it was as visionary as Kennedy's 'New Frontier' and perhaps equally unobtainable. 'But most of all, the Great Society is not a safe harbor, a resting place, a final objective, a finished work. It is a challenge constantly renewed, beckoning us toward a destiny where the meaning of our lives matches the marvelous products of our labor.'[74]

If the phrase never quite acquired the cachet of the New Deal, the concept caught on and became increasingly mentioned. Soon it would form the basis of Johnson's programme. Americans hungered for a renewed burst of idealism in the tragic wake of the assassination. And for many of them it was good to be alive in that spring and summer of 1964. There was a sense of the limitless potentialities of American life if their vision could match their power. And Johnson yearned to achieve. 'For half a century we called upon unbounded invention and untiring industry to create an order of plenty for all of our people. The challenge of the next half century is whether we have the wisdom to use that wealth to enrich and elevate our national life, and to advance the quality of our American civilization.'[75]

The election of 1964 did not merely give Johnson an unprecedented mandate; more practically it delivered in the shape of Democratic congressmen, the wherewithal to see his programme enacted. In the Senate the Democrats now outnumbered Republicans by 68 to 32: in the House by 295 to 140. Moreover, many of these were now real liberals, genuinely committed to the Great Society and to its author Johnson, on whose coat tails many had ridden to office. And the president, a political professional to his fingertips, would take nothing for granted. Remembering how his hero Franklin Roosevelt had squandered his great election victory of 1936 in a fruitless fight over the Supreme Court, he resolved to keep up the momentum. The resounding victory at the polls, he cautioned his congressional liaison team, 'might be more of a loophole than a mandate'.[76] Public opinion could be fickle; there was a tide in the affairs of men, and he resolved to take it on the flood.

The result was the most creative burst of legislation since the heady days of the first New Deal. Between January and August, Johnson sent sixty-five messages to Capitol Hill urging support for his proposals. In nine exhausting months, the extended first session of the Eighty-ninth Congress passed eleven major pieces of legislation and scores of lesser ones. By the end of his presidency, Johnson was proudly to reproduce in his Memoirs the list of 207 'Landmark Laws' that his Cabinet had had inscribed and presented to him as a record of his achievement between 1963 and 1969. This was activist government with a vengeance. It was liberalism's finest hour.[77]

The legislation came tumbling on to the statute book. The Gold Reserve Bill froze gold reserves to meet international claims and avoided a big run on the dollar. The Appalachia Redevelopment Bill aimed to alleviate distress in one of America's poorest regions. The Education Bill for the first time authorized federal funds for the general improvement of the nation's schools. An Excise Tax Reduction Bill cut taxes on luxury items and helped sustain the general level of 1960s prosperity. The Constitutional Amendment Bill that in due course became the Twenty-fifth Amendment to the Constitution allowed the appointment of a vice-president in the event of a presidential death or resignation and for the vice-president to become acting president in case of temporary presidential disability. The Medical Care–Social Security Bill at long last provided health care for the nation's aged and enhanced their pensions. The Voting Rights Bill complemented the Civil Rights Act of the year before and ensured that Americans in general, but African-Americans in particular, were guaranteed the exercise of their right to vote. A Department of Housing and Urban Development Bill created a new Cabinet Department. The Arts and Humanities Bill emphasized the all-embracing nature of the Great Society, by providing federal funds for them. An Immigration Bill liberalized the regulations and eliminated the national quota system that had operated for the previous forty years. And the Highway Beautification Bill set out to improve the scenic appearance of America's interstate highways. It is an interesting comment on Johnson's experience as a legislator, compared to Kennedy's ineptitude, that whilst the latter had hoped for a second term to demonstrate his effectiveness, Johnson achieved all the foregoing in the first year of his own presidency.

At times he touched greatness, as when he addressed Congress, urging passage of the voting rights legislation occasioned by the brutal quashing of a peaceful protest in Selma, Alabama. The city epitomized the flagrant injustice of the denial of the rights of its African-American citizens: of some 29,000 people, 15,000 were black of voting age, but only 355 were registered to vote. Martin Luther King had shrewdly chosen it for the predictable savagery of the authorities' response which, televised nationwide, sickened ordinary Americans. Now Johnson would eloquently give voice to that revulsion and their determination to end its occasioning.

I speak tonight of the dignity of man and the destiny of democracy... At times history and fate meet at a single time in a single place to shape a turning point in man's unending search for freedom...So it was last week in Selma, Alabama...There is no constitutional issue here. The command of the Constitution is plain. There is no moral issue here. It is wrong – deadly wrong – to deny any of your fellow Americans the right to vote in this country. There is no issue of states' rights or national rights. There is only the struggle for human rights...This time, on this issue, there must be no delay, no hesitation, and no compromise with our purpose...But even if we pass this bill, the battle will not be over. What happened in Selma is part of a far larger movement which reaches into every section and state of America. It is the effort of American Negroes to secure for themselves the full blessings of American life.

Their cause must be our cause too. Because it is not just Negroes, but really it is all of us who must overcome the crippling legacy of bigotry and injustice. And – we – shall – overcome.[78]

That the president, and a Southerner too, should use a phrase so significant with meaning for the cause of civil rights as 'We shall overcome' demonstrated the strength of Johnson's commitment. A century after the end of the Civil War, perhaps at last African-Americans would become full members of their society. The applause rolled on endlessly around the Chamber of the House of Representatives. Everyone was on their feet, both on the floor and in the galleries, to accord Johnson a standing ovation. Later he reflected: 'I remember the ride home from the Capitol that night. As we circled the reflecting pool, I looked toward the Lincoln Memorial. There had always been something haunting for me in that statue of Lincoln – so life-like and so clear cut a reminder of the persistent gap between our promises and our deeds. Somehow that night Lincoln's hopes for America seemed much closer.'[79]

Perhaps, indeed, at that moment something of Lincoln's greatness was within his grasp. If he had always measured himself against his mentor Franklin Roosevelt, some observers thought that it was only to surpass him. Had he succeeded, he would have displaced him from the trinity of the greatest presidents along with Washington and Lincoln. Yet Johnson's presidency ended in failure. The man who had been elected by a landslide in November 1964 abdicated the presidency three and a half years later, declining to seek re-election. The Democratic Party had been the party of liberalism and internationalism and on the latter, Johnson had foundered. If he had taken Rooseveltian liberalism to new heights, he had stretched internationalism beyond even America's capacity to support it; inevitably the two had become intermingled. Johnson himself had put it pithily: 'If I left the woman I really loved – the Great Society – in order to get involved with that bitch of a war on the other side of the world, then I would lose everything at home.'[80]

The tragedy was both personal and political. Somehow, for all his gifts Johnson never commanded the following that Franklin Roosevelt accepted almost as his birthright. Quite simply, he lacked that indefinable charisma that America's greatest leaders have possessed so often; equally, he lacked the more stalwart virtues, humdrum but reliable. He was never really popular, much as he craved affection and acceptance. Deep down, he was not very likeable. Perhaps he was not even very likeable on the surface. One of his aides noted: 'Lyndon Johnson could win votes, enact laws, maneuver mountains. He could not acquire that something beyond, which cannot be won, enacted or maneuvered but must be freely given. He could not command that respect, affection and rapport which alone permit an American President genuinely to lead.'[81]

By 1968 America was in turmoil. It was the year that everything went wrong. Optimism had given way to exhaustion, bitterness and resentment. Now restraint abroad would have to be matched by restraint at home. Four years before, conservatism had seemed to be marginalized; now it was moving back into the centre. For the first time for a generation it began to set the political agenda. In 1964 Goldwater had called for a choice, not an echo; even as he had gone down to crushing defeat, the Republican Party was beginning to come into its own. It was a development few would have predicted; only in retrospect can the outlines of this astonishing political realignment be clearly discerned.

3

The Attainment of World Power

1   The Background to Foreign Policy

In a striking passage in his *Democracy in America*, the French writer Alexis de Tocqueville predicted the rise of the United States to world power. The prophecy was all the more impressive because it was written in the 1830s and foretold the struggle with the Soviet Union which endured for most of the twentieth century. 'There are now two great nations in the world,' wrote Tocqueville, '...the Russians and the Anglo-Americans...The American fights against natural obstacles; the Russian is at grips with men. The former combats the wilderness and barbarism; the latter, civilization with all its arms...One has freedom as the principal means of action; the other has servitude...each seems called by some secret design of Providence one day to hold in its hands the destinies of half the world.'[1]

Perhaps this remarkable long-sightedness had a basis of commonsensical evaluation, furnished by the size of the United States, its potentiality for growth and the universalistic nature of its democratic ideology. Yet to the average American, it was its remoteness from, and even indifference to, the affairs of other nations that constituted one of its greatest attractions. The traditions of isolationism were deep and not easily repudiated. The schizophrenia in American foreign policy, the tension between the realists and the idealists, represented by Theodore Roosevelt on the one hand and Woodrow Wilson on the other, would not be resolved until the time of Franklin Roosevelt. His presidency would exorcize the ghost of isolationism that came back to haunt the American people even after 1917, the very year when American entry into the First World War and the Russian Revolution presaged the fulfilment of Tocqueville's remarkable prophecy.

144

Roosevelt's own background predisposed him to this role. Born of an upper middle-class East Coast family whose cultural sympathies lay across the Atlantic, he had first travelled to Europe at the age of three and very nearly yearly thereafter. As a young man he imbibed the imperial and naval doctrines of his cousin, who as president devoted himself to enhancing America's international status and naval power. Later, as a young politician, he had moved to Washington, to take up the post of assistant secretary of the Navy offered by Wilson. In 1913 the position was a showy backwater in a new administration bent on domestic reform. Eighteen months later the First World War began. Suddenly naval affairs became critical. Roosevelt, not always a particularly attractive figure, preached a big navy, preparedness for the World War and ultimately American involvement. Though never a combatant, he had a good war. By 1920 on the strength of his family name, his geographical base in New York, and his record in Washington, he was running as Democratic candidate for vice-president, committed to the League of Nations as Wilson's political heir.

The Republican victory of 1920 was a victory for isolationism; the American people had endorsed the Senate's rejection of the League. True, the decade saw some limited American involvement in postwar Europe. There were loans for reconstruction and a willingness to limit war exemplified by the Washington Naval Conference of 1921–2, or to outlaw it altogether as by the Kellogg–Briand Pact of 1928, meaningless though the latter might prove to be. Still, in general the forces of isolationism were triumphant. Nationalism was the order of the day. Nowhere was this more apparent than in the area of the economy, with disastrous consequences. European industry, struggling to get back on its feet after the First World War, was frozen out of the American market; Europe's nations retaliated likewise and international trade languished. The Great Crash of 1929 compounded the problem with further protectionism. It was putting the brake on with a vengeance when the world economy had gone into reverse. The consequences were predictable. By 1932 it was each nation for itself; they would hang separately rather than hang together.

2 Roosevelt and Isolationism

No aspirant to elective office could ignore such stark political realities. It was not Roosevelt's most glorious hour. Seeking the

Democratic nomination for president, he knew that his earlier internationalism was viewed with suspicion by certain influential isolationists. He therefore stated that he no longer favoured American
participation in the League of Nations, as 'the League of Nations
today is not the League conceived by Woodrow Wilson'.[2]

This was strictly true: it was now twelve years since the Senate
had voted down the treaty and the League had developed without
American participation. But the disclaimer was disingenuous: a political straddle recognized as such by the outraged old Wilsonians. Yet
it was in keeping with the public mood; four years of Depression had
concentrated the American mind wonderfully on home affairs. Whatever the cost in conscience, electorally it worked.

Worse was to come. In the summer of 1933 the London Economic
Conference took place. It began with high hopes; the nations of the
world would get together, talk over their economic difficulties and
agree a common programme for action. Roosevelt effectively sabo-
taged it. Of course, he was right, recognizing that such gatherings
are largely talking shops, and that the disparate range of special
interests represented often prevented any effective implementation
of anything but the lowest common denominator of agreed remed-
ies. Even more did Roosevelt fear that where action was purposeful,
it would force his hand and tie the United States to agreements
that would, in the unique circumstances of 1933, be inimical to the
flexibility he needed to achieve economic recovery. Winston Churchill, for one, agreed: 'Conferences exist for men and not men for
conferences.'[3] In terms of public relations, though, this stance was a
disaster. It did much to enhance suspicion of the United States.
Neville Chamberlain, closely involved as chancellor of the exchequer
in 1933, later commented: 'it is always best and safest to count on
nothing from the Americans but words.'[4]

Domestically, though, Roosevelt's action made good politics and
good economics; the American people had their own problems and
the First New Deal would be based on the premise of economic
nationalism. Not until 1934 would the Reciprocal Trade and Tariff
Act pioneered by that ardent internationalist Cordell Hull, the
secretary of state, reflect the latter's lifelong devotion to trading
agreements between nations as an aid to economic betterment and
international understanding. But it was Roosevelt who was more in
tune with the times. There was a public backlash against the First
World War: American entry in 1917 had long been seen as a mistake; now, in the wake of the Depression, it was viewed even more

critically. A spate of publications including Walter Millis's influential *Road to War* re-examined the causes.[5] American participation had, apparently, all been the fault of bankers, munitions manufacturers and allied propaganda.

Republican Senator Gerald Nye of North Dakota set up a committee that went on a fishing expedition through State Department papers, proving, at least to its own satisfaction, that such charges were justified. The upshot was the Neutrality Acts of 1935, 1936 and 1937, which set out to ensure it must never happen again. There would be no trading with belligerents in arms or munitions. Other goods would have to be paid in cash and carried in the purchasing nations' own ships; thus no American credit would be at stake and no American vessels sunk in war. Americans, to avoid a repeat of the *Lusitania* incident of 1915, could not travel on the ships of belligerents. It was the high-water mark of interwar isolationism. Perhaps one incident, in particular, illustrates the national mood. In 1935 it was proposed that America should join the World Court, a harmless gesture but, as it involved American adherence to an international body, technically a treaty requiring the consent of two-thirds of the Senate. Roosevelt was unable to muster sufficient votes. The phobia against the League of Nations died hard. It was to be a fateful legacy.

At first sight the inflexibility of American isolationism seems one of the mysteries of the decade. Even allowing for the reaction against the First World War and the settlement that followed it, the resentment occasioned by the Allies' non-payment of war debts, the consequences of the Depression, the illusion of geographic security, the praiseworthy desire for peace among nations, why did American isolationism remain so resolute? And in an era which saw Japan invade first Manchuria and then mainland China, Hitler tear up the Versailles Treaty, march into the Rhineland and begin the sequestration of his neighbours, Mussolini strut into Africa and Franco usurp the Spanish government! The answer partly lay in the tragedy of American idealism. American isolationism could be short-sighted and insular, when not downright selfish, even wilful. But there was also a genuine desire for peace by example: the belief that those who prepare for war invariably get it. Thus one must strain every nerve to avoid a repetition of the First World War, and if the ever-quarrelsome European powers recognized that never again would America help them out in a similar crisis, they too might learn to behave better. All the force of American

Christianity, pacifism and high-mindedness went into espousing and sustaining a policy that year by year became ever more misguided. Roosevelt, the latent internationalist, recognized as much but understood political reality. Though committing himself to 'the policy of the good neighbour' in his first term as president, it was clear that foreign affairs, of necessity, were of secondary importance.[6] Nor was this necessarily unwise, in the 1930s. If America could not be economically strong, she would be no use to anyone, least of all herself. The goal of economic recovery was paramount. He made a few initiatives. He recognized the Soviet Union in November 1933; it might help trade, serve as a warning to Japan, even drop a hint to Hitler. South of the Rio Grande, he embarked on a policy of assuaging bitter memories of 'Yankee imperialism'; here he could be a good neighbour in deed as well as name. American isolationism never embraced Latin America. He issued platitudes about peace and disarmament. Otherwise, domestic priorities were overwhelming. Yet were they merely domestic? Accepting renomination as president in 1936, his words may have had more than one level of meaning; in retrospect they seem a portent of future troubles: 'There is a mysterious cycle in human events. To some generations much is given. Of other generations much is expected. This generation of Americans has a rendezvous with destiny.' It was a brilliant phrase that epitomized his years in the White House. But Roosevelt also understood the international implications of his domestic policy.

> In ... other lands, there are some people, who, in times past, have lived and fought for freedom, and seem to have grown too weary to carry on the fight. They have sold their heritage of freedom for the illusion of a living. They have yielded their democracy ... only our success can stir their ancient hope. They begin to know that here in America we are waging a great and successful war ... not alone ... against want and destitution and economic demoralisation. It is more ... it is a war for the survival of democracy. We are fighting to save a great and precious form of government for ourselves and for the world.[7]

One must never discount the idealism in Roosevelt under the tough carapace of the practical politician obliged to confront world realities. Even in 1936 when interest in foreign affairs was at a low ebb, he could see the significance of the New Deal in global terms. No doubt he recalled the legacy of his cousin Theodore Roosevelt, that a strong America abroad necessitated a strong America at home. If the hunger-induced desperation and chaos of the Weimar Republic spawned a Hitler, all the more reason to show that there were other alternatives. Thus far, even the most pacifist of his countrymen might acquiesce; and here at least lay the seeds of future development. Nonetheless, the old Progressive equation between domestic health and foreign vitality was not one all his supporters would accept; indeed, the more ardent their desire for domestic reform, the more the fear that war would shatter it – the nemesis that had overtaken Wilson in 1917. Native isolationism was reinforced by the urge for home improvement; 'America First' would have a double meaning.[8]

'The Roosevelt Revolution', as it was termed, was dramatic enough in domestic affairs.[9] It was compounded by this increased importance of foreign policy. As the 1930s wore on, the stridency of the dictators penetrated even the American consciousness. Foreign affairs were, constitutionally, the prerogative of the president; his role as commander-in-chief was undisputed. Now a powerful president was about to see his powers enlarged still further, as a foreign crisis followed the domestic one. The activist presidency would find still further scope for its energies and, in so doing, subtly alter the nature of the presidency itself. From being an occasional concern of a president, as the Founding Fathers had envisaged, foreign affairs would become the pre-eminent, consistent concern; in that area where there was least restraint on his conduct, the president would be required to be constantly active. One might take that moment in October 1937, when Roosevelt warned his fellow-countrymen of the danger of aggressor nations and suggested that they might be quarantined, as the beginning of that concern with national security and foreign affairs that became the president's primary responsibility thereafter. Henceforth, one might argue, never again would an American president be able to free himself of the need to look to the nation's defence as his foremost priority. Through the approaches to the Second World War, the War itself, the Cold War, the nuclear age, never again would an American president enjoy the sole luxury of immersion in domestic politics: in comparison, even the Depression years paled in importance. Even after the ending of the Cold War, the American president, deploying the unique power of the United States as *de facto* global policeman, could only free himself of this encumbrance at the risk of being seen as failing in his responsibilities to the wider world community. A pattern of response would be set that would need to become permanent.

Nonetheless, Roosevelt began tentatively. His first real initiative, the so-called Quarantine Speech of October 1937, when he urged civilized nations to join together, was scarcely an aggressive proposal, merely recognition that there was a problem. 'It seems to be unfortunately true that the epidemic of world lawlessness is spreading. When an epidemic of physical disease starts to spread, the community approves and joins in a quarantine of the patients in order to protect the health of the community against the spread of the disease.'[10]

Yet public reaction was such that he had to backtrack immediately and suggest his words did not carry the meaning ascribed to them. It was a typical Roosevelt stratagem, to be endlessly repeated as he sought to penetrate the complacency of his countrymen. Three months later, in January 1938, he threw out a suggestion to Neville Chamberlain that the major powers meet and try and sort out their differences; this time it was the British prime minister who discounted it. When the latter flew to Munich later in the year, Roosevelt confided to his ambassador in Italy: 'Chamberlain's visit to Hitler today may bring things to a head or may result in a temporary postponement of what looks like an inevitable conflict within the next five years. Perhaps when it comes the United States will be in a position to pick up the pieces of European civilization and help them to save what remains of the wreck – not a cheerful prospect.'[11]

It was a prescient analysis. A fortnight later when Chamberlain prepared to go yet again, to return with the infamous agreement on which so much false hope would rest, Roosevelt cabled cryptically: 'Good Man.'[12] It was scarcely an enthusiastic endorsement of Appeasement. Yet Roosevelt was a spectator, not an actor, as the world moved with ever-increasing certainty to what Churchill later told him should be called 'the Unnecessary War'.[13] His countrymen would have brooked no other role for their president. War would not come and, if it did, it was no concern of America's.

Nor was this merely the reaction of the uninformed public. In mid-July 1939, Roosevelt called the members of the Senate Foreign Relations Committee to the White House, desperately seeking some modification of the Neutrality Laws that prohibited aid to belligerents. Cordell Hull the secretary of state outlined the gravity of the

European situation, assuring them that war was imminent. Senator Borah of Idaho, the Grand Old Man of the Republican Party and of isolationism, dissented. There would be no war. Hull stressed the danger: the cables coming in to the State Department all told the same story; Hull, indeed, offered to show them to Borah. The senator rejected the offer; 'I have my own sources of information,' he assured a furious Hull, 'and on several occasions I've found them more reliable than the State Department.'[14] It was Vice-President Garner who summed up the obvious: 'Well, Captain, we may as well face the facts. You haven't got the votes, and that's all there is to it.'[15] It was the rock of political reality Roosevelt would have to circumnavigate right up to Pearl Harbor. Every advance would have to be tenaciously fought for; when the moment was opportune, try to extract a concession. The isolationist bloc was simply too numerous to allow any other tactic and too intransigent to see reason without a struggle. Meanwhile, when, predictably, war came, Borah would dismiss it as a 'phony' war: a phrase that proved more durable than his foresight.[16]

This refrain, 'You haven't got the votes', was to be the theme song of two and a quarter years of presidential hesitancy and congressional indecision. When war broke out in Europe, American sympathy for the Allies was not in doubt: but only 2 per cent in an opinion poll taken that ominous September favoured American intervention. Roosevelt sought to make clear where justice lay; whilst urging American neutrality, he conceded that he could not ask Americans to be neutral in thought as well. Here the contrast with Wilson was manifest. Yet Roosevelt was in any case something of a spent force. Would he serve out his second term as president, a less than happy one compared to the achievements of the first, and retire in January 1941; or would he break the third term shibboleth that had endured since the days of Washington? Nobody knew: perhaps not even Roosevelt. Wisely, therefore, he decided to keep silent and keep friends and enemies guessing. It was the best strategy in the circumstances but one that, inevitably, made for caution. This was not the only consideration. In the last couple of years he had experienced a succession of rebuffs over enlargement of the Supreme Court, a plummeting economy and a futile attempt to remove conservatives from his party. His own prestige impaired, his enemies were now stronger than ever, bolstered by the Republican gains in the 1938 elections that made Congress less amenable than hitherto. The lesson had been harshly learned but was painfully clear: never again must he rush his fences. So, slowly, painstakingly, tentatively he followed events, seeking to discern their import. The stakes were too high to admit of error.

He had not forgotten the example of Wilson, who had taken a divided country into war, psychologically ill-prepared as to the reasons for its entry. The result was predictable; much of Wilson's troubles, when the conflict was ended and the peace failed to deliver the unrealistic hopes thus excited, could be traced back to this initial confusion. If and when Roosevelt went to war, he meant to lead a united country: only this could guarantee that the nation would stay the course. In the meantime, he would keep his ear close to the ground, content if necessary to follow public opinion rather than to lead it. True, he was not a passive observer; events and his own interpretation of them would nudge public attitudes in the way he wanted but the process would be a slow one, at times almost static.

At that very moment when Roosevelt seemed immobilized politically, he received a letter from Albert Einstein with a covering memorandum from Leo Szilard. Perhaps few more significant communications have ever been penned in history. Briefly, the famous scientists outlined the possibilities inherent in atomic fission; more practically, a presidential adviser able to paraphrase their significance delivered them personally. Roosevelt was no physicist but he had an intuitive grasp of the essential: 'What you are after is to see that the Nazis don't blow us up.' Summoning an aide, he emphasized 'This requires action.' In three words he had taken the most momentous decision of his presidency.[17]

Few then could have foretold what lay ahead. A few scientists perhaps might have had some presentiment but not the professional military, who were often sceptical and obstructionist, nor politicians, who feared the cost. Perhaps nothing vindicates more effectively the wisdom of Franklin Roosevelt or a Constitution that gave the chief executive such latitude. Widely perceived as a lame-duck president in a period when American foreign policy was at its least glorious, Roosevelt had set in train the building of a weapon of hitherto unimagined destructiveness, a weapon, moreover, that would terminate a war America had not yet entered, that would transform the assumptions and constraints of international relations, and would uniquely enhance the authority of the American president who alone had the power to decide to use it. Few revolutions have been implemented so casually or had such consequences. In such nonchalant ways is the course of history altered.

To the contemporary observer in 1939, however, it was Hitler not Roosevelt who was altering the course of history, and it was the latter's reaction to the German dictator that would shape the immediate direction of American foreign policy. Had it not been for Hitler, Roosevelt would almost certainly have retired in 1941. The election of 1940 was one of the few elections in American history where domestic considerations were not primarily important. And even here one must not discount the need to ensure the survival of the New Deal, the legacy of Hoover, and the liberalism of Roosevelt compared to other potential candidates. Still, in a crisis people often prefer continuity. Roosevelt was a proven leader, but he was supported on his claim to keep war away from America, not that she might become involved in it. It was a stance of some ambiguity. Fascism was to be deplored because it was the enemy of democracy; thus Britain and France might merit support out of self-interest, but only at the cost of non-intervention – otherwise the price was too high. The 'Committee to Defend America by Aiding the Allies', organized by internationalists, summed up in its title the appeal of non-belligerency.[18] Every measure Roosevelt took, therefore, that might be construed as one leading to war, had to be justified as making war less likely. It is hard to discern where the truth lay. Did Roosevelt really believe that Hitler could master Europe and that America could remain anxious but aloof? 'Some indeed still hold to the now somewhat obvious delusion that we...can safely permit the United States to become a lone island...in a world dominated by the philosophy of force. Such...may be the dream of...isolationists,' was Roosevelt's immediate comment after the Italian declaration of war on France in June 1940.[19]

Yet when the French prime minister pleaded for American intervention as catastrophe engulfed her, he was refused all assistance. Nor did Britain at first fare better. Not until September did Roosevelt engineer the Destroyer-Bases Deal, a direct exchange of fifty over-age American navy destroyers to help the hard-pressed British fleet, for bases in the New World to enhance American defence. It was the sole gesture Roosevelt made to Britain before his re-election. And even that was set in the context of American interests.

Roosevelt was on the horns of a dilemma. In many quarters the events of 1940 had not shattered isolationism but merely reinforced it. Since modern war was manifestly horrible – and here the American media provided ample corroboration – it was therefore best to avoid it, and avoidance was best achieved by non-entanglement.

It was as if Washington and Jefferson were still counselling their countrymen. The Atlantic was seen as a moat behind which one could shelter, not with the potentiality of a modern navy, more accurately a highway to a long, frequently defenceless coastline. This altered reality was, however, readily appreciated by Roosevelt. If there was one situation he dreaded, it was the possibility of the German navy acquiring the French fleet, augmented by Britain's fleet, bargained away in exchange for a softer peace. And if there was one factor that convinced him that Churchill's words of defiance, impressive though they were, were more than mere rhetoric, it was the latter's decision to sink those units of the French fleet that resisted the call to join the Allies. It was a political point, as Churchill well understood, purchased at the price of over a thousand French lives, but it was sufficient to convince Roosevelt. Britain at least was worth backing; she meant to fight, but to his countrymen Britain's fight was to be encouraged to keep the war at a safe distance. 'Your boys are not going to be sent into any foreign wars,' he famously assured a Boston audience, on the eve of the election. 'They are going into training to form a force so strong that ... will keep the threat of war far away from our shores. The purpose of our defense is defense.'[20] To those of long memory, it eerily resembled Wilson's campaign slogan of 1916: 'He Kept Us Out of War.' Wilson's promise proved good for less than six months; Roosevelt's lasted just over the year.

Doubtless, Roosevelt was influenced by the example; during the First World War, he had watched from the Navy Department, as German naval tactics on the Atlantic became increasingly intolerable. No doubt, he assumed that if war came to America, it would be through similar misunderstandings. Nor could there be any doubt that the Atlantic theatre was vital to Britain, if she were to obtain the supplies she so desperately needed. In the autumn of 1939, Roosevelt had at last achieved the amendment of the Neutrality Laws to alter the provision of 'cash and carry' aid to the Allies. A year later, when Britain was nearly broke, he conceived Lend-Lease. America would become the 'arsenal of democracy' supplying Britain with whatever she needed, to be returned later.[21] Imaginatively and disingenuously – even deceitfully – he likened the arrangement to the loan of a garden hose to help a neighbour put out a fire, lest it engulf one's own home. It fooled the public, perhaps even Congress, or at least saved face sufficiently to allow them to pass it. If, in Churchill's phrase, it was 'the most unsordid act in the history of any nation', it was also a commitment that might be construed as a precedent for more avowedly military help later.[22]

How long would this ambiguity continue, whereby every measure to aid the fight against Nazism was sold to the public as one for defence? For a start, it depended on the forbearance of Hitler. By 1941 the United States was in no way a neutral in any real meaning of the word, but it suited Hitler to suffer the increasing hostility of the United States rather than jeopardize his wider plans. He, too, remembered the First World War. Nonetheless, if a silent battle was going on across the Atlantic, unspoken but explicit, it was across America's other ocean, the Pacific, that events were coming to a head. Here American attitudes had been more decisive; the Japanese invasion of Manchuria and mainland China had aroused greater public antagonism, and a greater sense of the intolerability of Axis demands. Curiously, Americans were more isolationist about events 3,000 miles away than they were about happenings over twice that distance; most had never physically rejected Asia as so many had in leaving Europe. A sense of mission to the disadvantaged may also have been a factor; the American public had long had a sentimental love affair with China, scarcely based on reality, but compelling nonetheless. In contrast, they viewed the Japanese with wariness, and had done really since the time of Theodore Roosevelt. The very Senate Foreign Relations Committee that refused to lift the arms embargo was quite happy to recommend the abrogation of America's Commercial Treaty with Japan, thus aggravating an already fraught situation. Compared to the Germans, the Americans may have had cause to fear the Japanese less, but they disliked them more. Few would have thought that the Japanese would compound this dislike by an infamous, surprise attack on Pearl Harbor. Yet this had a certain strategic logic. If they needed to expand southwards for economic survival, the feuding with the Americans would inevitably intensify. For years Roosevelt had trod the delicate path between warning off the Japanese and driving them into a corner. Even the presence of the American Pacific fleet in her Hawaiian naval base rather than in home port in San Diego was a none-too-subtle reminder to them of American power. Better to strike now when there was some chance of quick victories, reasoned the Japanese, than drag on as the odds against them lengthened. The destruction of the American fleet would secure their flank until they had time to consolidate their gains. They lacked Hitler's patience, perhaps even his perception. Roosevelt could hardly have asked Congress for a declaration of war on behalf of the British or Dutch empires, more likely and more tempting targets. As it was, the Japanese solved Roosevelt's problem, and Hitler and Mussolini, unnecessarily and insanely – the Tripartite Pact only obliged them to furnish aid in the event of an attack on any of its signatories – rushed to their side. In an instant, Roosevelt was able to lead a hitherto isolationist nation united into war. At one fell swoop, the uncertainties of a decade had resolved themselves. Few American presidents, a cynic might observe, have had such a stroke of luck. The famed Roosevelt patience and masterly sense of timing had been rewarded by events.

In retrospect it was often said of the prewar years that public attitudes and congressional restraints tied Roosevelt's hands. In a sense, of course, this was undoubtedly true. But the vigilance of the isolationists, even their touchiness, their suspicions of the president's intentions, were itself a tribute to his power. It suggested that they at least knew who had the potential to chart the nation's direction in its dealings with foreign countries. And, of course, they were right. One can take as the last great victory of the isolationists that refusal of the Senate Foreign Relations Committee in July 1939 to amend the neutrality legislation in the face of Roosevelt's pleadings. Thereafter, throughout 1940 and 1941 isolationism fought a rearguard action as slowly, ineluctably, America's destinies and the anti-Axis coalition were intertwined. Moreover, they were up against a president who had demonstrated his power in a unique way; by persuading his fellow-countrymen to elect him for an unprecedented third term, breaking a tradition that had lasted since the days of the great Washington himself. No other man in American history had ever served in the presidency so long; and he had been elected yet again because in large part the world crisis of 1940 required that the American people had as their leader one in whom they placed their trust.

The presidential capacity for the evolution of a new direction in foreign policy in such circumstances was immense. Only Roosevelt could order the occupation of Greenland to forestall a German invasion, send American troops to Iceland, declare an Unlimited National Emergency, throw open American ports to British warships, or order the American fleet to shoot on sight German vessels. It was the president who could consistently seek to influence public opinion by words as well as deeds. Only Roosevelt could meet with Churchill to draw up the Atlantic Charter in a symbolic dis-

play of Anglo–American unity that gave expression to the respective leaders' hopes for the world in an era of Fascist aggression. In a
crisis, under the American system, the president must predominate;
if he does not, he is a failure as a president. And Roosevelt faced the
greatest crisis since the start of the Civil War in 1861. Pearl Harbor
settled many issues: not least, that on the central issue of foreign
policy, the president had been right and many of the leading congressmen wrong. Pearl Harbor ended American isolationism. The
moral authority of the presidency was assured, that of its critics
diminished.

3 Roosevelt as Wartime President

It was an authority that was not to be lost for a quarter of a century.
Firstly, there was the sheer scale of the achievement. Roosevelt
mobilizing a nation for war and putting himself at the head of a
worldwide coalition; Roosevelt at the Teheran and Yalta conferences
casually deciding the destinies of nations; Roosevelt as commander-
in-chief moving the armed forces around the globe. It was a role no
other American public figure could remotely compete with; even to
challenge presidential policy seemed vaguely unpatriotic. Moreover,
success throve on success and habit came from habit. The president
was his own secretary of state; the White House his personal State
Department. Harry Hopkins, Roosevelt's aide, clearly enjoyed much
more power and the confidence of his chief than Cordell Hull the
official secretary of state; the latter, indeed, was even undercut by his
own under secretary, Sumner Welles, whom Roosevelt preferred to
deal with. It gave Roosevelt a unique authority.

One incident illustrates this to perfection. In the autumn of 1943
George Kennan, then American chargé d'affaires in Lisbon, became
deeply concerned that his government's policy towards Portugal
was ill-conceived through misunderstanding at the highest level.
Accordingly, he felt obliged, at great personal risk to his career, to
take the issue over the heads of his superiors. Eventually he found
himself alone with Roosevelt, who promised to write a personal
letter to the Portuguese prime minister, to set the issues straight. 'I
replied,' Kennan recalled, 'that I could think of nothing better; but I
wondered whether there wasn't some misunderstanding here. I had
the impression, from the morning I spent in the Pentagon, that
people there were proposing to follow an entirely different course.

' "Oh, don't worry," said the President with a debonair wave of his cigarette holder, "about all those *people* over there" (having in mind, of course, no less than the Secretaries of War and Navy and the Joint Chiefs of Staff – in short, the entire high command of the American armed forces in wartime).'[23]

This authority of the American president bore little comparison with any parliamentary system. British observers noted at the Atlantic Charter meeting, how Churchill had to cable back and forth to the War Cabinet in London for approval as the document was drafted and amended: Roosevelt was a law unto himself. He had no need to carry his Cabinet with him; there would be no vote of confidence to win as Churchill later faced in the darkest days of the war. Indeed, once war had started this lofty eminence was exaggerated: his role as commander-in-chief gave him an even greater power. That role seemed to be more than a strictly military one, or at least the scope of that to which it pertained was unduly wide. 'The responsibilities of the President in wartime to protect the Nation are very grave,' Roosevelt proclaimed early in the war.

> This total war, with our fighting fronts all over the world, makes the use of the executive power far more essential than in any previous war ... I cannot tell what powers may have to be exercised in order to win this war. The American people can be sure that I will use my powers with a full sense of responsibility to the Constitution and to my country. The American people can also be sure that I shall not hesitate to use every power vested in me to accomplish the defeat of our enemies in any part of the world where our own safety demands such defeat.'[24]

And indeed, in a unique sense Roosevelt personified the American war effort. He was head of state; he was the chief executive elected by the whole of the American people; he was the leader who had brought the nation through the Depression and equipped it to meet this new challenge; he was the president of such enduring service. It was Roosevelt who both organized and benefited from that total coherence of purpose that the successful prosecution of the war demanded. It served to underline the wisdom of Tocqueville's comment a century previously:

> When a war has at length by its long continuance roused the whole community from their peacetime occupations and brought

all their petty undertakings to ruin, it will happen that those very passions which once made them value peace so highly become directed into war. War, having destroyed every industry, in the end becomes itself the one great industry, and every eager and ambitious desire sprung from equality is focused on it. For that reason those same democratic nations which are so hard to drag onto the battlefield sometimes perform prodigious feats once one has succeeded in putting arms in their hands.[25]

Or as a relieved and thankful Churchill, who had seen it thirty years before, recalled on the evening of Pearl Harbor: the United States is like 'a giant boiler. Once the fire is lighted under it there is no limit to the power it can generate.' And this power would be deployed at Roosevelt's behest.[26]

Equally, there was Roosevelt's good judgement. Essentially a civilian commander-in-chief with negligible military experience, he was content to leave tactics to subordinates. On matters of grand strategy he had, however, a sureness of touch events later vindicated. Even before Pearl Harbor, a decision had been taken that illustrated his grasp of fundamentals. If war came, Germany would be the major enemy; her defeat would lead inevitably to the defeat of Japan. The reverse did not necessarily follow. Roosevelt never departed from this Atlantic First strategy. Hitler's hope now lay in dividing the Grand Alliance; thus Roosevelt determined to work fully with his partners. There must be no repeat of the separate peace made by the Russians in the First World War.

When, for example, Stalin urgently wanted a Second Front to relieve pressure on the Soviet Union, whilst a cautious Churchill counselled delay, Roosevelt, alert to Stalin's suspicions of Anglo-American double-dealing, endeavoured to play the part of honest broker. True, no Western democratic leader could contemplate the butcher's bill in human casualties that a premature landing on mainland Europe might generate. Here Roosevelt's optimistic promise to the Soviet foreign minister, Molotov, in May 1942 that there would be a Second Front that year was wisely diverted by Churchill to landings in North Africa, advice Roosevelt sensibly followed. But Roosevelt understood Stalin's need for reassurance. Even the contentious commitment to 'Unconditional Surrender' made at Casablanca in 1943 was a recognition that Stalin needed to be certain that his Western allies would not run out from under him. There would be no separate deals with Fascist leaders.[27]

In 1917 America had entered the First World War as 'an Associated Power'; the implication was that her cause and that of the Allies were not necessarily identical; now America was a fully-fledged partner in the anti-Axis coalition, Roosevelt manifestly one of the big three. Soon the absence of foreign invasion, the prodigiousness of America's industrial resources, the freshness of its enthusiasm for war once the die was cast, made Roosevelt the senior partner. Stalin might be organizing a terrible resistance to German power, which ultimately would destroy it, but his was nonetheless a solely Russian war. Churchill, for all his grandeur, was still essentially the magnificent spokesman for a romantic cause that had defied hopeless odds with a vision sustained by memories of a glorious past. Roosevelt, however, fought for a world that was to come, to be born out of the suffering of the Second World War. It would be a new creation, better than, and different from, what had gone before. Roosevelt's world would witness a Pax Americana, operating through the United Nations, an end to colonialism and subject peoples, a trans-global free market economy and the triumph of democracy and liberal capitalism. It was a potent mixture of idealism and self-interest.

The war, of course, enhanced American strength as it weakened her allies; old colonial empires had fallen to invasion whilst back in Europe their rulers had experienced the horrors of enemy occupation. Even Britain, spared that particular ordeal, had had its Home Front subject to direct attack that had sapped its energy and exhausted its resources. As late as 1952 Secretary of State Dean Acheson, coming to Britain for King George VI's funeral, noticed the crowds and observed how 'They looked like a tired people'.[28] If 1940 had been Britain's finest hour, it had also been her swansong.

It was a truth Churchill knew innately even as he rejoiced in the relief of American intervention. Britain might still be one of the Big Three, but there was an even Bigger Two. However, the Soviet Union, even if militarily powerful, had at least 20 million of her population dead and was severely impoverished. It would need prodigious efforts by way of postwar reconstruction. Indeed, Europe generally was enfeebled by years of strife and destruction. In Asia, meanwhile, Japan lay prostrate under an American government of occupation that took control of her destiny, whilst the Chinese were divided in a civil war that seemed destined to last for years, if no way could be found to bring the warring parties together. America itself was to play a part in this ultimately futile enterprise. Elsewhere, the Europeans were in retreat: sometimes with relative graciousness as with the British in India: sometimes stubborn, resentful and uncomprehending, as with the French in Vietnam. All that remained for the old colonial empires was to decline and fall.

In contrast, never before had American power been so formidable. Now the United States had the atomic bomb and the scientific expertise that had developed that terrible weapon; behind this lay a unique industrial might further augmenting its exceptional military preponderance. America's economy was the strongest in the world; those of many of her erstwhile competitors shattered. Moreover, Roosevelt had not spent the first six years of his presidency combating the Depression to risk its return once the war had ended. In this respect the war itself had been a blessing, leading to American economic recovery, and so it was clear that once the conflict had ended the capitalist system had to be put on an international footing. The solution was to recognize American economic dominance by basing the world financial system on gold and the dollar. At the Bretton Woods Conference in 1944 this fact of life had been reluctantly accepted, backed by a World Bank and International Monetary Fund, largely financed by American money, to promote international trade and stabilize currencies. This was the historic moment of opportunity, but past precedent suggested that America might retreat back into itself. Yet by 1945, the prophecy, over a century earlier, of Tocqueville had come true; American and Russian troops had met on the Elbe and signalled the division of the world between two competing empires; two cities, Washington and Moscow, vied for influence.

In February 1945 the American delegation had left the Yalta Conference convinced that it was the dawn of a new era. Wartime cooperation was at its zenith; the Soviet Union would enter the war against Japan and join the new United Nations. Here Roosevelt had moved quickly. Unlike Wilson, he would not allow an interlude between war and peace before beginning the task of reordering international relations. Even in Poland some accommodation seemed possible between the Western desire for a freely elected government and Soviet need for security and co-operation. Ironically, only one cloud darkened their horizon. What if Stalin were to die and some unknown Soviet leader emerge out of the mysterious processes of the Kremlin? Would he be as cooperative? Few assumptions have been more misplaced. Two months later Roosevelt was dead; shortly thereafter, the British electorate ejected Churchill. Of the wartime Big Three leaders, only Stalin remained. Yalta, that had seemed a symbol of Allied cooperation, soon became, in popular legend, the Munich of American foreign policy.

On reflection, the four years of apparent American–Russian harmony, seemed in the long perspective since 1917, an aberration, brought about solely by the need to cooperate against Hitler. For this the Soviet Union incurred a major responsibility. In August 1939 the notorious Molotov–Ribbentrop pact had given the green light to Hitler for the War in the West; in April 1941 the Soviet five-year non-aggression pact with the Japanese had given Tokyo the go-ahead for the war in the East. The Soviet Union's record in international relations prior to the attack by Hitler scarcely inspired confidence. Once he was defeated, the alliance between America and the Soviet Union would dissolve; worse, there would be a power vacuum in Central Europe that only the Russians could fill. Talk, therefore, of American–Russian cooperation was probably unrealistic all along; certainly there were Americans who thought that Roosevelt verged on naivety. The implications for American foreign policy were profound. If Rooseveltian idealism were to have any meaning, the crusade might have to be continued against another foe. The Second World War was the start, not the finish; there was a continuity in American foreign policy that has sometimes been obscured by the rhetoric employed against its opponents. American foreign policy was not merely reactive, though it has sometimes been seen that way; the analogy between Hitler and Stalin does at least suggest a certain positive content to its philosophy. Roosevelt had taught the American people that freedom was worth defending; that America had a role to play in supporting democracy when threatened by totalitarianism – whether it was of the right or the left was a secondary issue. Had this purity of vision been sustained, American foreign policy after the war would have been clearer and more popular.

Roosevelt's willingness, even desire, to work with the Soviet Union after the war, was predicated on the assumption that their fight against Hitler did at least suggest certain shared values on which postwar cooperation might be built. Sometimes, it must be admitted, his enthusiasm involved some tortuousness. In one of his most inspiring speeches in January 1941, Roosevelt had looked 'forward to a world founded upon four essential freedoms ... freedom of speech and expression ... freedom of every person to worship God in his own way...freedom from want...freedom from fear'.[29]

Once challenged as to how the Soviet Union, officially an atheistic state, would embrace 'the freedom of every person to worship God in his own way', he rather lamely explained that this allowed the freedom not to believe in God. Nonetheless, if the United Nations was to work, one had to take a good deal on trust, perhaps even hope. One could argue that there was no alternative. The same spirit that had animated Roosevelt in the 1930s inspired him in the 1940s. The message was a positive one. Single-handedly he made America the spokesman for humanity. As Harry Hopkins, his closest aide, acutely noted, Roosevelt was supported 'because he's a great spiritual figure, because he's an idealist, like Wilson, and he's got the guts to drive through against any opposition to realize those ideals ...You can see the real Roosevelt when he comes out with something like the Four Freedoms. And don't get the idea that those are any catch phrases. *He believes them!* He believes they can be practically attained.'[30]

Consistently, both before America entered the war and thereafter, he had sought to emphasize the ideals that underlay his actions, maximizing support by appealing to the good intentions of his fellow-countrymen. This combination of principle and policy proved highly effective; what is remarkable in retrospect is how dramatically American public attitudes were turned around. The legacy was an activist foreign policy committed to internationalism; one of Roosevelt's greatest achievements was that his successors could do no other. America was and would remain the leader of the Free World. There would be no repetition of 1920. The Cold War had its positive as well as its negative features, a truth more apparent after it had ended than was always clear to Americans at the time, who so often defined their role in the light of the behaviour of their enemies.

Roosevelt, perhaps slightly fortunately, died at the height of his achievement, having ensured that the United Nations gained American acceptance. Unconditional surrender and postwar planning, *de facto* spheres of influence, if not openly admitted, reduced the area for disagreement amongst the victors to whom, indeed, belonged the spoils. The final act of the Second World War, which ended very much with a bang not a whimper, was the American president authorizing the obliteration of two Japanese cities with atomic weapons – a unique display of power. The decision may have been

Truman's; it had only been possible because years before Roosevelt had backed a hunch and invested vast resources in a project that many thought chimerical. Working in strictest secrecy, with funds fiddled through a Congress that little suspected the use to be made of them, armies of scientists in remote locations had expended 2 billion dollars in producing a weapon that would revolutionize human affairs. It was the outcome of that solitary meeting almost six years previously between Roosevelt and an adviser. It owed nothing to any other American politician, everything to the president. It was the ultimate vindication of Roosevelt's fitness for the presidency, the fitness that again and again he had exhibited to contemporaries, and consequently exalted the office that he exercised. 'Sitting calmly at his desk in the study of the White House, receiving constantly the reports of what was one of the blackest and most tragic episodes in all of American history,' wrote Sumner Welles, seeing him in the immediate aftermath of Pearl Harbor,

> he demonstrated that ultimate capacity to dominate and to control a supreme emergency which is perhaps the rarest and most valuable characteristic of any statesman. With complete grasp of every development, with full composure at the receipt of early, and fortunately, unfounded reports that Japanese landing operations in Hawaii were under way, with full realization of all that Pearl Harbour implied and all that it might still further imply to the future of the American people, the President never for one split-second ceased to be master of the fate of his country.[31]

Clearly, Roosevelt had set a standard to which few of his successors could aspire; none, indeed, achieved his level of greatness. Yet one only has to consider what the presidency had been under Hoover, let alone Coolidge or Harding, to see how far the office had grown in prestige and importance. Roosevelt's twelve years in the White House had witnessed a succession of crises; if the crises in some shape or form were to continue, even a lesser president would be enhanced by his office.

4   Truman and the Commitment to Internationalism

Roosevelt's immediate successor Harry Truman was a case in point. Few were more aware of his limitations than Truman himself, whose career demonstrated the role of chance and the rough ways of democratic politics. Actually only two years younger than Roosevelt, his path to the White House had nothing of that sense of predestined inevitability that encompassed his predecessor. There is a certain irony in the fact that Truman's first trip to Europe was with the American Expeditionary Force to France in the First World War; the second to the Potsdam Conference as president at the end of the Second World War. It was all of a part of his entry into politics. On demobilization in 1919 Truman returned to his native Missouri and started a men's haberdashers; the business failed and the need to earn a living drove him into the one profession which required no training, politics. It is ironic to reflect that had the business succeeded Truman might have spent a blameless life selling men's shirts, socks and underwear. Instead, attaching himself to one of the most notorious political machines in the country, by 1934 he had earned his passage sufficiently to be elected senator in the year that saw the nation endorse the policies of the New Deal. A Roosevelt loyalist who came from a state in the Midwest, the centre of isolationism, he was lucky to retain his seat in 1940. During the war he enhanced his hitherto mediocre reputation by chairing a Senate Committee to Investigate the National Defence Programme which, contrary to many such, was not an ego trip for its chairman, did useful work and is reckoned to have saved the American taxpayer 15 billion dollars. In 1944 the Democratic Party regulars were determined to have one of their own as vice-presidential candidate; this meant dropping vice-president Henry Wallace, a Progressive Republican and former secretary of agriculture chosen by Roosevelt in 1940 to broaden his electoral appeal. Truman, a party loyalist to his fingertips, got the job instead; three months after his fourth Inauguration Roosevelt was dead; Truman had inherited the greatest democratic office on earth.

Perhaps the first judgement on Truman is that he was right on the big decisions. He grew into the job, surprisingly so, and the hesitancies and insecurities of his early months gradually receded, to be replaced by a mature, stronger, more confident figure who executed a series of decisions that built on the legacy of Roosevelt. He never perhaps quite lost the image of the provincial and there was always a partisan streak to him that diminished him somewhat and made one always conscious of the fact that he was a politician rather than a statesman. In some ways he did himself an injustice for many of his achievements were considerable in adapting America to a postwar world that sought social progress at home and security from new dangers abroad, and were instrumental in securing Truman his unexpected election victory against the odds in 1948. Truman's unique quality was his courage; sometimes this could degenerate into belligerency or pigheadedness, but at its noblest it was a willingness to take unpopular decisions, come what may, and stick with them in the certainty that he was right. 'I am still inclined to think,' wrote one experienced observer, 'that Harry Truman is an overrated president, although he had more guts, more sheer, naked guts, than any leader the United States has had during this century, barring, perhaps, Theodore Roosevelt.'[32]

In many ways, his record was a remarkably good one. Dean Acheson, one of the leading participants in those years who ended his career as secretary of state, spoke of being 'Present at the Creation'. There is certainly a sense in which American foreign policy involved a great deal of new construction, perhaps a more fitting word than 'creation' for what was achieved. Truman was more a builder than he was an architect. He never appeared able to rise to the inspirational heights of Roosevelt; his speeches were unmemorable, and he never made the transition from American president to world statesman. In fact he lacked that true 'creativity' which is the mark of the genius, of opening up new possibilities inherent in a situation, of speaking for humanity in general; he lacked a certain generosity of spirit that had always saved his predecessor from pettiness.[33]

Still even if initially Truman seemed to find the mantle of Roosevelt an ill-fitting garment, if he never attained the stature of the latter, if he lacked inspiration and charisma, he acted decisively when the occasion warranted it. Indeed, he was required to confront a succession of problems that soon transformed him from the bumbling vice-president of popular mythology. Firstly, he had to insist that the Yalta Agreement be adhered to over Poland, then he was meeting and bargaining with Stalin at Potsdam, soon he had to determine the use of the atomic bomb. This last was an awesome decision from a man not four months in the White House, who had not even known of the bomb's development before taking office. There followed the need to face down the Russians in Iran and their aspirations for access to the eastern Mediterranean, and move tentatively as Truman felt his way from a policy of grudging, empty cooperation to open opposition to the Soviet Union. By 1947 he was promulgating the Truman Doctrine and urging Congress to grant funds to aid Greece and Turkey, thereby allowing America to take over Britain's traditional role in the Near East. Three months later he also backed the Marshall Plan, officially the European Recovery Programme, which provided the basis for a quarter of a century of sustained growth and prosperity for Western Europe. In 1948 the Berlin airlift signalled Western willingness to stand by its commitments, and the following year the North Atlantic Treaty Organization came into being. For the first time the United States would have a 'permanent' and indeed, 'entangling' alliance; she was committed to the defence of Western Europe and recognized the interdependence of the nations on both sides of the Atlantic. All in all, it was a remarkable record; manifest expressions, moreover, of presidential authority that tipped the balance still further in the direction of the Executive.

Much is made of the fact that Truman was an insecure figure who masked his insecurity in a display of aggression, a classic psychological ploy, and it was widely assumed at the outset that he would not be re-elected and might well, indeed, even be denied renomination by his party. Dean Acheson tells a revealing anecdote of finding himself the sole administration official on the platform in Washington to welcome back the president as he returned by train after the disastrous congressional elections of 1946 which restored power to the Republicans after sixteen years. Nobody likes a loser – least of all, apparently, ambitious politicians. Still, perhaps in some obscure way it was this that saved him. Somewhere along the line, Truman must have communed inwardly with himself and resolved that if indeed it was his fate to be ejected by the electorate then he could at least take with him back into private life his own integrity. At least he would know that he had done his best, according to his lights, to live up to the responsibilities of a job he had not sought; and that historians might think better of him than apparently did contemporaries. He would do what he thought right and calm his conscience, rather than what might please in a vain attempt to woo the voters, and in the end please nobody. And it was this honesty that his contemporaries too came to recognize and that persuaded enough of them to return him to the White House. Yet Truman's weak political position only serves to underline the powers inherent in his office. Notwithstanding the domestic constraints upon him, he was still able to act decisively when the situation demanded it. Hence the famous, though not perhaps wisest, advice of Republican Senator Vandenberg of Michigan, that if Truman wanted to get money out of a Republican-controlled, economy-minded Congress to fund his aid programme for Greece and Turkey, he should 'scare the hell out of the American people'. It illustrates how presidents could appeal over the heads of legislators to get them to do their bidding.[34]

Still there was a price to be paid. In a few short years a confident America, the undoubted victor of the Second World War, with all her territory intact and free of the experience of enemy occupation, that had serenely witnessed the inexorable triumph of her forces over all her enemies, became a fearful society. She seemed to many to be more an oppressor than a liberator. In something like a decade, America had moved from carefree isolationism, wanting to go her own way, to a threatened and threatening global superpower committed to a life-and-death struggle with the communist world. It was a result few would have anticipated when Roosevelt first moved to resist Fascism.

The trouble lay partly in the speed of the transition. Foreign policy and international involvement was a new concept for most Americans. Notwithstanding that their own national development had had its share of self-interested calculation – the war with Mexico for example – the concept of 'Manifest Destiny' had eased their consciences, whilst its speedy and successful conclusion made war seem an isolated event. Unlike most Europeans, who had learned over hundreds of years to live in close, watchful, proximity to their neighbours, where today's ally may be tomorrow's enemy and today's enemy tomorrow's friend – the pattern indeed of much of European history – Americans had moved from innocence to involvement too quickly. They had done so without developing the sophistication of older nations, who had lived out Clausewitz's dictum that 'War is the continuation of politics by other means.'[35]

This popular innocence had shown itself even in the way the American people had wished to prosecute the war: quickly, directly and with little thought for the aftermath. To the American public mind, wars solved problems; Europeans knew they merely gave rise to new ones. Given the abundance of the Americans' goodwill and their belief in the value of their own institutions and way of life, it was hard to accept that the world could not be made into their image. As Dean Acheson warned: 'We have got to understand that all our lives the danger, the uncertainty, the need for alertness, for effort, for discipline will be upon us. This is new to us. It will be hard for us.'[36] Fighting and winning a world war was a relatively easy challenge; it was far harder and less easily understood that the war against communism would be of a different calibre. Hence the Cold War psychosis that so soon gripped America and produced the paradox that the only power at least until 1949 to have atomic weapons, and thereafter clear superiority, was obsessed with the fear of the communist threat.

Roosevelt in 1936 had spoken of 'This generation of Americans' having 'a rendezvous with destiny'. Perhaps, inevitably, an element of messianism crept in. Roosevelt was the subtlest president of the twentieth century; none of his successors equalled his dexterity of thought. Roosevelt could blend profound truths, expressed in memorable phrases, with circumspect action. If he was the teacher, his successors were at best disciples. Truman, faced with a practical decision to take over from a bankrupt Britain and provide aid for Greece and Turkey, had turned that local issue into a worldwide commitment to support free governments everywhere. 'I believe that it must be the policy of the United States to support free peoples who are resisting attempted subjugation by armed minorities or by outside pressures. I believe that we must assist free peoples to work out their own destinies in their own way. I believe that our help should be primarily through economic and financial aid, which is essential to economic stability and orderly political processes.'[37]

Thus the 'Truman Doctrine' soon justified American intervention in the unlikeliest of places. First Truman fought to defend South Korea under the auspices of the United Nations; later presidents would regard the Lebanon, South Vietnam, the Caribbean and Central America as proper places for American intervention. It was a failure to balance means and ends that would become the besetting weakness of postwar American foreign policy. Where Roosevelt had thought in terms of cooperation between the Great Powers after 1945, this had turned into confrontation; and whereas a global campaign against fascism had secured worldwide endorsement, support for a global crusade against communism inspired more selective support. The dilemma of American foreign policy, never satisfactorily resolved, was how one advocated freedom, that is a revolutionary notion, and made oneself the spokesman for democracy, yet upheld an economic system that seemed to deny the egalitarianism advocated in the political sphere. Thus an uneasy tension existed between self-sufficiency at home and proselytizing abroad. Opposing communism, offering a better alternative, required a two-pronged attack, but the economic weapon always lagged behind the political. In a world where hunger was the prime consideration, a lot of the assumptions of American foreign policy were simply irrelevant. The United States often seemed a capitalist country first, a free country second.

In many ways this seems an unfair reaction, given American generosity as exemplified by aid programmes. The Marshall Plan, for example, was an inspired humanitarian attempt to underwrite the Truman Doctrine's economic side without discrimination.

Our policy is directed not against any country or doctrine but against hunger, poverty, desperation and chaos. Its purpose should be the revival of a working economy in the world so as to permit the emergence of political and social conditions in which free institutions can exist. Such assistance ... must not be on a piecemeal basis as various crises develop ... should provide a cure rather than a mere palliative.[38]

But that, however well intended, begged a lot of questions. For a start, there was clearly an element of self-interest: fear of a return to a 1930s-type Depression haunted American policy makers, and the promotion of markets for American goods had an obvious pay-off. Some would see it as economic imperialism. In any case this European Recovery Programme would have the effect of further dividing Western from Eastern Europe. In other parts of the world American assistance often seemed patronizing and insensitive or misdirected and exploitative, even if the characterization was an unfair one. Perhaps it reflected the gulf between industrial capitalist wealth and agrarian poverty, but for much of the Third World, the American experience offered no lessons of practical value; the transformation of Russia, from a semi-feudal agrarian society before 1917 to a modern industrial state in a generation, did. It was a path undeveloped nations hoped to emulate. The bafflement Americans showed in 1949 when they 'lost' China was a striking testimony to how far they still thought in Atlantic terms. In Europe, American policy was a success; in Asia, in Africa, in Latin America even, its own backyard as Americans liked to think, the record was more qualified. There was a lack of imagination in American understanding of Third World aspirations. Traditionally Americans had disliked colonialism, though they had certainly practised an economic version. The Second World War, however, had acted as a catalyst.

By the time of the Bandung Conference of 1955, where over 60 per cent of the human race was represented, the world was faced with a challenge as great as that posed to the Atlantic world in 1776 by the Declaration of Independence. Worse, with considerable tact and self-effacement, Chou En-lai, the Chinese foreign minister, had managed to place his country at the centre of the gathering. The ambitions of the African and Asian nations to achieve parity of status with the Europeans was blessed by Chinese communism.

One might contrast this ability to exploit an opportunity with the failure of American leadership after the Second World War to grasp this reaction against colonialism. Roosevelt had perceived clearly enough the tide of history; it was one of the areas where he clashed with Churchill, but his vision was not impaired by the need to service anti-communism. One example is especially poignant. Roosevelt, always the anti-colonialist, had toyed with the idea of some form of trusteeship for Vietnam after the war; he did not relish the return of the French as if nothing had happened since 1940. He knew that one could not put the clock back, that the days of European rule of subject peoples was numbered, and that the moral authority of the French, indeed of white men generally, had been destroyed by Japanese occupation. Tragically, his death and the multiplicity of problems in 1945 allowed the French to resume their rule. Soon Dean Acheson would be disparaging Ho Chi Minh, the Nationalist leader: 'The question whether Ho [is] as much nationalist as Commie is irrelevant. All Stalinists in colonial areas are nationalists', labelling him 'the mortal enemy of native independence in Indochina'.[39]

This was the same Ho Chi Minh who issued a Declaration of Independence modelled on the American; fought a guerrilla war against the Japanese with American assistance; and at least eight times pleaded with Washington after the war for help in securing his nation's independence. When one considers the subsequent tragedy of American–Vietnamese relations, one must regard the inability of the Americans to live up to their historic role of exemplar of freedom as nothing short of a disaster.

Faced with a bipolar world, or so initially it had seemed, as Acheson's comments bear witness, America had decided to 'contain' the Soviet Union:

...it is clear that the main element of any United States policy toward the Soviet Union must be that of a long-term, patient but

firm and vigilant containment of Russian expansive tendencies
... it will be clearly seen that the Soviet pressure against the free
institutions of the western world is something that can be contained by the adroit and vigilant application of counter-force at a
series of constantly shifting geographical and political points,
corresponding to the shifts and manoeuvres of Soviet policy, but
which cannot be charmed or talked out of existence.[40]

George Kennan, the progenitor of 'containment', saw it as a long-
term political response to a sustained political threat that might only
cease when the inherent tensions within the Communist Party
imploded to reveal the chaos and weakness of Soviet society underneath. This, at least, allowed the opportunity of a positive approach
in which what America stood for would have been a powerful
factor. The strength of American institutions, her self-confidence,
her prosperity, her belief in her own values would have conspired
to weaken her adversary by comparison. Instead, 'containment'
soon came to be conceived in military terms. This was, inevitably
far less flexible and appealing to uncommitted nations; it also made
an arms race between the major powers inevitable. The National
Security Act of 1947 creating a new Cabinet Department of Defence,
an advisory National Security Council, and a foreign intelligence-
gathering Central Intelligence Agency, was a new phenomenon for
a country that had only so recently been so intentionally uninvolved
in foreign and military concerns. It meant an ever-increasing commitment, indeed obsession, to a national defence that was less and
less reliable. Roosevelt had spoken of having 'nothing to fear but
fear itself'; soon American security was avowedly postulated on the
'balance of terror'.[41]

Truman had used the atomic bomb; the suspicion remained that it
was not only the Japanese he had in mind. The chance for America
to share her knowledge when she alone possessed it foundered on
irreconcilable conditions; America would not abandon the bomb
until the Russians agreed to open inspections; the Russians would
not agree to open inspections until the Americans abandoned the
bomb. The free transmission of scientific ideas was now hedged
around by governmental secrecy. By 1946 America would pass the
Atomic Energy Act which forbade the sharing of atomic secrets
even with the British who had played so important a part in their
earlier discovery and who had taken their considerable scientific
expertise across the Atlantic to cooperate on Project Manhattan.

Scientists were now governmental operatives, sometimes at considerable cost to their consciences – the freer spirits or the more disturbed retreated to their university laboratories. In the race to defeat Nazism, the goal of an atomic bomb had seemed justifiable; Project Manhattan had inspired a scientific camaraderie. 'When it went off, in the New Mexico dawn, that first atomic bomb,' recalled Robert Oppenheimer, its principal creator, 'we thought of Alfred Nobel, and his hope, his vain hope, that dynamite would put an end to wars. We thought of the legend of Prometheus, of that deep sense of guilt in man's new powers, that reflects his recognition of evil, and his long knowledge of it. We knew that it was a new world, but even more we knew that novelty itself was a very old thing in human life, that all our ways are rooted in it.'[42]

The American president now held a terrible power. Soon, the Soviet Union would have the bomb, sooner than was expected; espionage plausibly explained yet another apparent foreign policy failure. A 'Red Scare' orchestrated into a full-scale phobia by Senator Joseph McCarthy of Wisconsin, would shortly grip America; a president who had tried 'to scare hell out of the American people' discovered that it was easier to raise the political temperature than to reduce it. Fear is a bad counsellor, but as the 1940s ended it was not far below the surface across America. To Truman there seemed no alternative but further military commitment. For the first time in her history America joined a permanent peacetime alliance, NATO. Truman authorized the building of the hydrogen bomb in a desperate race to keep ahead of the Soviet Union. Then a fundamental review of defence strategy culminated in the famous planning paper produced by the National Security Council, NSC 68, which assumed an expansionist Russia bent on world conquest and subversion. Only America stood in her way; only military power was effective as a weapon; now America was committed to supporting the universalist policy of military containment of the Soviet Union. Almost before the ink was dry, North Korea invaded South Korea. To NSC 68's protagonists it was both a proof and an opportunity; under the auspices of the United Nations, America entered the Korean War. By 1952 there would be a million men under arms and the defence budget would reach 50 billion dollars. Worse still, the expenditure did not even prove effective. After initial successes in Korea, the American forces had moved north bent on achieving the country's reunification. Then upwards of 200,000 Chinese troops, almost as if from nowhere, entered the conflict, and the Americans were sent reeling back down the Korean peninsula; the result was deadlock and military stagnation.

Still, the decision to go to war, itself, was a particularly striking demonstration of presidential power; Truman did not even seek a congressional declaration of war. This was unwise. It is always a good idea to maximize one's support and when the war turned sour, as wars usually do, those who had not voted for it felt no need to support it, or at least, could indulge the luxury of criticism of decisions they did not like. One, the sacking of General MacArthur for what Truman deemed to be insubordination, was a striking reminder, as it was meant to be, of presidential authority. Truman was the commander-in-chief. If the war was to be fought, it would be fought on his terms. Similarly, it would be another presidential decision that ended it.

5 Eisenhower Assumes Control

If Truman took America to war, Eisenhower brought it back again. In fact, he clinched his election victory in 1952 by the promise to go to Korea. Faith in the ability of one man to negotiate a successful peace proved well founded, not in the sense that he achieved any great wonders but with his vast military authority, he was able to sell to the American people the less than perfect armistice that grew out of military deadlock. His Democratic opponent Adlai Stevenson, the governor of Illinois, would never have been able to emulate his assurances to his countrymen that the solution actually achieved was satisfactory, whilst Truman commented bitterly that had he himself proposed the same terms the Republicans 'would have tried to draw and quarter' him.[43]

Moreover, canny as usual, Eisenhower realized that unless the war was to be the albatross of his presidency, he had to end it quickly. Presidential initiative, including the oblique threat to the Chinese that unless they negotiated an agreement, resort might be had to nuclear weapons, achieved an armistice virtually within six months of his Inauguration. And the prestige of former supreme commander and first commander-in-chief of NATO qualified him uniquely to take over the presidency when the security of the nation and the free world generally seemed under threat.

It was Eisenhower's belief that Truman had cheapened the presidency. Partly, this was a matter of personal style; Truman was the most rumbustious chief executive since Teddy Roosevelt and enjoyed a scrap. But he had a deep reverence for the office he held and was determined to pass on to his successors the position without the slightest impairment of its powers and privileges. Here, very clearly, he succeeded. And though Eisenhower made great play of believing in the separation of powers and working with Congress, in part this was a reflection of the reality of domestic politics, where Democrats held sway. Accordingly, Eisenhower was committed to accepting twenty years of liberalism; but the reverse was that in foreign affairs he expected, and received, bipartisan support. It could hardly have been otherwise. The sources of information alone available to a president made any challenge to him faintly ridiculous; when these were allied to a depth of judgement that had been tested since the early days of the Second World War, they made criticism foolhardy. Quite simply, no congressman was remotely his equal.

Moreover, this congressional cooperation made for national strength. Eisenhower appreciated that a Joint Resolution of Congress, for example, could reinforce him in his dealings abroad. The American nation was seen standing together foursquare behind their president. Where he knowingly led, they would loyally and uncritically follow. Indeed Eisenhower had almost moved sideways into the presidency; he had a self-assurance that with the death of Stalin in 1953 and the departure of Churchill in 1955 made him the most experienced foreign policy expert in the world. The self-assurance, indeed, was such that Eisenhower could even afford to look incompetent if it suited his purpose; a revealing contrast with the early days of Truman in the White House, when inexperience and insecurity had to be masked by aggressive confrontation. Eisenhower allowed subordinates to appear to take decisions, notably the unpopular ones. He was more than happy to let John Foster Dulles, his cheerless secretary of state, act as a lightning conductor for hostile criticism. He was quite willing, if necessary, to mumble his way through press conferences and keep opponents guessing his intentions rather than give a straight answer that tied his hands; content to give an impression of grandfatherly complacency that cooled tensions and fitted the mood of the country. If by the end of his period in office the act had worn a bit thin, he had steered his country from Cold War to Cold Peace, lost no American lives in battle, and delivered a calmer, less tense nation, more at ease with itself, to his successor. Eisenhower was a Democrat's Republican; he understood the innate American desire for middle-of-the-road non-partisanship. If Roosevelt had a New Deal and Truman a Fair Deal, Eisenhower's might have been called the Same Deal. It suited the majority temper of the country; the liberal achievements of the previous twenty years were safe at home, the nation was safe abroad.

Nor was this the product of Coolidge-like inertia. The times demanded constant vigilance. But it was vigilance matched by prudence. Eisenhower understood the uses of power better, perhaps, than any twentieth-century president, with the exception of Franklin Roosevelt. Indeed, his sparing use of it was a reflection of his deep perception into its nature and limitations. As one adviser noted: 'Eisenhower had his own way of getting results, and although they were sometimes subtle, they were also sometimes uncommonly effective in the end.'[44]

Indeed, Eisenhower realized acutely that such was the power of the presidency that excessive activity might even diminish its effectiveness. The 1950s were, in fact, perilous years; for the first time mankind confronted the horrors of the H-bomb; reassurance at home and strength abroad were best supplied by a president who moved slowly and cautiously when confronted with a challenge, but who eschewed indecisiveness and vacillation. This was Eisenhower's forte. The product of a staff system learned in the army, he introduced a more methodical, even bureaucratic, organizational apparatus on entering the White House. The Cabinet, the National Security Council, even the probably superfluous Operations Coordinating Board, met regularly every week. Critics might find this over-complex compared to the free-wheeling days of Franklin Roosevelt, and it was easy to gibe that Eisenhower was endeavouring to run the Executive branch of government as if it were the Army. But this is to miss the reasons for the innovation. Eisenhower wanted close, methodical study of various policy options based on as full an appraisal of relevant information as possible; the raw material, as it were, for informed decisions. Such bureaucracies are only ineffectual if they impede or delay decisions, and Eisenhower's was predicated on the assumption that at its head was a president who could and would decide, and then ensure that his decisions were faithfully executed. If Eisenhower's system was more formal, it was also infused with his own capacity for ultimate decision making.

Sometimes this could be explicit; here Eisenhower's lofty eminence burnished the presidency. At other times, he worked behind the scenes, content to judge by results. Genuinely believing that a great deal could be achieved if one did not care too much who got the credit, Eisenhower used the delicate arts of influence, suggestion and persuasion, when more head-on tactics might have been counterproductive. His cautious patience and a willingness to let sleeping dogs lie hid proactive alertness. As he said about the eight years of peace America enjoyed under his leadership: 'It didn't just happen.'[45]

Eisenhower realized that the uniqueness of his office conferred a moral prestige that was international in scope; he understood that he was the leader of the free world, yet that ensuring its security was a more subtle process than mere military might. The hallmark of his presidency was its restraint. As the one professional soldier to become president in the twentieth century, war held no fascination for Eisenhower who had spent a lifetime mastering it. And though not afraid of force – on more than one occasion he threatened the use of atomic weapons – he saw the limitations of a policy that condemned vast proportions of the national budget to be utilized for defence. The price was seriously impairing the development of American society and permanently disrupting the economy.

Eisenhower, a more ambitious man than he liked people to realize, had really entered politics because of this concern for national security and a legitimate belief that he was uniquely qualified in the field of foreign affairs. Equally, he nurtured an anxiety about high spending which he thought inflationary and potentially as lethal a threat to the nation's integrity as danger from abroad. Thus he would plan to reduce the size of the American army and rely on nuclear weapons for national protection – in the defence review he undertook on taking office, concerned to cut costs and balance the budget without weakening American security. The reliance on nuclear weapons was a calculated gamble, one that perhaps only a man totally at ease with himself could have taken. Eisenhower could play military poker secure in the knowledge that many times before in his career he had demonstrated wise judgement and calculated the odds correctly. A man who had postponed the invasion of Europe for twenty-four hours at the last moment, and then decided to go ahead in circumstances that were not entirely propitious, was clearly level-headed.

A considerably more proactive president than the public at the time gave him credit for, Eisenhower successfully wielded American power without directly using it. The threat of 'massive retaliation', to use the jargon of the 1950s, was based on the calculated assumption that it would never be tested; this was a clever policy but a dangerous one. For a start it meant goodbye to the casual promise in the 1952 election of a 'liberation policy' for Eastern Europe. The East Germans in 1953, the Poles and, most tragically, the Hungarians in 1956 were to find out how empty these commitments were. 'Containment', the policy of the Democrats, was slated as 'negative, immoral, and futile': now Republicans would continue it.[46]

Increasingly, too, it meant that national security policy became a matter only for the initiate; an informed public debate became less and less possible in the arcane world of nuclear weapons strategy. Even the scientists were muzzled. 'It is a grave danger for us that these decisions are taken on the basis of facts held secret . . . wisdom itself cannot flourish and even the truth not be established, without the give and take of debate and criticism. The facts, the relevant facts, are of little use to an enemy, yet they are fundamental to an understanding of the issues of policy.'[47]

Thus Oppenheimer, 'the father of the atomic bomb', denied security clearance because of alleged communist connections and doubts about the H-bomb, retired to Princeton. Scientists now worked for the government on the latter's terms, not their own, and though Eisenhower pursued the hope of peaceful uses of atomic energy in the future and opening one's skies for others' inspection, for the present the arms race continued.

It was a problem Eisenhower grappled with to the end of his presidency. It was questionable whether for all its prodigious expenditure, America enjoyed any greater sense of security; the Russian launch of *Sputnik* in October 1957 was at the very least a remarkable propaganda coup which seemed to emphasize American vulnerability, all the more frightening because new in her experience. Now it was quite clear that neither the Atlantic Ocean, nor indeed the Pacific, were moats behind which America could shelter. If the Russians had the rocket thrust to launch an unmanned object in space, presumably they could do the same for intercontinental ballistic missiles (ICBMs), the first of which they had successfully fired two months previously; they could even be directed over the North Pole and across Canada. It was a salutary and frightening lesson in geography. The threat affected American society. 'Our military organization today,' Eisenhower conceded at the end of his presidency, bears little relation to that known of any of my predecessors in peacetime, or indeed by the fighting men of World War II or Korea. Until the latest of our world conflicts, the United States had no armaments industry... But now we can no longer risk emergency improvisation of national defense; we have been compelled to create a permanent armaments industry of vast proportions. Added to this, three and a half million men and women are directly engaged in the defense establishment. We annually spend on military security more than the net income of all United States corporations.

It was a tribute to the open-mindedness of the former general, and it gave his words added authority, that Eisenhower discerned the dangers in such a development to American democracy itself. 'In the councils of Government, we must guard against the acquisition of unwarranted influence, whether sought or unsought, by the military-industrial complex. The potential for the disastrous rise of misplaced power exists and will persist.'

The influence of science had come a long way since Einstein and Szilard had written to Roosevelt; now it was at the very heart of government. Again the implications were disturbing as Eisenhower warned: '... in holding scientific research and discovery in respect ... we must also be alert to the equal and opposite danger that public policy could itself become the captive of a scientific-technological elite.'[48]

In the 1830s Tocqueville had acutely noted how in a democratic society, men had a preference for practical, as opposed to theoretical science since 'Equality stimulates each man to want to judge everything for himself.'[49] Benjamin Franklin was the archetypal American scientist. How could this tradition be maintained when politicians, let alone the electorate, were totally unversed in the scientific expertise needed to understand sophisticated weapons systems and technology? There were scientific advisers galore but theirs was not the ultimate decision. In 1946 Dean Acheson, then under-secretary of state, together with John J. McCloy, the former assistant secretary of war, were briefed by Oppenheimer on nuclear physics. On a blackboard 'he drew little figures representing electrons, neutrons, and protons, bombarding one another, chasing one another about, dividing and generally carrying on in unpredictable ways. Our bewildered questions seemed to distress him. At last he put down the chalk in gentle despair, saying, "It's hopeless. I really think you two believe neutrons and electrons *are* little men!" We admitted nothing.'[50] Acheson tells the story against himself, but three years later he was one of those who, in the wake of the Russian atomic bomb, pressed hardest for the American development of the 'super' or hydrogen bomb, as it was later labelled. Again, the power of the Executive was enhanced; the president was saddled with a unique responsibility.

Sputnik had scared the American public, perhaps unreasonably, but Democratic allegations of a missile gap between the Americans and the Russians made good politics. Moreover, there was always the reverse danger that one could put too much faith in science; a concentration on missiles might induce a Maginot Line mentality that would merely invite a less frontal assault. This was to be the development of the 1960s; the wars of national liberation where nuclear forces were irrelevant. This was a style of war to which Eisenhower was unaccustomed, and with innate shrewdness he had avoided or limited those areas where such wars threatened. Thus his reluctance to bail the French out of Vietnam: privately he was scathing about the French, 'a hopeless, helpless mass of pro- toplasm', and their armies' stupidity in getting trapped in the up- country Highland Fortress at Dien Bien Phu.[51]

And Eisenhower's careful observance of the Geneva Accords after the French departure in 1954, limiting American military ad- visers to a maximum of 685, was the recognition of an old soldier that conventional battlefield warfare and guerrilla forces do not mix. Eisenhower understood the former; he did not intend to en- courage the latter, although he professed himself a believer in the 'falling domino' theory whereby if one country fell to communism it would lead to the collapse of another. But his method of dealing with the problem was through conventional alliances such as SEATO, the South East Asia Treaty Organization. Alternatively, he would use client rulers, economic assistance and covert CIA oper- ations.[52]

When Eisenhower did move, he moved in hard: Guatemala, for instance, in 1954, or the Lebanon in 1958. The efficacy of such inter- ventions lay in their infrequency. Eisenhower had turned to nuclear weapons as a way of cutting defence costs. But the economies this made – the defence budget initially dropped from 50 billion dollars to 34 billion and was kept to under 40 largely by reducing the size of the army – both required and encouraged restraint in the use of conventional forces. Eisenhower knew, at times even seemed obsessed with the thought, that bankruptcy at home could destroy America as effectively as communism abroad. Like the shrewder of his predecessors, he too understood the equation between a strong America at home and her effectiveness overseas. He was convinced that a healthy and vigorous economy was vital to winning the Cold War: 'We want democracy to survive for all generations to come, not to become the insolvent phantom of tomorrow.'[53]

6   Kennedy the Cold War Warrior

Still, even if 'massive retaliation' came to seem rigid and inflexible and scared America's friends almost as much as her enemies, nuclear weapons were irrelevant in wars of national liberation; thus John Kennedy encouraged the development of counter-insurgency forces capable of rapid deployment. Once developed, the temptation to use them was almost overwhelming; in a curious way the Eisenhower defence policy, because of the risks involved, had made for moderation. The acid test of this new approach was to be Vietnam; carelessly Kennedy broke the Geneva Accords and increased the number of American military 'advisers'. By his death there would be over 16,000.

Eisenhower had grown up under Franklin Roosevelt's tutelage; his vision was of an America slowly forced by circumstance to become the leading world power – 'a rendezvous with destiny' that had not been sought but forced upon it. This, together with his age, made for restraint and some sense of limitation, but it was not a restraint shared by 'a new generation of Americans' to whom, his successor in 1961 proudly claimed, 'the torch has been passed'; the phrase itself is indicative. Kennedy promised that America would 'pay any price, bear any burden, meet any hardship, support any friend, oppose any foe to assure the survival and the success of liberty'.[54] It was a staggering commitment. Instead of a piecemeal policy based on the demands of each situation, pragmatic, localized and restrained, any threat to American interests anywhere, however they were defined, would be seen as threatening them all.

Kennedy, at least when he entered the White House, was far more a Cold War warrior than his admirers have subsequently suggested; nor was this posture helped by the need to make good his campaign charges, wholly unfounded, that America lagged behind the Soviet

Union in nuclear warheads. The accelerated missile-building programme his administration launched, coupled with an emphasis on
first-strike capability and civil defence, not surprisingly frightened
the Russians. A defence budget of 40 billion dollars rose by 40 per
cent to 56 billion within two years. He also committed America to
put a man on the moon before the decade was out, an ambition
fulfilled in July 1969 at a cost of somewhere between 25 and 35
billion dollars. It was just the sort of proposal essentially designed
to outwit the Russians that had intense appeal to an American
public still smarting from *Sputnik*. Moreover, apart from the military implications – it is questionable how much the project augmented the scientific knowledge rather loosely claimed for it – there
were domestic advantages in a massive hike in military spending
generally in stimulating a still sluggish economy. It was a disturbing insight into Kennedy's more imprudent tendencies.

Meanwhile, Kennedy was fascinated by the notion of counter-
insurgency. Concerned, with some justice, that the Eisenhower
administration had been complacent about America's loss of standing in the Third World – Dulles, Eisenhower's secretary of state, had
disliked neutrals and often alienated them accordingly – Kennedy
wanted to win the battle for influence. There was an element of
youthful idealism here and, less attractively, messianism. At its
best, it produced schemes such as the Alliance for Progress, to
help Latin America, or the Peace Corps which allowed young
Americans to work in underdeveloped nations; at its worst it led
to direct intervention to oppose communist subversion. Early
warning of this ambiguity had already been given by the Bay of
Pigs fiasco when Kennedy had encouraged an attempt to topple
Castro by Cubans in exile. Kennedy determined to be an activist
president; there would be an element of glamour and role-playing.

Kennedy, however, understood the nature of his office. Few
occupants of the presidency have been more lyrical in their exposition of it; to Kennedy, 'The Presidency is the vital centre in our
whole scheme of government.'[55] His youthfulness suggested that his
supporters would not be disappointed. Perhaps the latter explains
his election; it gave him a charisma, a dynamism that contrasted with
a predecessor who had understood that non-interference was often
the highest wisdom and restraint the true test of statesmanship. It
was a policy based on strength, but its achievements, which were
considerable, involved much behind-the-scenes negotiation that
could seem dull, and watchful patience lacked the excitement of

public action. Moreover, it was almost thirty years since Roosevelt had campaigned for the presidency; the political order he had brought into being needed a fresh infusion. When Kennedy spoke in his Inaugural Address of 'a new generation of Americans', he cleverly contrasted his own youth with that of his predecessors. Roosevelt, Truman and Eisenhower had all been born within eight years of each other; Kennedy, born in 1917, the year America entered the First World War, was not so much a maker of modern America but its product.

It might be thought that in contrast to his predecessors, Kennedy's arrival in the White House would have represented a slackening in the growth of the presidency: his youth, his inexperience, even the fact that the Republicans gained some seats in the 1960 congressional elections, would all have told against him. He manifestly lacked the gravitas of Eisenhower or the political experience of Truman, let alone the greatness of Roosevelt. Partly, their occupancy of the office had exalted it to the point where any successor would be elevated by it. As Kennedy himself noted: 'The President bears the burden of the responsibility. No matter how many advisers you have, the President must finally choose. The advisers,' he added drily, 'may move on to new advice.'[56] It was a more elegant rendering of Truman's aphorism, 'The buck stops here.'[57] Moreover, whereas Truman had inherited the presidency and Eisenhower stepped into it, Kennedy had had to run hard for it. He could only offer promises. Hence, for Kennedy a sustained sense of crisis, if necessarily artificially induced, would facilitate his presidency. On his terms the presidency was 'the vital centre', and he committed himself to a role that was almost limitless in its assumptions: 'All this will not be finished in the first one hundred days. Nor will it be finished in the first thousand days, nor in the life of this Administration, nor even perhaps in our lifetime on this planet. But let us begin.'[58]

This was a breathtaking definition of the activist presidency. It was also the recognition that it was foreign affairs that gave the presidency virtually unrestricted scope. Here Kennedy's record contrasted with his domestic one where he simply lacked the manipulative powers to deliver the votes from a conservative-minded Congress. It was not the powers of a president that Kennedy lacked, but some of the skills. The result, therefore, in the domestic field was a sense of disappointment that put performance in foreign affairs even more at a premium. Here Kennedy did not disappoint, even if his achievements were not always the wisest or, in the case of the Bay of Pigs' abortive invasion of Cuba in April 1961, a humiliating rout. Kennedy was, in many ways, unimaginative even if towards the end of his presidency his attitudes were softening, but this stance allowed, even encouraged, a succession of crisis-management initiatives which accorded well with his concept of the presidency. From Laos, to Berlin, to Vietnam, to Cuba, the spotlight lay on Kennedy; that spotlight was at its brightest in the Cuban Missile Crisis of October 1962. An American president now risked blowing up half the world. None of the decisions that Roosevelt, Truman or Eisenhower had made throughout their years in the White House had singly been so momentous. Theirs had all allowed some possibility that error might be retrieved: Kennedy's was final.

In the greatest military threat to the United States since Pearl Harbor, reconnaissance flights over Cuba indicated that, with comparable stealth to the Japanese, but fortunately detected, the Russians were placing on the island missiles with nuclear warheads that could threaten the American mainland. In Kennedy's world view foreign issues were interdependent; even if the Russian move did not in fact upset the nuclear balance, given the megatonnage they could already unleash from Soviet bases, it appeared so to do. And as Kennedy well understood, 'in matters of national will and world leadership...such appearances contribute to reality'.[59]

The crisis evolved in secret and only became public when America chose to reveal to the world the information she had acquired and the steps she had taken in retaliation. Some subsequently questioned whether this was even necessary – whether tipping the wink to the Russians privately that America knew what they were up to wouldn't have saved face all round and facilitated a solution. It was a display of presidential power that took the world to the brink of nuclear destruction, yet America's allies were only informed, not consulted, after she had decided her course of action. In December 1950 the British prime minister had arrived hotfoot in Washington to deter Truman from any use of atomic weapons in Korea; now in 1962 even this modicum of influence was redundant. True, American policy was a restrained one. More hawkish voices calling for a pre-emptive strike had been ignored, since this would inevitably have killed Russians and Cubans, and a naval blockade had been imposed that allowed time for the Russians to turn back vessels bringing the weapons and offered a peaceable method of withdrawal. Even the notion of a naval 'quarantine' harked back to Roosevelt's speech a quarter of a century previously. In this sense American policy was non-provocative, but it relied on Khrushchev to take the path of moderation. A superpower was placing its destiny and that of its allies in the hands of its opponents; it is fortunate that Khrushchev was of an older generation and had a vivid memory of the horrors that his country had endured in the Second World War. Now he acted the part of the statesman, and in the end drew back, preferring loss of face to annihilation. The victory, however, was not all one-sided: for a start, Kennedy had to forswear any future invasion of Cuba, fear of which Khrushchev all along, not entirely plausibly, maintained was the reason the Soviet Union had installed missiles in the first place on behalf of their ally. As Nixon darkly queried, had it allowed them to 'bring an Iron Curtain down around Cuba'? It was a strange reversal within two years from when Kennedy had first criticized the Republicans for being too soft on Castro and then endeavoured to topple him to show them how it was done. Now, presumably, he was to be a permanent fixture.[60]

For their part, the Russians resolved privately never to be placed in a similar situation and took immediate steps to erase the difference in the two superpowers' respective forces. Soon they were embarked on a relentless building programme to catch up on America in strategic forces; a decade later they would have parity in numbers of strategic delivery vehicles and superiority in the total aggregate weight of warheads. For de Gaulle in France it was yet another reason not to put his country at the mercy of an American president, to develop a separate French nuclear deterrent and withdraw from NATO. The crisis, moreover, required Kennedy to promise to remove American missiles from Turkey, another NATO country. Khrushchev demanded their withdrawal, and though prestige compelled America to refuse to agree the measure publicly, Khrushchev had to be given private assurances that the missiles would be dismantled when the fuss died down. It was a frighteningly close-run thing.

The whole Cuban crisis, in fact, though it gave Kennedy the dramatic attention that he craved and placed him firmly in the centre of the action, had the most disturbing implications. In his Inaugural, Kennedy – with a certain high-school debating style – had urged, 'Let us never negotiate out of fear. But let us never fear to negotiate.' Now he began to re-examine American assumptions.

In one of the more hopeful speeches of an American president, in the year after the crisis, he suggested Americans re-examine their attitude towards the Soviet Union and the Cold War: 'We are not here distributing blame or pointing the finger of judgement. We must deal with the world as it is, and not as it might have been had the history of the last eighteen years been different.'[61]

This was a welcome revision and some relaxation of tension followed; a hotline was installed between Washington and Moscow to defuse misunderstandings and a nuclear test ban treaty was agreed, prohibiting the testing of weapons in the atmosphere. Yet the history of those last eighteen years had rested on the assumptions of the Truman Doctrine, and until America was prepared to reconsider its world role the pattern of the past seemed likely to continue. A change of heart would come about, but only as the fruit of bitter experience. The self-confidence of the United States in the 1960s required that the lesson would be a hard one.

7 The Vietnam War

The goodwill of Roosevelt had subtly over the years been transformed into what on occasions came very near to being American messianism. It was hard to assign to oneself the role of free-world defender without justifying one's actions to the point of self-righteousness. Some American politicians admittedly suffered from this trait more than others: Dulles had the disease particularly badly, but it had tended to beget an attitude that America knew best, and her power and wealth gave her a sense that her resources knew no limitation. 'We are willing to help people who believe the way we do,' Dean Acheson had vowed 'to continue to live the way they want to live,' but this was an ambiguous commitment.[62]

To fulfil it America would by the 1960s come to have military alliances with almost fifty nations, and forces stationed in well over twice that number. On reflection, it seemed unlikely that much of the 94 per cent of the world's population that was non-American would believe the way the Americans did or even share much community of interest. Traditionally, Americans had been anti-colonial, but they now inherited much of the odium reserved for former imperialists. This was in many respects unfair and certainly not understood by many Americans, but when it was the military aspect of the American presence that was so readily visible, it was fairly predictable.

The acid test was to come in Vietnam. By the time of Kennedy's assassination in November 1963, he had already increased the American military presence to over 16,000 'advisers'; some later argued that this was the first fatal misstep to disaster. His successor Lyndon Johnson was determined that Vietnam would not go the way of China. This way of thinking partly reflected Johnson's formative political experiences: as a new senator he had watched another Democratic president, Truman, berated for failing to stop the communist takeover in China, and believed that thereafter both he and Dean Acheson had lost their effectiveness. As so often, historical analogies were less than helpful: 'Everything I knew about history,' Johnson later mused, 'told me that if I got out of Vietnam and let Ho Chi Minh run through the streets of Saigon, then I'd be doing exactly what Chamberlain did in World War II. I'd be giving a big fat reward to aggression.'[63] Dean Rusk, the secretary of state of both Kennedy and Johnson, was another victim of the 'Munich syndrome', and would compare Ho Chi Minh to Hitler. Johnson, too, had lived through the Cold War; uncritically he had adopted its tenets and believed that politics stopped at the water's edge. In the 1950s as Senate Majority Leader, he had practised this faithfully, regularly supporting and ensuring Democratic votes for Republican President Eisenhower. Not surprisingly, he thought that as president the same courtesy would be extended, and he also believed that America's resolve was being tested and that the reliability of her word required that all her commitments should be equally respected. Thus in order to convince the people of West Berlin that their future was guaranteed by America, it became necessary to support rotten South Vietnamese regimes in their attempt to defeat communism. It was a curiously old-fashioned view of the world that for a start saw a global communist conspiracy and, of course, presupposed that America's resources were virtually endless. In this respect, not only did Americans misread the geopolitical intentions of their adversaries, but saw the South Vietnamese people and their leaders in the light of America's own commitment to democracy, whilst underestimating the force of nationalism in sustaining the North. It was a consequence of profound ignorance of the history, culture and politics of the area.

Moreover, America could not use the nuclear weapons that made for military superiority; instead she was forced to fight a jungle war with conventional forces, but did not modify her tactics accordingly. At first Johnson had thought he could have war on the cheap by relying on bombing; gradually he was forced to commit ground troops. In the end over half a million men would be in Vietnam and still the war seemed no nearer victory. As Clark Clifford, the dove-ish secretary of defence to whom Johnson turned when that painful truth was all too evident, reflected: 'We overestimated our allies, underestimated our adversary, and thought the American presence on the battlefield would be sufficient to change the situation in our favor. We were wrong.'[64]

It was ironic that Johnson, who had so admired Roosevelt and on whose domestic policy he had modelled his own, failed to follow his example in foreign affairs. Roosevelt had never moved far ahead of public opinion and sought always to educate it; Johnson soon divided America and never seemed able to convince enough of his countrymen that the sacrifice was worth the effort. There was never open debate with Congress and the public before policy initiatives were taken, and thus no cultivation of that necessary basis of sup-port which would have cushioned the impact of the unpredictable setbacks that long wars inevitably occasion. The appeal to American idealism that Roosevelt had always attempted seemed positively obscene in the context of the Vietnam War's miseries. A much chastened Robert McNamara, who as long-serving secretary of de-fence had been one of the war's most fervent advocates, later con-ceded: 'A nation's deepest strength lies not in its military prowess but, rather, in the unity of its people. We failed to maintain it.'[65]

Thus America was cast as the aggressor, in a war where her own security was not at stake. It seemed more the reflection of what Senator J. William Fulbright of Arkansas termed an 'arrogance of power' that 'confuses itself with virtue and tends also to take itself for omnipotence'. In this respect the desire to determine another nation's destiny accorded ill with reality: 'To go into a small, alien, undeveloped Asian nation and create stability where there is chaos, the will to fight where there is defeatism, democracy where there is no tradition of it, and honest government where corruption is almost a way of life.' It was a cause that attracted few allies abroad and much opposition at home. Even the traditional appeal to patri-otism in wartime rang increasingly hollow. There was a 'higher patriotism', which endeavoured to stop one's country doing itself harm by pursuing a wrong policy: and whereby 'to criticize one's country is to do it a service and pay it a compliment'.[66]

Already the war had shown up Executive bureaucratic confusion in endeavouring to implement so complex a policy – one, moreover, that involved a range of interlocking issues to provide a solution for a problem for which perhaps none existed. And in any case, the war itself was but part of a much broader range of foreign policies, though its increasing prioritization inevitably distorted them. Predictably, it caused other American interests to be neglected in pursuit of a victory that was in effect unattainable. Nor was the matter helped by the sort of simplistic macho posturing that had Johnson, on one celebrated occasion, letting his Texan ancestry show by telling a group of senior officers in Vietnam 'to go out there and nail that coonskin to the wall'.[67]

Soon even more muddled Executive thinking would surface. First Dean Rusk, the secretary of state, argued that 'a billion Chinese armed with nuclear weapons' were the real problem and 'if Hanoi were to take over South Vietnam by force, the effect would be to stimulate the expansionist ambitions of Communist China'. Then it was suggested that withdrawal was impossible anyway since America had never lost a war. As Senator George Aiken of Vermont wryly observed, why not 'declare victory and leave?' For the first time since Roosevelt Congress, not the president, seemed the wiser in its views on foreign issues.[68]

The war did immense damage to American society and its international position. The fact that it was a war between races did not help American standing with the coloured people of the underdeveloped nations; it helped even less with the coloured people of its own. It was American liberalism's greatest crisis. Since Roosevelt the Democratic Party had been internationalist, committed to a world order based on American power but not ruled by it. The rule of law was to be transcendent, the United Nations its visible expression; spheres of influence, at least in theory, were to be eschewed. The vision was a noble one at least in principle, if later circumscribed by Cold War realities and not always observed. Critics could point to many instances where power politics and American self-interest were pre-eminent. If support for military dictatorships, covert intervention against democratically elected but left-wing regimes, and an unfortunate tendency to believe that what was good for American business was good for the United States, were scarcely altruistic, still at best the furtherance of democratic values and social betterment had also been objectives. Moreover, Roosevelt had understood that politics was essentially a matter of education, that his task as a statesman was to persuade the electorate to share in his vision. Within a few years an isolationist nation had turned internationalist. It shared certain assumptions: that the American way of life was a desirable export; that an activist presidency might help achieve it; that the president might know best but he consulted with Congress and informed the public; that he spoke on their behalf and with their authority.

Vietnam called all this into question. Presidential authority became naked presidential power. The president led from the front, marshalling legislators in tow. Congressmen were persuaded, cajoled, bribed or threatened, pleaded with or appealed to on grounds of party loyalty, patriotism, or self-interest to support the presidential programme. That separation of powers beloved by the Founding Fathers, the keystone of the American Constitution, seemed to be dissolving. At one point Dean Rusk's deputy informed the Senate Foreign Relations Committee that events moved too quickly nowadays for the president to consult Congress before starting a war! Where then did the president's mandate end?

Ironically, it was thus in this very field of foreign affairs, where the president's authority had traditionally been strongest, that the check was to come. In 1964 if Johnson had a weakness, it was the suggestion that he lacked firmness of purpose in the field of foreign affairs. Hence his determination to take a tough line over Vietnam, which the apparently suspiciously convenient attack on American destroyers in the Gulf of Tonkin by North Vietnamese torpedo boats allowed him to do. Thus the passage of the South East Asia Resolution that summer, or the Tonkin Gulf Resolution as it became popularly known, authorizing him to defend American forces in South East Asia. Whether the incident was ambiguous, contrived, talked up, gladly seized upon or over-reacted to, has been much debated. But its importance is unquestioned. Although passed by eighty-eight votes to two in the Senate, it was, as one of the dissenters noted, a blank cheque for presidential authority. Never remotely, even in the days of congressional sycophancy towards the Executive in foreign affairs, was it assumed that this resolution would be used to legitimize over half a million American troops in South Vietnam. As the Senate Foreign Relations Committee three years later noted: 'Congress committed the error of making a *personal* judgment as to how President Johnson would implement the resolution when it had to make an *institutional* judgment, first, as to what *any* President would do with so great an acknowledgement of power, and, second, as to whether, under the Constitution, Congress had the right to grant or concede the authority in question.' As

Robert McNamara later stated: 'The fundamental issue of Tonkin Gulf involved not deception but, rather, misuse of power bestowed by the resolution.' Perhaps there is an element of self-exculpation in thus involving Congress, but it is striking testimony to the impact the President, any President, had come to have upon the Nation.[69] It was to be Johnson's undoing. The cost of the war – it would ultimately come to 141 billion dollars – proved prohibitive both in money and lives; it wrecked Johnson's ambitions for the Great Society and divided Americans more acutely than at any time since the Civil War. It also called into question the wisdom of the president, a president, moreover, who incurred immense unpopularity whilst claiming a legitimate mandate both from the electorate and from Congress. Over thirty years the president's position had been built up because of his ability to articulate the aspirations of the people; now the system seemed to have short-circuited.

Thoughtful critics, to whom a strong presidency had been a guarantor of all things good, now wondered whether this unquestioned liberal assumption had become outmoded. A strong president might lead in undesirable directions. Moreover, what the Executive was contriving was painfully visible. Television showed to a horrified public the face of modern warfare and what American forces were doing in apparent defence of democracy. The administration was at best being economical with the truth in how it reported the progress of the war, at worst downright dishonest. The president no longer spoke for the nation; for Johnson the consensus politician, this was a painful failure. He would sacrifice the presidency in atonement.

8 Nixon, Kissinger and the 1970s

The Vietnam War was a watershed in American foreign policy: the United States had attained world power apparently only to abuse it. America's allies were naturally disturbed, whilst her enemies publicly condemned and privately gloated; it was time to reassess her goals and objectives. This became the primary task of the 1970s under Richard Nixon and his National Security Adviser Henry Kissinger: to adopt a more restrained policy. It was clear that America's role would have to be more limited; and if she accepted mutual nuclear parity with the Soviet Union rather than superiority this could be compensated for by overtures to China. Thus far, the policy made sense; it aimed to drive a wedge, already widening, between the two communist powers, and arms agreements might place some limit on American–Soviet competition. The United States would play off one communist country against another. A historic trip to Peking, followed by one to Moscow, illustrated how skilfully one could balance competing interests, whilst the practice of 'linkage', in effect carrot and stick, enabled the resolution of a range of issues: concessions in one area might earn gains in another. It was a heady mixture of creative diplomacy and global geopolitics. Thus in the process of reordering superpower relations Vietnam became almost a side issue, and though one-third of American casualties were to occur under Nixon, the war which he had promised to end did eventually come to a conclusion. Yet the reordering was based on some very pragmatic assumptions: that it was in America's interests to preserve the *status quo* and that power, not law or justice, was the currency of international relations. There was a cynical realism here that was un-American in style if not always in content. It violated Americans' perceived self-image and the traditions of the nation's foreign policy since the earliest days of the Republic. This public idealism of American foreign policy could be, and often had been, woolly and muddle-headed. As critics have noted, there was underneath often a good measure of self-interest and self-deception, but at its best it did hold out the possibility of man's capacity for improvement. It also recognized the uniqueness of the American experience, what America stood for and had traditionally represented. In a way, the policy fell between two stools. As Kissinger grumbled:

> The liberal approach treated foreign policy as a subdivision of psychiatry; the conservative approach considered it an aspect of theology. Liberals equated relations among states with human relations. They emphasized the virtues of trust and unilateral gestures of goodwill. Conservatives saw in foreign policy a version of the eternal struggle of good with evil, a conflict that recognized no middle ground and could end only with victory... American idealism drove both groups to challenge us from different directions. The mainstream of liberalism found anything connected with the balance of power repugnant... we would organize mankind by a consensus of moral principles or norms of international law. Regard for the purity of our ideals inspired conservatives, contrarily, to put Communism

into quarantine. There could be no compromise with the devil. Liberals worried about the danger of confrontation; conservatives about funking it.[70]

Détente as a policy was an attempt to make Americans recognize reality – that there were limits on the nation's power, as Vietnam had demonstrated. Unfortunately, this military realism was reinforced by weaknesses in the American economy; by 1971 America was importing more goods than it exported. No longer would foreign banks be able to convert their dollars into gold as America's gold reserves were falling. With eyes fixed on the Soviet Union for a quarter of a century, the military rivalry had obscured the emergence of other economic superpowers, namely China, Japan and the European Community. In 1950 the American economy had represented just over half the world's Gross National Product; by 1960 it was 40 per cent; by 1970 it was down to 30 per cent. Since the closing years of the Second World War American political and military power had walked hand in hand with economic power. Now this predominance was being challenged: Nixon was reordering the world not from strength but from relative weakness.

This weakness was compounded by the energy crisis that hit the Western world in 1973, when the Arab OPEC nations determined to use oil as a weapon, quadrupling its price just when it was most needed. In the 1950s America had produced enough oil for her own purposes to be self-sufficient; perhaps this had encouraged an easy-come, easy-go attitude, but a decade later one in six barrels was imported from abroad, by the 1970s one in three. For an economy so dependent on oil a fourfold price increase was bound to fuel inflation; the cost of the Vietnam War had already started the increase, and now in the 1970s it was to reach double figures.

In retrospect, the 1970s were America's weakest moment, not because her problems if grave were overwhelming, but because for the first time since Roosevelt she had lost her self-confidence. Troubles had mounted: the impasse of the Vietnam War and its inglorious conclusion, the weakness of the economy and foreign competition, a reinvigorated Soviet Union using *détente* as a cover, and the Watergate scandal that undermined the Executive. In a crisis the president was supreme in foreign policy; now the loss of faith at the very least impaired his moral authority. It made Nixon unconvincing as spokesman for the free world and invited criticism of the viability of democratic institutions. Americans had set out to run the world; now apparently they could not even run their own country. If this was an unworthy gibe it was compounded by the American capacity for self-criticism.

In fact it was a hasty verdict and an unjust one. Indeed, even the way that Nixon was forced out of office was, paradoxically, a tribute to the health of American democracy. Yet it could not but have a paralysing effect on her foreign policy; the last sixteen months of Nixon's presidency were concentrated on saving his position and Gerald Ford, his successor, was limited and inexperienced. It also fell to Ford to preside over the closing chapter in the Vietnam saga: the 'peace with honor' Nixon had claimed he had obtained in 1973 was proved two years later to be a cruel illusion.[71]

Two hundred years previously, in April 1775, 'the embattled farmers' had 'fired the shot heard round the world'.[72] The War of American Independence had begun. Now in April 1975 the spectacle of the unseemly scramble from the American embassy in Saigon as Viet Cong units entered the city only underlined the humiliation inflicted on a once-idealistic anti-colonial power. It was worse than a military defeat; it was a spiritual one. And the dumping of the helicopters that carried out the evacuation over the sides of the ships of the Seventh Fleet into the South China Sea, at a cost of half a million dollars each to the American taxpayer, was testimony to the war's ultimate futility. The Vietnam War had become a national embarrassment best forgotten: not until a decade had passed would there be a Memorial to the 58,000 dead erected in Washington. Even then, it would be comparatively obscure and unnoticed: Americans unused to failure found the reality hard to accommodate.

Yet the ability to forget was a strength in the circumstances, nor did it preclude less confrontational ways of exercising influence. At its best it could lead to acting as peacemaker, in troubled parts of the world such as the Middle East and Africa. America ever since the foundation of Israel had endeavoured to support its ally without alienating the Arabs. Like all great powers, America sought stability: defusing tension where possible between the Jews and the Arabs and supporting those countries that might make a reliable ally, such as Iran or Saudi Arabia. In Africa the policy was far less successful; though in earlier years the Americans had backed the United Nations as it sought to deal with the aftermath of white colonialism, by the 1970s America was colluding with the South Africans and Portuguese as they faced wars of national liberation.

At its worst, the influence sought could be covert, through the machinations of the CIA, as in Latin America where the democratically elected Marxist Salvador Allende was toppled in Chile. Not surprisingly, these sorts of operation caused disquiet in the American public and the whole Nixon–Kissinger approach to foreign policy and the general troubles of the period led the electorate to turn against it almost as if in an attempt to revert to former innocence. The immediate beneficiary of this movement in public opinion was Jimmy Carter who, cleverly running against the Washington establishment as the outsider, promised a more moral foreign policy where human rights would be respected. It was a refreshing contrast to what had preceded it but it needed a more experienced president than Carter was, or at least one of firmer judgement. Good intentions were not sufficient and power was a factor in foreign policy that could not be lightly circumvented. Moreover, the equation between domestic and foreign strength remained valid, and the legacy of domestic problems Carter inherited and his inability to solve them made his stance on the international stage a comparatively weak one. Not, of course, that the United States did not possess awesome military might, as the various Strategic Arms Limitation Treaties of the 1970s such as SALT I and SALT II amply testified. Yet there was no doubting that American prestige, as opposed to military power, was being eroded and Americans who had grown up in the war and postwar years sensed the decline in their status.

Sometimes the signs were unmistakable. The Soviet invasion of Afghanistan in 1979 recalled the excesses of the early Cold War; the capture of American hostages in the US embassy at Teheran and the failure of the administration to release them underlined American impotence. Partly, there was a feeling of weariness, born of disappointment; for too long things had gone wrong and it induced a politics of nostalgia. Eisenhower was re-evaluated and his prestige rose accordingly, whilst the death of Kennedy seemed in retrospect to mark the end of an era. *Détente* came to be regarded as a one-way policy where America had made all the concessions and the Soviet Union had turned it to her advantage. Somehow American foreign policy seemed to lack a set of consistent principles; although Carter was a Democrat, he was also an outsider and no part of the bipartisan foreign policy establishment that had guided America's destinies since Roosevelt. Indeed, politically he was something of an aberration; there was never the coherence of purpose that had been the hallmark of previous administrations. Carter had little sense of history or historical understanding; like Hoover before him, he had the mind of an engineer more attracted to detail. True, Carter had his successes, as with the renegotiation of the Panama Canal Treaty, a courageous step which removed a source of Latin-American grievance of long duration. Then the patiently sought Camp David Accords brought about peace between Israel and Egypt, and the formalizing of relations with China (at the expense of Taiwan) rectified a long-standing absurdity. But in other respects Carter's policy was contradictory. Even his much-vaunted support of human rights had some notable blind spots, where American interests required that no action be taken. South Korea was too useful an ally to make effective protest and China too important to criticize its policy towards dissidents. Thus Carter fell between two stools; his policy's main characteristic was indecisiveness. Somehow he thought he could have the best of both worlds. 'I was familiar with the widely accepted arguments that we had to choose between idealism and realism, or between morality and the exercise of power; but I rejected those claims. To me, the demonstration of American idealism was a practical and realistic approach to foreign affairs, and moral principles were the best foundation for the exertion of American power and influence.' If only it had been that easy.[73]

At one level, it could be argued, Carter did put soul back into America's dealings with the world, his emphasis on morality and human rights echoing the Four Freedoms spirit of Franklin Roosevelt. At their best, liberal internationalists had married power and principle and the great age of American foreign policy making in the later Roosevelt and early Truman years had always recognized this idealistic side to the character of the American public, to whom old-fashioned power politics as such made limited appeal. In this respect Carter did at least breathe a fresh air of decency into the complexities of foreign policy, notwithstanding the muddle. Alas! This came with a naivety ill equipped to manage the waning of American power, the careful harbouring of influence and the delicate balancing of interests between friends and enemies. America faced a self-confident adversary in the Soviet Union of the later 1970s, exploiting the emergence of the Third World and the retreat from colonialism, profiting from *détente* but not always honouring it. So Carter sought accommodation with the Soviet Union, then admitted he had been mistaken; decided to build a neutron bomb, then countermanded the decision. Carter was soon perceived to be not only wrong in foreign policy but also, which was worse, weak. Nothing could erase the image of indecision, even incompetence, cruelly underscored by the Soviet invasion of Afghanistan to which Carter's major reply seemed to be to urge American athletes to boycott the 1980 Moscow Olympics and impose a self-damaging grain embargo. A few months later the abortive rescue of the Teheran hostages turned tragedy into farce. Democratic presidents might have taken the country into wars, even mistaken ones like Vietnam, but Roosevelt, Truman, Kennedy and Johnson were all, in their separate ways, seen to be strong leaders; Carter was not and it cost him the presidency.

9 Ronald Reagan and Anti-Communism

Faced with such confusion, even simplicity of vision seemed preferable; this was Ronald Reagan's moment. It was forty years since Roosevelt had committed the United States with Lend-Lease to be 'the arsenal of democracy'. From that time, this had been America's role either through war with the Axis powers, containment of the Soviet Union or direct intervention in local wars on the free world's periphery. Reagan, though a hard-line Republican and conservative right-winger, was a great admirer of Roosevelt, whose party he had originally supported. Though he had become disillusioned with the high cost of liberalism, the world view he had formed reflected both the naive optimism of the 1930s and the innocence that had been blighted by the Cold War. Moreover, he mourned the passing of the good old days of American pre-eminence. To Reagan, communism was the enemy and the Russians its exponents; he was always much more accommodating to the Chinese. Although committed to reducing federal expenditure and balancing the budget, he would happily plan to increase the defence budget from an incredible 1.1 trillion dollars to 1.5 trillion. America would 'find peace through strength'. It was necessary 'to speak out against those who would place the United States in a position of military and moral inferiority'. The 'evil empire', as Reagan labelled it, would be crushed by the competition. 'I believe that communism is another sad, bizarre chapter in human history whose last pages even now are being written.'[74]

There was undoubtedly a sense of public insecurity, which Reagan capitalized on to win the 1980 election. Like Kennedy twenty years before him he spoke of a missile gap, equally inaccurately. The concept of a strong America that would not be pushed around was undoubtedly appealing, an emotion Reagan played upon both to defeat Carter and to win re-election four years later. Yet it was a dangerous policy, almost trigger-happy, characterized by minor skirmishes such as clashes with Libya or the invasion of Grenada, that cheered public opinion but seemed as much for home consumption as a necessary part of foreign policy strategy. It was success on the cheap that scarcely befitted America's superpower status, but Reagan was able to carry it off because in the wider context of international relations he was enormously lucky.

Reagan's simplistic patriotism and old-fashioned bipolar vision might have been dangerous in another period but, as it happened, circumstances were with him. The election of a Polish pope in 1978, conservative and a committed anti-communist, gave added impetus and support for the Solidarity movement in Poland, and John Paul II's influence may have been the factor that persuaded the Polish authorities not to seek Russian aid in order to crush it. Equally, in the early 1980s the Soviet leadership was aged and ailing; Brezhnev, tired and sick after eighteen years in power, died in 1982; nor did his successors, Andropov in 1984 and then Chernenko in 1985, long outlive him. 'How am I supposed to get anyplace with the Russians,' Reagan complained to his wife Nancy, 'if they keep dying on me?'[75]

Thus the cumbersome Soviet administration, centralized and autocratic, was immobilized at the top throughout the first half of the 1980s. It was in no mood for adventurism. Had there been greater vigour, Reagan's provocation might have been challenged. Certainly the Kremlin was alarmed by his loose rhetoric. The Reagan administration in 'its imperial ambitions, goes so far that one begins to doubt whether Washington has any brakes at all preventing it from crossing the mark before which any sober-minded person must stop'. However, it had more pressing problems closer to home. Solidarity was the running democratic sore in Eastern Europe that helped ferment widespread dissidence, whilst beset with internal problems the Soviet leadership proved indecisive in meeting it.[76]

Reagan understood, too, that in the American system, especially in foreign affairs, the president had to give a lead. Successive presidents from Roosevelt onwards had understood this, but the debacle of the Vietnam War, Watergate, *détente* and the unhappy experiences of the later 1970s had weakened presidential self-confidence. Yet there was simply no alternative. The experiment with a reassertion of congressional authority in the 1970s was ultimately no more successful than the 1930s. True, there was a lot more wisdom in their policy, and their knowledge of this did a lot to restore their belief in the value of the role that they played. Congress had too often been supine in the face of successive presidents, with chairmen of the Senate Foreign Relations Committee, in particular, seeing it as their job to carry out presidential wishes. Fulbright in this respect had become a notable exception. This won them a lot of accolades in the White House but it is questionable whether it was the best service they could render their country. Alternatively, congressmen could be parochial, obstructionist, and ill-informed – members of the 'China lobby', for example, the so-called rabid Republican right, who were the despair of Eisenhower, and, of course, the infamous Joe McCarthy. Yet 100 senators and 435 representatives simply could not provide the central leadership or the speed of decision of the president. Gerald Ford, for example, had complained that the War Powers Act of 1973 limiting presidential freedom to commit troops in a crisis was impractical; the Supreme Court partly bore him out when they later ruled one of its central tenets unconstitutional. Presidents had faced attempts to restrict their powers before; in 1938 Roosevelt had had to fight off the Ludlow Amendment that would have required a national referendum before a declaration of war, a manifest absurdity. Almost twenty years later Eisenhower managed by one vote to defeat the Bricker Amendment that would have limited the president's ability to make Executive Agreements that did not need the consent of Congress. The plain fact was that the Constitution specified that the president had the power 'by and with the Advice and Consent of the Senate, to make Treaties'. Clearly, the balance had got out of kilter but there was no question from where, traditionally, the leadership should come.[77]

Leading, Reagan was plainly prepared to do, and by clever use of the Commander-in-Chief Clause of the Constitution he could move more matters under his unquestioned jurisdiction. Moreover, he had a piece of luck. His victory in 1980 might have been expected; what nobody could have foretold was that the Republicans would capture control of the Senate. They would keep the majority until 1986. Eisenhower had had this luxury for only two years; Nixon and Ford never. Reagan, for six whole years, could expect sympathetic support for his policies. Significantly, the most troublesome period of his presidency came when he lost this support after the 1986 elections.

Reagan, too, was the most amiable chief executive since Eisenhower; an ex-actor, he played his part well. In fact his message was often a harsh one, even with a touch of menace. The strident anti-communism and the willingness to suggest that domestic political opponents were smeared with it if they stood in his way suggested a very unamiable streak beneath the surface. One might expect it from the right-wing politician with the wealthy constituency that he undoubtedly appealed to, but it certainly succeeded in neutralizing the opposition. Reagan was not just temperamentally, but ideologically a conservative; in the atmosphere of the early 1980s after a decade of American self-doubt, simple convictions were preferred to complex uncertainties. And Reagan was too shallow a thinker to see his limitations.

By the time Reagan became president, the Cold War had lasted a generation, yet the views he propounded reflected the early stages of its development. Even in the darkest days of American–Russian confrontation, when 'containment' had moved from the political to the overtly military, there had been a core of belief that it was, at least, an unfortunate necessity. Reagan seemed to enjoy confrontation; no compromise was possible. Moreover, whereas previously some of America's anti-communist but manifestly undemocratic allies had been something of an embarrassment, Reagan willingly enlisted them in the crusade, provided that they were right-wing autocracies rather than left-wing totalitarian regimes, as the former sometimes evolved into democracies. It was a semantic distinction that convinced few non-believers and was a far cry from Roosevelt's belief in the essential 'Four Freedoms'.

In the 1980 election, Reagan had promised to increase defence spending by 7 per cent in real terms, whilst cutting taxes and balancing the budget, a set of policies George Bush for one, now his vice-president, had earlier denounced as 'voodoo economics' when campaigning for the Republican nomination against him. Reagan stuck to his first promise, dissimulated on his second and ignored his third; never had the military-industrial complex, which Eisenhower warned against, had it so good. The annual defence expenditure, even in the latter years when there was some attempt at curtailment, was almost 300 billion dollars. Thus by the end of the decade the National Debt had almost trebled from that inherited by Reagan in

1980 and had reached a fantastic, terrifying 2.6 trillion dollars. Reagan had accumulated more debt than all his predecessors put together; he was the most expensive president in American history.[78]

By the end of Reagan's first term, even if the American electorate felt more secure than four years previously, there was precious little in the way of achievement to justify this galloping expenditure. Forty years after Yalta American–Russian confrontation continued; Reagan even dreamed of SDI (the Strategic Defence Initiative). This, he hoped, would make America missile-impregnable, but the cost, if it worked, would be colossal and badly worry the Russians. It might even have encouraged a pre-emptive nuclear strike by them before it became operational, and nor were European allies cheered by the prospect of being without the nuclear umbrella. And presumably SLBMs (submarine-launched ballistic missiles) somewhere off the American coastline might still have slipped in under the cover. Moreover, the empty rhetoric of anti-communism, coupled with its practical application by intervention in parts of Latin America, constituted a poor record for the history books when Reagan's presidency came to be evaluated. A new Russian leader, Mikhail Gorbachev, was determined to modernize the Soviet Union; it would be of considerable help to the ailing Soviet economy if defence expenditure could be reduced. Logically, mutually agreed arms cuts between the superpowers would release money for domestic purposes.

Reagan's forbidding anti-communism of his first term now softened. Having gone the whole four years of it without meeting a Soviet leader, a unique postwar record, he would have no less than five meetings in his second term, and the man who had denounced 'the evil empire' would pay a visit to Moscow, its very heart. Consistency was never a Reagan hallmark. Admittedly, this was not the first time Reagan had suspended his principles: having denounced communism as such, he had soon found it expedient to continue the thaw in relations with China that had been begun by his predecessors. In 1984 he had even paid a visit to Beijing, which did his re-election chances no harm. Communism had been the enemy but only, apparently, the Russian variety. Now even Russian communism might be accommodated.

Some have contended that this was all part of some Reagan master plan. Genuinely appalled at the insanity that underlay Mutual Assured Destruction, Reagan was convinced that the only way forward was the wholesale elimination of nuclear weapons. But this would never be achieved until the Russians found the cost of the arms race prohibitive; thus the Americans would build up their armoury and negotiate from strength. Here even SDI, whether it worked or not, could be brought into play. Quite simply, the Russians could not afford to take the risk, nor could they afford to match it. It was, perhaps, the biggest bluff in history. Yet this happy analysis suggests an overall intellectual coherence and purposefulness not very obvious in other aspects of Reagan's policies; moreover, there was no guarantee that a modernizer would emerge in the Soviet Union just when Gorbachev did. Perhaps one should at least accord Reagan credit for seeing his opportunity when Gorbachev presented it. By 1987 the INF Treaty agreed to eliminate a whole class of weapons, intermediate-range nuclear forces. It was not only the first time that arms had actually been reduced, albeit by only 4 per cent; more significantly, it was clearly intended to serve as a precedent for future, more extensive reductions. The United States and the Soviet Union at long last were beginning to cooperate. Gorbachev, if his programme was to succeed at home, needed American benevolence. Reagan's luck still held; unwittingly, he had become the beneficiary of forty years of containment. That, not Reagan's strident anti-communism, is what finally paid off. But there was an American price to pay as well.

Thirty years before, Eisenhower had feared that the Soviet Union would frighten the United States into an arms race that would bankrupt the nation. Now the Reagan years told the story of how nearly this had been accomplished. By 1985 Americans were borrowing so much that for the first time since 1914 they became a debtor nation; by Reagan's last year in office they owed more than any other nation. Meanwhile, the trade deficits that had begun in 1971 relentlessly continued; and Americans made up for the shortfall in goods produced at home by importing from abroad, and borrowing to pay for the imports. The economy was unsound, a fact that did not escape the attention of investors. On Black Monday, 19 October 1987, the Stock Market crashed almost twice as far as in 1929 at the start of the Depression. At any other time it might have spelled disaster; but the lessons learned sixty years before had ensured that safeguards were built into the system. A 1930s-type Depression was not an immediate prospect unless the situation was allowed to worsen.

Meanwhile a rising tide of scandal threatened to engulf Reagan's administration. His anti-communism had particularly found expression in Latin America, almost a Reagan obsession. Here his principles didn't cost overmuch and his credentials were enhanced with his right-wing supporters. Still, it did cost money and when Congress cut off funds, resort had been had to illegal operations. Soon the Iran-Contra scandal would erupt: arms had been sold to the Iranians to secure the release of American hostages in the Lebanon and to raise funds to support the conservative forces endeavouring to overthrow the left-wing government of Nicaragua. It was a sordid story of deceit and chicanery; had not Reagan been personally popular and nearing the end of his term of office, he might well have suffered the fate of Richard Nixon. Nor did it actually impress that he wriggled out of blame, whilst taking 'full responsibility' by talking about 'activities undertaken without my knowledge'. Even so, there was a predisposition on the part of the American public to let him get away with it; too many presidents had been found wanting in recent years for another presidency to end in failure.[79]

It was thus a mixed legacy that Reagan bequeathed to his successor: a thawing of international tension bought at the price of crippling national indebtedness. Would America go the way of other great powers that had briefly achieved world hegemony, terminally weakened by the cost of financing her foreign adventures? How healthy was America beneath the military superstructure? Had the equation between domestic and foreign strength become unbalanced? Besides, Gorbachev posed another question: 'What are you going to do now that you've lost your best enemy?'[80]

10   George Bush and a New World Order

To George Bush would fall the task of providing the answers. It was to be a fortunate succession; Bush was the most experienced man in foreign policy to enter the White House since Eisenhower. Born in 1924, the product of an old-moneyed, established East Coast WASP (White, Anglo-Saxon, Protestant) family, the son of a US senator, preppy in style and upbringing, Bush had been a genuine war hero, the youngest volunteer naval pilot, flying fifty-eight combat missions and being decorated for bravery. Later he had moved to Texas to make a second fortune in the oil industry; thus patrician conservatism combined with Second World War internationalism to shape his outlook. Almost as a family tradition of public service, Bush entered politics, where he served two terms as US congressman and made a couple of unsuccessful runs for the US Senate. Then he was appointed successively ambassador to the United Nations, chairman of the Republican National Committee at the time of Watergate, head of the US Liaison Office in China and director of the CIA in the aftermath of unfavourable scrutiny of its activities. By 1980 he was making a bid for the Republican presidential nomination and served eight years as Reagan's loyal vice-president. It was a formidable CV as much for the safe pair of hands it betokened as for the range of jobs he had held.

Bush was never as beloved of the American right as Reagan, but his absence of ideology proved to be an advantage abroad. There was continuity in American foreign policy but with greater moderation, as he took up the presidency. In post-Second World War history 1989 was the miracle year. Freedom spread across Eastern Europe, from Poland to Hungary, to Czechoslovakia, to Bulgaria, to Romania as Soviet troops withdrew and the Warsaw Pact nations were left to seek their own destinies. Before the year was out the Berlin Wall itself, the very symbol of a Cold War-divided Europe, was dismantled. The euphoria seemed to echo the words of Wordsworth about a comparable revolution exactly 200 years previously: 'Bliss was it in that dawn to be alive, but to be young was very heaven!'[81]

In fact the retreat of Soviet power owed much to such older men as Bush, now well into his sixties. Bush and the brilliant foreign policy team he assembled, understood the parameters of Cold War politics; they had lived within them all their adult lives. The cautious hand Bush played, though criticized at the time for unadventurousness, was vindicated by results. For a start they had to be sure of Gorbachev. Brent Scowcroft, the national security adviser, with memories of the waning of *détente* under Ford, reflected:

I was suspicious of Gorbachev's motives and skeptical of his prospects ... In choosing Gorbachev, the old men of the Politburo clearly did not think they were selecting someone who would overturn the system, but one who would get it back on track ... I believed that Gorbachev's goal was to restore dynamism to a socialist political and economic system and revitalize the Soviet Union domestically and internationally to compete with the West. To me, especially before 1990, this made Gorbachev potentially more dangerous than his predecessors ...[82]

Thus an over-readiness to embrace arms reductions, for example, much of it perhaps intended for public consumption to win the propaganda battle with world opinion weary of the Cold War, might be to take receipt of a Trojan horse. Ironically, this had been one of the dangers of Reagan's pursuit of dramatic cutbacks in military forces, the zeal of the convert, buoyed up by the unrealistic hopes of an old man in a hurry, anxious to salvage his presidency. Equally dangerous was the Reagan rhetoric: to delineate the changes which were occurring in the context of an ideological crusade and gloat over one's victory. Nothing would have been more calculated to freeze Soviet reform dead in its tracks and to give comfort to those conservative forces inside the Soviet Union which looked askance at Gorbachev's methods, and perhaps hoped he would be unseated. America had to nudge him in the right direction; let him see that America harboured no ill intentions. There would be no desire to embarrass the Russians or take advantage of their difficulties; the Americans would be supportive, not exploitative, while they waited to see what Gorbachev intended and gently encouraged him in a peaceful direction. There would be no dancing on the Berlin Wall!

Thus Bush let events unfold as Soviet power retreated from Eastern Europe and their forces withdrew from Afghanistan. It was a masterly performance. Perhaps only Roosevelt's cat-like patience in 1940–1 and Eisenhower's sober-headed restraint in the 1950s were its equal. In 1990 Bush even achieved the seemingly impossible when the Russians with all their ancestral memories of what Germany had done to them, were yet induced to accept the unification of East and West Germany and for the new nation to remain in NATO. Precisely by not shaking the tree, the fruits of the Cold War fell gently into America's hands. Without firing a shot she watched the disappearance of her enemies.

The meeting between Bush and Gorbachev off Malta at the end of 1989 perhaps formally marked the end of the Cold War; it took some of the pressure off the American economy as this adjusted to the decline in international tension. After forty years containment seemed to have triumphed; the pace of change in Eastern Europe soon spread to the Soviet Union, as the post-Revolutionary centralized state was transformed into a commonwealth of independent nations. America had won the Cold War. Some argued that America should now be more supportive but with a crippled economy, the days when she could throw money around by the bucketful, as in the Marshall Plan, were long since over. Instead, there would have to be a patient, assiduous working with allies to construct a viable, coherent, long-term foreign policy perspective. In which direction now would Bush steer the nation? In September 1990 he essayed an answer:

> We stand today at a unique and extraordinary moment. The crisis in the Persian Gulf ... offers a rare opportunity to move toward an historic period of cooperation. Out of these troubled times ... a new world order – can emerge: a new era – free from the threat of terror, stronger in the pursuit of justice, and more secure in the quest for peace. An era in which the nations of the world ... can prosper and live in harmony ... A world where the rule of law supplants the rule of the jungle ... in which nations recognize the shared responsibility for freedom and justice ... where the strong respects the rights of the weak.[83]

Yet 'the rule of law' might need enforcing. American military power was still in place, the potential to organize it formidable. The Gulf War of 1991 was a tribute to America's ability to respond in a crisis: the alliance that liberated Kuwait the product of American foreign policy coordination. The whole exercise was brilliantly calibrated from the initial referral to the United Nations, which gave the operation international legitimacy. Here Bush's approachability – he was arguably the most good natured man to occupy the White House since Franklin Roosevelt – and long-standing willingness to consult with allies paid off handsomely. Firstly, the Saudi Arabian oilfields were secured even at the price of a quarter of a million foreign troops stationed on their soil, a remarkable feat of diplomatic persuasion. In due course these would rise to getting on for half a million prior to the liberation of Kuwait itself. It was an astonishing display of military logistics augmented by diplomatic finesse that evolved a coalition of 28 nations, 16 of whom committed ground troops, of which 10 were Islamic nations. After an air campaign that immobilized Iraqi defences through sheer technological efficiency, the land campaign was completed in a hundred hours. The speed of its execution was matched by its restraint. It would free Kuwait from the invader; it would not move beyond its mandate; there would be no march on Baghdad. It was statesmanship of the highest order, the more so for being popularly misunderstood. A defeated army would not be annihilated in a display of

American machismo that would only alienate Arab opinion in the age of war on television. Nor would America interfere in internal Middle East politics. If the American electorate had come to see national security as the province of the Republicans, Bush's performance vindicated their decision; it is hard to believe that his Democratic opponent in 1988, Michael Dukakis, would have matched his achievement.

Yet the same president seemed immobilized domestically, and attempts to tackle the budget deficit and trade imbalance, the legacy of the Reagan years, appeared weak and half-hearted. The Depression worsened and observers talked of a return to the 1930s. Clearly, if America was indeed to achieve 'a new world order' as Bush proposed, it could only realistically be done from a position of economic strength. The temptation, otherwise, would be to retreat into a 1930s-type new isolationism to match the economic crisis. Although it would be hard to overturn fifty years of American foreign policy all at once, Gorbachev had presciently diagnosed the American problem: what did America do now that she had lost her best enemy? In a curious way confrontation with the Soviet Union had acted as a stimulus, defining purposes and focusing energies. The Free World owed Bush a very great deal; he had overseen the transition successfully and, in this respect at least, he deserved better of his own countrymen. Now in the wrong hands this achievement could be dissipated.

11   Bill Clinton and the New Isolationism

Bush's displacement by Clinton was, in foreign policy at least, something of a tragedy. Born in 1946, Clinton represented a new generation in American politics, the postwar baby boomers who reached adulthood in the liberal 1960s. Skilfully he had evaded conscription in the Vietnam War, against which he had demonstrated outside the US embassy in London, while a student at Oxford. To old-fashioned patriots like George Bush, both the refusal to be called to the flag when one's country required it and, indeed, to repudiate it, were incomprehensible. It was a very different training for the role of commander-in-chief to that of his predecessor. Indeed, Clinton was the first president since Franklin Roosevelt to have no military experience and he, at least, had served in the Navy Department throughout the First World War.

Politically ambitious from his youth, Clinton gave every promise of emulating the other Democratic president of the post-liberal consensus, equally a Democratic governor of a minor state unskilled in foreign policy, Jimmy Carter. But even this similarity concealed an essential difference. Carter had been weak but stubborn; Clinton was weak but malleable. It would characterize the whole of his foreign policy. To some extent it was predictable. Bush had failed in domestic policy and Clinton's election had been narrowly achieved on promises to concentrate on the economy. The world was an inchoate place and if Bush's 'new world order' had substance it depended on the foreign policy skills of a very experienced president. It was not so much a policy as a procedure; the coherence came from how it was effected. What was evident was that Bush himself, at the level of action, if not abstractions, had some sense of what he might achieve. Here actions spoke louder than words. In contrast, Clinton might talk about 'American renewal', but how or when was never made clear.[84]

Thus particular issues such as American commitments in Bosnia, Haiti and Somalia, as far as Clinton was concerned, seemed determined more by their effect on public opinion. At times foreign policy appeared to be dictated by humanitarian concerns rather than America's strategic interests, and those concerns were at the whim of television reporting and the popular response it might arouse. Hence the humiliating withdrawal from Somalia when as few as eighteen servicemen were killed in a raid and their mutilated bodies openly displayed. All at once America would walk away from the civil war and famine their original intervention had intended to allay. At other times he pandered to special interest groups: the peace process in Northern Ireland was a particular example. Irish-American voters had often influenced Congress over the politics of their homeland; this was the first time in many years they had also influenced the Executive. Clinton was the first modern American president to succumb to their pressure. True, it might well be argued that in the bitter sectarianism of Northern Ireland politics only an outsider – and a high-profile outsider like the American president – had the necessary impact, even in Clinton's case charisma, to effect change in such deep-rooted antagonisms. Others would question whether, even if one gave him credit for trying, the end result would not be disappointment. Alternatively, the invasion of Haiti pandered to the concerns of the African-American caucus whose support Clinton needed in Congress. It reflected the weakness of a president with a slender mandate – in 1992 he had won but 43 per cent of the vote – and within two years faced a hostile Republican-dominated Senate and House. Even his victories were often in spite of his own party; both the North American Free Trade Agreement (NAFTA) approved by Congress, and the endorsement of the General Agreement on Tariffs and Trade (GATT) were only passed with Republican votes.

Moreover, though hard to define but easy to recognize, successful foreign policy also rested on the intangible of presidential authority. This was hard to accord a president whose campaign for the White House had been tarred by scandals even before he reached it and who would be constantly beset by them throughout his two terms. Nor did such policies as the lifting of the ban against homosexuals serving in the military, in face of much opposition, help him with his role as commander-in-chief. Very soon Clinton was perceived as weak and indecisive. Even his modest successes, such as bringing together the Palestine Liberation Organization's Yasir Arafat and Israel's prime minister at the White House or the Bosnian peace agreement negotiated in Dayton, Ohio, tended to be viewed as pleasant surprises rather than part of a coherent, overall plan.

To some extent, this failed to allow for how unstructured international relations had become in the 1990s. Superpower confrontation had at least had the merit of keeping the lid on the seething cauldron of ethnic and religious rivalries that had afflicted parts of Europe for generations; once American–Soviet rivalry was laid to rest, these tensions were likely to erupt. It was difficult to appear to be indifferent in the face of the cruelties these localized conflicts engendered, yet hard to act the world policeman when the American public had no stomach for a fight. Clinton understood the reluctance to commit American lives in battle; even the Gulf War had only been acceptable because it had been short and, in terms of casualties, inordinately sweet. The obvious solution was to resort to technology: hence the air war over the Serbian ethnic cleansing of Albanians in Kosovo in the spring of 1999. Yet to use NATO as an offensive alliance for the first time in its fifty-year history against a Slav people ran the risk of alienating Russia – a risk that was further exacerbated by the arguably too-early inclusion of Poland, Hungary and Czechoslovakia into NATO, which took Western forces to the very boundaries of the former USSR. Undoubtedly, it would sell well with former immigrant American voters and it was a cause on which one of them, Secretary of State Madeleine Albright, had clearly set her heart. But it was a form of foreign policy tokenism that ignored underlying realities and seemed more attuned to how it would play in the polls.

Once bipartisanship had been the basis of postwar American foreign policy; now even on the gravest issues Clinton lacked the moral authority to unify the nation. Not since the last years of the Truman administration had party differences been so bitter and the near-hatred Clinton aroused in some of his opponents cannot all be attributed to their fault. Clinton was a morally flawed president: he had to all but a legal casuist lied to the American people; he led a tawdry administration; the House of Representatives had voted that he be impeached. True, after trial he had escaped being convicted, but his survival and even political comeback had only enraged his enemies still further – had he even fired missiles at terrorist encampments to save his political skin? Monica Lewinsky's presence hovered over the political scene. In the most crushing rebuke to a president since the rejection of the Versailles Treaty submitted by Woodrow Wilson, the Senate defeated the Comprehensive Test Ban Treaty by 51 votes to 48, well below the two-thirds required for its ratification. Yet it had the support of over 80 per cent of the American people and had already been signed by 154 countries including 26 of the 44 nuclear-capable nations whose approval was needed before the treaty could come into effect. This was the new isolationism with a vengeance, an isolationism made worse by prosperity not depression. Here the Clinton years had seen a remarkable economic recovery. America could, quite literally, afford to go her own way.

Since Theodore Roosevelt the lesson has been clear. The president has to give a lead; equally, he has to educate public opinion to support him. But now there seemed to be an inability to make sense of changed conditions, no framework of understanding to guide the administration. Even if the Soviet threat had now departed, there was still a need for a proactive policy. Some saw in the conditions of the 1990s a unique chance to complete the work of liberal internationalism that had inspired an earlier American foreign policy, to set the parameters for democratic development in the third millennium. Yet the necessary leadership was lacking. The old order had run its course; a new one was not yet in place.

4

The Resurgence of Conservatism

1 The Conservative Conscience

In 1963, the very year that the oldest New Dealer of them all Lyndon Johnson reached the presidency, one historian, somewhat tongue in cheek, asserted: 'The collapse within half a generation of the fanatical hatred of the New Deal is certainly one of the marvels of American history. It would be easier to raise a regiment to fight for the Confederacy than against the New Deal.'[1] Today this judgement seems unduly optimistic. The New Deal has indeed found its critics and whilst those of the 1960s complained that the New Deal had not gone far enough, that it was largely a history of missed opportunities for real radical reform, later opponents saw in the New Deal the genesis of over-active government. As Ronald Reagan pithily put it: 'In this present crisis government is not the solution to our problem; government is the problem.'[2]

There is a certain irony that at the very moment when liberalism had reached its apogee, the forces that were beginning to undermine it were already starting to gather strength. Paradoxically, the changing politics of the 1960s are a tribute to the efficacy of the politics of the 1930s. The New Deal had done its work well and, sustained by Roosevelt's successors, the middle classes of America became the salient characteristic of American society. True, one-fifth of Americans might be an 'underclass', formally below the poverty line, submerged in a 'culture of poverty' passed on from one generation to the next, hidden from view and devoid of hope, as Michael Harrington's famously searing *The Other America*, published in 1962, amply demonstrated. But conversely, four-fifths were not.[3] It says much for America's liberals that the book truly shocked. It seemed an indictment of what had not yet been achieved: of pockets of poverty in the midst of plenty, out of sight, forgotten

212 President and Nation

or ignored. It acted as a catalyst and inspiration even, for those who would aim yet further to fulfil the promise of American life. However, given that it is the underclass who are less likely to turn out in elections, at what point did the crusading values of the Great Society, with its war on poverty targeted at the most deserving, become an insupportable burden of taxation for those who paid for it? Had the Vietnam War not occurred, the disillusionment might have been delayed, but the plain fact was that the war did occur and Lyndon Johnson could not, as he came to recognize, expect his countrymen to pay the cost of both a domestic and a foreign war.

Of course, conservatism had never lacked for spokesmen; Senator Robert Taft, the Midwestern conscience of the Republican Party, was its resident Washington intellectual after 1938. But stiff, humourless, intractable – whatever his private merits, Taft seemed personally too redolent of the spirit of Herbert Hoover to appeal to the uncommitted. Perhaps the Republicans themselves knew as much; again and again he was left standing at the altar when his party's presidential nomination came round, always the bridesmaid never the bride, sustaining his party in its long years of minority, but never achieving its official leadership.

Some of Taft's Senate allies lacked even his saving grace of rectitude. Provincial politicians, partisan and narrow-minded, they had a limitation of outlook that reminds one that America is indeed a continent not just to be interpreted through the eyes of Washington. Even Eisenhower, the titular leader of their party, found them wearisome. Indeed, one only has to compare some of the leading party spokesmen of the period with the great Republican luminaries who had dominated the political scene of an earlier generation, to see how far it had fallen. It bore all the characteristic hallmarks of a party that had been diminished philosophically by years of electoral defeat. Indeed, Eisenhower ruefully noted early on in his presidency that 'Republican Senators are having a hard time getting through their heads that they now belong to a team that includes rather than opposes the White House.'[4]

Taft's death in July 1953 removed the Republican Party's compass; not the least of Eisenhower's omissions was a failure to identify what precisely modern Republicanism stood for. A president of the United States is, whether he likes it or not, not only head of state and chief executive but, less exaltedly but necessarily, a party leader. But Eisenhower's personal success masked the need for this question to be answered. Whilst he himself had evolved a creed that very much matched his personality that

> it would be impossible for me ever to adopt a political philosophy so narrow as to merit the label 'liberal,' or 'conservative,' or anything of the sort. I came to believe . . . that an individual can only examine and decide for himself each issue in a framework of philosophic conviction dedicated to responsible progress – always in the light of what he believes is good for America as a whole . . .

It didn't make it easy to translate into an identifiable political programme.[5] Loose talk about 'the middle way' or being 'liberal on human issues, conservative on economic ones', was probably good politics for a minority party in the short term whose greatest asset was its leader.[6] Yet looking to the future, what was the sort of party that he would bequeath his successor? what would be his political legacy? who would be his ideological heir? Admittedly, none of the answers to these questions is entirely within the gift of any president, however powerful or popular; but it would have been reasonable to make the effort. Had he done so, the result of the 1960 election might, given its ultimate closeness, have been very different, and might have anticipated the eventual Republican dominance of the presidency. Nixon's defeat paved the way for others to try instead.

The Republicans, returning to their customary place outside the White House, found as always that defeat led to introspection. In such cases the party faithful work on a different set of assumptions from the average voter; being more committed, they place a greater premium on ideological fidelity. An objective observer looking at the sorry Republican record since the advent of Franklin Roosevelt in 1932 might have concluded that if Republicanism was to be made attractive it needed a consensus politician such as Eisenhower to be its standard bearer. Irrespective of whether or not Nixon had run a good campaign in 1960 – and he very probably had not – Nixon's partisanship, the sense that he was little more than a successful professional politician, clearly counted against him. The message the party faithful drew, however, was entirely different: that the weakness of Republicanism was that it was a milk-and-water affair that failed to offer an effective contrast to the Democrats. If only Republicans would be true to their roots, would have the courage of their convictions, there was outside in the vast American hinterland a whole army of conscripts waiting to be recruited. All that was needed was a charismatic standard bearer to make the dream a reality.

Senator Barry Goldwater of Arizona filled the role to perfection. An uncomplicated man, he was not ashamed to call himself a conservative. The year 1960, when Nixon was narrowly defeated by Kennedy, saw the publication of his *The Conscience of a Conservative*. Here was the creed of the true believer.

I have little interest in streamlining government or in making it more efficient, for I mean to reduce its size. I do not undertake to promote welfare, for I propose to extend freedom. My aim is not to pass laws, but to repeal them. It is not to inaugurate new programmes, but cancel old ones that do violence to the Constitution, or that have failed in their purpose, or that impose on the people an unwarranted financial burden. I will not attempt to discover whether legislation is 'needed' before I have first determined whether it is constitutionally permissible. And if I should be later attacked for neglecting my constituents' 'interests,' I shall reply that I was informed their main interest is liberty and that in that cause I am doing the very best I can.[7]

For Goldwater the great mistake of the Republican Party had been precisely that adaptation to political moderation that had enabled the only Republican presidential victories since 1928. Indeed, he positively, exultingly, repudiated it. *'Extremism in the defense of liberty is no vice! ... Moderation in the pursuit of justice is no virtue'*, proclaimed Goldwater (who had underlined the phrase in his own text), as he accepted the Republican presidential nomination in 1964.[8]

Goldwater was at least quite an attractive personality underneath all the rhetoric, if undeniably a somewhat simplistic one. As befitted a politician from a newer, even rawer part of the country, he saw politics in much simpler terms than sophisticates from the East Coast, a part of the country he openly disdained. As he famously put it: 'Sometimes I think this country would be better off if we could just saw off the Eastern Seaboard and let it float out to sea.'[9]

In the still developing Southwest individualism was a force to be reckoned with, so that governmental interference and budget deficits seemed the high price the nation paid for liberalism. In no sense a profound thinker, Goldwater articulated the frustrations and the resentments of those to whom modern America was complex, complicated and controlled by forces they did not understand. Goldwater and his supporters, who worshipped him, would undo the shabby compromises of a generation of American politics. Their agenda was straightforward: get government off the backs of the American people; roll back the communist threat; and revert to the virtues of the frontier to which the nation owed her greatness. Goldwater breathed a fresh air into American politics, the more exhilarating for its manifest headiness. He would offer the American people 'A Choice, Not an Echo'; in other words, another sun not a pale moon.[10]

His capture of the party was not only a tribute to the organizational powers of his followers, who had plotted their triumph since the defeat of the much less attractive, if far more complex, Nixon, but also compelling evidence of how far conviction politics can galvanize grassroots support. 'I find that America is fundamentally a Conservative nation,' Goldwater noted. 'The preponderant judgement of the American people, especially of the young people, is that the radical, or Liberal approach has not worked and is not working. They yearn for a return to Conservative principles.'[11] Indeed, Goldwater's adherents openly delighted in provoking the East Coast Republican moderates who had long regarded presidential politics as their particular preserve. This time there would be no shifting to the middle ground once the nomination was safely secured, none of the reaching out to the uncommitted voter that the politics of electoral pragmatism necessarily and customarily dictated. One observer commented incredulously: 'He's going to run as Barry Goldwater.'[12]

True believers court martyrdom. Thus Goldwater's predictable landslide defeat at the hands of Lyndon Johnson in the election of 1964 was inevitably the subject of much mockery, not helped by the candidate's own blunders that contributed to what one commentator labelled *The Goldwater Caper*.[13] It was easy to laugh. In a campaign where everything went wrong, the Republicans were reduced to the slogan: 'In your heart, you know he's right', as if support for Goldwater defied rational analysis. (The Democrats responded: 'In your guts you know he's nuts' – reasonably.)[14]

2 The Turning Conservative Tide

Yet in a curious way the much-derided Goldwater supporters appear to have had the last laugh. It was in 1964 that a rather second-rate film actor, called Ronald Reagan, made a famous speech on national television attacking the New Deal, in support of Goldwater. The publicity thus generated was to launch an astonishing career, when the acolyte himself assumed the prophet's mantle. For in retrospect it appears that Goldwater's main fault was that while he was ridiculed for wanting to lead his countrymen back to the nineteenth century, the Old Frontier his critics contended as opposed to the New, he was in fact ahead of his time. How crucial were to be those two years between the Kennedy assassination in November 1963 and the autumn of 1965 for the future of modern America! It was almost as if they were the very fulcrum on which America swung away from its liberal present to its conservative future; but the first stirrings of this movement could only just be discerned and only later gathered momentum.

Looking back, 1964 was a year of portents. Lyndon Johnson first enunciated his vision of the Great Society; the Civil Rights Act was passed into law; the Tonkin Gulf Resolution slid through Congress; the Democratic landslide occurred. In New York the World's Fair opened, a testimony to American prosperity, economic well-being and technological know-how, and the cultural and commercial dominance of the United States' most famous city. But that same year, California surpassed New York State in the size of its population; for the first time in American history, the most populous state in the Union lay on the Pacific, not the Atlantic Coast. This was significant for the present and symbolic for the future. By chance, the Republican Party sensed the signs of the times; their Convention, the one that nominated Goldwater was held in San Francisco, gateway to the Pacific; the Democrats had to make do with Atlantic City, a downmarket East Coast resort.

Gradually the centre of American political gravity was shifting; the older industrial states of the North and the East, the frostbelt, lost population; the numbers in the sunbelt states of the South and West increased. According to the census of 1960 America was a nation of just under 180 million people; forty years later it was over 280 million. It had taken the first 60 years of the twentieth century to add 100 million, only the last forty to add another. Where this later growth took place was even more striking; every decade the Northeast's share of the nation's population diminished; that of the South and West increased. Some increases were almost astronomical. In forty years California went from a little under 16 million to almost 34 million: Texas from 9.5 to almost 21 million: Florida from 5 to almost 16 million. Arizona virtually quadrupled its population in the same period: Nevada spectacularly increased sevenfold: between 1990 and 2000 its numbers soared by two-thirds! On the other hand New York could only manage an increase of 2 million, picking up steam in the closing decade of the century, though ceding second place in population to Texas. Pennsylvania could not even make a million; West Virginia actually lost population, a melancholy statistic she shared alone with the District of Columbia. The Midwest's performance was also lacklustre, states such as Iowa, Kansas, Nebraska and Ohio making little headway. The Dakotas (North and South), perhaps a special case, told a similar story.

The flight from frostbelt to sunbelt came from a variety of causes. At one level it was simply the search for a better climate, to escape the severities of northern winters; Florida in part resembled an old people's home. By 1980 over half its population was born out of state; in the South generally it was one in five. California had always been the El Dorado of American myth. 'Go West, young man' had been a much-quoted, piece of mid-nineteenth-century advice to those in search of success.[15] Now the retired and the elderly also packed their bags. In any case, moving was so much easier: the automobile and the new interstate highways made mobility routine. In the quarter of a century between the end of the Second World War and 1970 car registration rose from 26 million to 89 million; total car mileage from 250 billion to 1 trillion plus.

Industries, too, preferred to relocate and start afresh with new factories, cheaper Southern labour and laxer labour laws. In the South, too, the unions were notably less militant; it was a combination any employer would find attractive. The changing pattern of the American economy made these areas ripe for development; the new defence industries, aerospace, oil and electronics all flourished. Southern congressmen on the relevant committees made sure that military bases and contracts came to the South. Out West, 'Silicon Valley' in California or the huge Boeing works in Seattle told the same story; by 1990 the metropolitan areas around Los Angeles and San Francisco together had well over 20 million people; Seattle's over half the population of Washington State. Clean, modern, expanding, self-confident sunbelt cities made a refreshing contrast to the old urban centres, crime-infested jungles struggling with epidemics of hardship and deprivation. Meanwhile, the latter's problems were compounded by loss of revenue due to suburban migration, leaving large tracts of waste land, boarded-up shops and derelict factories, sub-standard housing and neighbourhood ghettos. When even New York, albeit financial irresponsibility arguably having played its part, had to go cap in hand to the federal government to be bailed out in the 1970s, the message of failure was there for all to hear.

Long-term, these changes in population were to have profound implications for political arithmetic; increased population meant greater representation in Congress and hence in the Electoral College that chooses presidents; diminished population meant reduced representation and loss of presidential voting power. In the 1960 election, the last to be regulated by the statistics of the postwar 1950 Census, New York had 45 votes against California's 32, a total the latter shared with Pennsylvania. In 1964, with the 1960 Census returns taking effect, the comparable figures were 43 to 40, with Pennsylvania now trailing with 29. And so each decade the imbalance continued. In 1992, 1996 and 2000, following the 1990 Census, California with 54 would have precisely one-fifth of the votes needed to elect a president. Texas with 32 votes had only 1 less than New York: Florida with 25, more than Pennsylvania (23), Illinois (22), or Ohio (21). Indeed, one might be pardoned for thinking that the Confederacy had won after all; their states now provided 54 per cent (146) of the Electoral College votes (270: i.e. a majority of 538) needed to elect a president.

The Southern states had traditionally had a suspicion of federal government; this attitude remained even when, as during the New Deal, they were happy to receive federal handouts. The Western states, newer, rawer even, more individualistic, too, found no contradiction in supplicating Washington for what it had to offer, grants for irrigation or access rights to public lands, for example, whilst at the same time disdaining it and preaching self-reliance and independence. Both regions were ripe for conservative proselytizing. Significantly, even in the debacle of 1964 Goldwater carried, apart from his home state of Arizona, five states of the Deep South; what seemed at first the political equivalent of Pickett's doomed charge at Gettysburg, in fact heralded a major political earthquake.

The demise of the Republican Party in general and conservatism in particular, widely predicted in the wake of the Johnson landslide which was amply replicated in the congressional and state elections, was instead the first stirrings of the party's resurrection. The 1964 election was for American liberalism both its triumph and its turning point. Thereafter its path ran steadily downhill, relieved only by an intermittent plateau in its descent, until its nadir was reached in 1994. Yet this descent was concealed because there was no great turning point immediately visible; no election of 1860 and a Civil War, no 1932 and a Depression, whereby one political party and its creed directly displaced another. Only in retrospect can it be seen that the Vietnam War was the foreign policy trauma of modern America that would equally effect a major electoral realignment. But whereas the Civil War had had its Lincoln and the Depression its Franklin Roosevelt, who had drawn order out of chaos, the Vietnam War would produce no such political genius. Would that it had! Instead, lesser men would find themselves afloat in uncharted political waters, drifting in directions that were at first merely dimly perceived and but partially understood. The capital of Franklin Roosevelt had not yet been expended; more accurately, it was to be frittered away.

Foreign affairs, it must be admitted, only gradually played their part in this decline, or at least hastened its onset. The Vietnam War slowly came to overshadow the Great Society and destroyed the liberal consensus from within; liberalism's greatest champions at home were the least enthusiastic about pointless foreign wars, whilst those most in favour of foreign commitments often looked askance at domestic reform politics. By 1967 about a dozen senators of both parties opposed the war. The tragedy of the war for the Democratic Party and the liberalism it espoused was nowhere more starkly demonstrated than in the private agony of Hubert Humphrey. He was a consistent liberal standard bearer, in season and out, now vice-president and forced by loyalty to Lyndon Johnson to endorse a war that threatened the very causes to which he had devoted his life.

The war also threatened the Democratic Party. When a meeting was arranged in Manila between the American and South Vietnamese presidents a fortnight before the 1966 congressional elections, scepticism was widespread. 'Is this a quest for peace or a quest for votes?' asked Richard Nixon. Already Lyndon Johnson sensed his vulnerability; so, too, did his enemies. Nixon added: 'I realized for the first time how worried Johnson was beneath his booming exterior.' Quite early on, the perennial presidential hopeful had carefully calculated: 'Republicans had good reason to be optimistic about the 1966 elections, and if I had a hand in a sweeping party victory, it would not go unnoticed in the party ranks.'[16]

In the event, the Republicans made up much of the losses of two years previously, 47 seats in the House of Representatives, and 3 in the Senate. They also gained 8 state governorships, of which the most significant would be Ronald Reagan's victory in California. Even if this was to some extent the natural swing of the political pendulum, still it contrasted with Franklin Roosevelt's off-year triumph of 1934 as the New Deal got under way. Moreover, one can make too much of the war. Disillusionment with the Great Society even without it had set in early. Significantly this preceded the widespread public opposition to the Vietnam imbroglio, which did not really come to a head until a year later. As Gerald Ford, the Republican leader in the House, claimed just before the election: 'Congress now is a pawn in the hands of the White House and 50 per cent of the members are puppets who dance when the President pulls the strings.' With obvious satisfaction he later noted: 'On election day that November voters showed that they agreed.'[17]

Perhaps the Johnson coalition of 1964 had been just that; it was easy to attract Republican votes and conservative Democrats who a few years previously had been Democrats for Eisenhower, if Goldwater could be portrayed as the enemy of consensus. Johnson had sensed this, too, urging passage of his legislation in the first session of the Eighty-ninth Congress in 1965 before his support began to evaporate. After a lifetime's experience as a legislator he knew the need to seize the moment when a law might be enacted. Less happily, he did not always perceive that a parliamentary majority, and it only takes a majority of one to pass a bill, is not the same as genuine consensus. He could never educate the public to accept his programme, the way his great mentor Franklin Roosevelt had done; in the end he ran ahead of public opinion and the Great Society never had the inspirational quality that marked the best of the New Deal. Perhaps too many Americans were too well-off. This is not to devalue the genuine achievements of the Great Society, but sometimes it could seem a law too much. No liberal had doubted the need for the Civil Rights Act of 1964 or the Voting Rights Act of 1965; but racial tension thereafter rose, not lessened; the explosion of riots in the city ghettos across the nation in the next years tempered white liberal enthusiasm. As Gerald Ford again questioned: 'How long are we going to abdicate law and order – the backbone of any civilization – in favor of a soft social theory that the man who heaves a brick through your window or tosses a fire bomb into your car is simply the misunderstood and underprivileged product of a broken home.'[18]

At other times the legislation, if not superfluous, seemed unduly interventionist, or at least dependent on intrusive federal bureaucrats for its implementation. This was a line of argument that Republican leaders like Ford shrewdly recognized might generate non-partisan support. 'The performance of the Eighty-ninth Congress, I felt, had been disgraceful. It had enacted irresponsible legislation that gave the federal bureaucracy unprecedented control over the lives of private citizens. It had passed spending bills without imposing restraints.'[19] Neither did such legislation necessarily have widespread popular backing. Thus anti-poverty programmes were as much a tribute to the influence of elite policy makers within the administration as they were to a wholesale demand to help the disadvantaged. They were often seen as discriminating against those very people who made some effort to help themselves. Their consequences were often to set white against black; and, ultimate irony for all the disproportionate criticism they attracted from those who questioned whether government should permanently subsidize an underclass, they failed in their objective. Thus the Office of Economic Opportunity, predicated on the assumption that free enterprise was the way out of poverty, never really had enough funds, even less as the Vietnam War escalated; and seemed constantly involved in bureaucratic tangles. The Community Action Programmes targeting assistance at the most needy, with their emphasis on Maximum Feasible Participation at the community level, seemed too often to be at the mercy of those with an axe to grind or, alternatively, failed to enlist the help of those they were meant to assist.

America was also getting older and more prosperous. The New Deal and its successors had been effective. Older people tend to be more conservative, to reflect values that the social liberal ethic of the 1960s sorely challenged. Only perhaps in concern for social security were senior citizens likely to be natural Democratic supporters. Perhaps only Goldwater could have campaigned in a state like Florida and discoursed to an audience of senior citizens on the wrongs of provision of hospital care for the aged under social security; predictably, Florida's electoral votes went to Lyndon Johnson. A more politically astute Republican like Nixon would never have made such a mistake; besides, being a centrist of lower-middle-class and small-town background growing up in the Depression, he had no difficulty in accepting that social security was here to stay.

Increasing prosperity, however, inevitably weakened the Democratic ranks. True there was the politics of loyalty and nostalgia, but gradually as former blue-collar workers, urban immigrants and ethnics or their children, by now college graduates, made it professionally or socially into the middle class, the older ties would weaken. The Servicemen's Readjustment Act of 1944, better known as the GI Bill of Rights was one of the last great imaginative domestic proposals of the Roosevelt administration. By providing long-term low-interest mortgages and a $2,000 bonus towards the purchase of a new home, it helped stimulate a postwar housing boom and laid the foundations for the growth in home ownership that is an essential prerequisite for a middle-class society. Even more significantly, it put a college education within the reach of millions who would otherwise have returned to civilian life and thought themselves lucky to have found a blue-collar job or one on a farm. Of the almost eight million returning servicemen, about a half went on to some form of higher education. Its success is best summed up by the fact that, notwithstanding its astronomical cost, some twenty billion dollars all told, the government recouped the lot through the higher taxes that such graduates paid in consequence of the better jobs they secured. America was upwardly mobile. Hubert Humphrey, Nixon's opponent in 1968, the last of the old New Dealers, was already looking a somewhat dated figure; he appealed to a constituency that was already in the process of dissolution.

Liberalism might have set the agenda of politics since the 1930s, but the fact that it took a generation to complete suggests the conservative capacity to obstruct. Eisenhower had won by clear majorities in the 1950s, Kennedy in 1960 by the thinnest margin of victory since 1888. (Eisenhower would certainly have won again had he been able to be a candidate.) What had pushed America leftwards in so short a period? The 'feel-good' factor in this case clearly worked for Johnson, but such emotions are an unlikely basis for crusading, reform politics. Neither the slavery abolitionists of the 1840s and 1850s, nor early twentieth-century Progressives, let alone Depression-inspired Democrats of the 1930s relied on such capital. True, at times Johnson could wax genuinely lyrical on the subject of poverty, and his speeches often reflected the idealism that, if often buried, had always been a part of his make-up. But to many he was still the conservative Southerner, and the very reasons why liberals had objected to his selection as Kennedy's running mate in 1960 made him for others a reassuring figure. It was the liberals who had nowhere else to go in 1964, not the uncommitted, the middle-of-the-roaders, and the less ideologically conservative. It was these Johnson had to attract if he were to build his consensus. Such support, inevitably, was scarcely rock-solid; soon there were other reasons why it began to melt away.

Liberals had assumed that their battle would be with right-wing conservatives; soon they discovered that they were being undercut on the left. To the more radical, the price of increased liberalism was the unacceptable acceptance of capitalism; ironically, some of its most affluent children now sought a wholesale restructuring of American society. Deeming it to be economically exploitative, culturally repressive, socially racist and militarily aggressive, disparate dissenters against the prevailing liberal ethos made common cause. Often more united in what they were against than in what they were for, their opposition was at best corrosive and at worst violent, anarchic and destructive. But it created a counter-culture that alienated traditional, older liberal sympathizers and pushed them rightwards, whilst offering little that practical politics could encompass instead. At one level it might be diagnosed as a sickness brought on by a surfeit of affluence, at another resentment occasioned by a sense of political and social alienation. Whatever the cause, it undermined Johnson's hopes of a truly integrated 'Great Society'. Worse, it became subsumed into the wider anti-war movement that provided it with a convenient unity, a common cause that individual groups had been unable to make.

Opposition to the Vietnam War was initially confined to minority groups of the professionally committed: Quakers, pacifists, anti-war Christians. Slowly it gathered momentum as the war escalated and the draft increased. The war's carnage could be itemized by one terrifying statistic: by the end of Johnson's presidency the United States had dropped more bombs on Vietnam than in the whole of the Second World War. The war's cost in human resources could equally briefly be recorded: 184,000 American soldiers in Vietnam in 1965; an additional 200,000 in 1966; a further 100,000 in 1967; a grand total of a little under 540,000 in 1968. The 225 Americans killed in action about the time Johnson resolved to widen the war in early 1965 had become 1,594 by the year's close; 15,979 at the end of 1967; and 30,568 as of 31 December 1968. Opposition in principle moved to opposition in practice when the middle classes found themselves involved. Hitherto, deferment had usually enabled college-bound students to evade the draft legitimately; it was an escape route that benefited the middle classes at the expense of high-school drop-outs from the lower socio-economic groups accustomed to getting all the kicks, unused to political organizing and powerless to protest. African-Americans were particularly at risk here, along with the poorer whites, but though these might be liberalism's natural constituency, they were largely inarticulate. Real trouble came within liberal ranks when the selfsame college students whose predecessors on graduation had flocked to Washington in the heady days of the New Deal and staffed government agencies, now stayed on campus organizing massive anti-war protests directed at Franklin Roosevelt's spiritual heir. Like the mythical Cretan Minotaur, the draft boards inexorably required their annual tribute. Now even under-performing college students were finding that their lacklustre grades could be used as evidence against them to cancel their deferments; soon liberal professors, opposed to the war and outraged at such a misapplication of academic procedures, would artificially inflate grades to protect their (male) students. Parental protest against their sons' forcible induction into the army might be less dramatic than a campus sit-in; but letters to congressmen or newspapers, hostile responses to opinion-poll surveys, all gnawed away at the administration's support. In this respect hawks might be as disenchanted as doves, finding in Johnson's ambiguous strategy of bombing pauses, embargoed targets and professed desire for peace, a failure of will to go all-out for victory. Johnson was damned if he did and damned if he didn't.

Thus a dangerous coalition was forming. There was increasing middle-class adult disillusionment with redistributive taxation, aimed at coddling an apparently permanent dependent underclass that might readily explode in manifestations of urban ethnic violence. Graphic reporting of the race riots in the Watts section of Los Angeles in 1965, or Detroit and Newark in 1967, or even Washington, DC, itself in 1968 in the wake of the assassination of Martin Luther King, only fuelled their resentment. This, when combined with the middle-class young hostility to an unjust war which demanded the sacrifice of their lives for a cause which they neither approved nor considered viable, inevitably spelled the end of the Democratic political ascendancy. As Johnson himself had divined, even before his troubles, it was simply too good to last. Yet one must not begrudge him the success he merited. If 1965 was his *annus mirabilis*, he battled on mightily even as the liberal tide receded. Up until the end he worked his legislative legerdemain, compiling a record 207 Acts on the statute book.

Perhaps one of his initial failures underlines both the reach of Johnson's vision, the compassion of his proposals, and the cruel blindness of his opponents. It was one of the few occasions when he missed a trick, and typically Johnson never rested until he had redeemed it. In July 1967 the Rat Extermination and Control Bill was debated in the House of Representatives, a simple, straightforward measure which aimed to provide federal grants to local neighbourhoods for implementing rat control and extermination programmes. Johnson had deliberately separated this proposal from his other recommendations in his message on urban and rural poverty, to stir the conscience of more affluent Americans. As Johnson himself explained:

Every year thousands of people, especially those living in the slums of our cities, are bitten by rats in their homes and tenements. The overwhelming majority of victims are babies lying in their cribs. Some of them die of their wounds. Many are disfigured for life. Rats carry a living cargo of death. Directly and indirectly, more human beings have been killed by rats than have been killed in all the wars since the beginning of time. In their travels from sewers to trash heaps to kitchens, rats carry the germs of fatal epidemic jaundice and typhus.

But the greatest damage cannot be measured in objective terms. You cannot measure the demoralizing effect that the plague of rats has on human beings – a mother wakened by a cry in the middle of the night to find her child bleeding with rat bites on his nose, lips, or ears... a father reluctant to repair his damaged property, knowing that rats will only destroy it again... the disgust, fear, and hatred intrinsic to rodent-infested warrens of substandard living.

The debate that followed was a travesty, one Republican urging, 'I think the "rat smart thing" for us to do is to vote down this rat bill "rat now".' Jokes followed about the new 'civil "rats" bill', 'throwing money down a rathole', 'discriminating between city and country rats'. Johnson had relied on the self-evident logic of the proposal; defeated by the old Republican–conservative Democratic coalition, he used every ounce of publicity to shame the conservatives to change their minds; two months later the House reversed itself.[20]

3 The Election of 1968

Clearly, on self-evident moral issues the liberal creed still counted large numbers of adherents. Nor can one discount the role of accident or bad luck in occasioning its demise. The year 1968 was strange and disturbed by any standard. What if Senator Eugene McCarthy of Minnesota, having unseated Lyndon Johnson when he entered the Democratic presidential primaries, had been able to capture the nomination itself? What if Senator Robert Kennedy of New York had not been assassinated and had run for president? What if Hubert Humphrey had been a little quicker at distancing himself from Lyndon Johnson when he became the Democratic candidate? What if the announcement of a total bombing pause in Vietnam had come a little earlier than Hallowe'en? What if even the first Tuesday after the first Monday in November, the traditional date for the election, had been, say, the 7th or 8th rather than the 5th, and had let the gathering Democratic swing move still further? Nixon's victory was not predetermined. Yet Nixon read the public mood well. His whole campaign both for the Republican nomination and for the presidency itself was based on the notion that he was a healer and a unifier. It was an improbable stance for one of the most partisan of politicians, made credible only by the discord occasioned by Lyndon Johnson, from whose shadow the luckless Hubert Humphrey could never quite escape. 'As we look at America, we see cities enveloped in smoke and flame. We hear sirens in the night. We see Americans dying on distant battlefields ... hating each other; killing each other at home,' Nixon proclaimed as he accepted the Republican presidential nomination. And so he would make his pitch to ' ... the great majority of Americans, the forgotten Americans, the nonshouters, the nondemonstrators'. The appeal of a candidate who could invoke traditional values, 'They're good people ... decent people; they work ... save ... pay taxes ...', cannot be gainsaid. Nixon, the professional politician, went with the tide.[21]

Central to Nixon's victory was his 'Southern strategy'. Just as in the 1920s, the Democratic pluralities in the big cities, even in the midst of general Republican victory, presaged the later urban bedrock of Franklin Roosevelt's support, so the Goldwater victories in the South suggested future Republican pickings. The race issue was at last beginning to bite. The realignment of which Franklin Roosevelt had dreamed would at last become a reality, though it would be to the detriment of the Democratic Party. In presidential politics, conservative white Southerners would see that the logic of their situation made the Republican Party their natural home. Congressional realignment would come later; here incumbency, seniority, habit, tradition, sentiment, vested interest would retard the process. But even in 1964 Strom Thurmond of South Carolina, the Dixiecrat presidential candidate of 1948, switched from the Democrat to the Republican Party after ten years in the Senate, a straw in the wind of change. Nixon, with his promise to appoint 'conservative' federal judges, with soothing noises about school desegregation and an unenthusiastic attitude to school busing (which was also an issue in the North), sedulously cultivated this constituency, weaning it away from its traditional Democratic Party base. But for the accident of Lyndon Johnson's Texas ancestry, it is possible that more of the South might have deserted to Goldwater in 1964. There had already been early portents in the 1950s when Eisenhower had garnered Southern support. But in 1957 he had also, albeit with reluctance verging on distaste, sent federal troops into Little Rock, Arkansas, to prevent civil disorder occasioned by the legally sanctioned admission of black students to a hitherto all-white school. Now Nixon would construe the need for adherence to the law somewhat differently. 'To those who say that law and order is the code word for racism, here is a reply: Our goal is justice – justice for every American. If we are to have respect for law in America, we must have laws that deserve respect. Just as we cannot have progress without order, we cannot have order without progress.'[22] Nixon was not a racist, but if the cause of Civil Rights had been advanced by civil disobedience, this was a game others could play, albeit without eschewing violence. In this respect law and order was a genuine, widespread issue. But the political pay-off for Nixon was obvious, especially when George Wallace, the governor of Alabama, was running as an Independent, appealing to the cruder partisans of white disaffection. Hence Nixon's surprise choice of Maryland's governor, Spiro T. Agnew, for vice-president. He had made no bones about his views on rioters in the wake of the assassination of Martin Luther King; he might appeal to the North whilst being acceptable to the South. As one of the few African-American Republican delegates to the Republican Convention sadly noted: 'The Republican party reckons it can do without the Negro. It feels it can win on the white backlash.'[23]

Besides, the South had always been more traditionally militaristic: Goldwater's nuclear trigger-happy rhetoric had never offended Southern ears quite so badly; now the anti-war protests of Vietnam liberals had even less appeal. This, too, was a reason for deserting the Democratic fold. In any case, the Vietnam War was the dominant issue throughout 1968. Here Nixon, the most experienced of all the candidates in foreign policy, enjoyed the luxury of opposition. He could criticize the conduct of the war, he could intimate that he alone could end it honourably, but be piously vague about exactly how he would achieve this. 'As a candidate it would have been foolhardy, and as a prospective President, improper, for me to outline specific plans in detail. I did not have the full range of information or the intelligence resources available to Johnson. And even if I had been able to formulate specific "plans," it would have been absurd to make them public. In the field of diplomacy, premature disclosure can often doom even the best-laid plans.'[24]

Finally, coalition politics depends on consensus. When the Democratic Party was fighting amongst itself in public, when Eugene McCarthy challenged Lyndon Johnson for the presidential nomination and Robert Kennedy hesitatingly followed, the game was up, as Johnson implicitly recognized when he determined not to seek re-election. He had failed to unify the country. The bloodletting, literally, in the streets of Chicago at the Democratic Convention later that turbulent summer of 1968, when anti-war protesters clashed with the police and National Guard, merely confirmed the party's sorry state. When so partisan a politician as Richard Nixon could pose as the man who would heal the nation by courting the once 'solid South' and George Wallace could run as an Independent appealing to the prejudices of Southern whites and Northern blue-collar workers, Franklin Roosevelt's political construction was in ruins.

4   Richard Nixon in the White House

Yet if the edifice had gone, the foundations were seemingly still in place; Richard Nixon was the first president sine 1848 to come into office with both Houses of Congress arrayed against him; the first since 1880 not even to have his party win the House of Representatives. Moreover, his election had been a narrow one, his margin of victory of 500,000 in the popular vote a mere seven-tenths of 1 per cent. Not since 1912 had so small a proportion of Americans elected their president. This stark fact concealed a deeper understanding not immediately appreciated: that Wallace with almost 10 million votes, had not just freakily captured traditional Democratic sympathizers, but uncovered a core of future conservative support. It was thus easy for Democrats to see the result as something of an aberration; 1968 was apparently not a 1932 with a major electoral realignment. Certainly the Democrats were to continue their congressional ascendancy. Not until 1980 would the Republicans capture the Senate (and lose it again in 1986): not until 1994 would both Chambers be in their control. Yet the White House in retrospect was now their fiefdom; the pattern of almost forty years was to be reversed. Only Jimmy Carter in 1976 and Bill Clinton in 1992 and 1996 would upset this arrangement; significantly, neither of them were liberal Democrats in the Rooseveltian mould. In effect, liberalism was to fight a losing battle; the long-drawn-out twilight of Democratic ascendancy had begun.

The logic of this situation would also not have been recognizable to many Republicans; they could only count their good fortune at the Democratic Party's internecine warfare and keep their fingers crossed for 1972. Nixon himself saw that domestic politics offered little scope for manoeuvre; a Democrat-controlled Congress would block him at every turn. But just as Eisenhower had ended the war in Korea and given the nation a sense of security in crisis, so Nixon would end the war in Vietnam and develop his true love, foreign affairs. A pattern was beginning to emerge that would reflect the wishes of the electorate; the Republicans were best trusted with the presidency and issues of national security; but liberal programmes already enacted and wanted were safer in Democratic congressmen's hands. Some believed that Nixon's own margin of victory might have been wider had doubts not lingered under the surface about his attitude to social security. Thus if conservatism was to have any long-term chance of survival, its agenda would have to appeal beyond individual economic self-interest to encompass changing public attitudes towards other aspects of the liberal creed that might inspire less personal loyalty. Here Nixon might follow the prescriptions of one of his 1968 campaign aides, Kevin Phillips, who perceptively noted the trend of the times:

Far from being the tenuous and unmeaningful victory suggested by critical observers, the election of Richard M. Nixon... in November, 1968, bespoke the end of the New Deal Democratic hegemony and the beginning of a new era in American politics... the vastness of the tide (57 per cent) which overwhelmed Democratic liberalism – George Wallace's support was clearly an even more vehement protest against the Democrats than was Nixon's vote – represented an epochal shifting of national gears... This repudiation visited upon the Democratic Party for its ambitious social programming, and inability to handle the urban and Negro revolutions, was comparable in scope to that given conservative Republicanism in 1932 for its failure to cope with the... Depression.[25]

Here, then, far from a fluke victory, was on the contrary a historic opportunity. Nixon could set out to reverse what he saw as liberalism's recent aggrandisement. Here, clearly, he perceived a mandate:

As I saw it, America in the 1960s had undergone a misguided crash program aimed at using the power of the presidency and the federal government to right past wrongs by trying to legislate social progress. This was the idea behind Kennedy's New Frontier and Johnson's Great society. The problems were real and the intention worthy, but the method was foredoomed. By the end of the decade its costs had become almost prohibitively high in terms of the way it had undermined fundamental relationships within our federal system, created confusion about our national values, and corroded American belief in ourselves as a people and as a nation.

The 1960s had been a decade of great restlessness and change. Prodded by the emotional power of Kennedy's liberal rhetoric, new sensitivities – some sincere, some merely fashionable – developed regarding the black, the poor, and the young in our society.[26]

Yet if these three groups seemed to have dominated the politics of the 1960s, for all the noise they made they were not, in fact, representative. Voters under 25 had cast only 7.4 per cent of the nation's ballots in 1968, and whilst the African-Americans were clearly lost to the Republican Party, they were not necessary to secure victory. Some 60 per cent of low-income workers were in fact white. Later

Nixon was to suffer some political embarrassment from civil-rights groups with a leaked memorandum advising him: 'The time may have come when the issue of race could benefit from a period of "benign neglect." The subject has been too much talked about. The forum has been too much taken over by hysterics, paranoids, and boodlers on all sides. We may need a period in which Negro progress continues and racial rhetoric fades.' Yet many would have privately – or not so privately – agreed.[27]

And besides, how many Americans were both actually poor and, equally significantly, regular voters? The underclass of American society is the least reliable of political footsoldiers. Indeed, the very character of the American polity was changing. The census of 1920 had signified the emergence of an urban nation; now it was fast becoming a suburban one. As increasing numbers of socially aspiring Americans fled the cities, another pillar of the Democratic Party ascendancy was crumbling. Kevin Phillips's analysis looked towards a golden Republican Party future: 'Now it is Richard Nixon's turn to build a new era on the immense middle-class impetus of Sun Belt and suburbia.'[28]

The Sunbelt was the natural focus of a new political realignment; so too, was urban, white working-class disillusionment with seeming pro-black liberal policies – the Wallace supporters of 1968. Add to that conventional middle- and working-class distaste for the socially relaxed and morally permissive ethos of 1960s liberalism, and the fact that America is a very Christian country as evidenced by formal church attendance, then a new conservative coalition might be in the making. Would Irish or Italian Roman Catholics of the big cities, and now increasingly of the suburbs, the very people Franklin Roosevelt had appealed to, be content to support a Democratic Party that appeared to harbour some of the more unconventional radical chic attitudes? These, however beguiling to East-West sophisticates in Washington or New York or San Francisco or Los Angeles, profoundly alienated the conservative social mores of the average voter. And did middle-class suburbanites with their respect for, and need of, law and order, their socially conformist habits and relaxation, their conventional career aspirations and concern for professional self-advancement, still find a spiritual home inside the Democratic Party? A party that seemed increasingly to condone or passively encourage violence and criminal disorder, the counter-culture and libertarian lifestyles, social drop-outs and protest movements. The perception may not always have been a fair one, but the reality was that such perceptions became increasingly common. Richard Nixon was superbly fitted to appreciate these attitudes and capitalize on them. Born in 1913, the epitome of small-town America, his birthplace Yorba Linda and upbringing and college education at Whittier were both in California. This, together with his law-school studies at Duke University in North Carolina, foreshadowed that combination of South and West that gave the sunbelt its political predominance. Indeed, within hours of being elected president he announced that he was transferring his voting residence from New York to Florida. An ambitious, lower-middle-class self-achiever, Nixon exemplified the values of Middle America with which he constantly identified. Hard-working, ruthlessly determined, with a pitiless eye to the main chance, a loner posing as a joiner, Nixon's somewhat philistine virtues and countervailing vices aptly fitted the postwar America in which he had risen to national prominence. Nixon, as a lawyer and young ex-serviceman, first won a seat in the House of Representatives in 1946 by defeating an incumbent Democrat whose impressive liberal record was maliciously construed by his opponent to furnish evidence of communist sympathies. Thus from the outset Nixon gave clear indications of his street-fighter style of politics. A seat on the bigoted House Un-American Activities Committee, the relentless prosecution of Alger Hiss, a former State Department official who denied charges of Communist Party membership and espionage, gave the young congressman welcome publicity which Hiss's subsequent conviction and imprisonment for perjury Nixon turned to his political advantage. By 1950 he was senator for California after a vicious campaign waged against the background of the Korean War and red-scare politics. Now he alleged that his opponent, the lovely former musical star Helen Gahagan Douglas, was another communist sympathizer; to liberals it appeared almost as the classic encounter between beauty and the beast. Certainly it underscored Nixon's reputation as a political infighter, who pulled few punches and slung more than a few low ones. Two years later the ex-naval lieutenant was vice-president under former supreme commander and five-star general, Dwight Eisenhower. It was a meteoric rise in a political career of six years. Success was seemingly achieved at the price of integrity, and perhaps no other Republican was so hated by his opponents as Nixon, with the unenviable exception of Joe McCarthy, who at least had the merit of not being a heartbeat away from the presidency. If Eisenhower seemed to be above politics, Nixon appeared to be their most partisan exponent; while the president held the political high ground, his vice-president, it was alleged, took the political low road. Even more cruelly, it was asked: 'Would you buy a used car from this man?'[29]

The falseness of the man seemed palpable. In the 1952 campaign he had been obliged to go on nationwide television to defend himself against charges that he had improperly used political expenses for personal benefit. It was an unappealing, if successful, exercise in self-justification that mixed sentimentality, self-pity and self-righteousness in equal proportions; even his young daughter's dog Checkers was conscripted for the defence. Eight years later, television was to prove his downfall when in debates with John Kennedy he appeared shifty, evasive and unable to match the cool, calm self-control of his opponent. If unseeing radio audiences thought that Nixon had the better of the encounter, viewers thought otherwise. In retrospect, perhaps the body language was a primitive portent, not a trick of the camera. Yet one must come back to electoral reality; 34 million of his countrymen wanted him as their president in 1960; in 1968 some 2 million less were sufficient to elect him; in 1972 a massive 47 million, over 60 per cent of those voting, confirmed him in office. Is this a comment on Nixon, on his opponents, or on those who supported him? Is it perhaps a somewhat unsettling comment on all three?

Nixon's progression from narrow loser to narrow winner to triumphant victor clearly reflects the rising conservative tide; he understood the increasing mainstream disenchantment with excessive governmental activism, an enlarged bureaucracy, and specific minority interest-targeted policies paid for by the majority. The dispossessed, the disadvantaged, the dissatisfied wielded undue influence; it was time for 'the great silent majority' to assert itself.[30]

If Nixon played his cards well, 'the great silent majority' might become a Republican one. An interesting combination of pragmatism and prejudice, Nixon was acutely aware of his minority status as a president and the uncertainty of his re-election in four years' time unless he could permanently cut the ground from under the Democrats' feet. Having been written off politically in the 1960s, after being defeated for the presidency in 1960 and the governorship of California in 1962, Nixon knew that his first term as president would be his last unless he could capitalize on the disenchantment with liberalism. Yet the congressional results had told a different story; was there some way of combining the two? Given his separate initiatives in foreign policy, and here the Executive has the right and indeed the duty to lead, Nixon might present an image of a president strong and decisive in foreign policy, but moderately conservative at home. He would wind down an unpopular war and reorder the basic structure of international relations, while sustaining liberal programmes that enjoyed majority support but curtailing those that moved beyond this consensus. Republicans had accepted the New Deal; they would not accept the Great Society. Thus the 1970s would witness conservatism in transition. The ideological conservatism of Goldwater or his acolyte Ronald Reagan, who now as governor of California made his first bid for the presidency in 1968, would be tempered by the pragmatic conservatism of 1950s Republicanism. If the former preached to the converted, there were still too few of these to construct a new consensus: Reagan's moment had not yet arrived, even if liberalism's had departed.

Symptomatic of Nixon's approach would be such initiatives as the Family Assistance Plan, designed to place a floor under poverty through direct cash payments to those too poor to be liable for federal income tax. Such a scheme bypassed the Great Society bureaucrats and social workers administering the multitude of specifically targeted programmes which appealed to particular interest groups and, by implication, certain ethnic constituencies. Moreover, the scheme did not penalize those who worked, minimized the attractions of welfare dependency and encouraged social stability by making two-parent families eligible for such assistance. It discouraged the absentee father whose desertion ensured welfare payments to his family. With its concentration on workforce not welfare, the proposal appealed to the work ethic both of Nixon and his professional middle-class and blue-collar worker supporters. They had watched with increasing distaste the expansion of welfare and its consequential rising cost, aggravated by the increasing awareness of the poor that welfare was a right not a privilege. The professional administrators of the Great Society had done their work too well for the comfort of ordinary tax-paying Americans.

It was a clever proposal, even an imaginative one. Had it been accepted, it might have represented the best chance ever to eliminate poverty in the United States before the belt-tightening of the 1970s and 1980s made such ideas financially impossible. As it was, Nixon was to spend more on human resource programmes in every one of the five budgets for which he was responsible than on defence spending, in contrast to the federal budgets of the previous quarter of a century since the Second World War. Yet Nixon seemed to liberals a suspect convert, whilst to shore up his conservative base he had to package his programmes in right-wing rhetoric that alienated the Democratic majority in Congress. In consequence, he fell between two stools, and though the measure passed the House of Representatives, it was defeated in the Senate in both 1971 and 1972 by an unholy alliance of conservatives and liberals who thought the proposals either went too far or not far enough. (Some liberal ambitions for anti-poverty measures were financially fantastic and would have bankrupted the country.) Perhaps, had Nixon had a more favourable party balance in Congress or had he been better at the art of congressional arm-twisting, the result might have been different. As it was, he had to make do with a limited scheme in 1972 to help the elderly, the disabled and the blind, thereby ensuring a small victory both for principle and common sense.

Nixon's other major initiative was the concept of the New Federalism that promoted revenue-sharing among the separate states and moved power away from the centre. Very much in line with Republican thinking over the need to restrict the enlarged role of government, its emphasis on the individual state was also part of Nixon's Southern strategy. Unfortunately, here neither principle nor common sense coincided. For a start there was no guarantee that states would necessarily use the revenues thus shared – 16 billion dollars in all – for the purposes deemed advisable by Washington. Welfare programmes administered by the states lacked the cadre of top-flight bureaucrats commonplace in the federal government, and a desirable form of patronage now bypassed Congress; the power of the purse is as much a congressional perk as congressional prerogative.

Besides, it was questionable whether even the old federalism worked very well under Nixon. Jimmy Carter, governor of Georgia during much of Nixon's presidency, recalled:

I had been frustrated and angered by the absence of even minimal cooperation between the Nixon White House and state and local leaders around the nation. The system of federalism had almost completely broken down. It had also been extremely difficult – sometimes impossible – for us to obtain information about the federal programs that so directly affected our state and for which we were at least partially responsible.[31]

Again, amalgamating Cabinet departments might nominally reduce their number but smacked of administrative musical chairs; the likelihood was that with greater areas of responsibility they would merely expand their operations under other names. Doubtless, federal agencies had proliferated and bureaucratic muddle sometimes resulted. Equally, fewer bigger ones would cloak accountability in anonymity. It seemed odd to preach the virtues of dispersion at local level to abet popular participation and advocate concentration at federal level to ensure the same. Nixon might dress up the proposal as a 'New American Revolution', and call for 'a complete reform of the federal government' but the 'most comprehensive and constructive statement on my domestic policy that I made as President' earned but a bare half page in Nixon's *Memoirs*. Congress would not move and Nixon could not move them.[32]

Perhaps, deep down, the problem was that in domestic politics, Nixon was not really a conviction politician. It is always hard for an opposition party to run in effect on another party's programme subject to certain limitations – more of the same but not quite as much. That inability to define what modern Republicanism stood for, that was one of Eisenhower's greatest limitations, also handicapped Nixon. At one level domestic politics bored him; he had not become president to have the New Federalism as his monument. Indeed, for any Republican president there was little political mileage to be had in just tinkering with liberalism's legacy. Conservative themes such as law and order were doubtless opportune. A brake on social engineering exemplified by the busing of schoolchildren to achieve racially integrated schools was welcome in some quarters. The appointment of strict constructionist judges to the federal courts, disposed to stick closely to the written Constitution and take a cautious view of judicial activism, was a legitimate strategy. The lambasting of the liberal media by members of the administration such as Vice-President Agnew clearly had some favourable response. But collectively, these initiatives were less a philosophy of government than an attitude of mind. Nixon and his entourage seemed to be clearer about what they were against than what they were for. The Republicans were still running against the prevailing liberal ethic and whilst this stance might be popular and capture the public disillusionment, it lacked that positive, forward-looking conviction that presaged a genuine political revolution. Nixon, the supreme political pragmatist, might advocate conservatism in practice, but conservatism as a philosophy had still to find its feet.

The first requirement, it was clear, was for New Deal liberalism to forfeit its right to govern, for the activist executive to be found wanting; it was the ultimate irony that this was to come from the actions of Nixon himself. Already there had been stirrings, even amongst those liberals who had been brought up to believe as an article of faith that a strong president would promote desirable liberal goals. Clearly, when untrammelled executive power could put over half a million men into Vietnam and conduct a less than honest war, this belief had to be rethought. And the very intellectuals that made up the liberal elite could never identify personally with the less than charismatic figure of Lyndon Johnson; they might support him with their heads but scarcely with their hearts.

5 The Imperial Presidency

Similarly, Nixon had succeeded to what would soon be termed the 'imperial presidency'.[33] But he lacked that popular backing and the personal gifts that were necessary to live up to the expectations that so exalted an office inspired. He seemed the beneficiary of a negative reaction to the previous administration, with relatively little to offer in domestic affairs. Thus Nixon had to end the Vietnam War, yet not at the risk of losing his right-wing supporters. Paradoxically, he had, therefore, to widen the war to restrict it, substituting aerial warfare for ground troops and pursuing the enemy beyond South Vietnam's boundaries. Such a policy provoked domestic dissent that to Nixon verged on the treasonable; with a phobia about the liberal media he was prepared to outflank the opposition illegally, believing that the end justified the means. The genesis of Watergate and its abuse of power lay in the unit set up to ensure loyalty within his administration, the Plumbers – to plug the leaks and see that the secrets of his government remained secure. Nixon was playing for high stakes. As president he was committed to reversing the direction of American foreign policy. If he succeeded, the Vietnam War itself would shade into insignificance; meanwhile, he would use all the powers of his office and a few others besides to impose his policies.

It was a far cry from the open government of Roosevelt. Nixon, too, was a very different personality. His successor Gerald Ford noted that 'he seemed to prefer dealing with paper work to dealing with people'. More ominously, for everyone has faults in their

238   *President and Nation*

make-up, 'In Nixon's case, that flaw was pride. A terribly proud man, he detested weakness in other people.' Thus Nixon's furtiveness, his isolation, his willingness to conduct a covert foreign policy, his vindictiveness towards his opponents and his willingness to resort to illegality in pursuing them, made for the whole malaise of his presidency that erupted into Watergate. 'His pride and personal contempt for weakness had overcome his ability to tell the difference between right and wrong.'[34]

This, far more persuasively than any conservative spokesman, argued for the necessity of curtailing the Executive. Liberals had been hoisted with their own petard. True, it might be possible to argue that one should distinguish between domestic reform and foreign excesses, but one could not have a schizophrenic presidency, as Nixon amply demonstrated when he impounded funds voted by Congress for causes which they might approve, but he thought undesirable. Put simply, the legislative power reserved to Congress could be frustrated by executive fiat; Nixon would decide what monies appropriated by Congress should be spent or withheld, what federal programmes should be continued or terminated. When this sum of money reached 15 billion dollars affecting over 100 programmes or nearly 20 per cent of such legislated funding, it was clear that an activist presidency could be equally over-mighty when it acted in a negative direction. Nixon might argue that the public endorsed his desire for economy, but even if some of the savings were made in defence, where the president's responsibility was manifest, a lot of the impoundments were from funds earmarked for education, the environment, health, housing and urban regeneration. In any case, it was unconstitutional. Then, presidents could veto entire bills, not particular items of them.

Even this was no obstacle to Nixon. A president does have the right to veto a bill, but that veto can be overturned by a two-thirds vote of Congress. Alternatively, if he refuses to return a bill to Congress, it automatically becomes law after ten days unless Congress has adjourned in the interim; in this case a so-called 'pocket veto' takes place. Such a veto cannot be overturned. Up until Nixon, this procedure was exercised rarely, and usually over specific private bills or ones of no public consequence. Some ambiguity existed as to what constituted an adjournment: the end of each Congress clearly, the end of one of its sessions as well, but not, presumably, when it was little more than a brief holiday recess. Nixon, however, used a five-day Christmas break to pocket-veto the Family Practice of Medicine Act of 1970, costing 225 million dollars. A bipartisan measure passed 64 to 1 in the Senate, 345 to 2 in the House, it was clear that a straightforward presidential veto would almost certainly have been overturned. Nixon would just have to be his own constitutional lawyer.

To some, Nixon's undemocratic, even unconstitutional tendencies had a long ancestry. As ex-President Harry Truman had observed before Nixon entered the White House, he did not know whether Nixon had read the Constitution but 'If he has, he doesn't understand it.'[35] Of course, Truman had hated Nixon, who had been a running sore during his own presidency. Yet Nixon's earlier career did not augur well for his occupancy of the White House. Those who had seen him at close quarters discerned an amorality of conduct that deeply troubled them. Sam Rayburn, the long-serving Speaker of the House of Representatives, considered him 'The meanest face I've ever seen in the House' and had dreaded the thought of a Nixon presidency in 1960 and what it would mean for the country. A dozen years after his death, the old man's forebodings were amply vindicated.[36]

Firstly, Nixon had been a president on the defensive, conscious of his narrow electoral base, fearful that he would be defeated for re-election. Then Senator Edward Kennedy of Massachusetts's embarrassment over the Chappaquiddick incident, with the never satisfactorily explained drowning of a young woman assistant, foreclosed the possibility of his candidacy in 1972 was a stroke of political good fortune for Nixon that was augmented when Governor George Wallace was disabled in an assassination attempt. To cap it all, the Democrats proceeded to commit electoral suicide by nominating Senator George McGovern of South Dakota as their candidate. Widely seen as representative of all that was most suspect to ordinary Americans in liberalism, his campaign never got off the ground when he was saddled with the burden of advocating the three As: acid (i.e. drugs), amnesty (for Vietnam War draft-dodgers), and abortion. And it was virtually buried when his first choice for vice-president had to stand down after it was revealed he had sought electric shock therapy for depression. Thus the outcome of the 1972 election, which few would have predicted four years earlier, was a landslide victory for Nixon. He swept the country with over 60 per cent of the popular vote and 49 of the 50 states. The luckless McGovern was left with liberal Massachusetts and the District of Columbia.

The election result seemed, too, an endorsement of Nixon's apparent successes in foreign policy. 'The great silent majority' to whom Nixon had made his appeal in the first year of his presidency had clearly been true to their name. Once again Nixon had read the political runes aright. If the war in Vietnam had not been ended 'in a way that we could win the peace' that Nixon and Kissinger resolutely demanded as an American face-saver, it had certainly been wound down. Only 39,000 American troops remained in the country on election eve, almost an irrelevance in the context of the historic normalizing of relations with China and *détente* with the Soviet Union which would surely be Nixon's greatest legacy.[37]

Nixon now believed himself unassailable. Interviewing him in March 1973, a reporter found him 'reflective, almost serene, an American President at the height of his authority'. 'My judgment,' Theodore White continued,

> suspended at that date, would have cast Richard Nixon as one of the major Presidents of the twentieth century, in a rank just after Franklin Roosevelt, on a level with Truman, Wilson, Eisenhower, Kennedy.
>
> Thus the view from Olympus, on March 17 1973, as Nixon described his use of a President's power. And then, within a few days, the view was to be shattered. I was to be brought down from Olympus to consider, with the President and millions of other Americans, the housekeeping of power – and its abuse.[38]

Watergate was a unique crisis. For a start, whatever hopes the conservative cause had of building on 1972, of constructing a natural Republican majority, were to be dashed. That overworked phrase, a Greek tragedy, hubris followed by nemesis, does seem particularly fitting for what was to happen subsequent to Nixon's victory. Already the Watergate burglary had been effected, even before Nixon's renomination, in retrospect a pointless exercise as much as an illegal one. It was inherently unlikely that any great Democratic Party secret would be discovered and the whole operation was a tribute to the vast campaign funds that Nixon had amassed, which in consequence had to be spent on more and more improbable ventures. And elections always attract political adventurers, operating in a twilight world of campaign chicanery and dirty tricks; in 1972 the Republican Party with money to burn would not lack for seamy underlings. One justification was that if Nixon ran strongly, he would benefit his party: a belief that was not borne out in practice and compounded his problems when the scandal broke. Indeed, there still remained the entrenched Democratic majorities in Congress. Nixon's own victory might rival the great Roosevelt successes of 1936 or Johnson's of 1964, but they had swept scores of Democrats into office with them – in this respect Nixon was still a circumscribed president.

A darker fear lurked beneath the surface: that Nixon the perennial loser who had made enemies over a quarter of a century would blow even this apparently foregone election. Thus any measure was permissible in the ugly war he believed it necessary to wage to outflank his opponents. There was the paradox at the heart of the man. After a quarter of a century in politics played out before the television cameras he was, as an aide observed, 'probably the best-known human being in the history of the world'; yet as Henry Kissinger noted, 'the essence of this man is loneliness.'[39]

Nixon was not a likeable exponent for conservatism, and inevitably its spokesman tainted the cause. Yet the abuse of power was not in itself a conservative prerogative; if anything, it underscored the general direction that liberal governments had taken since the days of Franklin Roosevelt. The Democrats might be the immediate beneficiaries of Watergate, yet the long-term losers. If ever conservatism could be given an attractive electoral face, it might continue where Nixon, enmeshed in Watergate, had been obliged to leave off. If Watergate undermined the Nixon presidency, it also undermined big government. It was a fact both political parties would come to appreciate.

There were those who argued that Nixon's alleged criminality could be justified; but the issue was much broader than legal niceties. Indeed, the very fact that Nixon would have faced an impeachment trial in the Senate, not in a court of law, was indicative of the political nature of the process. In effect, it supplied the body politic with a safety valve. The impeachment clause of the Constitution enumerated 'treason, bribery or other high crimes and misdemeanours' as reason for removal from office.[40] The formula was so vague precisely because it was intended to allow for expulsion on grounds of unworthiness, instantly recognizable if difficult to define. This Nixon manifestly was. Such a man was not worthy of the trust of his fellow citizens, but his disgrace posed a problem for the American system.

6   **Presidential and Party Politics after Watergate**

One could not put the clock back; the president had to be, needed to be powerful. When Congress sought to reassert its authority, it took steps to limit presidential initiative, such as in the War Powers Act of 1973 against 'undeclared wars', or the Budget Reform Act of 1974 curtailing impoundments. There was a revulsion against Washington centralization, but it would never quite carry conviction. Gerald Ford, Nixon's replacement, might represent a more decent, relaxed, likeable presidency; Jimmy Carter might get elected in 1976 by parading his virtues as a Washington outsider: still the system depended on one man. The conundrum remained: how did one ensure that the President was up to the job, yet could not become too powerful? Could one limit the Presidency without weakening it? The presidency had grown in response to crisis; there was no sign that the era of crisis had in any sense diminished.

As so often in politics, necessity would prevail. The 1970s may have been a decade of disillusionment for Americans, but the world moved on. Problems still abounded: at home, inflation and the shortage of oil; abroad, Soviet expansion into the Third World and the fiasco of Vietnam. Overshadowing all was the arms race, as threatening as ever, with nuclear annihilation a constant danger. This last alone made talk of a more limited presidency or greater consultation with Congress unrealistic. Nor did it make unassuming presidents any more credible: it was this which was to sink Jimmy Carter. The former one-term governor of Georgia and peanut farmer simply lacked the stature of a president. It made being a Washington outsider attractive in theory, ineffectual in practice. Too much was expected of the president; he had to deliver.

Thus the pattern that began to emerge in 1968 seemed increasingly to be confirmed. From 1932 until 1968 Democrats occupied the White House, with the exception of Eisenhower, and he was an atypical Republican. The strength of the modern presidency had first been built on domestic liberalism, subsequently augmented by foreign affairs. This, it was clear, was what the nation wanted; the Democratic Party would still run well locally by appealing to its traditional supporters, catering for their special interests. In foreign affairs, however, the Democratic Party record was more mixed: Truman's failures, real or perceived, had opened the way for Eisenhower; Johnson's over Vietnam had led to Nixon. Sometimes the Democratic Party's ability to deliver on national security had appeared questionable: George McGovern, the Democratic Party standard bearer in the 1972 campaign, had seemed suspect; later, Carter in office would have a dismal record. The Teheran hostages would be the final encumbrance of a weak presidency: a humiliatingly public symbol of American impotence. If the years 1932 to 1968 had seen the presidency dominated by the Democrats, with the exception of Eisenhower, the years from 1968 until 1992, with the exception of Carter's one-term victory in 1976 in reaction to Watergate, would be Republican. Where national security and foreign affairs were concerned, Republican presidents seemed safer.

Yet a lingering doubt remained. Even if, as the years passed, the weight of government bureaucracy seemed increasingly a legacy of the New Deal state, a fact on which Ronald Reagan would capitalize so effectively in 1980, the welfare aspects were deeply entrenched in people's affections. Though the middle classes might balk at paying ever more taxes to fund anti-poverty programmes, thereby obviating the liberal agenda of the 1960s, they did not want, and nor did blue-collar workers, labour, ethnic minorities, lower socio-economic groups generally, the abolition of welfare, only perhaps its curtailment. Here the Democrats had the safer hands. If the impetus for further reform had run its course, if the Great Society had represented the apogee of liberalism, nonetheless its consolidation and continuance enjoyed considerable support. The enduring popularity of the Democratic Party in congressional elections would be both the cause and the consequence of this sentiment. The Republicans remained the minority throughout Nixon's presidency; this was to be the consistent misfortune of Republican presidents thereafter, with the exception of Reagan, who at least had a slender majority in the Senate for the first six years of his presidency. Even he, for all his rhetoric, was to find when it came to cutting the cost of the federal budget that the leeway for retrenchment was limited; certain welfare programmes had too strong a constituency to risk curtailment. If the Republicans controlled the presidency, the Democrats controlled the Congress.

Thus the eighteen months between the opening revelations of administration misconduct in the concealment of Watergate and Gerald Ford's well-intentioned but ineptly timed pardon of his predecessor, March 1973 to September 1974, effectively scuppered any hopes of a Republican victory in 1976. The damage they would inevitably sustain was presaged by the Democrats' gains in the midterm elections of 1974. In retrospect, it is remarkable and significant how well Republicans did do, given the unique disgrace of Nixon's resignation and the limitations of his successor. Gerald Ford was not a Harry Truman, though he assiduously cultivated the analogy of unsought promotion. Hence the Republican setback was not necessarily an indication that the conservative tide had receded; indeed, in a curious way Watergate helped it forward. For a start even the anticipated Republican drubbing in the off-year elections did not demonstrate a renewed liking for liberalism on the part of the electorate; the 'new Democrats' elected in that year – and the phrase took on a life of its own – were self-consciously not old New Deal liberals. If they shared the latter's beliefs on international and social issues, on labour, spending and taxation, they reflected the attitudes of the younger, more affluent professional classes, which increasingly made up their constituencies. The old Roosevelt coalition had broken up. In 1972 the AFL-CIO (American Federation of Labor-Congress of Industrial Organizations) had actually endorsed Nixon for president, an astonishing volte-face. Those older Democrats who still held power in Congress were often viewed as akin to dinosaurs by the freshmen of 1974. Large Democratic majorities, sustained in 1976, hid an internecine warfare that was no longer just one between urban liberals and rural conservatives, the old Democratic fissure of long standing. Indeed, these latter groups often made common cause against the newcomers, bent on reforming Congress and its rules of seniority and committee structures that benefited the long-serving.

This same ambiguity showed itself in the Democrats' selection of their presidential candidate in 1976. There was the elder statesman Hubert Humphrey, a likeable, warm-hearted man, whose philosophy harked straight back to Roosevelt and could be relied upon to safeguard liberal orthodoxy. At the end of his life he gave eloquent expression to his creed: 'The moral test of government is how it treats those who are in the dawn of life, the children; those who are in the twilight of life, the aged; and those who are in the shadows of life – the sick, the needy and the handicapped.' Humphrey, 'a liberal who never changed his stripes', half thought that the party would be obliged to turn to him, as the natural candidate in waiting.[41] Although it was an assumption interestingly shared by Gerald Ford, his putative opponent, it ignored political reality. Watergate had not merely blighted the Republican Party but Washington and all its works in general. The old politics was suspect, of whatever persuasion.

It was this mood of disillusionment with the old order and a yearning for a fresh start that facilitated the rise of Jimmy Carter to the White House from the relative obscurity of one term as governor of Georgia. Carter was no New Deal liberal, though he came from Franklin Roosevelt's adopted Southern state. Indeed, he might never have entertained the thought of the presidency had a winnable Senate seat been available when his term as governor ended in 1974; his candidacy for the presidency initially provoked widespread derision for a presumption based on inexperience. Yet Carter had correctly discerned the direction of the political tide. Anybody untainted by Washington politics would have a head start in the revulsion against Watergate. In the unique circumstances of 1976 relative inexperience, as long as it had a fresh face, might be an advantage. 'If I ever lie to you, if ever I ever make a misleading statement, don't vote for me. I would not deserve to be your President.'[42]

The promise never to tell a lie, whilst it might invite scepticism from all but the credulous, revealed a capacity to judge the mood of the electorate every bit as accurately as Warren Harding when he had called for 'normalcy' a half century and more previously. The American people wanted a president who would not lie to them, and in large part were half willing to believe that such a man was possible. It made the suspension of disbelief easier if the candidate in question was a relative unknown with no long political record to call their faith into question.

If Carter appealed to the electorate in general, he appealed to Democrats in particular. Inevitably, his candidacy had to be based on straddle, a Southern base, shades of the old Roosevelt coalition, sufficiently middle-of-the-road not to threaten the true liberals but contemporary and footloose enough from the old power blocs to seem something of a New Democrat. This ambiguity was to cause trouble in the long run when Carter was in office, but in the immediate quest for nomination and election there were distinct advantages in apparently being nobody's man but his own. In running against Washington, Carter initiated a ploy that others were to use to ever greater advantage subsequently, and for the Democrats it was, long-term, a high-risk strategy; they, if anybody, were the party of Washington, had been indeed for almost half a century. It was the political equivalent of calling stinking fish. For the moment, however, it prised open the Republican grip on the White House that had threatened to become permanent; more dangerously, it obscured the immensity of the change that had already taken place.

In fact, Carter's narrow victory over Gerald Ford might have served as a warning. Even Nixon's disgrace, the debacle in Vietnam, the increasing sense of a rudderless administration – Ford vetoed more significant legislation than any previous president – compounded by record postwar unemployment and almost as severe inflation, were not in themselves apparently sufficient cause alone to jettison the Republicans. No matter that even WIN (Whip Inflation Now), a cause on which Ford had set his heart – 'our inflation, our public enemy number one, will, unless whipped, destroy our country, our homes, our liberties, our property and finally our national pride as surely as will any well-armed wartime enemy' – had proved unavailing.[43]

Indeed, Ford might well have overcome even these handicaps, had conservative Republicans not chosen this of all moments to advance their cause by challenging the president for the nomination. Ford was a Republican of older ancestry who had, in effect, been appointed to the presidency, initially as replacement vice-president after Spiro Agnew left office in disgrace when, to avoid more serious charges, he pleaded guilty to income tax evasion in October 1973; he then succeeded Nixon in August 1974. Although a Midwesterner from Michigan who had led his party in the House of Representatives, where he had served for a quarter of a century, Ford represented mainline Republicanism. His political moderation was symbolized by his own appointment of Nelson Rockefeller as his vice-president, the archetypal eastern Republican governor of New York whom the conservative wing of the party cordially detested. Thus in 1976 Ronald Reagan, having served eight years as governor of California and an old man in a hurry, determined to wrest the nomination from Ford. Such challenges, if serious and made to an incumbent president, are usually doomed but invariably benefit the opposition, as the Democrats found in 1968 and 1980, the Republicans in 1976 and 1992. Ford, notwithstanding he was already in the White House, was reduced to canvassing for the support of individual delegates to the Republican Convention. The outcome as to the nomination was in suspense to the last, and the wounds thus created inevitably weakened the party as it tried to present a united front to the electorate in the subsequent campaign. Too many hostages to fortune had been given which the Democrats, predictably, were not slow to exploit. Still, it was a close run thing.

And the fact that it took such a double whammy of poor policies and party divisions to defeat narrowly a very average candidate, who did not hold the presidency in his own right and was overshadowed by the crimes of his predecessor, suggests a surprising latent Republican strength. There was clearly a bedrock of support that would have been incomprehensible for a minority party only a few years previously.

Indeed, in spite of the result – Carter defeated Ford by 2 per cent of the popular vote: with 50.1 per cent he just had a majority as president, and a mere 56 electoral college votes' margin – it was clear that the palmy days of Democratic dominance were at an end. The Roosevelt coalition was a thing of the past; only vestiges of it survived. Even the South was no longer solid, that is, if white votes are counted. Misleadingly, Carter, a Southerner, retained the region for the Democratic party. Nixon's Southern strategy seemed to have come unstuck, but unlike Roosevelt, Carter held on to the South because of black votes – the white South was inexorably moving rightwards. Similarly, the old ethnic loyalties were no longer reliable, whilst the poorest groups such as African-Americans and Mexican-Americans went overwhelmingly for Carter, the increased affluence of such groups as Irish-Americans and Italian-Americans, once solidly Democrat, weakened their loyalty to the party of FDR. Though labour recanted from its 1972 flirtation with the Republicans and went back to its traditional political home, alarmingly, the Democrats ceased to be geographically a national party, failing to win a single Western state. It was a striking reminder that the frostbelt–sunbelt division, if allowance is made for Carter the Southerner, was a potent factor that would increasingly weaken a Democratic Party that was receding from its days of glory. Even the fact that in what was widely regarded as a certain Democratic year, the party could find no other candidate than Carter, suggested a party that had lost its way.

Put simply, Carter, in many ways a decent man, was not up to the job of president. At one level this is to do him an injustice: 'When it came to understanding the issues of the day', a friendly critic noted, 'Jimmy Carter was the smartest public official I've ever known. The range and extent of his knowledge were astounding.' But Tip O'Neill, the powerful Democratic Speaker of the House added: 'His mind was exceptionally well developed, and it was open, too. He was always willing to listen and to learn. With one exception. When it came to the politics of Washington, D.C, he never really understood how the system worked. And although this was out of character for Jimmy Carter, he didn't want to learn about it, either.'[44]

Having run against the Washington establishment, Carter took his rhetoric – or perhaps his principles – seriously, forgetting that the great strength of the party he had inherited was precisely in that ability to wield the levers of federal power that it had practised with such conspicuous success since the 1930s. The first president since Woodrow Wilson to have no previous experience of Washington whatsoever, it was essential that Carter set out to understand its inner politics. He would have to work with the congressional leadership of his own party. Thus he could try to create a political agenda around which Democrats, and hopefully the country, might unite as they sought to find their way in the troubled 1970s. Battered by Watergate, the aftermath of the Vietnam War, and the economic disruption induced by OPEC's (Organization of Petroleum Exporting Countries) quadrupling of oil prices, America faced a crisis of confidence it was imperative Carter resolved. His election in 1976 had been based on the promise of a fresh start, but Carter was a political technician more than a political artist; if he had some good ideas in theory, he never had the consistency of purpose or the skill in implementation to translate his promises into performance. He remained the one-term governor of a conservative Southern state, endeavouring to apply his limited powers nationwide. Nor was he helped by the provincial, not to say parochial, Georgian mafia who made up too many of his advisers and lacked the wider perspective vital in counsellors to an inexperienced president. Even this liability might have been overcome, had he reached out to his natural allies in Washington. Instead, Tip O'Neill complained constantly at Carter's unwillingness to help the passage of vital legislation by employing the political arts of persuasion, patronage and punishments that successful presidents must do if they are to see their programmes implemented by the legislators. Too often O'Neill was left fighting for the president's programme without adequate backing; indeed, some of the Georgia mafia had an ability, amounting to near genius, to tread on congressmen's toes.

Moreover, even had Carter and his aides been able to fashion an effective political relationship with the Democrats in Congress, it was never quite clear where the president planned to lead them. Perhaps the tension between being an avowed economic and fiscal conservative but a moderate, social liberal proved too confusing.

Revealingly, Carter confided in his diary: 'In many cases I feel more at home with the conservative Democratic and Republican members of Congress than I do with the others, although the others, the liberals, vote with me much more often.'[45]

At first, Carter looked as if he might be a traditional Democrat in the Roosevelt-Johnson mould. Unemployment was running at near 8 per cent and it was the hope that a Democratic president might react with typical Democratic concern that helped win Carter the election. Indeed, Carter even revived the old FDR formula of the fireside chat, this time on television, where the American public was regaled with the spectacle of the president, clad in a cardigan sweater, at ease in a chair by his fireside, chatting about the problems of the nation. Typically, it seemed to have escaped Carter that it was by their own firesides that Roosevelt's audiences had assembled. Roosevelt himself spoke from the desk in his study. Moreover, a single log burning in the fireplace invited ridicule unless the urgency of the energy problem, the subject of the first talk, was even worse than was suspected! On another occasion the fire in the grate actually went out! It seemed symbolic of liberal hopes for the success of Carter's presidency.

After a while Carter decided that inflation, not unemployment, was the number one problem facing the nation; thus unbalanced budgets with large deficits, tax cuts and increased public spending were out, reduced government expenditure and delayed tax reductions in. A $79 billion budget deficit in 1976 was cut to $27 billion in 1979. By the second half of his presidency he was vetoing the very spending programmes he had proposed in the first. The inevitable mishmash pleased nobody. By 1979 Senator Edward Kennedy had resolved to run against him for the Democratic presidential nomination as a genuine liberal candidate; Carter was derided as a conservative, even a closet Republican. What was inescapable was that by 1980, his last full year in the presidency, Carter faced an ever-deepening recession with unemployment at 7.5 per cent (in other words, little progress had been made throughout his time in the White House in getting people back to work). Meanwhile, inflation averaged over 12 per cent; mortgage rates were 15 per cent; and interest rates a record 20 per cent.

Worse, Carter compounded his problems by his failure to pass effective energy conservation and oil deregulation measures. Though proclaiming the energy crisis 'the moral equivalent of war', his legislation was a sorry version of its pristine self after special-interest lobbyists had got to work on their congressional allies already at sixes and sevens due to an absence of firm party leadership. If Carter's proposals had any chance of success he needed to practise precisely those political skills he so conspicuously lacked. Moreover, he had underscored the gravity of his failure by his assertion that 'Our decision about energy will test the character of the American people and the ability of the President and the Congress to govern this nation.' And it was precisely that 'ability' that would increasingly be called into question.[46]

Well into the third year of his presidency, Carter himself acknowledged his failure and treated the American people to an extraordinary display of political naivety. Retiring to the presidential retreat at Camp David, for ten days Carter consulted with a wide range of supporters and advisers before addressing the nation. To Carter, 'These next few days were destined to be some of the most thought-provoking and satisfying of my Presidency.' To his loyal vice-president, 'It was an unorthodox thing to do, and he was convinced that it would result in political catastrophe.'[47]

Finally on 15 July 1979 Carter addressed the nation. Subsequently dubbed the 'malaise' speech, though the word was never used, it took on the characteristics of a sermon that mixed damaging admissions of failure and exhortations to national rededication in equal part. Weakly he conceded: 'I realize more than ever that as president I need your help.' It was scarcely an auspicious start; nor did his frank avowal of some of the advice he had received while on retreat give an impression of strong leadership: 'Mr. President, you are not leading this nation – you're just managing the government. You don't see the people enough any more. Some of your Cabinet members don't seem loyal. There is not enough discipline among your disciples....' All in all, it was an extraordinary exercise in soul-searching self-incrimination. And when he went on to assert: 'Looking for a way out of this crisis, our people have turned to the federal government and found it isolated from the mainstream of our nation's life. Washington D.C. has become an island. The gap between our citizens and our government has never been so wide', Carter had virtually written the Republican Party programme for the 1980 election. Little wonder that he lost it![48]

It cost liberalism a lot more. Carter's defeat elevated to the White House the true spiritual heir of Barry Goldwater. This time it really was Ronald Reagan's last chance. Ever since he had made the speech in the 1964 election on nationwide television from Los Angeles on behalf of Goldwater, he had been the darling of the American right. If the 1964 election broke Goldwater, it made Reagan. Two years later he was elected governor of California, ousting a popular two-term incumbent who four years previously had defeated Richard Nixon; by 1968 he was already challenging for the Republican presidential nomination. His hour had not yet come; instead, he remained in Sacramento, re-elected in 1970, practising what critics called the politics of symbolism. Thus he promised to lower taxes and reduce state governmental expenditure; in fact he raised the former and more than doubled the budget of the latter. Having attacked abortion, he signed one of the nation's most liberal abortion laws. He criticized welfare dependency but the number of recipients nearly doubled; even when, later, he reduced the number of beneficiaries, the size of their payments was substantially increased. Reagan even managed the trick of seemingly running against the government he had just headed when he sought re-election in 1970.

Yet in spite of all, Reagan was a conviction politician and this was the source of his strength. He believed in what he said, and the very simplicity of his message made it easier to comprehend. Moreover, though not without guile, Reagan was a man without subtlety; the very two-dimensional nature of his understanding made it easier for him to accept contradictions between his words and his actions that would have embarrassed a more acute thinker. And if he was intellectually lazy, he was socially relaxed: if simple in his perceptions, genial in his manner. The actor was always aware of the need to be amiable to his fans, unstuffy and good-humoured: qualities he took with him into politics and which ensured his popularity. Reagan never forgot who his ultimate paymasters were or to whom he owed his part. It was one he acted to perfection.

Reagan had very nearly wrested the nomination from Gerald Ford in 1976; four years later he was more successful against all the odds that age stacked against him. Born in 1911, he was almost seventy when elected president, the age Eisenhower had been as the oldest chief executive in the nation's history when he left the White House. This, too, helped his conservative image. Reagan's adult lifetime had spanned modern America; he could speak on behalf of a generation, which had seen their hopes gone awry; he had voted for Franklin Roosevelt and found liberalism to have been a god that failed. It gave force to his criticism of the New Deal state.

For the potency of its appeal was still strong; there were many Democrats who believed that Carter's great mistake had been to turn his back on the traditional full-blooded liberalism of his party; Kennedy was one of them. Moreover, to Kennedy liberalism implied the need for activist government: the one required the other. It was here particularly that he thought Carter had failed. He simply did not know how to utilize the power of the presidency. There was an enormous, unique potential to the office; Carter did not understand his obligations. He had to be proactive; it was a president's duty to lead: 'A President has got to stay ahead of the curve. The one institution in this government that has the ability not to be crisis-crushed is the presidency of the United States... this *outsider* can't solve our problems... Even on issues we agree on, he doesn't know how to do it.'[49]

It was rotten luck that the very day that, greatly daring, Kennedy launched his candidacy against an incumbent president, Iranian extremists should have captured the American embassy personnel in Teheran. The presidency is always shown to best advantage in a foreign crisis; there is a natural rallying round the president. Carter initially benefited from this public gut instinct, and even a weak president like Carter could deploy all the powers of his office to stifle an opponent. Kennedy, morally flawed after Chappaquiddick, not to mention an undercurrent of rumour about his private life, showed himself a surprisingly poor candidate at the outset. There were some painful television performances. Even the Kennedy aura could not save him. Yet the failure was more personal than political, and the failure was redeemed by a stunning speech at the Democratic Convention when Kennedy, unburdened of the quest for the nomination, never looked more like a president than in the moment when he knew he had failed to make it. Unleashing all the liberal aspirations of the old New Deal–Great Society traditions of the Democratic Party, which was his second home, Kennedy galvanized the delegates:

My fellow Democrats, I have come here tonight not to argue as a candidate but to affirm a cause...

Our cause has been, since the days of Thomas Jefferson, the cause of the common man and the common woman. Our commitment has been, since the days of Andrew Jackson, to all those he called 'the humble members of society – the farmers, mechanics, and laborers...'

We are the party of the New Freedom, the New Deal, and the New Frontier. We have always been the party of hope...

For me, a few hours ago, this campaign came to an end. For all those whose cares have been our concern, the work goes on, the cause endures, the hope still lives, and the dream shall never die![50]

If the Carter forces had retained control of the body of the Democratic Party, it was arguable that the Kennedy supporters had captured its soul, and thus the ostensible victors were obliged to mollify their opponents by conceding a large number of liberal policies in the party platform. Indeed, one cannot but regret what might have been. How would the election of 1980 have turned out, and what an exciting one it would have been, had it been a straight liberal–conservative contest. Had Kennedy, against all the odds, won the nomination and stepped into the election arena as an old-style liberal champion against Reaganite conservatism, what direction would America have taken? Was such a possibility American liberalism's last frail chance?

7 Reagan, Bush and Conservatism

The important thing to grasp about the election of 1980, if it was a turning point, was that it was partly so by default. Perhaps that is true of all great turning points. But it was clear whom the American people were voting against, even if they were not entirely sure what they were voting for. Of course, to some extent that was true in 1932 when Roosevelt ousted Hoover, but the subsequent Roosevelt policies showed a general consistency of purpose, if not of detail, quite different from the subsequent so-called Reagan revolution. Although 1980 marked the coming of age of American conservatism, there was a gulf between its leader and his followers, which it was to take a dozen more years or so to resolve. All political parties have their ginger groups; all party loyalists sometimes wish their leader would go faster than those who exercise responsibility can safely dare. What is remarkable about Reagan and his conservative followers is how often he led them in directions diametrically opposed to the ones he had promised them. Equally remarkable is that they still followed him. Such ambiguity suggests either a polished sleight-of-hand or a vacuity at the heart of American conservatism.

The politics of the 1980s reflected this ambiguity. Reagan's great strength lay in his promise of a strong, respected America abroad and making people feel good at home. Growing up in the Depression, where Roosevelt had been his hero, it was only in middle age that increasing wealth turned him from the Democrats to the Republicans. In this respect, perhaps, his voyage of self-discovery was typical of many of his countrymen. Thus he caught the tide of conservatism, nor was this merely political; equally powerful was the emergence of the religious right, concerned at what appeared a wholesale repudiation of much of America's Christian moral heritage. By the late 1970s some 70 million Americans described themselves as 'born-again Christians': reinforced by television evangelists, they became a potent political force. At one level it was an odd phenomenon: a sometimes strident reaction against the institutionalizing of social liberalism, a curious mixture of piety and patriotism, that seemed almost fundamentalist in its creed. Even odder was Reagan as its standard bearer: a remarried divorcee who was not particularly noted for the regularity of his church-going, running against a real born-again Christian like Carter whose deep religious commitment was not in doubt. But it undoubtedly gave Reagan a core constituency, as he astutely recognized; evangelist Billy Graham told him: 'I would think you have talked about God more than any other president since Abraham Lincoln.'[51]

And the very simplicity of Reagan's message acted as a powerful antidote to the confusion of the post-Watergate years. In 1980 he promised an end to the apparent drift and decline of the 1970s. His achievement reflected both the strengths and the dangers that the growth of the presidency now offered. Government was apparently the problem; so too, however, was indecisive leadership. It was an interesting paradox. The American people had invested great trust in the presidency; now they needed someone who could live up to their expectations. Each election would be an opportunity to realize these hopes, but would any candidate live up to his promise? Not since Eisenhower had a president served a normal two-term presidency: disappointment seemed almost inevitable as the reality of practical politics destroyed the reputation of any candidate chosen. No human being could accommodate all the hopes placed in him; only perhaps by transcending politics could failure be averted. This was to be Reagan's forte. Roosevelt had harnessed the public mood to support his programmes; Eisenhower had avoided party politics; Reagan preserved his popularity by a clever deflection of responsibility. It was a style that suited his lackadaisical attitude to his duties. In the short term, it was effective.

After the traumas of the 1970s, the nation yearned for equilibrium; one might even call it 'normalcy'. A strong America that did not get kicked around abroad, a prosperous society that provided middle-class comforts without middle-class obligations at home, would be balm for the wounds inflicted on the national psyche by a decade of self-doubt. When Reagan in a breathtaking piece of political effrontery could accept the nomination for president in 1980 and quote copiously from Franklin Roosevelt in his acceptance speech, enlisting him as a patron for some unlikely liberal causes, he could ensure the succession whilst dramatically departing from it. Roosevelt had made America the world power, Reagan would renew it; Roosevelt had augmented the powers of government, Reagan would reduce them, arguing that the solution had by now become the problem. Where Roosevelt had sown, Reagan would reap. The New Deal had done its work well; a middle-class society had come into being, sufficiently satiated to call a halt to further reform. In the words of J. K. Galbraith, it was 'the culture of contentment'.[52]

Personally amiable, Reagan's popularity was undoubted; in 1984 he was triumphantly re-elected. It illustrated how powerful a figure the president could be if he read aright the mood of public opinion, told the American people what they wanted to hear, gave them at least the sense of security that once had been their birthright. At other times, security exacted too high a price, as when bent on carrying on his own obsessive vendetta against the Nicaraguan Sandinistas, the Iran-Contra affair organized in his name stretched to breaking point the legal powers of the presidency. Personal popularity, the eruption of the scandal when he was but two years from compulsory retirement, a weary public who did not want yet another of their idols to be found to have feet of clay, probably saved him from public humiliation, if not outright impeachment.

Nor was this playing to the gallery confined to posturing in foreign policy. The Reagan years were remarkable above all for their inconsistency; here indeed they make a contrast with the years of Franklin Roosevelt. Of course the New Deal was noted for its inconsistency, but it was an inconsistency of method, not of content. Only in the so-called Roosevelt recession of 1937–8, when Roosevelt got cold feet and listened to his conservative advisers, did he backtrack on what he had done before, and the conservative experiment did not last; by the spring of 1938 he had come to his liberal senses. With Reagan the programme was fundamentally incoherent from the start: 'voodoo economics' as George Bush, his rival for the presidential nomination in 1980, aptly termed it. There was no way that Reagan could cut taxes, balance the budget and increase defence expenditure. And the pious belief that heavy tax-cutting for the wealthy would benefit the lower echelons of taxpayers, the 'trickle down' theory, rested more on economic faith than economic experience. To Reagan, however, it was all too simple:

> you reduce tax rates and allow people to spend or save more of what they earn, they'll be more industrious; they'll have more incentive to work hard, and money they earn will add fuel to the great economic machine that energizes our national progress. The result more prosperity for all – and more revenue for government. A few economists call this principle supply-side economics. I call it common sense.[53]

The result could have been anticipated. Whilst taxes were cut and defence expenditure was increased, the budget went even further out of balance; Reagan put America into greater debt than all his predecessors together. All one could do was admire his insouciance. Faced with the stark political reality that the much-vaunted notion of governmental economies simply disappeared in the face of national need or vested interest, Reagan was soon forced into euphemistic 'revenue enhancements', in effect indirect taxes, to make up for tax cuts and consequent loss of government revenue. If Reagan would not touch the defence budget, in fact increased it, his opponents in Congress would not let him touch welfare. In the end, only some 17 cents in every dollar spent by the government came from programmes where cuts could be contemplated.

Indeed, even his Economic Recovery Tax Act, passed in August 1981 in the honeymoon period most newly elected Presidents enjoy, might never have got out of the halls of Congress. But Reagan pluckily survived an attempted assassination in the spring, which inevitably earned him a good deal of public sympathy. There is no doubt that Reagan practised the political arts to perfection, giving conservatism an attractive face. And when the economy faltered, what saved him was partly the old Reagan luck. The OPEC nations fell out and oil prices plummeted. Meanwhile, increased defence spending would in effect be a militarized version of Keynesian deficit spending reminiscent of the public works programmes of the New Deal – though this time the 'public works' thus built were military hardware.

Reagan actually made a mess of the American economy and caused much hardship in consequence. To save money, anti-poverty programmes were cut back wherever they had the fewest defenders, occasioning real, even shameful deprivation for the most needy. For example, more than 400,000 people lost their AFDC (Aid For Dependent Children) coverage, and Medicaid for good measure. There was a callous side to American conservatism that too easily equated dependency with fecklessness. By 1989, the year Reagan left office, almost 13 per cent of the population lived below the poverty line, defined as $12,674 for a family of four. By contrast, 20 per cent had incomes of $50,000 or above. It rather called into question his successor's assertion that 'class is for European democracies or something else – it isn't for the United States. We are not going to be divided by class.'[54]

Nor was Reagan even successful within his own terms of reference. It did not, however, appear to faze him unduly. Certainly, in Congress he faced some wily and determined Democratic opponents. There were still many 'bread-and-butter liberals'. They would not lightly surrender the gains of half a century. Nor, if they had affection, did they have much respect for their opponent. 'Ronald Reagan lacked the knowledge he should have had in every sphere, both domestic and international. Most of the time he was an actor reading lines, who didn't understand his own programs... it was sinful that Ronald Reagan ever became president.'[55]

Even if one conceded that there was much congressional special-interest pleading, not all of it high-minded, it was not just confined to Democrats. Republicans, too, were not slow in coming forward on behalf of their constituents. They might have recalled that in 1980 only 11 per cent of those who voted for Reagan did so because he was a real conservative. If he had any natural constituency, it was white males under 35 who liked his promise to stand up to the Soviet Union. The over-65s and women generally were more concerned about social programmes. Government spending, therefore, would always find its defenders. That, his director of the Budget conceded, 'may not be wise, but it is the only real and viable definition of what the electorate wants'. Nonetheless, he added,

I cannot be so patient with the White House. By 1984 it had become a dreamland. It was holding the American economy hostage to a reckless unstable fiscal policy, based on the politics of high spending and low taxes. Yet rather than acknowledge that the resulting massive buildup of public debt would generate serious economic troubles, the White House proclaimed a roaring economic success. It bragged that its policies had worked as never before when, in fact, they had produced fiscal excesses that had never before been imagined.[56]

If tax cuts made for poor economic strategy, however, they made for good political tactics. They helped the Republican Party to expand its own influence and diminish that of its opponents; spending cutbacks, for example, often hit hardest those institutions that normally sided with the Democrats, such as social service and regulatory agencies. Equally, higher taxes had at least allowed Congress to enact preferential tax legislation by way of mitigation; clearly, this was going to be difficult with less money to go round and the deficit ever rising. In 1986 a Tax Reform Act outlawed many of them officially. Congress, with at least a Democrat-controlled House, found it impossible to pass so much as one major new spending programme during the first six years of Reagan's presidency. 'I had always thought of government as a kind of organism with an insatiable appetite for money,' Reagan later noted, 'whose natural state is to grow forever unless you do something to starve it. By cutting taxes, I wanted not only to stimulate the economy but to curb the growth of government and reduce its intrusion into the economic life of the country.'[57]

The 1986 tax cuts were certainly dramatic. Fourteen tax brackets were reduced to two, and the rates themselves were the lowest since Coolidge. Perhaps this had more than a touch of symbolism. For Reagan also conjured up a vision of a return to the 1920s in the amount of corruption that touched his administration. All in all, it was quite a Republican tradition. The Teapot Dome scandal under Harding – the leasing of naval oil reserves to private development plus all the other influence-peddling and chicanery – would be followed by Watergate, Iran-Contra and the general sleaziness of the Reagan years. Since these were all Republican embarrassments, one may reasonably ask whether this is mere coincidence or a reflection on American conservatism? Perhaps it was the inevitable concomitant of wealth allied to political power, but it suggests that the spirit that at its lowest animated the Republican Party in the Gilded Age has had several reincarnations. Certainly, not since the days of Progressivism have Republican domestic policies as such been able to capture the moral high ground; in the final analysis Jeffersonianism is more intuitively in tune with the principles that are enshrined in the American Republic than Hamiltonianism. The former spoke for the many, the latter for the few.

Where Reagan was considerably more effective – here the hard work was continued by his successor – was in making sure that political conservatism, lest it be a passing phase, should receive judicial approbation. The twelve years of Republican ascendancy, 1981–93, were to see half the membership of the Supreme Court and the lower federal judiciary profoundly altered by conservative appointments. This was a powerful legacy for the future. Given that long after Reagan and Bush had gone to their reward, such judges might still be in office, one might cynically observe that not only ideological orthodoxy but also youth, a good heart and lungs, and a family history of longevity were useful requisites for appointment. It threatened to enact or reverse a pattern of judicial development not seen since Roosevelt's fight with the Supreme Court in 1937. If in the intervening years the Court had accepted the enlargement of federal authority, a cause dear to, and indeed a necessary prelude to, political liberalism, it had also gone on to accept, or indeed encourage, the development of social liberalism.

The real turning point was Eisenhower's nomination of the apparently safe Republican governor of California and 1948 vice-presidential nominee Earl Warren as chief justice in 1953. The following year came the momentous *Brown v. Board of Education of Topeka, Kansas*, ruling that outlawed separate but equal educational facilities for whites and blacks, and a year later ordered school integration with all deliberate speed. Soon Southern governors were standing in well-publicized school doorways while black parents walked their small children to register for school in front of howling white mobs. But the Supreme Court, perhaps partly as a welcome corrective to enlarged governmental power, increasingly cherished individual liberties that of necessity supported minority causes at the expense of mainstream attitudes. With the surging conservative tide of opinion reinforced by the American religious right, the feeling that the law leaned too much towards libertarian causes took hold. In 1973 the Supreme Court in the famous *Roe v. Wade* case asserted a constitutional right to abortion during the first trimester, though in effect abortion on request throughout pregnancy soon became accepted in practice. It became the touchstone of the division between social liberals and conservatives; once again the argument that the Court was playing politics was heard, this time from the right. The charge was that the judges were making law, not interpreting the Constitution. Soon a battle-royal was being waged. Conservatives argued that judges should uphold the doctrine of original intent, that is, they should read the Constitution as the Founders had intended or one might suppose they had intended it to be read. Against them were ranged liberals who suggested that the Constitution, to survive, had to be seen as a living document, to be interpreted creatively in the light of modern circumstances. When such issues as abortion or affirmative action programmes for historically disadvantaged minorities or racial, gender or sexual discrimination cases seemed to depend on individual judicial philosophies, the stakes were clearly high. One nomination, indeed, the attempted appointment of Robert Bork to the Supreme Court by Reagan in 1987, was to be a nomination too far and marked the waning of his power. After 1986 the Senate, which had to approve the nomination, was once again controlled by the Democrats, thus enabling the liberals, led by such stalwarts as Kennedy, to obstruct a president who would soon leave office and whose authority was eroded by the Iran-Contra scandal. It was a salutary reminder that if the liberals were dead they would not lie down; if the days of big government, high taxes and heavy federal expenditure had formally been rejected, lots of liberal causes still had their champions. Political conservatism was more attractive than social conservatism to the average voter. It was a warning sign that Republicans would ignore at their peril. However, Reagan's luck would hold to see him safely out of office.

Thus George Bush entered the White House with the same atmosphere of complacency that had marked Herbert Hoover's first six months in office: in Bush's case the honeymoon was to last two years. True, he faced a Democratic Congress that would soon prove obstructive, and warning voices had already been raised about America's parlous economic and social condition. Yet Bush had boxed himself in by a pledge not to levy new taxes. It implied that his opponent Michael Dukakis, the governor of Massachusetts, was a 'tax and spend' liberal, which helped win Bush the election. Indeed, the Bush victory was clear-cut if not as complete as Reagan's had been; but there was comfort for the Democrats who reinforced their hold on Congress. Thus Bush's pledge would come back to haunt him.

For the moment, however, Bush prospered. Here war proved, as usual, the health of the presidency; Bush was the first president to lead his country to war twice within two years of taking office. The invasion of Panama may not have been much more than one of the routine Latin-American police actions that had consistently marked American interventionist policies south of the Rio Grande whenever it suited her interests; the Gulf War was clearly of a superior order. Perhaps nothing better exemplifies just how far the presidency had become a virtual law unto itself, that only for the second time in fifty years, the first in fact since Roosevelt's request after Pearl Harbor, did the Executive seek from Congress a formal declaration of war. Had America been at peace in between? Moreover, almost half a million men had been moved to Saudi Arabia, resolutions put through the United Nations, allies sought and a coalition constructed, even before Congress narrowly gave its approval. Even that was a courtesy. 'In truth, even had Congress not passed the resolutions', Bush later conceded, 'I would have acted and ordered our troops into combat. I know it would have caused an outcry, but it was the right thing to do. I was comfortable in my own mind that I had the constitutional authority.'[58]

The speed and the success of the war seemed further to enhance the president and undercut his critics. It did not help them that all the Democratic leadership in both Houses of Congress voted against it. Only a sublime indifference to troubles nearer home could jeopardize the Bush presidency. But the Reagan years had left their dread legacy in acute social problems and a soaring budget deficit. Nor was the latter helped by the collapse of the deregulated Savings and Loan industry, which left the American taxpayer to foot the $500 billion bill to bail out the depositors. The White House wanted spending cuts to finance the deficit; Congress wanted tax increases. In the end a compromise was reached whereby the Democrats stomached cutbacks and Bush rescinded his tax promises. It was to cost him re-election.

The high tide of Bush's presidency concealed a powerful undertow. Whilst he bestrode the world the American economy was collapsing. Unemployment was rising while corporations were 'restructuring'; consumer confidence was declining and, uncharacteristically, American expectations were diminishing. Prosperity, where it existed, was often based on two incomes. Meanwhile a functional underclass was expanding, condemned to low-paid repetitive work with little hope of advancement. Nor did it help that too many African-Americans were found within its ranks, often victims, so it seemed, of persistent racism. And their resentment was only exacerbated by the apparent greater social mobility of more recent immigrants from the Near East and Asia, among whom Koreans were a particular source of grievance. It would not take much for the frustrations thus engendered to break out. In 1992 Los Angeles exploded in an orgy of violence and destruction.

An all-white jury cleared four white policemen of beating an African-American motorist notwithstanding that the assault had been captured on video. There followed the worst race riot in American history in which 55 people were killed, 4,000 injured and over 12,000 arrested. The rioting that went on for three days is estimated to have cost over a billion dollars. It seemed symptomatic of governmental indifference to deeply imbedded cancers in American society whose existence called into question the validity of non-interventionist politics.

The cycle had run its course; after two generations Americans witnessed a re-run of the lassitude of the 1920s. Bush was the last president who operated in the shadow of Franklin Roosevelt. As a young man he had gone away to the Second World War, Roosevelt's war; his successor was not born until a year after Roosevelt's death and the war's conclusion. If Bush operated within the foreign policy parameters laid down by Franklin Roosevelt as the world the latter had made began to dissolve and form new structures, in domestic affairs a passive presidency proved to be his undoing. It might be plausible to talk of gridlock, to blame a Democratic Congress for obstructionism and inactivity but that only highlighted the failure of presidential leadership. Roosevelt and his best successors had understood this; others had ignored it at their peril. Bush seemed not so much unable to implement a programme as to be lacking one. 'The first rule of economic policy,' Bush told an audience in North Carolina just a year before the 1992 election, 'puts me in mind ... the Hippocratic Oath: Do no harm.' And four months later in election year itself, he said of welfare dependency, 'The government's first duty is like that of the physician: Do no harm.'[59]

It wasn't good enough. Overwhelmingly, the American voter was concerned about the economy; Americans looked for a lead when times were hard. The issue spelt political death for George Bush as it had for Herbert Hoover. America needed another Roosevelt. Would she again be so fortunate?

8 Clinton and the 1990s

The problems of the 1990s clearly cried out for leadership. It was sixty years since Roosevelt had first been elected to the presidency. Now his version of internationalism had finally triumphed; America had won the Cold War. The economic cost, however, had proved enormous; America's National Debt the day Bill Clinton was inaugurated president stood at 4,177,365,738,326 dollars, a sum so large as to be meaningless. More comprehensibly, it rose at a rate of 13,000 dollars a second, and cost the nation 292 billion dollars in annual interest payments. The social problems were less easily quantifiable, a by-product of the economic decline that national indebtedness signified. There were other changes. In 1920 both major parties' presidential candidates had come from the Midwestern state of Ohio; now in 1992 all three leading candidates were Southerners by birth or adoption. That the election had attracted a third-party candidate was itself significant. Ross Perot was a billionaire businessman who scorned Washington and professional politicians. He was clearly a maverick. Yet in spite of pulling out of the campaign in a dudgeon in July and returning to it in October, Perot polled more votes than any third-party candidate since Teddy Roosevelt in 1912 and better than Robert La Follette in 1924. It testified to the bankruptcy of traditional politics. His candidature undoubtedly assisted Clinton. With a mere 43 per cent of the vote and running behind his party, the new president scarcely had a mandate for anything.

It was an inauspicious start and only worsened. Clinton had run as a moderate Democrat politically but also as a social liberal. This required the lifting of discrimination against homosexuals in the armed forces and the appointment of ethnic minorities to positions in the administration. Both were easier said than done. The former made unnecessary enemies over what was a secondary issue, whereby the compromise 'Don't Ask, Don't Tell', if workable, both lost him credibility with the homosexual constituency and alienated the military. The need to fill posts with suitable candidates from minorities simply foundered on their shortage. The result was an absence of key personnel that slowed the administration. Meanwhile, on so major a plank of the Clinton programme as reform of the nation's health care system, all the efforts ended dismally. True, it had few supporters in Congress and aroused the wrath of the insurance industry; equally, it was probably too complicated a scheme and too costly. That the combined efforts of the president and his wife Hillary, who was put in charge of the scheme, achieved nothing scarcely augured well for the future.

This was amply confirmed later when there was a wholesale slaughter of Democratic congressmen in the off-year elections. Was this just a vote against Democrats or a vote against those who had held power but failed to lead? If Rooseveltian liberalism had run its course, was Reaganite conservatism a creative force or Coolidgism run rampant? If the making of modern America had required an expansion of presidential government, could a deliberate limiting of its role be any more than an interlude, in which problems would necessarily surface, the inevitable penalty for reactive rather than proactive politics? The whole tenor of modern America had been towards recognizing that only the federal government could exercise sufficient power nationwide to meet the challenges American society faced. Eisenhower, for all his stand pat attitudes, had in fact recognized reality; Nixon's New Federalism and return of power to the states never carried much conviction; Reagan's deliberate dismantling of governmental programmes had doomed his successor. Bush, in turn, had failed because domestically he was seen as a 'do-nothing' president. Throughout all those years there had been enough believers of the liberal creed in Congress to keep alive the notion of an activist government. Was it credible that a mere two years later, the party that had won the 1992 election should be massacred in the name of governmental rollback and the curtailment of the centre? Was the issue ideology or incompetence? Was Newt Gingrich's conservatism, and his Contract with America, the authentic voice of a desire to devolve power from Washington or rather the popular instinct to deny power to those who did not know how to use it?

Clinton had turned his back on traditional Democratic Party liberalism in politics and economics, only to embrace a sixties liberalism in social and cultural affairs. Here he was the reverse of Franklin Roosevelt. In stepping out of FDR's shadow, had he restored the sun of conservative Republicanism? If moons are but pale reflections, could a Democrat afford to be anything but a liberal? Carter had given way to Reagan, Clinton in effect to Gingrich. Had not the whole tenor of sixty years, of two generations, been that problems required solutions, that national problems required national solutions? That power was there to be used, that the Democratic ascendancy had been brought about because Hoover had not used the potentialities of his office in the face of a crisis, and that in politics as in life nothing succeeds like success? Similarly, nothing fails like failure. Had Roosevelt's first two years in office resembled Clinton's, then 1934 would also have been a Democratic disaster. Perhaps to paraphrase Reagan, it was not that government was the problem; it was that bad government was the problem, and lack of government no solution. Even the fact that Clinton moved even further right, stole the conservatives clothes to win in 1996, an astonishing comeback, suggested that what he was really pandering to was a political self-satisfaction among the politically committed groups in American society. It was ironic that in 1997 it fell to Clinton to dedicate the long-delayed Memorial to Franklin Roosevelt in Washington. 'It's hard to visit the memorial', a commentator sadly noted, '... without being reminded of the hollowness of the president who dedicated it, comparing his own accomplishments to those of FDR, even as he dismantles the last remnants of the New Deal.'[60]

The disenchantment with politics was widespread, a disturbing sign in a nation like America. Critics uneasily noted the fragmentation and lack of harmony that characterized the United States in the 1990s. The fragmentation took various forms. One was gender. Possibly unfairly, the Republican Party became identified with – or had too many within its ranks – who appeared, unsympathetic or out of touch with the aspirations of modern women. This would harm both Bush and Dole when they ran for the presidency in 1992 and 1996. Moreover, as white, Anglo-Saxon, Protestant males of the generation formed by the Second World War they seemed passé figures in dealing with the social attitudes of the 1990s; here Clinton was a much more modern figure. He was a child of the 1960s.

Another cause of disharmony was race. America had always been a melting pot; that indeed had been its strength and its glory. But now multiculturalism was based on a disinclination to assimilate. The increasing ethnicization of the United States by Asians and Hispanics was a case in point. Between 1980 and 1990, the number of the former officially more than doubled from some 3.5 million to over 7 million; the latter rose from over 14 million to more than 22 million, an increase of more than 50 per cent. One in five Americans was now of non-white descent. Many others were illegal immigrants, attracted by the wealth of the United States but outside its political deliberations. Disturbingly, a helot class was forming who would take low-paid jobs serving American citizens, but assume none of the responsibilities or enjoy any of the privileges of citizenship itself. Moreover, the Reagan–Bush years had pushed the disadvantaged down still further, a trend that conservative Democrats like Clinton had neither the wish nor the mandate to arrest. Indeed, to secure re-election in 1996 Clinton had to outbid the conservative Republicans in Congress in his willingness to cut back on welfare; it was hard to believe that he belonged to the party of Roosevelt, Truman, Kennedy or Johnson. It was a 'sad day', said the head of the American Federation of Labor, when Clinton signed into law a bill that was 'anti-poor, anti-immigrants, anti-women and anti-children – unravelling the safety net Franklin Roosevelt had put in place sixty years before'.[61]

Poverty took its toll in the form of crime, lawlessness, drugs and social alienation. Americans increasingly were on guard against each other, turning their homes, estates and suburbs into armed, protected enclaves against the outside world. Even the proliferation of the home computer, which enabled one in five American families to have internet access, only furthered the true human isolation under a specious social relationship whereby technology substituted for community and neighbourliness. The traditional divisions between haves and have-nots were exacerbated. Was the United States now threatened, as the Populists alleged it had been a hundred years previously, by 'the two great classes – tramps and millionaires'?[62]

If there were many of the former, equally the latter prospered in the 1990s. In the first year of Clinton's presidency the Dow Jones stock market index was 3,500; by the 2000 election it was hovering at the 11,000 mark. By the classic economic indicators, it was a period of sustained economic growth. Employment rose, inflation fell, business profits soared. Moreover, the burgeoning budget deficit of the Reagan–Bush years was first matched, then mastered; soon swelling tax revenues generated a budget surplus for the first time in thirty years. How much this had to do with Clinton is questionable: many assigned credit to Alan Greenspan, the chairman of the Federal Reserve Board. Moreover, there was an insouciance about personal indebtedness; in 1950 Americans had owned 75 per cent of their homes; by 2000 it would be just 50 per cent. It was, for many, a prosperity based on less than prudent borrowing, supportable only if the good times continued. What the long-term cost was in terms of social polarization and the blighting of human resources was more questionable. It smacked of the selfishness of the 1920s, or

1950s complacency; in the long run, economic prosperity might come at a very high national price.

The conundrum for liberalism was that big government required governmental spending; it was, therefore, comparatively easy for opponents to mount an assault on the redistributive taxation measures which liberal policies inevitably imply. Since, except in periods of recession, the poor will be a minority, this crudely requires taking money from the many for the few. However, economic imperatives can be over-ridden if other values can be put in their stead. A nation might be persuaded that health care or education, the environment or space exploration, or simply an integrated, compassionate community based on justice, were worth paying for; in this respect what therefore is needed is an overarching vision of society and a statesman to set it out. Theodore Roosevelt, Woodrow Wilson and above all Franklin Roosevelt had this; even Lyndon Johnson tried. The problem for the 1990s was that American society had become too fragmented and that its politics had largely lost its soul. Special interests and group causes too often motivated the more affluent voters, whilst the most needy and desperate were not even included at all. Much is made of 280 million Americans within a federal system, but diversity in unity has often in the past been an American strength. In this respect the president must in the last resort be a politician above party and speak for all his countrymen. For this, he must have moral authority; it must be seriously doubted whether Clinton had.

Clearly, from the outset Clinton was a suspect figure from whom the taint of scandal was never far removed. Some of the scandal was marital and sexual, some was financial, some went back to his days as governor of Arkansas, some related to campaign contributions and the soliciting of donors, some was governmental. It made the presidency look sleazy. Soon it became clear that what worked politically was for Clinton the limit of his ideology; the lack of principle now extended to what, in so far as it is possible in the White House, could be deemed his personal life. In what must be considered the most sordid scandal in American history, Clinton surpassed even his murky record. It emerged that he had indulged in sexual contact, if not intercourse, with a young woman White House intern and later Pentagon employee in a relationship that had lasted the best part of two years. He was exposed as unquestionably a liar and a philanderer. The archetypal image of the Clinton presidency that will endure is the wagging finger of the television broadcast: 'I want to say one thing to the American people. I want you to listen to me. I'm going to say this again: I did not have sexual relations with that woman, Miss Lewinsky. I never told anybody to lie, not a single time. Never. These allegations are false.'

In due course the shameful details reduced him to a laughing stock. Then more seriously, even, with respect to his office, it was argued: 'There also is substantial and credible information that the President's actions with respect to Monica Lewinsky constitute an abuse of authority inconsistent with the President's constitutional duty to faithfully execute the laws.' There were 'eleven possible grounds for impeachment'. Severally, he had 'lied under oath ... obstructed justice ... improperly tampered with a potential witness ... abused his constitutional authority'.[63]

For the first time since 1868 and for only the second time in American history, a President was impeached. After a trial in the Senate reduced to two general counts of perjury and obstruction of justice, he was acquitted 55 to 45 on the first and 50 to 50 on the second, a two-thirds vote being needed to convict. In essence the impeachment clause, as Nixon's shrewder supporters had recognized, is about more than legal offences. It is about the general presumption of fitness for office. On these grounds Clinton appeared highly vulnerable; on the question of character the Republican right and so-called moral majority had long ago marked his card. Besides, Republicans generally hated Clinton: first for stealing the White House, then for stealing their clothes. It is hard to see how he got away with it. Perhaps the impeachment was too partisan; it never really had sufficient voter support. Perhaps in the long run Americans didn't care; perhaps prosperity dulled the edge of public indignation. A political climate that wishes to minimize the role of government suggests a low expectation of politicians.

It was a far cry from the great heroes of the past. But Clinton held the office once occupied by Washington and Jefferson, Lincoln and Franklin Roosevelt; it was a sorry comment on how low the presidency, and by implication the government, had sunk. The American political system seemed deadlocked, an impression the 2000 election only confirmed. Intense partisan bitterness suggested just how far Americans had become polarized; yet neither candidate seemed to offer a clear vision of exactly where they would lead the nation. Even the confusion, once the polling was over, seemed an apt comment on the period. For a generation conservatism had set out to diminish government; in many respects it had succeeded. It was a philosophy that implicitly resulted in Americans becoming frustrated with politics. Now the political process compounded the frustration even more.

Conclusion

In November 2000 the American people commemorated two bicentennials. The first was John Adams's move on 1 November 1800 into the still-unfinished White House that thereafter became the presidential home. The second was his defeat in the election of that same month by Thomas Jefferson and Aaron Burr which, due to an anomaly in the Constitution, made no distinction between their votes in the Electoral College for president and vice-president. Thus the election was automatically decided by the outgoing House of Representatives, where Adams's Federalist Party, though repudiated at the polls, still held a majority. Although Jefferson was obviously the intended president he was so detested by his opponents that they were tempted to select Burr. Wiser heads finally prevailed; if the Federalists disliked Jefferson's principles the more, they distrusted him the less, rightly fearing the unprincipled Burr still further. Exhaustingly, on the thirty-sixth ballot, Thomas Jefferson was finally confirmed as third president of the United States and the Constitution itself was later amended to preclude any future such ambiguity.

It was not the last time that the resolution of an inconclusive presidential election would prove contentious. In 1824 John Adams's son John Quincy Adams was preferred by the House of Representatives to frontiersman Andrew Jackson, who had gained more votes in the Electoral College than Adams, and indeed more popular votes, but not a majority sufficient to elect him. It was not an auspicious start to a presidency, made worse by suggestions of corruption, and four years later the moral winner from Tennessee had his revenge and won conclusively. In 1876 the outcome was uncertain for months. In the aftermath of the Civil War the Electoral College votes of three Southern states were disputed; a clearly partisan commission awarded all to the Republican candidate Rutherford Hayes, electing him president by just one vote, an acceptance for which the Democrats exacted concessions. The

South was finally freed of Northern troops at the price of conceding the White House.

These events might have given comfort to Americans as they contemplated the election of 2000. That the loser Al Gore manifestly had some 300,000 more popular votes nationwide than George W. Bush, the declared victor, was in itself merely a comment on the fact that on occasions democratic societies will be almost equally divided between two candidates for office. True, that itself was perhaps a telling comment on the politics of the 1990s, a strange mixture of partisan bitterness and voter indifference, occasioned by the politics of opportunism rather than of principle. When politicians themselves cease to believe in the potentialities of government, the electorate will draw the obvious conclusion. Still, not every president has had a popular majority. A similar event had occurred in 1888 and America rightly acknowledges the federal system through the device of the Electoral College, thereby respecting the interests of the less populated states. Even the fact that Gore won more states in total only further underscored the division in the nation, replicated in the congressional elections, which resulted in a Senate divided equally between Republicans and Democrats and a House of Representatives with the narrowest of Republican margins.

Far more disturbing, indeed deeply so, was the determination of the final Electoral College vote, that hinged on the counting of votes in one state, Florida, and the recourse to the courts including the nation's highest, to determine their tallying. It raised doubts about the legitimacy of the whole electoral process. Who really won in Florida? The Supreme Court in what seemed like a partisan and manifestly divided decision, suspended a vote recount while it deliberated, and then likewise confirmed its decision citing shortage of time as a supporting factor. How far did George W. Bush owe his narrowest of margins in the Electoral College to the voters of Florida, or to five out of nine Supreme Court justices, was a question that would surely reverberate for years. It was a decision that could not fail to undermine the moral authority both of the declared winner and of the Court itself. And in the last resort it was the latter that was more serious. There have been failed presidents, and indeed flawed ones, but presidential elections take place regularly every four years. The American people can always rectify what they deem to be earlier mistakes. But the integrity of the democratic process, the reputation for impartiality of Courts and judges, once doubted, is not so easily restored. The 2000 election was not a happy one.

If presidential elections since 1800 had not always gone smoothly, neither had the White House from the time of John Adams's occupancy always enjoyed an untroubled existence. In 1814 it had actually been set on fire by an invading British army during the War of 1812. Indeed, the total destruction of the house might well have resulted, had the flames not been quenched by a violent thunderstorm. Perhaps that providential occurrence might be taken as symptomatic of the fortunes of the American Republic in general, and the white paint liberally used to cover the scorch marks, that gives the house its name, testimony to Americans' ability to move on from misfortune.

For America has always proceeded on hope. Indeed, one of its lessons has been that however apparently insurmountable its problems, it has always survived them. The serene optimism of Jefferson, who spoke of 'some wave ever ahead threatening to overwhelm us and yet passing harmless under our bark' and predicted that the United States would 'go on, puzzled and prospering beyond example in the history of man' appears to have been vindicated.[1]

In the nineteenth century it survived, and was indeed ultimately strengthened and confirmed even by a terrible Civil War. Modern America, too, met a multiplicity of challenges. The pressure for reform at home with a growing and changing population, redefinition of the powers of government, urbanization, industrialization, the increasing assimilation of ethnic minorities into the American polity, civil rights and the emancipation and equalization of the position of women in society, were all confronted. Abroad, the United States expanded, entered two world wars, developed nuclear weapons and lived for half a century with mortal danger, the threat of which only receded in the 1990s. It was by any standards a remarkable achievement. It is also a remarkable testimony to their political institutions, of which in this period the most notable was the presidency.

Yet there is at the same time another characteristic, though it may be a consequence of the innate hope in American history, and that is its restlessness. Americans have never stopped pushing back a frontier even if that long ceased to be merely a geographical one. Americans like a challenge. Along with that goes a tendency to self-dramatization, a self-importance even, that sees the issues of their lives and their resolution, as having significance beyond the confines of America itself. When George Kennan urged his countrymen in 1947 to take up the task of containing the Soviet Union and the threat she represented to the free world, he concluded that

> the thoughtful observer of Russian–American relations will find no cause for complaint in the Kremlin's challenge to American society. He will rather experience a certain gratitude to a Providence which, by providing the American people with this implacable challenge, has made their entire security as a nation dependent on their pulling themselves together and accepting the responsibilities of moral and political leadership that history plainly intended them to bear.[2]

In the circumstances, it is perhaps not surprising that a note of messianism crept in. It may be that, as Senator Fulbright later alleged, Americans reached that stage in their national development that 'is one of the uniformities of history: power tends to confuse itself with virtue and a great nation is peculiarly susceptible to the idea that its power is a sign of God's favor, conferring upon it a special responsibility for other nations'.[3]

Yet at the same time it might be argued that the undoubted fact of American power has also induced in it a certain nobility that the best of its presidents have aspired to and sometimes exemplified. If the position of the United States at the beginning of a new century gives rise for concern, if in some respects its combination of complacency and absence of purpose disturb, its long-term prospects based on its experience in the last century also give rise to some guarded optimism.

It was something that Americans, and indeed the world in general, could take comfort from in the wake of the terrorist outrage of 11 September 2001, itself almost a hundred years to the day from when Teddy Roosevelt became president. Just as that sad transition had left Americans momentarily confused and bewildered, so even more would the terrible loss of life in the aftermath of the surprise attacks in New York and Washington understandably occasion panic and fear. The analogy with Pearl Harbor sixty years previously was irresistible. Yet the real comparison to be made was the spectacle of the presidency in a crisis. How he responded would make or break George W. Bush's presidency and, indeed, very possibly the future prospects of America and the free world generally. Such a challenge illustrates the unique role the office has played in the life of the nation and in the making of modern America.

Perhaps the last word should rightfully be Franklin Roosevelt's; the greatest president modern America produced and its principal maker: they were the last words he ever wrote. Appropriately, they were intended to commemorate Thomas Jefferson: 'The only limit to our realization of tomorrow will be our doubts of today. Let us move forward with strong and active faith.'[4]

Notes

The full titles of the works cited have been left to the bibliography since these are the real sources for an understanding of the presidency and its role in modern American history but quotations have been identified. Wherever possible when quoting from primary documents, not only has the source been given but also a more accessible version of the same so that any reader so minded will be able to read the original that is part of the raw material of American history. Not the least reason for seeing for oneself is to avoid a handed-down version that too often substitutes for what was actually said. Thus Henry Steele Commager's invaluable *Documents of American History* (2 vols), a vade-mecum for all American historians, has been cited as a supplementary source for quotations (it is cited as 'Commager'), even when the original source has been identified. Similarly, Janet Podell and Steven Anzovin's *Speeches of the American Presidents*, a very useful collection, has also been utilized as a convenient alternative work of reference as I have quite deliberately let America's presidents speak for themselves. *Theodore Roosevelt's Works* are cited as TR Works except for the more accessible edition of his *Autobiography*. Similarly, the *Public Papers and Addresses of Franklin D. Roosevelt* are cited as FDR Papers.

Introduction

1 Theodore Roosevelt, 'The New Nationalism', Osawatomie, Kansas, 31 August 1910: *TR Works*, vol. XVII, p. 5; *Speeches of Presidents*, p. 335.
2 Franklin D. Roosevelt, New York City, 28 October 1936: *FDR Papers*, vol. V, p. 541.
3 F. Scott Fitzgerald, *The Crackup*, p. 197.
4 The Declaration of Independence, Philadelphia, 4 July 1776: *Commager*, vol. I, p. 100.
5 Abraham Lincoln, Annual Message to Congress, 1 December 1862: *Lincoln Works*, vol. V, p. 537; *Commager*, vol. I, p. 405; *Speeches of Presidents*, p. 193.
6 Lyndon B. Johnson, Washington, DC, 15 March 1965: *Speeches of Presidents*, p. 638. See also Johnson, *Vantage Point*, pp. 161–6; Dallek, vol. 2: *Flawed Giant*, pp. 218–20, for the general context.
7 Abraham Lincoln, Annual Message to Congress, 1 December 1862: *Lincoln Works*, vol. V, p. 537; *Speeches of Presidents*, p. 192.
8 Franklin D. Roosevelt, Acceptance Speech, Philadelphia, 27 June 1936: *FDR Papers*, vol. V, p. 235. Herbert Hoover, New York City, 31 October 1932: *Memoirs*, vol. III, pp. 336, 343.
9 See Leuchtenburg, *In the Shadow of FDR*, for the phrase and its stimulating exposition.

10 Credit for this quite brilliant analogy must go to Thomas Mann via George Kennan in X, 'The Sources of Soviet Conduct', *Foreign Affairs*, vol. 25 (July 1947), p. 580.
11 The Constitution of the United States, *Commager*, vol. I, p. 138.
12 Woody Guthrie, *This Land is your Land*.
13 Lyndon B. Johnson, Washington, DC, 15 March 1965: *Speeches of Presidents*, p. 642.
14 Franklin D. Roosevelt, 1 November 1937: *FDR Papers*, vol. II, p. 10.

Chapter 1 The Development of Modern America

1 Cited in Morris, *Theodore Roosevelt*, p. 724; Leech, *McKinley*, p. 537. There is some confusion whether Hanna said 'this' or 'that'. Cooper, *Warrior and Priest*, p. 40, substitutes 'White House' for 'Presidency' as does Pringle, *Theodore Roosevelt*, p. 223.
2 Cited in Riis, *Theodore Roosevelt*, p. 237.
3 The description of the War is cited in Smith, *Spanish–American War*, p. 212. The comment is in D. W. Brogan, 'A Fresh Appraisal of the Civil War', in *American Aspects*, p. 27.
4 Cited in Morris, *Rise of Theodore Roosevelt*, p. 705.
5 See Theodore Roosevelt, *Autobiography*, pp. 279–91; Brogan 'The First Roosevelt', in *American Aspects*, p. 82; Harbaugh *Roosevelt*, p. 107.
6 Thomas Jefferson to John Adams, 21 January 1812: Jefferson, *Writings*, p. 1259.
7 Mark Twain and Charles Dudley Warner, *The Gilded Age*, a novel published in 1873 that gave its name to an era.
8 Cited in Melissa L. Meyer 'We can not get a living as we used to: Dispossession and the White Earth Anishinaabeg, 1889–1920', *American Historical Review*, vol. 96, p. 394.
9 Turner, *Frontier*, p. 1.
10 Thomas Jefferson, First Inaugural Address, 4 March 1801: Jefferson, *Writings*, p. 494; *Commager*, vol. I, p. 187; *Speeches of Presidents*, p. 39.
11 Turner, *Frontier*, p. 30.
12 Walt Whitman, *Democratic Vistas*, p. 11.
13 Turner, *Frontier*, p. 9
14 *Ibid.*, p. 1; for Jacob Riis, *How the Other Half Lives* (1890), see Theodore Roosevelt, *Autobiography*, pp. 185–8.
15 Thomas Jefferson, *Notes on the State of Virginia*: Jefferson, *Writings*, p. 291.
16 Emma Lazarus's famous words inscribed on the Statue in New York harbour when it was completed in 1886 actually concluded: 'Send the homeless, tempest-tost to me / I left my lamp beside the golden door.'
17 Thomas Jefferson, *Notes on the State of Virginia*: Jefferson, *Writings*, p. 290.
18 Thomas Jefferson, First Inaugural Address, 4 March 1801: Jefferson, *Writings*, p. 495; *Commager*, vol. I, p. 186; *Speeches of Presidents*, p. 39. Andrew Carnegie, *The Gospel of Wealth*, p. 4.

19 The Populist Party Platform, 4 July 1892: *Commager*, vol. II, p. 143.
20 Henry Adams, *Democracy; Education*, pp. 988, 976.
21 Riis, *Theodore Roosevelt*, pp. 48–9; see also Theodore Roosevelt, *Autobiography*, p. 63.
22 Cited in Nevins, *Cleveland*, p. 182; Morris, *Rise of Theodore Roosevelt*, p. 291.
23 Cited in Werner, *Bryan*, pp. 67, 86.
24 Cited in Coletta, *Bryan*, vol. I, p. 152.
25 Cited in Hofstadter, *American Political Tradition*, p. 230.
26 Cited in Jones, *Limits of Liberty*, p. 372.
27 Henry Adams, *Education*, p. 1101.
28 Cited in Morris, *Rise of Theodore Roosevelt*, p. 18; cited in Brown, *Westerners*, p. 275.
29 Thomas Jefferson to Dr Benjamin Rush, 16 January 1811: *Jefferson, Writings*, p. 1236.
30 Cited in Mitchell, *Hamilton*, vol. I, p. 491.
31 Abraham Lincoln, Gettysburg Address, 19 November 1863: *Lincoln Works*, vol. VII, p. 23; *Commager*, vol. I, p. 429; *Speeches of Presidents*, p. 193.
32 Abraham Lincoln, Annual Message to Congress, 1 December 1862: *Lincoln Works*, vol. V, p. 537; *Speeches of Presidents*, p. 192.
33 Bryce, *American Commonwealth*, pp. 69–75, 1314–15.
34 Cited in Cooper, *Warrior and Priest*, p. 86; Gould, *Presidency of Theodore Roosevelt*, p. 10.
35 Theodore Roosevelt, *Autobiography*, p. 389.
36 Cited in Morris, *Rise of Theodore Roosevelt*, p. 11.
37 Cited in Cooper, *Warrior and Priest*, p. 114.
38 Cited in ibid., p. 83; Pringle, *Theodore Roosevelt*, p. 256.
39 Cited in Cunliffe, *American Presidents and Presidency*, p. 134.
40 La Follette, *Autobiography*, p. 166.
41 Cited in Cunliffe, *American Presidents and Presidency*, p. 198.
42 Theodore Roosevelt, Washington, DC, 14 April 1906: *TR Works*, vol. XVI, p. 416; *Speeches of Presidents*, p. 326.
43 Theodore Roosevelt, Provincetown, Massachusetts, 20 August 1907: *TR Works*, vol. XVI, p. 84.
44 Cited in Cooper, *Warrior and Priest*, p. 69.
45 Theodore Roosevelt, 'How I Became a Progressive', 12 October 1912: *TR Works*, vol. XVII, pp. 318–19.
46 Theodore Roosevelt, *Autobiography*, p. 580.
47 Cited in Tindall and Shi, *America: A Narrative History*, p. 996.
48 Theodore Roosevelt, 'The Expansion of the White Races', Washington, DC, 18 January 1909: *TR Works*, vol. XVI, pp. 264–5.
49 Theodore Roosevelt, 'What a Progressive Is', Louisville, Kentucky, 3 April 1912: *TR Works*, vol. XVII, p. 184.
50 Woodrow Wilson, 'The Old Order Changeth', *The New Freedom*, pp. 26–7.
51 Cited in Clements, *Wilson*, p. 93.
52 Woodrow Wilson, Annual Message to Congress, 8 December 1914: *Wilson Papers*, vol. 31, p. 423.

278   *Notes*

53 Woodrow Wilson, 'An Appeal to the American People', 18 August 1914: *Wilson Papers*, vol. 30, p. 394; *Commager*, vol. II, p. 276.
54 Cited in Cooper, *Warrior and Priest*, p. 275.
55 Cited in Jones, *Limits of Liberty*, p. 414.
56 Bertrand Russell, *Autobiography*, pp. 250–1.
57 George Washington, Farewell Address, Philadelphia, 17 September 1796: *Commager*, vol. I, p. 174; *Speeches of Presidents*, pp. 19–20.
58 Thomas Jefferson, First Inaugural Address, 4 March 1801: Jefferson, *Writings*, p. 494; *Commager*, vol. I, pp. 187–8; *Speeches of Presidents*, p. 39.
59 James Monroe, Annual Message to Congress, 2 December 1823: *Commager*, vol. I, p. 236; *Speeches of Presidents*, p. 70.
60 Cited in Cooper, *Warrior and Priest*, p. 307.
61 Woodrow Wilson, War Message to Congress, 2 April 1917: *Wilson Papers*, vol. 41, p. 525; *Commager*, vol. II, p. 311; *Speeches of Presidents*, p. 393.
62 *Ibid*: *Wilson Papers*, vol. 41, pp. 526–7; *Commager*, vol. II, p. 312; *Speeches of Presidents*, p. 394.
63 Cited in Taylor, *Struggle for Mastery*, pp. 557–8.
64 Woodrow Wilson, 21 July 1917: *Wilson Papers*, vol. 43, p. 238.
65 For the Fourteen Points see, *Commager*, vol. II, pp. 317–24; *Speeches of Presidents*, pp. 394–8.
66 Hoover, *Ordeal of Woodrow Wilson*, pp. 300–1.
67 Cited in ibid., p. 266. See *Commager*, vol. II, pp. 340–2; *Speeches of Presidents*, pp. 405–12, for the general context.
68 Cited in Smith, *Cheering Stopped*, p. 219.
69 Cited in Schlesinger, *Age of Roosevelt*, vol. I: *Crisis of Old Order*, p. 378.
70 The Constitution of the United States, *Commager*, vol. I, p. 143.
71 The phrase itself is from F. Scott Fitzgerald's *Tales of the Jazz Age* (1922); Fitzgerald is almost its spokesman.
72 Herbert Hoover, Acceptance Speech, Stanford, California, 11 August 1928: Hoover, *Memoirs*, vol. II, p. 201; *Speeches of Presidents*, p. 459.
73 Warren Harding, Boston, 14 May 1920: cited in Hicks, *Republican Ascendancy*, p. 24.
74 Coolidge, *Autobiography*, p. 168.
75 Ibid., p. 133.
76 Herbert Hoover, *American Individualism*, p. 63.
77 Herbert Hoover, 'The Philosophy of Rugged Individualism', New York City, 22 October 1928: Hoover, *Memoirs*, vol. II, p. 203; *Commager*, vol. II, p. 404.
78 Coolidge, *Autobiography*, p. 243.
79 Herbert Hoover, Acceptance Speech, Stanford, California, 11 August 1928: *Speeches of Presidents*, p. 455.
80 Calvin Coolidge, 'Government and Business', New York City, 19 November 1925: Coolidge, *Foundations of the Republic*, p. 320; *Speeches of Presidents*, p. 435.
81 Cited in Venn, *New Deal*, p. 9.
82 Cited in Kennedy, *Freedom From Fear*, p. 39.
83 Herbert Hoover, New York City, 22 October 1928: *Commager*, vol. II, p. 403.

Chapter 2   The Achievement of Liberalism

1   Franklin D. Roosevelt, Oglethorpe University, Georgia, 22 May 1932;
    Radio Address, Albany, New York, 7 April 1932: *FDR Papers*, vol. 1,
    pp. 646, 625.
2   Herbert Hoover, New York City, 31 October 1932: *Memoirs*, vol. III,
    pp. 336–43; *Hoover State Papers*, vol. II, pp. 408–28.
3   Franklin D. Roosevelt, Acceptance Speech, Chicago, 2 July 1932: *FDR
    Papers*, vol. I, pp. 647–59; *Speeches of Presidents*, pp. 481–86.
4   Moley, *First New Deal*, p. 364.
5   Moley, *After Seven Years*, p. 48.
6   Franklin D. Roosevelt, San Francisco, 23 September 1932: *FDR Papers*,
    vol. I, pp. 742–56.
7   Cited in Schlesinger, *Age of Roosevelt*, vol. I: *Crisis of Old Order*, p. 494.
8   Cited in Terkel, *Hard Times*, pp. 46, 77.
9   Orsi, *St Jude*, p. 54.
10 Cited in Kamphoefner et al., *Land of Freedom*, p. 516.
11 Franklin D. Roosevelt, First Inaugural Address, 4 March 1933: *FDR
    Papers*, vol. II, p. 13; *Commager*, vol. II, p. 420; *Speeches of Presidents*,
    p. 487.
12 Moley, *First New Deal*, p. 127.
13 Cited in Perkins, *Roosevelt*, p. 73.
14 Cited in Sherwood, *Hopkins*, vol. 1, p. 72.
15 Franklin D. Roosevelt, First Fireside Chat, 12 March 1933: *FDR Papers*,
    vol. II, p. 65.
16 Perkins, *Roosevelt*, p. 81.
17 Cited in ibid., p. 330.
18 Cited in ibid., p. 108.
19 *The Times*, 17 June 1933.
20 Moley, *After Seven Years*, p. 155.
21 Franklin D. Roosevelt, First Fireside Chat of 1934, Washington, DC, 28
    June 1934: *FDR Papers*, vol. III, p. 313.
22 Cited in Sherwood, *Hopkins*, vol. 1, p. 52.
23 See Perkins, *Roosevelt*, pp. 218–21, for an interesting example.
24 Franklin D. Roosevelt, Annual Message to Congress, 4 January 1935:
    FDR Papers, vol. IV, p. 20.
25 Ibid., p. 17.
26 John Steinbeck, *The Grapes of Wrath*.
27 Cited in Bartley, *New South*, p. xi.
28 James Agee and Walker Evans, *Let Us Now Praise Famous Men*.
29 Perkins, *Roosevelt*, pp. 204, 208.
30 Franklin D. Roosevelt, 209th Press Conference, Washington, DC, 31
    May 1935: *FDR Papers*, vol. IV, p. 209.
31 Cited in Leuchtenburg, *Roosevelt and New Deal*, p. 145.
32 Roosevelt, 209th Press Conference: *FDR Papers*, vol. IV, p. 200.
33 Franklin D. Roosevelt, First Inaugural Address, 4 March 1933: *FDR
    Papers*, vol. II, p. 15; *Commager*, vol. II, p. 422; *Speeches of Presidents*,
    p. 489.

34 Franklin D. Roosevelt, Chicago, 14 October 1936: *FDR Papers*, vol. V, p. 488.
35 Thomas Jefferson, *Notes on the State of Virginia*: Jefferson, *Writings*, p. 291.
36 Moley, *First New Deal*, p. 4.
37 Claude G. Bowers, *Jefferson and Hamilton*; cited in Peterson, *Jefferson Image*, p. 352.
38 Cited in Ellis, *Passionate Sage*, p. 210; Peterson, *Jefferson Image*, p. 3, has 'still survives'.
39 *FDR Papers*, vol V, p. 486.
40 Franklin D. Roosevelt, Annual Message to Congress, 4 January 1935: *FDR Papers*, vol. IV, p. 25.
41 Franklin D. Roosevelt, Annual Message to Congress, 4 January 1939: *FDR Papers*, vol. VIII, p. 6.
42 Franklin D. Roosevelt, First Inaugural Address, 4 March 1933: *FDR Papers*, vol. II, pp. 15–16; *Commager*, vol. II, p. 422; *Speeches of Presidents*, p. 489.
43 Franklin D. Roosevelt, Washington, DC, 8 January 1940: *FDR Papers*, vol. IX, p. 31.
44 Moley, *First New Deal*, p. 4.
45 Cited in Rossiter, *American Presidency*, p. 128.
46 Acheson, *Present at Creation*, p. 41.
47 Cited in Sherwood, *Hopkins*, vol. 1, p. 73.
48 Cited in Schlesinger, *Age of Roosevelt*, vol. II: *The Coming of the New Deal*, p. 14; but see also Morgan, *FDR*, p. 377.
49 *Economist, New Deal*, p. 149.
50 Franklin D. Roosevelt, Acceptance Speech, Philadelphia, 27 June 1936: *FDR Papers*, vol. V, p. 235.
51 Cited in Sherwood, *Hopkins*, vol. 1, pp. 100–1.
52 Freedman, *Roosevelt and Frankfurter*, pp. 282–3.
53 Cited in Perkins, *Roosevelt*, p. 333.
54 Franklin D. Roosevelt, Second Inaugural Address, 20 January 1937: *FDR Papers*, vol. VI, p. 5; *Speeches of Presidents*, p. 495.
55 Franklin D. Roosevelt, First Inaugural Address, 4 March 1933: *FDR Papers*, vol. II, pp. 14–15; *Commager*, vol. II, p. 422; *Speeches of Presidents*, p. 489.
56 Cited in Schlesinger, *Imperial Presidency*, p. 1.
57 Cited in Bork, *Tempting of America*, p. 176.
58 Cited in Leuchtenburg, *Roosevelt and New Deal*, p. 234.
59 Franklin D. Roosevelt, Washington, DC, 24 June 1938: *FDR Papers*, vol. VII, p. 209.
60 Cited in Leuchtenburg, *Roosevelt and New Deal*, p. 319.
61 Ibid., p. 187.
62 Cited in Heale, *Roosevelt*, p. 67.
63 Harry Truman, Elizabeth, New Jersey, 7 October 1948; Framlingham, Massachusetts, 27 October 1948; *Speeches of Presidents*, p. 55.
64 See Mayer, *Republican Party*, pp. 485–91.
65 Eisenhower, *Mandate*, p. 320.

66 Cited in Larson, *Eisenhower*, p. 21.
67 John F. Kennedy, Acceptance Speech, Los Angeles, 15 July 1960: *Speeches of Presidents*, p. 602.
68 Cited in Wicker, *JFK and LBJ*, p. 23.
69 Cited in Dallek, *Lone Star Rising*, p. 266.
70 Cited in Weisbrot, *Freedom Bound*, p. 82.
71 Cited in Patterson, *Grand Expectations*, p. 546.
72 Lyndon B. Johnson, Washington, DC, 16 March 1964: *Speeches of Presidents*, p. 631.
73 Ibid., p. 632.
74 Lyndon B. Johnson, Ann Arbor, Michigan, 22 May 1964: *Speeches of Presidents*, p. 635.
75 Ibid.
76 Johnson, *Vantage Point*, p. 323.
77 Ibid., front inside cover.
78 Lyndon B. Johnson, Washington, DC, 15 March 1965: Johnson, *Vantage Point*, p. 165; *Speeches of Presidents*, pp. 637–42.
79 Johnson, *Vantage Point*, p. 166.
80 Cited in Kearns, *Lyndon Johnson*, p. 251.
81 Goldman, *Tragedy of Lyndon Johnson*, p. 531.

Chapter 3 The Attainment of World Power

1 Tocqueville, *Democracy*, pp. 412–13.
2 Cited in Dallek, *Roosevelt Foreign Policy*, p 19. Interestingly, the relevant comment is not included in the extract from the speech in the *FDR Papers*, vol. I, pp. 723–6.
3 Cited in Schlesinger, *Age of Roosevelt*, vol. II, p. 215.
4 Cited in Feiling, *Chamberlain*, p. 325.
5 Walter Millis, *Road to War: America 1914–1917*.
6 Franklin D. Roosevelt, First Inaugural Address, 4 March 1933: *FDR Papers*, vol. II, p. 14; *Commager*, vol. II, p 421; *Speeches of Presidents*, p. 488.
7 Franklin D. Roosevelt, Acceptance Speech, Philadelphia, 27 June 1936: *FDR Papers*, vol. V, pp. 235–6.
8 Cited in Sherwood, *Hopkins*, vol. 1, p. 131.
9 Ernest K. Lindley, *The Roosevelt Revolution: First Phase*.
10 Franklin D. Roosevelt, Address at Chicago, 5 October 1937: *FDR Papers*, vol. VI, p. 410.
11 Franklin D. Roosevelt to William Phillips, 15 September 1938: Roosevelt, *FDR Personal Letters 1928–1945*, vol. II, p. 810.
12 Franklin D. Roosevelt to Joseph Kennedy, 28 September 1938: ibid., pp. 826–7.
13 Churchill, *Second World War*, vol. I, p. x.
14 Cited in Dallek, *Roosevelt Foreign Policy*, p. 192; see also Cordell Hull, *Memoirs*, vol. I, pp. 649–50.
15 Cited in Sherwood, *Hopkins*, vol. 1, p. 134.

16   Cited in Welles, *Time for Decision*, p. 62.
17   Cited in Rhodes, *Making of Atomic Bomb*, p. 314.
18   Cited in Sherwood, *Hopkins*, vol. 1, p. 167.
19   Franklin D. Roosevelt, University of Virginia, Charlottesville, 10 June
     1940: *FDR Papers*, vol. IX, p. 261; *Commager*, vol. II, p. 611.
20   Franklin D. Roosevelt, Boston, 30 October 1940: *FDR Papers*, vol. IX,
     p. 517.
21   Franklin D. Roosevelt, Fireside Chat, 29 December 1940: *FDR Papers*,
     vol. IX, p. 643; *Speeches of Presidents*, p. 507.
22   Churchill, *Second World War*, vol. II, p. 451.
23   Kennan, *Memoirs*, p. 161.
24   Franklin D. Roosevelt, Fireside Chat, 7 September 1942: *FDR Papers*,
     vol. XI, p. 373.
25   Tocqueville, *Democracy*, p. 657.
26   Churchill, *Second World War*, vol. III, p. 477.
27   Cited in Sherwood, *Hopkins*, vol. 2, pp. 692–3.
28   Acheson, *Present Creation*, p. 613.
29   Franklin D. Roosevelt, Annual Message to Congress, 6 January 1941:
     FDR Papers, vol. IX, p. 672; *Commager*, vol. II, p. 629; *Speeches of Presi-
     dents*, p. 511.
30   Cited in Sherwood, *Hopkins*, vol. 1, p. 266.
31   Welles, *Time for Decision*, p. 229.
32   Alsop, *Best of It*, p. 267.
33   Acheson, *Present Creation*.
34   Cited in Patterson, *Grand Expectations*, p. 128.
35   Karl von Clausewitz, cited in *Oxford Dictionary of Quotations*, (4th edn,
     1992), p. 205.
36   Cited in Hugh Brogan, *United States of America*, p. 519.
37   Harry S. Truman, Address to Congress, 12 March 1947: *Years of Trial
     and Hope*, p. 111; *Commager*, vol. II, p. 721; *Speeches of Presidents*, p. 540.
38   George C. Marshall, Commencement Address, Harvard University, 5
     June 1947: *Commager*, vol. II, p. 729.
39   Cited in La Feber, *The American Age*, p. 520; cited in McNamara, *In
     Retrospect*, p. 31.
40   Kennan, 'Sources of Soviet Conduct', pp. 575–6.
41   Cited in Sherry, *Shadow of War*, p. 223.
42   Cited in Rhodes, *Making of Atomic Bomb*, p. 676.
43   Cited in Whelan, *Drawing the Line*, p. 369.
44   Larson, *Eisenhower*, p. 22.
45   Cited in Ambrose, *Eisenhower the President*, p. 626.
46   The phrase 'massive retaliation' is strictly a misnomer, juxtaposing a
     word Dulles used elsewhere in his speech; cited in Moss, *Men who Play
     God*, p. 110; for 'liberation policy', see Hoopes, *Devil and Dulles*, p. 131;
     for the comment on containment, see Acheson, *Present Creation*, p. 690.
47   Cited in Schweber, *Shadow of the Bomb*, p. 160.
48   Dwight D. Eisenhower, Farewell Address, Washington, DC, 17 January
     1961: *Speeches of Presidents*, p. 595; see also Eisenhower, *Waging Peace*,
     p. 616.

49 Tocqeville, *Democracy*, p. 459.
50 Acheson, *Present Creation*, p. 153.
51 Cited in La Feber, *American Age*, p. 549.
52 Cited in Ambrose, *Eisenhower the President*, p. 180.
53 Dwight D. Eisenhower, Farewell Adddress, Washington, DC, 17 January 1961: *Speeches of Presidents*, p. 595.
54 John F. Kennedy, Inaugural Address, Washington, DC, 20 January 1961: *Speeches of Presidents*, p. 604; Sorensen, *Kennedy*, pp. 245–6.
55 Cited in Schlesinger, *A Thousand Days*, p. 108.
56 Cited in ibid., p. 594; Cunliffe, *American Presidents and Presidency*, p. 228.
57 Cited in Acheson, *Present Creation*, p. 730.
58 John F. Kennedy, Inaugural Address, Washington, DC, 20 January 1961: *Speeches of Presidents*, p. 605; Sorensen, *Kennedy*, p. 247.
59 Sorensen, *Kennedy*, p. 678.
60 Cited in Ambrose, *Nixon*, p. 12.
61 John F. Kennedy, American University, Washington, DC, 10 June 1963: Sorensen, *Kennedy*, p. 732.
62 Cited in Ambrose, *Rise to Globalism*, p. xix.
63 Cited in Kearns, *Lyndon Johnson*, p. 252.
64 Cited in Clifford, *Counsel to President*, p. 614.
65 McNamara, *In Retrospect*, pp. 322–3.
66 Fulbright, *Arrogance of Power*, pp. 3–4, 15, 23, 25.
67 Cited in Clifford, *Counsel to President*, p. 443. Interestingly, the remark is not recorded in Johnson's account of his trip. See Lyndon B. Johnson, *Vantage Point*, p. 363.
68 Cited in Cohen, *Dean Rusk*, p. 288; cited in Schulzinger, *Time for War*, p. 332.
69 Cited in McNamara, *In Retrospect*, p. 141; ibid., p. 142.
70 Kissinger, *Years of Upheaval*, p. 239.
71 Richard Nixon, *Memoirs*, p. 757.
72 Ralph Waldo Emerson, cited in *Oxford Dictionary of Quotations*, (4th edn, 1992), p. 276.
73 Jimmy Carter, *Keeping Faith*, p. 147.
74 Ronald Reagan, Orlando, Florida, 8 March 1983: *An American Life*, pp. 569–70; *Speeches of Presidents*, pp. 759–60.
75 Ronald Reagan, *An American Life*, p. 611.
76 Cited in Hersh, *Target is Destroyed*, p. 176.
77 The Constitution of the United States, *Commager*, vol. I, p. 143.
78 Cited in Schaller, *Reckoning with Reagan*, p. 28.
79 Ronald Reagan, Television and Radio Address, Washington, DC, 4 March 1987: *Speeches of Presidents*, p. 788.
80 Cited in Powell, *Soldier's Way*, p. 375.
81 William Wordsworth cited in *Oxford Dictionary of Quotations*, (4th edn, 1992), p. 744.
82 George Bush and Brent Scowcroft, *A World Transformed*, p. 13.
83 George Bush, Address to Congress, 11 September 1990: ibid., p. 370.
84 Cited in Sherry, *Shadow of War*, p. 482.

Chapter 4   The Resurgence of Conservatism

1   Rauch, *New Deal*, p. vi.
2   Ronald Reagan, First Inaugural Address, 20 January 1981: *Speeches of Presidents*, p. 747.
3   Michael Harrington, *The Other America: Poverty in the United States*.
4   Cited in Ambrose, *Eisenhower President*, p. 55.
5   Eisenhower, *Mandate*, pp. 8–9.
6   Eisenhower, *Mandate*, p. 51; cited in Ambrose, *Eisenhower President*, p. 115. See also Barry Goldwater, *Conscience of a Conservative*, p. 9.
7   Barry Goldwater, *Conscience of a Conservative*, pp. 22–3.
8   Cited in White, *Making President, 1964*, p. 217.
9   Cited in Rovere, *Goldwater Caper*, p. 11.
10   Cited in White, *Making President, 1964*, p. 218.
11   Barry Goldwater, *Conscience of a Conservative*, p. 5.
12   Cited in White, *Making President, 1964*, p. 217.
13   Rovere, *Goldwater Caper*.
14   Cited in Tindall and Shi, *America*, p. 1417.
15   Horace Greeley's advice was often, of course, reversed by those who necessarily looked to Washington, DC, or New York. See, for example, William O. Douglas, *Go East Young Man*.
16   Richard Nixon, *Memoirs*, pp. 273, 275–6, 272.
17   Gerald Ford, *Time to Heal*, pp. 83–4.
18   Cited in Patterson, *Grand Expectations*, p. 649.
19   Gerald Ford, *Time to Heal*, p. 83.
20   Lyndon B. Johnson, *Vantage Point*, p. 84.
21   Cited in Chester et al., *American Melodrama*, p. 496.
22   Cited in ibid., p. 497.
23   Cited in ibid., p. 499.
24   Nixon, *Memoirs*, p. 298.
25   Phillips, *Republican Majority*, p. 25.
26   Nixon, *Memoirs*, p. 352.
27   Ibid., p. 437.
28   Phillips, *Republican Majority*, p. 474.
29   Cited in Hugh Brogan, *United States of America*, p. 612.
30   Richard Nixon, *Memoirs*, p. 409; *Speeches of Presidents*, p. 669.
31   Jimmy Carter, *Keeping Faith*, p. 47.
32   Richard Nixon, State of the Union Address, 22 January 1971; *Memoirs*, p. 533; *Speeches of Presidents*, pp. 679, 678.
33   Schlesinger, *Imperial Presidency*.
34   Gerald Ford, *Time to Heal*, p. 35.
35   Miller, *Plain Speaking*, p. 364.
36   Hardeman and Bacon, *Rayburn*, p. 382.
37   Richard Nixon, Television and Radio Address, Washington, DC, 3 November 1969; *Memoirs*, pp. 409–11; *Speeches of Presidents*, p. 669.
38   White, *Making President, 1972*, pp. 353, 360.
39   Cited in ibid., pp. 224, 234.
40   The Constitution of the United States: *Commager*, vol. I, p. 143.

41 Hubert Humphrey, last speech, Washington, DC, 1 November 1977: cited in O'Neill, *Man of the House*, pp. 203, insert 214–15. For the comment on Humphrey as a liberal, see ibid., p. 203.
42 Jimmy Carter, *Keeping Faith*, p. 69.
43 Gerald Ford, *Time to Heal*, p. 195.
44 O'Neill, *Man of the House*, p. 297.
45 Jimmy Carter, *Keeping Faith*, p. 107.
46 Jimmy Carter, Television and Radio Address, Washington, DC, 18 April 1977: *Keeping Faith*, p. 96.
47 Jimmy Carter, *Keeping Faith*, p. 121.
48 Jimmy Carter, Television and Radio Address, Washington, DC, 15 July 1979: *Keeping Faith*, pp. 121–7; *Speeches of Presidents*, pp. 730–1.
49 Cited in White, *America in Search*, pp. 274–5.
50 Cited in ibid., p. 338.
51 Cited in Reeves, *Twentieth-century America*, p. 237.
52 Galbraith, *Culture of Contentment*.
53 Ronald Reagan, *An American Life*, p. 232.
54 Cited in Galbraith, *Culture of Contentment*, p. 30.
55 O'Neill, *Man of the House*, pp. 376, 360.
56 Stockman, *Triumph of Politics*, p. 403.
57 Ronald Reagan, *An American Life*, p. 232.
58 George Bush and Brent Scowcroft, *A World Transformed*, p. 446.
59 Cited in Mervin, *George Bush and the Guardianship Presidency*, p. ix.
60 Cited in Garson and Kidd, *The Roosevelt Years*, p. 201.
61 Cited in ibid., p. 196.
62 The Populist Party Platform, 4 July 1892; *Commager*, vol. II, p. 143.
63 Bill Clinton, Televised Education News Conference, Washington, DC, 26 January 1998; cited in *Starr Report*, p. 151; Grounds for Impeachment, ibid., pp. 153–5.

Conclusion

1 Thomas Jefferson to John Adams, 21 January 1812: Jefferson, *Writings*, p. 1259.
2 George Kennan, 'The Sources of Soviet Conduct', *Foreign Affairs*, July 1947, p. 582.
3 Fulbright, *Arrogance of Power*, p. 3.
4 Franklin D. Roosevelt, Undelivered Address prepared for Jefferson Day, 13 April 1945: *FDR Papers*, vol. XIII, p. 616; *Commager*, vol. II, p. 694; *Speeches of Presidents*, p. 532.

Bibliography

Any historian who works in this field is under a considerable debt to his predecessors, as much for ideas as for information. Thus in no sense is this list a comprehensive one, but it includes books found to be particularly helpful or enjoyable and will hopefully give some idea of the variety available and encourage those who wish to explore further to do so. Collectively, they testify to the immensity of the history of the American presidency in the making of modern America and its inherent interest and importance.

Acheson, Dean, *Present at the Creation: My Years in the State Department* (New York: W.W. Norton, 1969).

Adams, David K., *Franklin D. Roosevelt and the New Deal* (London: Historical Association, 1979).

Adams, David K., 'The New Deal and the Vital Center: A Continuing Struggle for Liberalism'. In Herbert D. Rosenbaum and Elizabeth Bartelme (eds)', *Franklin D. Roosevelt: The Man, the Myth, the Era, 1882–1945* (Westport, CT: Greenwood Press, 1987).

Adams, Henry, *Democracy: An American Novel; The Education of Henry Adams* (New York: The Library of America, 1983).

Agee, James and Evans, Walker, *Let Us Now Praise Famous Men* (Boston, MA: Houghton Mifflin, 1960).

Allswang, John, *The New Deal and American Politics: A Study in Political Change* (New York: John Wiley, 1978).

Alsop, Joseph W., *I've Seen the Best of It* (New York: W.W. Norton, 1992).

Ambrose, Stephen E., *Rise to Globalism: American Foreign Policy since 1938* (Harmondsworth: Penguin, 1993).

Ambrose, Stephen E., *Eisenhower*, vol. 1: *Soldier, General of the Army, President-Elect, 1890–1952*; vol. 2: *Eisenhower the President* (New York: Simon & Schuster, 1983, 1984);

Ambrose, Stephen E., *Nixon: The Triumph of a Politician, 1962–72* (New York: Simon & Schuster, 1989).

Badger, Anthony J., *The New Deal: The Depression Years, 1933–40* (Basingstoke: Palgrave Macmillan, 1989).

Bartley, Numan V., *The New South, 1945–1980* (Baton Rouge, LA: Louisiana State University Press, 1995).

Basler, Roy P. *et al.* (eds), *The Collected Works of Abraham Lincoln*, 9 vols (New Brunswick, NJ: Rutgers University Press, 1953–5).

Bennett, G. H., *The American Presidency, 1945–2000: Illusions of Grandeur* (Stroud: Sutton, 2000).

Berman, Larry, *Lyndon Johnson's War* (New York: W.W. Norton, 1989).

Bernstein, Barton J. and Matusow, Allen J., *Twentieth-Century America: Recent Interpretations* (New York: Harcourt Brace Jovanovich, 1972).

Bishop, Jim, *FDR's Last Year: April 1944–April 1945* (London: Hart-Davis, MacGibbon, 1975).

Blum, John Morton, *Years of Discord: American Politics and Society, 1961–1974* (New York: W.W. Norton 1991).

Blum, John Morton, *Liberty, Justice, Order* (New York: W.W. Norton, 1993).

Bork, Robert H., *The Tempting of America: The Political Seduction of the Law* (London: Sinclair-Stevenson, 1990).

Bowers, Claude G., *Jefferson and Hamilton: The Struggle for Democracy in America* (New York: Houghton Mifflin, 1925).

Boyle, Peter G., *American–Soviet Relations: From the Russian Revolution to the Fall of Communism* (London: Routledge, 1993).

Brock, W. R., *The Character of American History* (London: Macmillan, 1960).

Brogan, D. W., *American Aspects* (London: Hamish Hamilton, 1964).

Brogan, Hugh, *The Longman History of the United States of America* (London: Longman, 1999).

Brown, Dee, *Bury my Heart at Wounded Knee: An Indian History of the American West* (London: Barrie & Jenkins, 1970).

Brown, Dee, *The Westerners* (London: Michael Joseph, 1974).

Bryce, James, *The American Commonwealth,* 2 vols (Indianapolis: Liberty Fund, 1995).

Burns, James MacGregor, *Roosevelt: The Lion and the Fox: Roosevelt the Soldier of Freedom, 1940–45* (New York: Harcourt Brace Jovanovich, 1956, 1970).

Burns, James MacGregor, *The Crosswinds of Freedom* (New York: Vintage Books, 1990).

Bush, George and Scowcroft, Brent, *A World Transformed* (New York: Alfred A. Knopf, 1998).

Carnegie, Andrew, *The Gospel of Wealth and other Timely Essays* (London: Frederick Warne, 1901).

Carter, Jimmy, *Keeping Faith: Memoirs of a President* (Fayetville: University of Arkansas Press, 1995).

Chester, Lewis, Hodgson, Godfrey and Page, Bruce, *An American Melodrama: The Presidential Campaign of 1968* (London: Literary Guild, 1969).

Childs, Marquis, *Eisenhower: Captive Hero* (London: Hammond, 1959).

Churchill, Winston S., *The Second World War*, vol. I: *The Gathering Storm*; vol. II: *Their Finest Hour*; vol. III: *The Grand Alliance*; vol. IV: *The Hinge of Fate*; vol. V: *Closing the Ring*; vol. VI: *Triumph and Tragedy* (London: The Reprint Society, 1950–4).

Clements, Kendrick A., *The Presidency of Woodrow Wilson* (Lawrence, KS: University of Kansas Press, 1992).

Clifford, Clark, *Counsel to the President: A Memoir* (New York: Anchor Books, Doubleday, 1991).

Cobb, James C. and Namorato, Michael V. (eds), *The New Deal and the South* (Jackson: University Press of Mississippi, 1984).

Cohen, Warren I., *Dean Rusk* (Totowa, NJ: Cooper Square Publishers, 1980).

Coletta, Paolo, *William Jennings Bryan*, vol. 1: *Political Evangelist, 1860–1908*; vol. II: *Progressive Politician and Moral Statesman, 1909–1915*; vol. III: *Political Puritan, 1915–1925* (Lincoln, NB: University of Nebraska Press, 1964–9).

288   *Bibliography*

Commager, Henry Steele, *Documents of American History* (New York: Appleton-Century-Crofts, 1949).

Coolidge, Calvin, *Foundations of the Republic: Speeches and Addresses* (New York (Charles Scribners' Sons, 1926).

Coolidge, Calvin, *The Autobiography of Calvin Coolidge* (London: Chatto & Windus, 1929).

Cooper, John Milton Jr, *The Warrior and the Priest: Woodrow Wilson and Theodore Roosevelt* (Cambridge, MA: Belknap Press, 1983).

Cooper, John Milton Jr, *Pivotal Decades: The United States, 1900–1920* (New York: W.W. Norton, 1990).

Cray, Ed, *General of the Army: George C. Marshall, Soldier and Statesman* (New York: W.W. Norton, 1990).

Cunliffe, Marcus, *American Presidents and the Presidency* (London: Eyre & Spottiswoode, 1969).

Dallek, Robert, *Franklin D. Roosevelt and American Foreign Policy, 1932–1945* (Oxford: Oxford University Press, 1979).

Dallek, Robert, *Lone Star Rising*, vol. 1: *Lyndon Johnson and his Times, 1908–1960*; vol. 2: *Flawed Giant: Lyndon Johnson and his Times, 1961–1973* (Oxford: Oxford University Press, 1991, 1998).

Degler, Carl N., *Out of our Past: The Forces that Shaped Modern America* (New York: Harper & Row, 1984).

Diggins, John Patrick, *The Proud Decades: America in War and Peace, 1941–1960* (New York: W.W. Norton, 1988).

Divine, Robert A., *Eisenhower and the Cold War* (Oxford: Oxford University Press, 1981).

Passos, John Dos, *Mr Wilson's War* (London: Hamish Hamilton, 1963).

Douglas, William O., *Go East Young Man: The Autobiography of William O. Douglas*, vol. 1: *The Early Years*; vol. 2: *The Court Years, 1939–1975* (London: Random House, 1974, 1980).

Dumbrell, John, *The Carter Presidency: A Re-evaluation* (Manchester: Manchester University Press, 1995).

Drew, Elizabeth, *Portrait of an Election: The 1980 Presidential Campaign* (London: Routledge & Kegan Paul, 1981).

Dulles, Foster Rhea, *America's Rise to World Power, 1898–1954* (New York: Harper & Row, 1954).

Economist, The, The New Deal: An Analysis and Appraisal (New York: Alfred A. Knopf, 1937).

Eisenhower, Dwight D., *The White House Years*, vol. 1: *Mandate for Change, 1953–1956*; vol. 2: *Waging Peace, 1956–61* (London: Heinemann, 1963, 1966).

Ellis, Joseph J., *Passionate Sage: The Character and Legacy of John Adams* (New York: W.W. Norton, 1994).

Feiling, Keith, *The Life of Neville Chamberlain* (London: Macmillan, 1970).

Ferrell, Robert H., *Truman: A Centenary Remembrance* (London: Thames & Hudson, 1984).

Fitzgerald, F. Scott, *The Crackup*, ed. Edmund Wilson (New York: New Directions, 1931).

Fitzgerald, F. Scott, *Six Tales of the Jazz Age and other Stories* (New York: Simon & Schuster, 2000).

Ford, Gerald R., *A Time to Heal: The Autobiography of Gerald R. Ford* (London: W. H. Allen, 1979).

Freedman, Max (ed.), *Roosevelt and Frankfurter: Their Correspondence, 1928–1945* (London: Bodley Head, 1967).

Freidel, Frank, *Franklin D. Roosevelt: A Rendezvous with Destiny* (New York: Little, Brown, 1990).

Freud, Sigmund and Bullitt, William C., *Thomas Woodrow Wilson: A Psychological Study* (London: Weidenfeld & Nicolson, 1967).

Fulbright, J. William, *The Arrogance of Power* (London: Jonathan Cape, 1967).

Galbraith, John Kenneth, *The Culture of Contentment* (New York: Houghton Mifflin, 1992).

Garraty, John A., *Henry Cabot Lodge* (New York: Alfred A. Knopf, 1953).

Garson, Robert A. and Kidd, Stuart S. (eds), *The Roosevelt Years: New Perspectives on American History, 1933–1945* (Edinburgh: Edinburgh University Press, 1999).

Ginsberg, Benjamin and Shefter, Martin, *Politics by other Means: Politicians, Prosecutors, and the Press from Watergate to Whitewater* (New York: W.W. Norton, 1999).

Goldman, Eric E., *The Tragedy of Lyndon Johnson* (London: Macdonald, 1969).

Goldwater, Barry, *The Conscience of a Conservative* (London: Fontana Books, 1964).

Gould, Lewis L., *The Presidency of Theodore Roosevelt* (Lawrence, KS: University of Kansas Press, 1991).

Graham, Otis L. Jr and Wander, Meghan Robinson (eds), *Franklin D. Roosevelt, his Life and Times: An Encyclopedic View* (New York: G. K. Hall, 1985).

Greenstein, Fred I., *The Hidden-hand Presidency: Eisenhower as Leader* (New York: Basic Books, 1982).

Hagedorn, Hermann (ed.), *The Works of Theodore Roosevelt* (New York: Charles Scribners', 1926).

Harbaugh, William H., *The Life and Times of Theodore Roosevelt* (Oxford: Oxford University Press, 1975).

Hardeman, D. B. and Bacon, Donald C., *Rayburn: A Biography* (Austin: Texas Monthly Press 1987).

Harrington, Michael, *The Other America: Poverty in the United States* (London: Macmillan, 1962).

Harrison, Robert, *State and Society in Twentieth-century America* (London: Longman, 1997).

Heale, M. J., *Franklin D. Roosevelt: The New Deal and War* (London: Routledge, 1999).

Hersh, Seymour, *The Target is Destroyed: What Really Happened to Flight 007 and what America Knew about It* (London: Faber & Faber, 1986).

Hicks, John D., *Republican Ascendancy, 1921–1933* (New York: Harper & Row, 1960).

Hofstadter, Richard, *The American Political Tradition and the Men who Made It* (New York: Alfred A. Knopf, 1948).

Hoopes, Townsend, *The Devil and John Foster Dulles* (London: André Deutsch, 1974).

Hoover, Herbert, *American Individualism* (New York: Doubleday, Page, 1922).

Hoover, Herbert, *Memoirs*, vol. I: *Years of Adventure, 1874–1920*; vol. II: *The Cabinet and the Presidency, 1920–1933*; vol. III: *The Great Depression, 1929–1941* (London: Hollis and Carter, 1952–3).

Hoover, Herbert, *The Ordeal of Woodrow Wilson* (London: Museum Press, 1958).

Hull, Cordell, *Memoirs*, 2 vols (London: Hodder & Stoughton, 1948).

Humphrey, Hubert H., *The Education of a Public Man: My Life and Politics* (London: Weidenfeld & Nicolson, 1976).

Jefferson, Thomas, *Writings* (New York: Library of America, 1984).

Johnson, Haynes, *Sleepwalking through History: America in the Reagan Years* (New York: W.W. Norton, 1991).

Johnson, Haynes, *Divided We Fall: Gambling with History in the Nineties* (New York: W.W. Norton, 1994).

Johnson, Lyndon Baines, *The Vantage Point: Perspectives of the Presidency, 1963–1969* (New York: Holt, Rinehart & Winston, 1971).

Jones, Maldwyn, *The Limits of Liberty: American History, 1607–1992* (Oxford: Oxford University Press, 1995).

Kalb, Marvin and Kalb, Bernard, *Kissinger* (New York: Little, Brown, 1974).

Kammen, Michael, *A Machine that would Go of Itself: The Constitution in American Culture* (New York: Alfred A. Knopf, 1986).

Kamphoefner, Walter D., Helbich, Wolfgang and Sommer, Ulrike (eds), *News from the Land of Freedom: German Immigrants Write Home* (New York: Cornell University Press, 1991).

Kearns, Doris, *Lyndon Johnson and the American Dream* (New York: Harper & Row, 1976).

Kelly, Alfred H., Harbison, Winfred A. and Beltz, Herman, *The American Constitution: Its Origins and Development* (New York: W.W. Norton, 1991).

Kennan, George, *Memoirs, 1925–1950* (London: Hutchinson, 1968).

[Kennan, George] 'X' 'The Sources of Soviet Conduct', *Foreign Affairs*, July 1947.

Kennedy, David M., *Freedom from Fear: The American People in Depression and War, 1929–1945* (Oxford: Oxford University Press, 1999).

Kennedy, Robert F., *Thirteen Days: A Memoir of the Cuban Missile Crisis* (New York: W.W. Norton, 1969).

Kissinger, Henry, *White House Years: Years of Upheaval* (London: Weidenfeld & Nicolson and Michael Joseph, 1979, 1982).

Ladd, Everett Carll Jr with Hadley, Charles D., *Transformations of the American Party System: Political Coalitions from the New Deal to the 1970s* (New York: W.W. Norton, 1978).

La Feber, Walter, *The American Age: US Foreign Policy at Home and Abroad, 1750s to the Present* (New York: W.W. Norton, 1994).

La Feber, Walter, *America, Russia, and the Cold War, 1945–1996* (New York: McGraw-Hill, 1997).

La Follette, Robert M., *La Follette's Autobiography: A Personal Narrative of Political Experiences* (Madison: University of Wisconsin Press, 1968).

Larson, Arthur, *Eisenhower: The President Nobody Knew* (London: Leslie Frewin, 1969).

Leech, Margaret, *In the Days of McKinley* (New York: Harper & Brothers, 1959).

Leuchtenburg, William E., *Franklin D. Roosevelt and the New Deal, 1932–1940* (New York: Harper & Row, 1963).

Leuchtenburg, William E., *In the Shadow of FDR: From Harry Truman to Ronald Reagan* (New York: Cornell University Press, 1985).

Levy, Leonard W., *Original Intent and the Framers' Constitution* (Basingstoke: Palgrave Macmillan, 1988).

Lindley, Ernest K., *The Roosevelt Revolution: First Phase* (New York: Viking Press, 1933).

Link, Arthur S. (ed.), *The Papers of Woodrow Wilson*, 69 vols (Princeton, NJ: Princeton University Press, 1966–).

Link, Arthur S., *Woodrow Wilson and the Progressive Era, 1910–1917* (New York: Harper & Row, 1954).

Lubell, Samuel, *The Future of American Politics* (New York: Harper & Row, 1965).

McCoy, Donald R., *Coming of Age: The United States during the 1920s and 1930s* (Harmondsworth: Penguin, 1973).

MacDonald, Callum A., *Korea: The War before Vietnam* (Basingstoke: Palgrave Macmillan, 1986).

McNamara, Robert S., *In Retrospect: The Tragedy and Lessons of Vietnam* (New York: Times Books, 1995).

Maney, Patrick J., *The Roosevelt Presence: A Biography of Franklin Delano Roosevelt* (New York: Twayne, 1992).

Matusow, Allen J., *The Unravelling of America: A History of Liberalism in the 1960s* (New York: Harper & Row, 1984).

Mayer, George H., *The Republican Party, 1854–1966* (Oxford: Oxford University Press, 1967).

Mervin, David, *George Bush and the Guardian Presidency* (Basingstoke: Palgrave Macmillan, 1996).

Miller, Merle, *Plain Speaking: An Oral Biography of Harry S. Truman* (London: Coronet, 1976).

Millis, Walter, *Road to War: America, 1914–1917* (London: Faber & Faber, 1935).

Mitchell, Broadus, *Alexander Hamilton*, vol. I: *Youth to Maturity, 1755–1788*; vol. II: *The National Adventure, 1788–1804* (London: Macmillan, 1957, 1962).

Moley, Raymond, *After Seven Years* (New York: Harper & Brothers, 1939).

Moley, Raymond, *The First New Deal* (New York: Harcourt, Brace & World, 1966).

Morgan, Iwan W., *Beyond the Liberal Consensus: A Political History of the United States since 1965* (London: Hurst, 1994).

Morgan, Ted, *FDR: A Biography* (New York: Simon & Schuster, 1985).

Morris, Edmund, *The Rise of Theodore Roosevelt* (London: Collins, 1979).

Moss, Norman, *Men Who Play God: The Story of the Hydrogen Bomb* (London: Victor Gollancz, 1968).

Mowry, George E., *Theodore Roosevelt and the Progressive Movement* (New York: Hill & Wang, 1946).

Mowry, George E., *The Era of Theodore Roosevelt, 1900–1912* (London: Hamish Hamilton, 1958).

Myers, Walter Starr (ed.), *The State Papers and Other Public Writings of Herbert Hoover*, vol. I: *March 4, 1929 to October 1, 1931*; vol. II: *October 1, 1931 to March 4, 1933* (New York: Doubleday, Doran & Company, 1934).

Nash, George H., *The Life of Herbert Hoover: Master of Emergencies, 1917–1918* (New York: W.W. Norton, 1996).

Nevins, Allan, *Grover Cleveland: A Study in Courage* (New York: Dodd, Mead, 1932).

Nixon, Richard, *Memoirs* (New York: Grosset & Dunlap, 1978).

Nye, Russel B., *Midwestern Progressive Politics: A Historical Study of its Origins and Development, 1870–1958* (East Lansing: Michigan State University Press, 1959).

Oates, Stephen B., *With Malice toward None: The Life of Abraham Lincoln* (London: George Allen & Unwin, 1978).

O'Neill, Tip, *Man of the House* (London: Bodley Head, 1987).

Orsi, Robert A., *Thank You, St Jude: Women's Devotion to the Patron Saint of Hopeless Causes* (New Haven, CT: Yale University Press, 1996).

Parrish, Michael E., *Anxious Decades: America in Prosperity and Depression, 1920–1941* (New York: W.W. Norton, 1992).

Patterson, James T., *Congressional Conservatism and the New Deal* (Lexington: Kentucky University Press, 1967).

Patterson, James T., *The Welfare State in America, 1930–1980* (Durham: British Association for American Studies, 1981).

Patterson, James T., *Grand Expectations: The United States, 1945–1974* (Oxford: Oxford University Press, 1996).

Perkins, Frances, *The Roosevelt I Knew* (New York: Viking Press, 1946).

Peterson, Merrill D., *The Jefferson Image in the American Mind* (Oxford: Oxford University Press, 1960).

Phillips, Kevin P., *The Emerging Republican Majority* (New Rochelle, NY: Arlington House 1969).

Podell, Janet and Anzovin, Steven (eds), *Speeches of the American Presidents* (New York: H. H. Wilson, 1988).

Potter, Jim, *The American Economy between the World Wars* (London: Macmillan, 1974).

Powell, Colin, *A Soldier's Way: An Autobiography* (London: Hutchinson, 1995).

Pringle, Henry F., *Theodore Roosevelt* (London: Jonathan Cape, 1931).

Rauch, Basil, *The History of the New Deal, 1933–1938* (New York: Octagon Books, 1963).

Reagan, Ronald, *An American Life* (London: Hutchinson, 1990).

Reeves, Thomas C., *Twentieth-century America: A Brief History* (Oxford: Oxford University Press, 2000).

Renshaw, Patrick, *The Longman Companion to America in the Era of the Two World Wars, 1910–1945* (Harlow: Longman, 1996).

Rhodes, Richard, *The Making of the Atomic Bomb* (Harmondsworth: Penguin, 1988).

Rhodes, Richard, *Dark Sun: The Making of the Hydrogen Bomb* (New York: Simon & Schuster, 1995).

Riis, Jacob A., *How the Other Half Lives: Studies among the Tenements of New York* (New York: Dover, 1971, reproduces 1901 edition of Charles Scribners' Sons, originally published 1890).

Riis, Jacob A., *Theodore Roosevelt the Citizen* (London: Macmillan, 1912).

Romasco, Albert U., *The Poverty of Abundance: Hoover, the Nation, the Depression* (Oxford: Oxford University Press, 1965).

Roosevelt, Elliott (ed.), *FDR his Personal Letters, 1928–1945*, vol. II (New York: Duell Sloan & Pearce, 1950).

Roosevelt, Theodore, *Autobiography* (London: Macmillan, 1913).

Rosenman, Samuel I. (ed.), *The Public Papers and Addresses of Franklin D. Roosevelt*, 13 vols (New York: Random House, 1938–50).

Rosenman, Samuel I., *Working with Roosevelt* (London: Hart-Davis, 1952).

Rossiter, Clinton, *The American Presidency* (London: Hart-Davis, 1960).

Rovere, Richard H., *Senator Joe McCarthy* (London: Methuen, 1960).

Rovere, Richard H., *The Goldwater Caper* (London: Methuen, 1966).

Russell, Bertrand, *Autobiography* (London: Routledge, 1998).

Russell, Francis, *President Harding: His Life and Times, 1865–1923* (London: Eyre & Spottiswoode, 1969).

Schaller, Michael, *Reckoning with Reagan: America and its President in the 1980s* (Oxford: Oxford University Press, 1992).

Schlesinger, Arthur M. Jr, *The Age of Roosevelt*, vol. I: *The Crisis of the Old Order, 1919–1933*; vol. II: *The Coming of the New Deal*; vol. III: *The Politics of Upheaval* (New York: Houghton Mifflin, 1957–1960).

Schlesinger, Arthur M. Jr, *A Thousand Days: John F. Kennedy in the White House* (London: Deutsch, 1965).

Schlesinger, Arthur M. Jr, *The Imperial Presidency* (London: Deutsch, 1974).

Schlesinger, Arthur M. Jr, *The Cycles of American History* (London: Deutsch, 1987).

Schlesinger, Arthur M. Jr, *The Disuniting of America: Reflections on a Multicultural Society* (New York: W.W. Norton, 1992).

Schulzinger, Robert D., *A Time for War: The United States and Vietnam, 1941–1975* (Oxford: Oxford University Press, 1998).

Schweber, S. S., *In the Shadow of the Bomb: Bethe, Oppenheimer, and the Moral Responsibility of the Scientist* (Princeton, NJ: Princeton University Press, 2000).

Sherry, Michael S., *In the Shadow of War: The United States since the 1930s* (New Haven, CT: Yale University Press, 1995).

Sherwood, Robert E., *The White House Papers of Harry L. Hopkins*, 2 vols. (London: Eyre & Spottiswoode, 1948).

Smith, Gene, *When the Cheering Stopped* (London: Hutchinson, 1964).

Smith, Joseph (ed.), *The American Constitution: The First 200 Years, 1787–1987* (Exeter: Exeter University Press, 1987).

Smith, Joseph, *The Spanish–American War: Conflict in the Caribbean and the Pacific, 1895–1902* (Harlow: Longman, 1994).

Smith, Joseph, *The Cold War, 1945–1991* (Oxford: Blackwell, 1998).

Sorensen, Theodore C., *Kennedy* (London: Hodder & Stoughton, 1965).

Starr Report, The (New York: Public Affairs, 1999).

Steel, Ronald, *Walter Lippmann and the American Century* (London: Bodley Head, 1980).

Steinbeck, John, *The Grapes of Wrath* (London: Heinemann, 1939).

Stockman, David A., *The Triumph of Politics* (London: Bodley Head, 1986).

Sundquist, James L., *Dynamics of the Party System: Alignment and Realignment of Political Parties in the United States* (Washington, DC: Brookings 1983).

Taylor, A. J. P., *The Struggle for Mastery in Europe, 1848–1918* (Oxford: Clarendon Press, 1954).

294   *Bibliography*

Terkel, Studs, *Hard Times: An Oral History of the Great Depression* (London: Allen Lane, The Penguin Press, 1970).

Tindall, George Brown and Shi, David E., *America: A Narrative History* (New York: W.W. Norton, 1996).

Thompson, J. A., *Progressivism* (Durham: British Association for American Studies, 1979).

Tocqueville, Alexis de, *Democracy in America*, ed. J. P. Mayer (London: Fontana, 1994).

Truman, Harry S., *The Memoirs of Harry S. Truman*, 2 vols; vol. 1: *Year of Decisions, 1945*; vol. 2: *Years of Trial and Hope, 1945–1953* (London: Hodder & Stoughton, 1955, 1956).

Turner, Frederick Jackson, *The Frontier in American History* (New York: Henry Holt, 1920).

Twain, Mark and Warner, Charles Dudley, *The Gilded Age: A Tale of Today* (Oxford: Oxford University Press, 1996, reproduces the American Publishing Company edition of 1873).

Venn, Fiona, *The New Deal* (Edinburgh: British Association for American Studies 1998).

Ward, Geoffrey C., *Before the Trumpet: Young Franklin Roosevelt, 1882–1905; A First Class Temperament* (New York: Harper & Row, 1985, 1989).

Weinberg, Gerhard L., *A World at Arms: A Global History of World War II* (Cambridge: Cambridge University Press, 1994).

Weisbrot, Robert, *Freedom Bound: A History of America's Civil Rights Movement* (New York: W.W. Norton, 1990).

Welles, Sumner, *The Time for Decision* (London: Hamish Hamilton, 1944).

Werner M. R., *Bryan* (London: Jonathan Cape, 1929).

Weymouth, Lally (ed.), *Thomas Jefferson: The Man...His World...His Influence* (London: Weidenfeld and Nicolson, 1973).

Whelan, Richard, *Drawing the Line: The Korean War, 1950–1953* (London: Faber and Faber, 1990).

White, Mark J., *The Cuban Missile Crisis* (Basingstoke: Palgrave Macmillan, 1996).

The White House Transcripts (New York: Bantam Books, 1974).

White, Theodore, *The Making of the President 1960; 1964; 1968; 1972* (London: Cape, 1961–74); *American in Search of Itself: The Making of the President 1956–1980* (London: Cape, 1983).

Whitman, Walt, *Democratic Vistas and Other Papers* (London: Walter Scott, 1888).

Wicker, Tom, *JFK and LBJ: the Influence of Personality upon Politics* (New York: Morrow, 1968).

Wilson, Woodrow, *The New Freedom: A Call for the Emancipation of the Generous Energies of a People* (Englewood Cliffs, NJ: Prentice-Hall, 1961).

Index

Index